AF819884

QUE Bee

From Doubts to Distinction
Your ICSE 2026 Exams Partner

GIST OF THE TEXTBOOK
Crisp & Complete Theory - No need to go back to bulky textbooks!

ALL TYPES OF LATEST PATTERN QUESTIONS
MCQs | Case-based | Assertion-Reason; All in one place!

KEYWORDS HIGHLIGHTED
Important points and key words are neatly Underlined; Never miss what matters

COUNCIL-STYLE ANSWERS
Write responses like an examiner expects

SAMPLE PAPER
Practice in real-exam mode. Perfect your timing, strategy, and confidence.

arihant
SUCCESS AND NOTHING LESS

ARIHANT PRAKASHAN
(School Division Series)

卐 **ADMINISTRATIVE & PRODUCTION OFFICES**
Regd. Office
'Ramchhaya' 4577/15, Agarwal Road, Darya Ganj, New Delhi -110002
Tele: 011- 47630600, 43518550; Fax: 011- 23280316

卐 **Head Office**
Kalindi, TP Nagar, Meerut (UP) - 250002, Tel: 0121-7156203, 7156204

卐 **SALES & SUPPORT OFFICES**
Agra, Ahmedabad, Bengaluru, Bareilly, Chennai, Delhi, Guwahati, Hyderabad, Jaipur, Jhansi, Kolkata, Lucknow, Nagpur & Pune.

PO No : TXT-XX-XXXXXXX-X-XX

Published By Arihant Publications (India) Ltd.

For further information about the books published by Arihant, log on to www.arihantbooks.com or e-mail at info@arihantbooks.com

Follow us on

卐 **PRICE** ₹ 250.00

PRODUCTION TEAM

Publishing Manager
Keshav Mohan

Project Head
Shivam Gupta

Cover Designer
Bilal Hashmi

Inner Designer
Ankit Tyagi

Page Layouting
Sundar Bisht

Proof Reader
Priya Kumari

QUE Bee

ICSE
HISTORY & CIVICS
Class 9

Types of Questions & their Respective Number

Type of Questions	Total Number
Multiple Choice Questions (MCQs)	229
Assertion-Reason (A-R)	82
Very Short Answer Questions (VSA)	186
Short Answer Type Questions (SA)	98
Long Answer Type Questions (LA)	80
Structured Questions	62
TOTAL NO. OF QUESTIONS	**737**

Created by

Kamlesh Charan

B.A., M.A, B.Ed.
30 Yrs. Experienced
TGT(History), St. Thomas English Medium School

Contributor

Nazma Ansari

From Learner to Leader

Step-Into the Spotlight

QUE Bee is more than just a book - it's a platform for young achievers like you to guide future toppers. If you've cracked the code to smart study or have insights that can make learning easier for others, this is your moment to shine!

What Can You Share?

- Your study techniques, time management tips, or motivation hacks
- Feedback or suggestions to make QUE Bee even better
- Real experiences that can guide other students through the exam maze

What's in It for You?

- Your name will be featured in our exclusive Student Panel in the next edition
- Win exciting & surprise rewards for impactful suggestions
- **Get published** - your photo, Ideas-or even interviews can be featured in the book
- **Become a student icon** - recognized and followed by peers across schools

Let your learning become someone else's ladder.
Be remembered. Be featured. Be the guide.

SCAN TO SHARE YOUR IDEA

QUE Bee

Index

CIVICS	**1-48**
Our Constitution	
1. Our Constitution and its Features	3-11
2. Fundamental Rights and Duties	12-22
3. Directive Principles of State Policy	23-31
Elections	
4. Elections	32-40
The State Legislatures	
5. The State Legislatures	41-48
HISTORY	**49-206**
1. The Harappan Civilisation	51-64
2. The Vedic Period	65-79
3. Jainism and Buddhism	80-95
4. The Mauryan Empire	96-107
5. The Sangam Age	108-117
6. The Age of the Guptas	118-129
Medieval India	
7. The Cholas	130-140
8. The Delhi Sultanate	141-153
9. The Mughal Empire	154-166
10. Composite Culture	167-178
Modern Age in Europe	
11. The Modern Age in Europe : Renaissance	179-190
12. The Modern Age in Europe : Reformation	191-198
13. Industrial Revolution	199-206
ICSE Sample Question Paper	**207-216**

Latest
Course Structure

There will be one paper of two hours duration carrying 80 marks and an Internal Assessment of 20 marks.

SECTION A : CIVICS

An elementary study is required of this section without verbatim study of the Constitutional Articles in detail.

1. **Our Constitution**

   Definition of Constitution - date of adoption, date of enforcement and its significance.

   Features: Single Citizenship, Universal Adult Franchise, Fundamental Rights and Fundamental Duties, Directive Principles of State Policy (meaning), Difference between Fundamental Rights and Directive Principles, Meaning of a Welfare State.

2. **Elections**

   Meaning; Composition and functions of Election Commission of India; Direct and Indirect election; General election; Mid-term election and By-election.

3. **The State Legislatures**

   The Legislative Assembly and the Legislative Council. Meaning of Unicameral and Bicameral Legislatures, term, composition, qualification for membership, powers and functions.

SECTION B: HISTORY

1. **The Harappan Civilisation**

   Sources: Great Bath, Citadel, seals, bearded man, dancing girl, dockyard, granaries, script. Urban planning, trade, art & craft, and its decline.

2. **The Vedic Period**

   Sources: Names of the four Vedas and importance of epics.

   Early Vedic Period- Social Organisation- Family, Position of the king; Rig Vedic Assemblies- Sabha, Samiti, Vidhatha. Brief comparative study of the position of women in Early and Later Vedic society.

   A brief comparison between the economy of Early and Later Vedic Period.

   The four class divisions, the four Ashramas and the education system.

3. **Jainism and Buddhism**

   Sources: Angas, Tripitikas and Jatakas (brief mention). Causes for their rise in the 6th century B.C. Doctrines- Jainism-Tri-ratnas, Karma, Equality, Moksha Buddhism- The Four Noble truths, The Eight-fold path, Nirvana.

4. **The Mauryan Empire**

   Sources: Arthashastra, Indika, Ashokan Edicts, Sanchi Stupa. Names of the kings in chronological order and administration; Ashoka's Dhamma - Principles and Impact

5. **The Sangam Age**

   Sources: Tirukkural and Megaliths. Society – Position of women Economy - Agriculture and Trade

6. **The Age of the Guptas**

   Sources: Account of Fa-hien; Allahabad Pillar Inscription.Names of the kings in chronological order; administration; Contribution to the fields of Education (Nalanda University), Science (Aryabhatta), Sushrutha (medicine) and Culture (works of Kalidasa, Deogarh temple).

7. Medieval India

(a) The Cholas

Sources: Inscriptions; Brihadishwara Temple. Names of the kings in chronological order and administration; Chola art.

(b) The Delhi Sultanate

Sources: Inscriptions; Qutab Minar. Names of the dynasties in chronological order Alauddin Khilji – Market Regulations, Deccan Expedition, Measures against nobility, Military reforms, Revenue reforms Muhammad Bin Tughlaq-Transfer of capital, Token Currency, Taxation in Doab, Plan of conquests.

(c) The Mughal Empire

Sources: Ain-i-Akbari, Taj Mahal, Jama Masjid and Red Fort.Names of the kings in chronological order. Babur- The three battles waged to consolidate his empire. Akbar-Rajput Policy, Steps towards integration, social and educational reforms, mansabdari system.

(d) Composite Culture

Factors responsible for composite culture, principles of the Bhakti and Sufi movement impact of composite culture, impact of the Bhakti Movement, the Sufi Movement and Christian missionaries.

8. The Modern Age in Europe

(a) Renaissance

Definition, causes (capture of Constantinople, decline of Feudalism, new trade routes, spirit of enquiry and invention of the printing press) and impact on art, literature and science (Leonardo Da Vinci, William Shakespeare and Copernicus). Consequences of Renaissance.

(b) Reformation

Meaning, Causes of reformation (dissatisfaction with the practices of the Catholic Church and new learning); Martin Luther's contribution, Counter Reformation.

(c) Industrial Revolution

Definition of the term. Causes of Industrial Revolution, meaning of capitalism and causes for the rise of capitalism, meaning of socialism and causes for the rise of socialism.

Civics

OUR CONSTITUTION AND ITS FEATURES

Definition of Constitution

- Constitution is a comprehensive document which contains laws and rules through which a country/nation is governed.
- The Constitution is the basic principles and laws of a nation, state, or social group that determine the powers and duties of the citizens.
- It is also known as the Fundamental Law of the Land.
- The Constitution aims to ensure the welfare of its citizens through good governance.

Implementation of the Indian Constitution

- The Constitution of India was framed by the members of Constituent Assembly which were elected indirectly by the Provincial Legislature Assemblies.
- **Date of Adoption** 26th November, 1949
- **Date of Enforcement** 26th January, 1950
- At the time of enforcement, the Constitution had 395 Articles, 22 Parts and 8 Schedules.

Significance of the Indian Constitution

- It aims for social, economic and political justice for all people of the country.
- It promotes a sense of brotherhood among all citizens.
- It aims at the unity of the nation being the hallmark of the efforts of the government.
- It ensure freedom of thought and expression, freedom of faith, freedom of belief and worship.

The Preamble

- It is an introduction to the Constitution which tells us about the source, the object and the ideals of the Constitution.
- Objective Resolution was introduced by Pt. Jawaharlal Nehru on 22nd January, 1947. This resolution proposed to make India a 'Sovereign Democratic Republic'.
- The Preamble is considered as the Soul and Spirit of our Constitution.
- According to the 42nd Constitution Amendment Act, 1976 'Sovereign Democratic Republic' was changed to 'Sovereign Socialist Secular Democratic Republic'.

Features of the Indian Constitution

Single Citizenship

- It is an idea that a person can only be a citizen of one country, and not of any particular state or region within that country.
- The Indian Constitution provides single citizenship which means that all Indians, irrespective of the state of their domicile are the citizens of India.

Universal Adult Franchise

- The Constitution guarantees every Indian citizen of the age 18 and above to vote or contest in the elections irrespective of their caste, colour, religion, etc.
- This system is aimed at curbing communal politics and fostering communal harmony.

Fundamental Rights

- Fundamental Rights are basic human rights, which provide the conditions essential for the all-round development of a human being.
- The Fundamental Rights are given in Part III of the Indian Constitution (Articles 12-35).
- The Indian Constitution has guaranteed six Fundamental Rights to all its citizens which are
  - (i) **Right to Equality** (Articles 14 to 18) It includes equality before the law, prohibition of discrimination and equal opportunity in employment, abolition of untouchability and abolition of titles.
  - (ii) **Right to Freedom** (Articles 19 to 22) This includes freedom of speech and expression, freedom of assembly, freedom of movement, protection of life and liberty.
  - (iii) **Right Against Exploitation** (Articles 23 and 24) It is a fundamental right in India that protects people from being exploited, prohibition of employment of children under the age of 14 in factories, mines etc.
  - (iv) **Right to Freedom of Religion** (Articles 25 to 28) It includes the right to practice, propagate, and have a conscience about any religion. Freedom to manage religious affairs.
  - (v) **Cultural and Educational Rights** (Articles 29 and 30) It promotes equality and respect for all cultures, religions and languages. It also includes right to establish and administer minority educational, social and cultural institutions.
  - (vi) **Right to Constitutional Remedies** (Article 32) It grants every individual the right to approach the Supreme Court for the enforcement of their Fundamental Rights.
- These rights are enforceable in the High Courts and the Supreme Court.

Fundamental Duties

- They are moral obligations of Indian citizens to uphold the unity of India and promote patriotism.
- They are specified under Article 51A (Part IV A) of the Indian Constitution.
- The Indian Constitution lists 11 Fundamental Duties for the people of the country.
- The Constitution of India originally had 10 fundamental duties. The 86th Amendment Act, 2002 added the 11th duty to the Constitution.
- Fundamental Duties were added to the Constitution by the 42nd Amendment Act, 1976. The Swaran Singh Committee recommended the addition of these duties.
- 6th January is celebrated as 'Fundamental Duties Day' in India.

EXAM ORIENTED QUESTIONS

TYPE - 1 1 Mark

Multiple Choice Questions

Q.1 The Cabinet Mission which proposed setting up of Constituent Assembly arrived in India in which year?

(a) 1944 (b) 1945
(c) 1942 (d) 1946

Ans. (d) 1946

Exp. The Cabinet Mission arrived in India in 1946 to plan the transfer of power from British rule to Indians. It proposed forming a Constituent Assembly to draft India's Constitution.

Q.2 Which of the following principles is/are added by the 42nd Constitutional Amendment?

P : Sovereignty
Q : Socialist State
R : Secular State
S : Liberty

Codes

(a) Only Q (b) Q and R
(c) P and S (d) P, Q and R

Ans. (b) Q and R

Q.3 The Constitution of India is the supreme legal authority which binds the legislative, executive and judicial organs of government. The Constitution grants all citizens Fundamental Rights and empowers the independent judiciary to invalidate legislation or government actions which violate the Constitution. What information about the Constitution can we obtain from the above passage? *The Supreme Court of India*

(a) It ensures smooth governance for the welfare of its citizens.
(b) It regulates the position of the citizens.
(c) It dictates terms to the states working under the central government.
(d) It provides rules and regulations for the smooth functioning of various commercial establishments in the country.

Ans. (a) It ensures smooth governance for the welfare of its citizens.

Q.4 The Constituent Assembly was truly national in character. In this context, identify the categories which were given membership of the Constituent Assembly.

P : General Category, Muslims and Sikhs
Q : Christians, Anglo-Indians and Parsees
R : General Category and Sikhs
S : Christians and Parsees

Codes

(a) P and Q (b) R and S
(c) P and R (d) Q and S

Ans. (a) P and Q

Exp. The Constituent Assembly represented India's diversity, including General Category, Muslims, Sikhs, Christians, Anglo-Indians, and Parsees, ensuring fair representation of all communities. Hence, categories in P and Q were included.

Q.5 In the picture given below, some members are signing the Indian Constitution. How many members of the Constituent Assembly signed the Indian Constitution on 24th January, 1950?

(a) 200 (b) 280 (c) 284 (d) 300

Ans. (c) 284

Q.6 A Constitution is a very long and detailed document. Therefore, it needs to be amended quite regularly to keep it updated. Those who drafted the Indian Constitution felt that it has to be in accordance with people's aspirations and changes in society. They did not see it as a sacred, static and unalterable law. So, they made provisions to incorporate changes from time to time. *Atomic Energy Education Society*

How many articles are there in Indian Constitution at the time of its enforcement?

(a) 395 (b) 448 (c) 411 (d) 400

Ans. (a) 395

Q.7 Identify the odd one out of the following features of the Constitution.

(a) Written and the Lengthy Constitution
(b) Fundamental Rights
(c) Committed Judiciary
(d) Fundamental Duties

Ans. (c) Committed Judiciary

Exp. Committed judiciary is not a feature of the Indian Constitution. Instead, the Constitution ensures an Independent Judiciary, free from external influence or bias.

Q.8 Who was the Chairman of the Drafting Committee of the Indian Constitution?

(a) Pandit Jawaharlal Nehru
(b) Mahatma Gandhi
(c) Vallabh Bhai Patel
(d) Dr. B.R. Ambedkar

Ans. (d) Dr. B.R. Ambedkar

Q.9 The Constitutional Advisor to the Constituent Assembly of India was

(a) Vallabh Bhai Patel
(b) B.N. Rau
(c) Mahatma Gandhi
(d) Lal Bahadur Shastri

Ans. (b) B.N. Rau

Q.10 Fundamental Rights: Part III of the Constitution:: Directive Principles : ?

(a) Part IV (b) Part II
(c) Part V (d) Part VI

Ans. (a) Part IV

TYPE - 2 — 1 Mark

Assertion-Reason Questions

Q.1 Read the statements given below about the Fundamental Law and select the option that shows the correct relationship between (A) and (R)

Assertion (A) The Constitution is referred to as the 'Fundamental Law of the Land'.

Reason (R) It contains laws and rules that govern the nation and ensure the welfare of its citizens through good governance.

(a) R contradicts A
(b) R is the reason for A
(c) A is true but R is false
(d) A and R are independent of each other

Ans. (b) R is the reason for A

Q.2 Read the two statements given below about the Constitution and select the option that shows the correct relationship between (A) and (R).

Assertion (A) The Constitution of a country is a set of rules that are accepted by all the people living in a country.

Reason (R) It generates a degree of trust and coordination among people that is necessary for different kinds of people living together.

(a) R contradicts A
(b) R is the reason for A
(c) A is true but R is false
(d) A and R are independent of each other

Ans. (b) R is the reason for A

Q.3 Read the two statements given below about the Constitution and select the option that shows the correct relationship between (A) and (R).

Assertion (A) The Indian Constitution came into force with effect from 26th January, 1950.

Reason (R) 26th January is celebrated as the Independence day.

(a) A is true but R is false
(b) R contradicts A
(c) R is the reason for A
(d) A and R are independent of each other

Ans. (a) A is true but R is false

Q.4 Read the two statements given below about the Constitution and select the option that shows the correct relationship between (A) and (R).

Assertion (A) The Preamble of the Constitution seeks to spread justice among all Indians.

Reasons (R) The Preamble of the Constitution of India guarantees to all citizens of India, Social, Economic and Political Justice

(a) R contradicts A (b) R is the reason for A
(c) A is true but R is false
(d) A and R are independent of each other

Ans. (b) R is the reason for A

Q.5 Read the statements given below about the Preamble and select the option that shows the correct relationship between (A) and (R)

Assertion (A) The Preamble is considered the 'Soul and Spirit of our Indian Constitution'.

Reason (R) It outlines the objectives, ideals and the source of the Indian Constitution.

(a) R contradicts A (b) R is the reason for A
(c) A is true but R is false
(d) A and R are independent of each other

Ans. (b) R is the reason for A

TYPE - 3

2 Marks

Very Short Answer Type Questions

Q.1 With reference to the Indian Constitution, answer the following questions.

(i) When was the Indian Constitution adopted and passed?

(ii) When did the Indian Constitution come into force?

Ans. (i) The Constitution of India was adopted and passed on 26th November, 1949.

(ii) The Constitution of India came into force on 26th January, 1950.

Q.2 Mention any two key features of the Indian Constitution?

Ans. 'Fundamental Rights' and 'single citizenship' are the two key features of the Indian Constitution.

Q.3 Give any two reasons why the Indian Constitution is termed as the 'Supreme Law of the Country'.

Ans. The Indian Constitution is termed as the 'Supreme Law of the Country' because

- it establishes the framework of the Constitution.
- it guarantees the Fundamental Rights to its citizens.

Q.4 Name two prominent members of the Constituent Assembly.

Ans. B.R. Ambedkar and Jawaharlal Nehru are among the two prominent members of the Constituent Assembly.

Q.5 Imagine you were a member of the Constituent Assembly on 26th November, 1949. How would you describe the atmosphere in the Assembly as the Constitution was adopted and signed?

Ans. The atmosphere was one of celebration. I witnessed that the temporary Chairman called upon the members to sign the register and present their credentials. Provisions like citizenship, elections and provisional parliament adopted immediately. People were all happy and became independent from the British rule.

Q.6 What do you understand by Secularism? Why is India called a secular country?

Ans. Secularism in India means equal treatment of all religions by the state. India is called a secular country because its Constitution guarantees religious freedom to all citizens and the government does not favour any religion.

Q.7 Mention two advantages of the principle of a Socialist State.

Ans. Two advantages of the principle of a Socialist State are

(i) It creates a society that focuses on economic equality.

(ii) In a socialist state, exploitation and discrimination are absent.

Q.8 Explain any two significance of the Preamble?

Ans. The Preamble to the Indian Constitution is significant because

- It sets the framework and provides guiding principles for the constitutional laws.
- It contains ideals that the Constitution seeks to achieve.

Q.9 Mention the words added to the Preamble according to the 42nd Amendment.

Ans. The words 'Socialist', 'Secular', and 'Integrity' were added to the Preamble according to the 42nd Amendment of the Indian Constitution.

Q.10 How does citizenship in India differ from that of the USA?

Ans. The main difference between citizenship in India and the United States is that India practices 'single citizenship', while the United States practices 'dual citizenship'.

Q.11 Read the extract given below and answer the question which follows.

The adoption of universal suffrage is a great and bold venture of faith of the Constituent Assembly in the people of the country and in the principle of democracy. *Hindustan Times, 12th January, 2020*

What is Universal Adult Franchise or Universal Suffrage? What is its importance in India?

Ans. Universal Adult Franchise refers to the right of all adult citizens to vote in an election. It guarantees every Indian citizen of the age 18 and above to vote or contest in the elections irrespective of their caste, colour, religion, etc.

Q.12 Mention any two advantages of Fundamental Rights given in the Constitution.

Ans. Two advantages of Fundamental Rights given in the Constitution are

- It ensures protection from discrimination.
- It ensures the protection of cultural and educational rights

Q.13 **Which committee recommended the addition of Fundamental Duties in the Constitution and when it was added to the Constitution?**

Ans. The Swaran Singh Committee recommended the addition of Fundamental Duties to the Constitution. It was added to the Constitution by the 42nd Amendment Act, 1976.

TYPE - 4 3 Marks

Short Answer Type Questions

Q.1 **"26th January in India's struggle is very important". Explain why?**

Ans. 26th January is significant in India's struggle for independence because, on this day in 1930, the Indian National Congress declared Purna Swaraj (Complete Independence) from British rule.

Later, in 1950, India adopted its Constitution, making 26th January as the Republic Day of the country. Since then, it has been celebrated as Republic Day, symbolising India's sovereignty and democratic values.

Q.2 **Why was 26th January chosen as the date for the enforcement of the Indian Constitution?**

Ans. The date 26th January was chosen as the date for the enforcement of the Indian Constitution for the following reasons

- **Symbolic Importance of Purna Swaraj Day** On 26th January, 1930, the Indian National Congress had declared 'Purna Swaraj' (Complete Independence) as India's ultimate goal and marked it as a significant date in the freedom struggle.
- **Tribute to the Independence Movement** Choosing this date to honour the sacrifices of freedom fighters and connected the Constitution's enforcement to the historical journey toward self-rule.
- **Establishing the Republic** The Constitution officially came into force on this day in 1950, declaring India a sovereign democratic republic.

Q.3 **Write a short note on Dr. Ambedkar's contribution to the Indian Constitution.**

Ans. Dr. B.R. Ambedkar, as the Chairman of the Drafting Committee, played a crucial role in shaping the Indian Constitution. He is often called the 'Father of the Indian Constitution' for his contributions to ensuring justice, equality and liberty for all citizens.

Ambedkar focused on protecting the rights of marginalised groups, including Scheduled Castes, Scheduled Tribes and Other Backward Classes, and advocated for the abolition of untouchability.

Q.4 **What is known as the 'Objective Resolution'? When and by whom was it proposed?**

Ans. The Objective Resolution was a key document that outlined the fundamental principles and goals for the newly independent India.

The resolution was proposed by Jawaharlal Nehru in the Constituent Assembly on 13th December, 1946. It served as the guiding framework for the drafting of the Constitution and was later adopted by the Assembly.

Q.5 **Article 32 of the Indian Constitution is known as the 'Heart and Soul' of the Constitution. Justify.**

Ans. Article 32 of the Indian Constitution is known as the 'Heart and Soul' of the Constitution because it provides individuals the right to approach the Supreme Court directly for the enforcement of their fundamental rights. It guarantees the right to constitutional remedies, ensuring that if any fundamental right is violated, citizens can seek justice through the highest court in the country.

TYPE - 5 4 Marks

Long Answer Type Questions

Q.1 **The Indian Constitution provides single citizenship. Justify this by mentioning any four points.**

Ans. The Indian Constitution provides single citizenship, meaning that every Indian citizen is a citizen of the entire country, rather than of individual states. This concept of single citizenship is justified by the following points

(i) Single citizenship ensures uniformity in the legal status and rights of all citizens, regardless of the state they reside in.

(ii) It fosters a sense of collective national identity, where all citizens are considered equal participants in the democratic process, irrespective of their regional backgrounds.

(iii) Single citizenship simplifies the legal system by avoiding multiple citizenships, making it easier for citizens to enjoy fundamental rights across the country without confusion or conflict.

(iv) The Indian Constitution avoids the complexities and potential issues associated with dual citizenship, which could lend to conflicts of loyalty and rights.

Q.2 What was the significance of the Kesavananda Bharati case (1972-1973) in establishing the status of the Preamble in the Indian Constitution?

Ans. The Kesavananda Bharati case (1972-1973) was a landmark judgement by the Supreme Court of India. It was significant as it impacted the status of the Preamble in the Indian Constitution. The Court stated that while the Preamble is part of the Constitution, it cannot be enforced in courts. However, it laid down the principle that the basic structure of the Constitution cannot be altered by any amendment, even by Parliament.

The significance of this case is that it highlighted the importance of the Preamble's values, justice, liberty, equality, and fraternity, as the core principles of India's Constitution. Although the Preamble itself cannot be directly enforced, it serves as a guiding framework for interpreting the Constitution.

Q.3 How did the provisions related to civil liberties, a strong centre and a unified judicial system contribute to the strength and unity of India as envisioned by the framers of the Constitution?

Ans. The provisions related to civil liberties, a strong centre, and a unified judicial system were crucial in ensuring the strength and unity of India in the following ways

- **Civil Liberties** The Constitution guarantees fundamental rights like freedom of speech, equality before the law and protection from discrimination. These civil liberties promote individual freedoms, equality and justice, which are essential for social harmony and unity across India's diverse society.
- **A Strong Centre** The framers of the Constitution established a strong central government to maintain national unity and ensure uniformity in laws and policies. This centralised authority helped prevent the fragmentation of the country into regional conflicts and ensured that all states functioned within a cohesive framework.
- **Unified Judicial System** A single, unified judiciary, with the Supreme Court at its apex, ensures that justice is administered fairly across the country. It upholds the Constitution, protects citizens' rights, and resolves disputes between states and between the central government and states, promoting legal consistency and unity.

TYPE - 6

10 Marks

Structured Questions

Q.1 The Constituent Assembly framed the Constitution of India. With reference to this, answer the following questions.

(i) Describe the composition of the Constituent Assembly. **(3)**

(ii) A public declaration was made on 26th January, 1930. What is the historical significance of 26th January? Mention any three events that made this day memorable. **(4)**

(iii) Explain the six Fundamental Rights guaranteed by the Indian Constitution. **(3)**

Ans. (i) The composition of the Constituent Assembly was as follows

- A total of 389 members, formed the Constituent Assembly.
- Out of these, 292 members were from British India, 93 from Princely States and 4 from Commissioner's Provinces.
- The first sitting of the Constituent Assembly was held on 9th December, 1946.

(ii) 26th January is a significant day in India's history, marking important events in the freedom struggle and the creation of the Indian Republic. Here are three key events that make this day memorable

(a) **Purna Swaraj Declaration (1930)** On 26th January, 1930, the Indian National Congress, under the leadership of Jawaharlal Nehru, declared Purna Swaraj (Complete Independence) from British rule. This marked a major turning point in the freedom struggle, moving beyond demands for constitutional reforms to a call for full independence.

(b) **Adoption of the Indian Constitution (1950)** On 26th January, 1950, India officially adopted its Constitution and became a Republic. This day marks the transformation of India into a sovereign, democratic, republic with a new political and legal framework.

(c) **Republic Day Celebrations** Since 1950, 26th January has been celebrated as Republic Day every year, with a grand parade in New Delhi showcasing India's cultural heritage, military strength and democratic values. This event has become a symbol of national pride and unity.

(iii) The Indian Constitution guarantees six Fundamental Rights to its citizens. These are

(a) **Right to Equality** Ensures all people are treated equally before the law.

(b) **Right to Freedom** Gives freedom of speech, movement, and expression.

(c) **Right Against Exploitation** Protects people from forced labour and child labour.

(d) **Right to Freedom of Religion** Allows individuals to follow any religion.

(e) **Cultural and Educational Rights** Protects the rights of minorities to conserve their culture and education.

(f) **Right to Constitutional Remedies** Allows people to approach the courts to protect their rights.

Q.2 The Indian Constitution is a written document. It is one of the most lengthy and detailed Constitution of the world. With reference to the Indian Constitution answer the following questions.

(i) India to Reconsider Single Citizenship Policy as 'Global Indians' Continue to Dominate International Business.

Henley & Partners, 13th August, 2019

What is single citizenship and how is it different from dual citizenship? (3)

(ii) "The Constitution was given shape by some of the finest minds of the country, the one was Pt. Jawaharlal Nehru". Mention his contribution in drafting the Indian Constitution. (3)

(iii) Explain the significance of the Indian Constitution. (4)

Ans. (i) **Single citizenship** means that a person is a citizen of the entire country, not just of a particular state or region. In India, every citizen is an Indian citizen, regardless of the state they live in. The Indian Constitution provides for single citizenship, ensuring equal rights and responsibilities for all citizens across the nation.

Dual citizenship, on the other hand, refers to a person being a citizen of two countries simultaneously, with the legal rights and obligations of both. India does not allow dual citizenship, meaning an individual cannot hold Indian citizenship along with the citizenship of another country.

(ii) **Jawaharlal Nehru** popularised the demand for a Constituent Assembly to draft India's Constitution and made it a central issue in the 1937 elections.

- He moved the Objectives Resolution, which aimed to declare India as an Independent Sovereign Republic.
- He headed various important committees in the Constituent Assembly of India which are - Union Power Committee, States Committee, Union Constitution Committee.

(iii) The significance of the Indian constitution is

- It aims for social, economic and political justice for all people of the country.
- It promotes a sense of brotherhood among all citizens.
- It aims at the unity of the nation being the hallmark of the efforts of the government.
- It ensures freedom of thought and expression, freedom of faith, freedom of belief and worship.

Q.3 Look at the picture given below and answer the following questions.

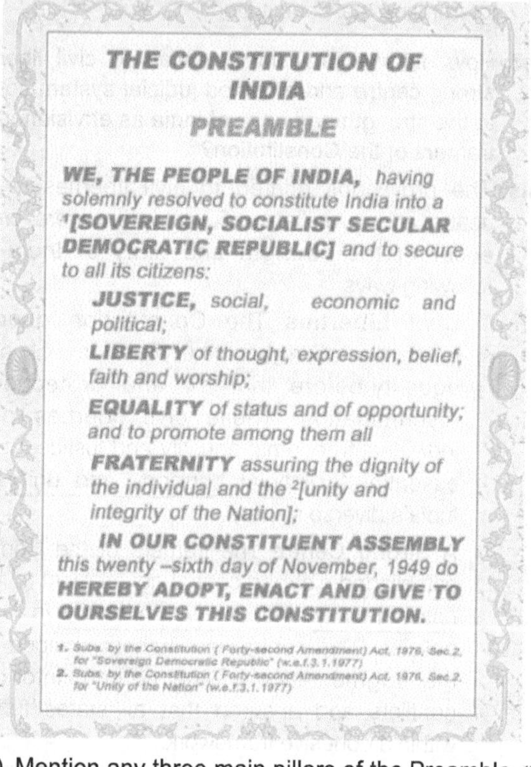
THE CONSTITUTION OF INDIA

PREAMBLE

WE, THE PEOPLE OF INDIA, having solemnly resolved to constitute India into a [1][SOVEREIGN, SOCIALIST SECULAR DEMOCRATIC REPUBLIC] and to secure to all its citizens:

JUSTICE, social, economic and political;

LIBERTY of thought, expression, belief, faith and worship;

EQUALITY of status and of opportunity; and to promote among them all

FRATERNITY assuring the dignity of the individual and the [2][unity and integrity of the Nation];

IN OUR CONSTITUENT ASSEMBLY this twenty –sixth day of November, 1949 do HEREBY ADOPT, ENACT AND GIVE TO OURSELVES THIS CONSTITUTION.

1. Subs. by the Constitution (Forty-second Amendment) Act, 1976, Sec.2, for "Sovereign Democratic Republic" (w.e.f.3.1.1977)
2. Subs. by the Constitution (Forty-second Amendment) Act, 1976, Sec.2, for "Unity of the Nation" (w.e.f.3.1.1977)

(i) Mention any three main pillars of the Preamble. (3)

(ii) The preamble of the Indian Constitution is also known as the 'soul of the Constitution'. Justify. (3)

(iii) What does the word sovereign, socialist, secular, democratic, republic mean in the Preamble? (4)

Ans. (i) The three main pillars of the Preamble of the Indian Constitution are

(a) **Justice** It emphasises social, economic, and political justice, ensuring that all citizens are treated fairly and equally under the law.

(b) **Liberty** It guarantees freedom of thought, expression, belief, faith, and worship, allowing individuals to lead their lives with dignity and autonomy.

(c) **Equality** This pillar ensures that all citizens are treated equally, without discrimination based on religion, caste, gender, or any other status, and that opportunities are available to all.

(ii) The Preamble of the Indian Constitution is often referred to as the 'soul of the Constitution' because it expresses the core values, objectives, and vision of the Constitution that guide the nation. It reflects the aspirations of the Indian people and sets the guiding principles for the functioning of the nation.

The Preamble outlines essential ideals like justice, liberty, equality, and fraternity, which form the foundation of India's democratic framework.

It also highlights the commitment to securing Fundamental Rights and promoting social, economic, and political justice for all citizens.

(iii) In the Preamble of the Indian Constitution, the words sovereign, socialist, secular, democratic, and republic have the following meanings

- **Sovereign** India is an independent nation, free to make its own decisions without interference from outside forces or other countries.
- **Socialist** India aims to promote social and economic equality, striving for the welfare of all citizens, especially the underprivileged, and reducing the gap between the rich and poor.
- **Secular** India does not favour any religion, and all religions are treated equally. The state remains neutral in religious matters.
- **Democratic** India follows a system of government where the people elect their leaders through free and fair elections. It ensures participation and representation of all citizens in decision-making.
- **Republic** The head of the state (President) is elected, not a hereditary monarch. The country is governed by elected representatives and the power rests with the people.

2

FUNDAMENTAL RIGHTS AND DUTIES

Fundamental Rights

- Fundamental Rights are basic human rights, which provide the conditions which are essential for the all-round development of a human being.
- The Fundamental Rights are enshrined in Part III of the Indian Constitution (Articles 12-35).
- These rights are enforceable in the High Courts and the Supreme Court and cannot be changed or removed by regular legislation.

Features of Fundamental Rights

1. **Universal** Fundamental Rights are provided to all citizens irrespective of their caste, creed, colour, sex, faith, religion, property, qualifications, place of residence or education.
2. **Unchangeable** Fundamental Rights provide certain safeguards that cannot be changed by ordinary legislation.
3. **Justiciable** These rights are justiciable in nature i.e. citizens can ask or file case for justice in the High Court or **Supreme Court** if their rights are violated.
4. **Not Absolute** These rights can be enjoyed until they do not go against the rights of others. Parliament has the right to impose certain restrictions on these rights if a larger issue is concerned.
5. **Suspension** Fundamental Rights can be suspended during a National Emergency as per Article 359, but the rights guaranteed under Articles 20 and 21 cannot be suspended.

Classification of Fundamental Rights

The Indian Constitution guarantees six fundamental rights to its citizens. They are classified into the following categories.

1. Right to Equality (Articles 14 to 18)

(a) **Equality before Law** (Article 14) It basically means that all persons are equal in the eyes of the law. It guarantees equality before law and the equal protection of law within the territory of India.

(b) **Prohibition of Discrimination** (Article 15) It forbids discrimination against any individual on the basis of caste, colour, creed, sex, religion, place of birth etc. This ensures social and economic equality.

(c) **Equality of Opportunity** (Article 16) This ensures equal job opportunities for all citizens in Central or State Government offices.

(d) **Abolition of Untouchability** (Article 17) It declares that 'untouchability' is abolished and its practice in any form is forbidden.

(e) **Abolition of Titles** (Article 18) The State is prohibited to confer any titles like 'Raja', 'Maharaja', 'Rai Sahib', 'Khan Bahadur', etc. Citizens of India are also not allowed to accept any titles from Foreign states. Titles can only be conferred for Military, Sports or Academic distinctions. For example, 'Bharat Ratna', 'Padma Bhushan', 'Padma Shri', etc.

2. Right to Freedom (Articles 19 to 22)

(a) Under Article 19, the Constitution of India guarantees six basic freedoms to its citizens

(i) Freedom of speech and expression
(ii) Freedom to assemble peacefully and without arms
(iii) Freedom to form associations or unions
(iv) Freedom of movement throughout India
(v) Freedom to reside and settle in any part of India
(vi) Freedom to practice any occupation or carry out any profession

- **'Right to Information' (RTI)** has been included in Article 19(1) of the Constitution of India. This is an implied Fundamental Right.
- On 24th August, 2017, the Supreme Court of India declared the Right to Privacy as a fundamental right, subject to reasonable restrictions.

3. Right Against Exploitation (Articles 23 and 24)

(a) **Prohibition of Forced Labour and Traffic in Human Beings** (Article 23) This provides freedom from slavery, beggary or any other forms of forced labour.

(b) **Prohibition of Employment of Underage Children** (Article 24) This prohibits employment of children below the age of 14 years in factories, mines and other hazardous occupations. The practice of bonded labour has also been declared unlawful.

4. Right to Freedom of Religion (Articles 25 to 28)

(a) **Freedom of Conscience and Free Propagation** (Articles 25) All citizens of India have the freedom of conscience and the right to profess, practice and propagate their religion.

(b) **Freedom to Manage Religious Affairs** (Articles 26) This provides for the freedom to manage the religious affairs of the citizens and is subject to public order, morality and health.

(c) **Freedom from Payment of Taxes** (Article 27) This provides that no person can be morally or forcefully compelled to pay taxes for the propagation of a particular religion.

(d) **Freedom from Attending Religious Instruction** (Article 28) It protects the freedom of religion in educational institutions.

5. Cultural and Educational Rights (Articles 29 and 30)

(a) **Right to Conserve Language, Script and Culture** (Article 29) It gives a section of the people or whole of them the right to preserve their distinct language, script and culture.

(b) **Right to Establish Educational Institutions** (Article 30) It gives all the minorities the right to establish and administer the educational institutions of their choice.

6. Right to Constitutional Remedies (Article 32)

(a) This right allows people to approach the Supreme Court to enforce their Fundamental Rights.

(b) Dr. B.R. Ambedkar referred to this right as the heart and soul of the Constitution.

(c) Under Article 32, if any Fundamental Right is violated, citizens can directly approach to the Supreme Court.

Right to Property (Article 300 A)

- Previously, it was a Fundamental Right under the Article 31 but it was removed by the 44th Amendment Act, 1978.
- A new Article 300A, was added and according to this article, the Right to Property is a constitutional and legal right.

Limitations to Right to Constitutional Remedies

(a) **Protection in Case of Conviction for an Offence (Article 20)**

Any person who is accused or convicted for an offence has three protections

(i) Punishment only for a lawful offence, with no penalty beyond what the law prescribes.

(ii) No double punishment or prosecution for the same offence.

(iii) No compulsion to be a witness against himself.

(b) **Protection of Life and Personal Liberty (Article 21)**

- A person cannot be deprived of his life and liberty except in accordance with the law.
- Personal liberty is the freedom to make life choices without interference, except for legal limits to protect others' welfare.

(c) **Protection against Arrest and Detention (Article 22)**

This right protects citizens under the following circumstances

(i) Ordinary Circumstances (ii) Preventive Detention

Writs

- A writ is an official order from the court to provide legal help to individuals.
- Article 226 of the Constitution of India gives High Courts the power to issue writs to enforce Fundamental Rights.
- These writs can be issued to any person or authority, including the government to protect rights of the citizen. The important writs are
  (i) **Habeas Corpus** It means 'to have the body'. It orders the state to bring a person who has been arrested to court and explain the reason for arrest. If the arrest is unlawful, the person is released.
  (ii) **Mandamus** In Latin, it means 'we order'. It is a command or an order from a superior court to a lower court or government official who has refused or neglected to perform a specific duty.
  (iii) **Prohibition** Orders a lower court to stop a case, if it is beyond its powers or violates natural justice.
  (iv) **Certiorari** Orders a lower court to send the case records to a higher court for review after the decision has been made.
  (v) **Quo-Warranto** It means 'by what order'. It prevents a person from holding a position they are not legally qualified for, and asks them to prove the legal authority to hold that position.

Fundamental Duties

- The Fundamental Duties are listed in Article 51A of the Indian Constitution, under Part IVA of the Constitution.
- These were added by the 42nd Amendment Act, 1976, based on the recommendations of the Swaran Singh Committee.
- They are moral obligations of Indian citizens to uphold the unity of India and promote patriotism.
- The 11 fundamental duties of Indian citizens are as follows
  (i) Defend the country and render national service when called upon.
  (ii) Cherish and follow the noble ideals that inspired the national struggle for freedom.
  (iii) Value and preserve the rich heritage of the country's composite culture.
  (iv) Protect and improve the natural environment, including forests, lakes, rivers and wildlife.
  (v) Develop the scientific temper, humanism and the spirit of enquiry and reform.
  (vi) Safeguard public property and avoid violence.
  (vii) Promote harmony and the spirit of common brotherhood among all citizens.
  (viii) Strive towards excellence in all spheres of individual and collective activity. So, that the nation constantly rises to higher levels of endeavor and achievement.
  (ix) Protect the sovereignty and integrity of India.
  (x) Provide opportunities for education to his child or ward between the ages of six and fourteen years.
  (xi) Follow the Indian Constitution and respect its ideals, institutions, the National Flag and the National Anthem.

EXAM ORIENTED QUESTIONS

TYPE - 1 — 1 Mark

Multiple Choice Questions

Q.1 If a male and a female are selected for the same post but the female candidate gets less salary, which of her following rights is violated?

(a) The Right to Freedom
(b) The Right Against Exploitation
(c) The Right to Education
(d) The Right to Equality

Ans. (d) The Right to Equality

Exp. The female candidate's Right to Equality (Article 14 and Article 15) is violated as it ensures equal treatment and prohibits discrimination based on gender in employment and wages.

Q.2 Given below are details of few persons with their Rights.

Person	Article	Description
W	14	Is equal in the eyes of the law
X	17	Can prevent other person from entering a public place of worship
Y	18	Not allowed to accept any titles from Foreign States
Z	30	Can establish Educational Institutions

Select the person who does not have the correct Fundamental Right under the mentioned Articles of the Indian Constitution.

(a) W (b) X
(c) Y (d) Z

Ans. (b) X

Q.3 Identify the Fundamental Rights enshrined in the Indian Constitution

P : Freedom of speech and expression
Q : Freedom to disobey laws in the country
R : Freedom of movement throughout India
S : Freedom to issue illegal arms and ammunitions

(a) P and Q (b) R and S
(c) P and R (d) Q and S

Ans. (c) P and R

Q.4 Complete the given analogy.

Equality of Opportunity: Article 16 : : Protection of Life and Personal Liberty : ?

(a) Article 19 (b) Article 20
(c) Article 21 (d) Article 22

Ans. (c) Article 21

Q.5 Which of the following articles deals with Right to Education?

(a) Article 19 (b) Article 20
(c) Article 31 (d) Article 21A

Ans. (d) Article 21A

Q.6 Read the description and identify the Article related to it.

"The heart and soul of the Constitution".

(a) Article 21 (b) Article 25
(c) Article 27 (d) Article 32

Ans. (d) Article 32

Exp. Article 32 is called the 'heart and soul of the Constitution' because it allows people to go to the Supreme Court to protect their Fundamental Rights.

Q.7 Identify the odd one out of the following Articles related to Fundamental Rights.

(a) Article 13 (b) Article 25
(c) Article 30 (d) Article 51A

Ans. (d) Article 51A

Exp. Articles 13, 25, and 30 are part of Fundamental Rights, while Article 51A deals with the Fundamental Duties, which are moral obligations, not enforceable rights.

Q.8 After the 44th Amendment, the Right to Property became a legal right under which article of the Indian Constitution?

(a) Article 31A (b) Article 300A
(c) Article 15 (d) Article 19

Ans. (b) Article 300A

Q.9 Right to Freedom : Articles 19 to 22 : : Right to Freedom of Religion : ?

(a) Articles 29 to 30
(b) Article 32
(c) Articles 25 to 28
(d) Article 23 and 24

Ans. (c) Articles 25 to 28

Q.10 Which of the following writs, a person in India can opt for, against illegal detention as shown in the image below?

(a) Prohibition (b) Habeas corpus
(c) Certiorari (d) Quo-warranto

Ans. (b) Habeas corpus

Q.11 In a judgement, the Supreme Court issued a writ when an inferior tribunal has acted in a way that is not in accordance with the law or has exceeded its jurisdiction. Which of the following writs do you think the Supreme Court in this case, would likely to issue?

(a) Habeas corpus (b) Certiorari
(c) Quo-warranto (d) Mandamus

Ans. (b) Certiorari

Exp. The Supreme Court issues a writ of certiorari when a lower court or tribunal has made a decision that goes beyond its powers or violates the law. It is used to correct errors made by inferior courts.

Q.12 On 13th August, 2024, Rudal Shah filed a writ petition under Article 32 of the Constitution seeking his release and compensation for his unlawful detention. The Court held that the prolonged detention of Rudal Shah without any legal justification was a clear violation of his Fundamental Rights under Article 21.

The Supreme Court of India, 1st August, 1983

What information about a writ can we obtain from the above passage?

(a) Rudal filed a Prohibition petition in the higher court to issue an order to a lower court to prevent it from proceeding with a case that is outside of its jurisdiction.
(b) Rudal filed a quo-warranto petition in this Court to prevent the abuse of public offices.
(c) Rudal filed a certiorari petition in this court to a higher court to review a lower court's decision or a government agency's action.
(d) Rudal filed a habeas corpus petition in this court for his release from illegal detention.

Ans. (d) Rudal filed a habeas corpus petition in this court for his release from illegal detention.

Exp. A habeas corpus petition is filed when someone is detained unlawfully, and it ensures their release. In this case, Rudal Shah used it to challenge his illegal detention and seek justice.

Q.13 Which of the given descriptions is not aligned with the reference of the picture given below?

(a) The President can declare a National Emergency under Article 352.
(b) During a National Emergency in India, no Fundamental Rights of citizens can be suspended.
(c) The President can declare a National Emergency when he is satisfied that the safety of India or a part of it is threatened, even before the actual threat occurs.
(d) The order of Emergency must be laid before both Houses of Parliament for approval.

Ans. (b) During a National Emergency in India, no Fundamental Rights of citizens can be suspended.

Q.14 Which of the following describes the fundamental duty as per Indian Constitution?

(a) Casting a vote in an election
(b) Following all religious norms
(c) Protecting and improving the natural environment
(d) Residing and settling in any part of India

Ans. (c) Protecting and improving the natural environment

TYPE - 2 1 Mark

Assertion-Reason Questions

Q.1 Read the two statements given below about the Fundamental Rights and select the option that shows the correct relationship between (A) and (R).

Assertion (A) The Fundamental Rights are justifiable in nature.

Reason (R) These when violated, the aggrieved individual cannot move the courts for their enforcement.

(a) R contradicts A
(b) R is the reason for A
(c) A is true but R is false
(d) A and R are independent of each other

Ans. (a) R contradicts A

Q.2 Read the statements given below about the Fundamental Rights and select the option that shows the correct relationship between (A) and (R)

Assertion (A) Fundamental Rights are not absolute and can be restricted by the government in certain situations.

Reason (R) These rights can be limited if the larger public interest, such as national security or public order, is at stake.

(a) R contradicts A
(b) R is the reason for A
(c) A is true but R is false
(d) A and R are independent of each other

Ans. (a) R contradicts A

Q.3 Read the statements given below about the Right to Equality and select the option that shows the correct relationship between (A) and (R)

Assertion (A) The Right to Equality ensures that all persons are treated equally before the law.

Reason (R) It prohibits discrimination based on caste, religion, sex, or place of birth, ensuring social and economic equality.

(a) R contradicts A
(b) R is the reason for A
(c) A is true but R is false
(d) A and R are independent of each other

Ans. (b) R is the reason for A

Q.4 Read the two statements given below about the writs and select the option that shows the correct relationship between (A) and (R).

Assertion (A) The writ of quo-warranto is issued by the court to enquire into the legality of claim of a person to a public office.

Reason (R) It prevents illegal control of public office by a person. Hence, it literally means 'By what authority or warrant'.

(a) R contradicts A
(b) R is the reason for A
(c) A is true but R is false
(d) A and R are independent of each other

Ans. (b) R is the reason for A

TYPE - 3 — 2 Marks

Very Short Answer Type Questions

Q.1 Read the extract given below and answer the question which follows.

Supreme Court recognises Fundamental Right against Climate Change. The judgment noted that the right to a healthy environment, safe from the ill-effects of climate change, was a "fundamental human right".

The Hindu, 8th April, 2024

Which Article link the above distinct Fundamental Right? What interconnection does it highlight?

Ans. The Supreme Court recognises Fundamental Right against Climate Change, linking it to Articles 21 (Right to Life) and 14 (Right to Equality). It highlights the interconnection between Climate Change and various Human Rights.

Q.2 Read the extract given below and answer the question which follows.

Right to privacy is 'intrinsic to life and liberty,' rules the Supreme Court of India. *The Hindu, 25th November, 2022*

What is the Right to Privacy and under which Article of Indian Constitution it has been protected?

Ans. The Right to Privacy is a fundamental right that protects an individual's personal information from unauthorised access. It is protected under Article 21 of the Indian Constitution

Q.3 With reference to the National Emergency, answer the following questions.

(i) The Power of the President of India
(ii) The Power of Parliament

Ans. (i) The President of India can declare a National Emergency when the security of India is threatened by war, external aggression, and armed rebellion. He can also suspend Fundamental Rights during a National Emergency.

(ii) The proclamation of a National Emergency must be approved by both Houses of Parliament with a special majority of the two-third of the members are present and voting in favour of the motion within one month from the date of its issue.

Q.4 Imagine you were in a society where untouchability was practiced. Mention any two cases where you might face discrimination based on your caste.

Ans. If I were in a society where untouchability was practiced, I might have faced discrimination under the following two circumstances

(i) **Social Segregation** I might be denied access to public places like temples, bathing ghats and water wells.

(ii) **Job Restrictions** I might be forced to do the lowest jobs, which are traditionally considered 'unclean' or menial.

Q.5 To whom can the citizens of India file an application if they wish to seek any information from the Government authorities?

Ans. Citizens of India can apply for Public Information Officers (PIOs), Assistant Public Information Officers (APIOs) under RTI to seek any required information from the government authorities.

Q.6 **Mention the two Articles that relate to Cultural and Educational Rights.**

Ans. The two Articles that relates to Cultural and Educational Rights are

(i) **Article 29** This right protects the interests of minorities including the right to preserve their language, script and culture.

(ii) **Article 30** This right gives minorities the right to establish and administer their own educational institutions.

Q.7 **'Fundamental Rights are universal in nature'. Explain this statement.**

Ans. The above statement means that Fundamental Rights are granted to all citizens of a country without distinction based on caste, class, gender, colour, religion, or any other status.

Q.8 **How are Fundamental Rights justiciable?**

Ans. Fundamental Rights in India are justiciable, meaning that individuals can enforce them in court if they are violated. A suit can be filed under Article 226 in a High Court or under Article 32 in the Supreme Court in case there is dissatisfaction.

Q.9 **Mention two Fundamental Rights that indicate that India is a 'secular state'.**

Ans. Two Fundamental Rights that indicate that India is a 'secular state' are as follows

(i) **Article 25** Freedom of Conscience and Free Propagation

(ii) **Article 26** Freedom to Manage Religious Affairs

Q.10 **By which Act of Parliament were the Fundamental Duties included in the Constitution? Mention the Fundamental Duty which has been added by the Constitution (86th Amendment) Act, 2002.**

Ans. The 42nd Amendment Act, 1976 of Parliament added the Fundamental Duties of citizens to the Constitution of India. The 86th Constitution Amendment Act, 2002 added a fundamental duty which states that "Parents and guardians are required to provide educational opportunities for their children between the ages of six and fourteen."

Q.11 **Give two reasons why Fundamental Duties are important in life.**

Ans. Fundamental Duties are important in life because they

(i) remind citizens of their responsibilities.

(ii) promote a sense of discipline and commitment.

TYPE - 4 3 Marks

Short Answer Type Questions

Q.1 **What was the Right to Property in the Indian Constitution? When was it removed from the list of Fundamental Rights? Mention the position of the Right to Property in India?**

Ans. Right to Property was a Fundamental Right that guaranteed all the citizens of India the right 'to acquire, hold and dispose of property.'

The Right to Property was removed from the list of Fundamental Rights in India in 1978 by the 44th Constitutional Amendment.

The Right to Property in India is a 'constitutional and legal right' under Article 300A of the Constitution of India.

Q.2 **Write a short note on the Right to Education in India.**

Ans. The Right to Education in India has been granted by the Constitution (86th Amendment) Act, 2002. By this Act, a new Article 21A has been inserted in the Constitution, which states, "The state shall provide free and compulsory education to all children of the age of 6 to 14 years".

Q.3 **Mention the three wrong practices which have been declared illegal under Right Against Exploitation.**

Ans. The three wrong practices declared illegal under the Right Against Exploitation are

(i) **Forced labour** No one can be forced to work without pay.

(ii) **Child labour** Children cannot be employed in hazardous work.

(iii) **Human Trafficking** The trade of people for exploitation is prohibited.

Q.4 **'India is a Secular State'. Justify by giving three examples.**

Ans. India is considered a Secular State, which means it does not have any official state religion, and the government treats all religions equally.

Three examples that justify this are

(i) **Religious Freedom (Article 25)** The Constitution of India guarantees freedom of religion to all citizens. People have the right to practice, profess, and propagate their religion without any interference from the state.

(ii) **Non-Discrimination on Religious Grounds (Article 15)** The state cannot discriminate against any citizen on the basis of religion. This ensures equal treatment for all citizens, regardless of their religious beliefs.

(iii) **Equal Treatment in Public Services (Article 16)** In India, appointments to government jobs and positions are not based on religion. The government ensures that people of all religions have equal opportunities in public services.

Q.5 What is the role of Article 32 in protecting Fundamental Rights? Why did Dr. B.R. Ambedkar call it the 'heart and soul' of the Constitution?

Ans. Article 32 plays a key role in protecting Fundamental Rights by allowing people to directly approach the Supreme Court if their rights are violated. It empowers the court to issue writs (formal orders) like habeas corpus, mandamus, prohibition, certiorari, and quo-warranto to restore rights.

Dr. B.R. Ambedkar called this article as the 'heart and soul' of the Constitution because it ensures that citizens can seek justice and the enforcement of their rights.

TYPE - 5 — 4 Marks

Long Answer Type Questions

Q.1 Mention any four Fundamental Rights enshrined in the Indian Constitution.

Ans. Fundamental Rights enshrined in the Indian Constitution are as follows

- **Article 14** It ensures that every citizen is treated equally before the law, guaranteeing equality and fairness. It means that no individual or group can be discriminated against unfairly by the state.
- **Article 16** It provides equality of opportunity in matters of public employment. It ensures that no citizen is denied a job or position in government service based on discriminatory grounds.
- **Article 18** It abolishes titles that are awarded by the state, except for military and academic honors. It ensures that no one can claim superiority based on inherited titles.
- **Article 20** It provides protection against arbitrary arrest and detention. It ensures that no person can be convicted for an offence that was not defined as a crime at the time of commission (ex post facto law).

Q.2 Briefly explain the following writs.

(i) Writ of Mandamus (ii) Writ of Prohibition

Ans. (i) The writ of mandamus is as follows

- The writ of mandamus is a command issued by a higher court to a lower court or government official, instructing them to perform their legal duty or correct an omission.
- It ensures that public officials or bodies follow the law and fulfill their responsibilities as required.

(ii) The writ of prohibition is as follows

- The writ of prohibition is issued by a higher court to prevent a lower court from continuing a case that exceeds its jurisdiction or violates legal procedures.
- It ensures that lower courts operate within the limits of their authority and uphold the principles of justice and fairness.

Q.3 The Fundamental Duties promote a spirit of patriotism and uphold the unity of India. Which committee recommended the inclusion of Fundamental Duties in the Constitution? Mention any three Fundamental Duties enshrined in the Indian Constitution.

Ans. The Swaran Singh Committee, set up in 1976 recommended the inclusion of Fundamental Duties in the Indian Constitution.

Three Fundamental Duties enshrined in the Indian Constitution (under Article 51-A) are

(i) **To respect the Constitution, the national flag, and the national anthem** Citizens are expected to honor the symbols of India's sovereignty and unity.

(ii) **To uphold and protect the sovereignty, unity and integrity of India** It is the duty of every citizen to ensure that India's integrity and sovereignty are maintained.

(iii) **To promote harmony and the spirit of common brotherhood** Citizens must work to foster a sense of unity, peace, and mutual respect among all people, irrespective of differences of religion, language, or region.

TYPE - 6 10 Marks

Structured Questions

Q.1 With reference to the 'Fundamental Rights' enshrined in the Indian Constitution, answer the following.

(i) Why are Fundamental Rights referred to as fundamental in the Indian Constitution? **(3)**

(ii) "Fundamental Rights are basic human freedoms where every Indian citizen has the right to enjoy a proper and harmonious development of personality and life." State their three characteristic features. **(3)**

(iii) "The laws apply in the same manner to all, regardless of a person's status." On the basis of this statement, explain any four components of the Right to Equality. **(4)**

Ans. (i) Fundamental Rights referred to as 'fundamental' in the Indian Constitution because

- The Constitution mandates that the state cannot infringe upon these rights, except under specific conditions prescribed by law.
- Fundamental Rights are enforceable in a court of law. Citizens can approach the judiciary if their rights are violated, and courts can intervene to protect these rights.
- The justiciable nature of these rights makes them an important tool for ensuring justice and preventing abuse of power by the state.

(ii) Three characteristic features of Fundamental Rights are

(a) **Integral part of the Constitution** Fundamental rights are enshrined in the Constitution and cannot be revoked by regular legislation.

(b) **Qualified Rights** Fundamental rights are not absolute, but qualified with reasonable restrictions and constraints in the collective interest of society.

(c) **Justiciable** Fundamental rights are justiciable, meaning people can move to the courts to enforce them if they are violated.

(iii) Four components of the Right to Equality are

(a) **Equality before the Law** It states that everyone is equal before the law and should receive equal protection under the law.

(b) **Prohibition of Discrimination** It prohibits discrimination based on race, religion, gender, caste, or place of birth.

(c) **Equality of Opportunity** It guarantees equal opportunity in employment and public office.

(d) **Abolition of Untouchability** It abolishes the social practice of untouchability.

Q.2 Article 20 provides for protection in respect of conviction for offences. In this respect, answer the following.

(i) What protections are available to the citizens against conviction? **(3)**

(ii) Preventive detention is also known as 'detention without trial'. What is meant by preventive detention? State the rights of citizens in this respect. **(3)**

(iii) "Right to Protection is the right to be free from harm and to live in a safe and supportive environment." Explain any four of its limitations. **(4)**

Ans. (i) Article 20 of the Constitution of India provides citizens with the following protections against conviction for offences

(a) **No Retrospective Law** A person cannot be convicted of an act that was not a crime at the time it was committed.

(b) **No Double Jeopardy** A person cannot be prosecuted and punished for the same offence more than once.

(c) **No Self-incrimination** An accused person cannot be compelled to be a witness against themselves.

(ii) Preventive detention is the imprisonment of a person without a trial or conviction for the purpose of preventing them from committing further crimes or to maintain public order.

The Indian Constitution's Article 22 protects citizens from arbitrary arrest and detention, and provides the following rights for those detained under preventive detention laws

(a) Right to be informed

(b) Right to legal representation

(c) Right to prompt judicial review

(iii) The four limitations of Right to Protection are

(a) Not all human rights are equally protected

(b) Absolute safety is unattainable

(c) Environmental threats to health

(d) Increased vulnerability to environmental hazards

Q.3 Read the excerpt given below and answer the questions that follow.

"Article 32 of the Constitution gives an extensive original jurisdiction to the Supreme Court for enforcement of Fundamental Rights. It is empowered to issue directions, orders or writs, including writs in the nature of habeas corpus, mandamus, prohibition, quo-warranto and certiorari to enforce them." *The Supreme Court of India*

(i) What is a writ? Mention any two ways in which the writs can be filed. **(3)**

(ii) "A special form of legal action used to resolve if a person has the legal right to hold the public office that he or she occupies." Which writ is associated with this statement? Mention its two important purposes. **(3)**

(iii) Explain the following writs. **(4)**

(a) Prohibition

(b) Certiorari

Ans. (i) A writ is a formal written order issued by a court to an individual, organisation, or the state to perform or stop performing a specific action.

The two ways in which the writs can be filed include

(a) A writ petition can be filed in the High Court under Article 226 of the Constitution of India.

(b) A writ petition can be filed in the Supreme Court of India under Article 32 of the Constitution of India.

(ii) The 'writ of quo-warranto' is a legal action used to determine if someone has the legal right to hold a public office.

The two important purposes of the writ of quo-warranto include

(a) It upholds the integrity of public offices

(b) It protects citizens from being deprived of the public office they are legally entitled to.

(iii) (a) A 'writ of prohibition' is a legal order issued by a higher court to a lower court to prevent it from proceeding with a case that is outside of its jurisdiction. It is also known as a 'Stay Order'.

(b) A 'writ of certiorari' is a legal document that requests a higher court to review a case that has already been heard in a lower court.

Q.4 Look at the picture given below and answer the following questions.

(i) Describe the incident depicted in the cartoon. **(3)**

(ii) Mention any three points to analyse the conditions of the people who are there in the cartoon. **(3)**

(iii) "The Supreme Court observed that the exploitation of childhood is harmful to the democracy as well as the social stability, unity and the integrity of the nation." Give any four reasons to justify this statement. **(4)**

Ans. (i) The cartoon clearly depicts the following

- **Children working in brick factories** The cartoon clearly shows young children performing tough and hazardous tasks like carrying and arranging bricks, which are unsuitable for their age and physical capacity.
- **Loss of education and childhood** Their faces reflect fatigue and despair, symbolising stolen opportunities for education, play and personal growth.
- **Highlighting exploitation** This cartoon underscores the harsh reality of child labour and stresses the urgent need for strict laws and action to protect children from such exploitation.

(ii) The three points to analyse the conditions of the people who are in the cartoon are

(a) They are working in a hazardous environment where their safety and stability are concerned.

(b) They look malnourished.

(c) They seem to be under 14 years of age.

(iii) Reasons to justify the given statement are

(a) Child labour can lead to slavery and sexual or economic exploitation.

(b) This keeps children away from schooling and health care, restricting their Fundamental Rights.

(c) This can result in extreme bodily and mental harm, and even death.

(d) This can promote the risk of abuse and trafficking.

Q.5 With reference to the 'Fundamental Duties' enshrined in the Constitution of India, answer the following.

(i) What do you mean by Fundamental Duties? (3)

(ii) Citizens should obey their Fundamental Duties. Justify the statement by mentioning three points. (3)

(iii) Explain any four importance of Fundamental Duties. (4)

Ans. (i) Fundamental Duties are a set of moral obligations for citizens of India that are outlined in Part IV-A of the Constitution. They are intended to promote patriotism and unity in India. They are not enforceable by Courts. They are listed in Article 51A of the Indian Constitution.

(ii) Citizens should obey their Fundamental Duties because these duties are essential for the smooth functioning of society and the well-being of the nation. The above statement can be justified by the following points

(a) Fundamental Duties promote unity and integrity by encouraging citizens to respect the Constitution, the national flag, and the national anthem, which symbolise the nation's sovereignty.

(b) Duties like promoting the spirit of common brotherhood and respecting diversity help maintain peace and harmony among citizens of different backgrounds, religions and cultures.

(c) By fulfilling their Fundamental Duties, citizens contribute to maintaining the environment of freedom and justice, which allows the Fundamental Rights of all individuals to be respected and protected.

(iii) Four importance of Fundamental Duties are

(a) **Promoting National Unity** Fundamental duties promote national unity by encouraging citizens to respect the Constitution, the national flag and anthem, and the country's ideals and institutions.

(b) **Protecting the Country** Fundamental duties include defending the country and performing national service when required.

(c) **Preserving Cultural Heritage** Fundamental duties include preserving and valuing India's rich cultural heritage.

(d) **Promoting Harmony** Fundamental duties promote harmony and brotherhood among people of different regions, languages, customs and beliefs.

3

DIRECTIVE PRINCIPLES OF STATE POLICY

Meaning of Directive Principles of State Policy

- The Directive Principles of State Policy (DPSPs) are the guidelines to be followed by the government in the governance of the country.
- They are non-justiciable in nature, which means they are not enforceable by the courts of law.
- Part IV of the Constitution of India (Article 36-51) contains the DPSP.
- The concept of DPSP was inspired by Article 45 of the Irish Constitution.

Classification of DPSPs

Directive Principles can be classified into three categories based on their content and orientation

(i) **Socialist Principles** These principles aim to ensure social and economic justice and guide the establishment of a welfare state.

(ii) **Gandhian Principles** These principles promote social justice, rural development and the upliftment of the marginalised.

(iii) **Liberal-Intellectual Principles** These principles focus on individual rights, freedom and rule of law.

Implementation of DPSPs

The implementation of Directive Principles of State Policy can be seen in the following reforms of union and state governments

Social Equality and Justice

- The Right to Education Act ensures free education for children aged 6-14 years in government and aided schools.
- Reserved seats in jobs and education are provided for Scheduled Castes and Scheduled Tribes.
- Untouchability has been made illegal and punishable by law.

Economic Welfare

- The government abolished the Zamindari system and implemented land reforms to eliminate rural feudal structures.
- Major banks, insurance firms and key industries were nationalised to serve the public good.
- MGNREGA (2005) guarantees 100 days of paid labour annually for rural workers.
- PMSNY, PMUY and Ayushman Bharat (2018) are the health protection scheme, which focuses on health and wellness of the people.

Political, Legal and Administrative Reforms

- Panchayati Raj promotes local self-governance in remote villages.
- Free legal aid ensures justice for those who are unable to afford lawyers, with advisory boards in some states.
- One/third of seats in Panchayats and local bodies are reserved for women.

Foreign Policy

- India opposes colonialism, apartheid and racism globally. It supports international peace, fosters just relations and promotes global cooperation.
- India wants the world to get rid of all nuclear weapons and believes that nuclear power should only be used for making energy and doing peaceful things.

Importance of DPSPs

- They guide the government in making laws and policies.
- They ensure stability in a democracy.
- They guide the government towards creating a welfare state.
- They uphold the values of liberty, justice, equality, and fraternity.
- They educate people about their rights and what to expect from elected leaders.

Criticisms of DPSPs

Some scholars have criticised the Directive Principles on the following basis

- **Not enforceable** DPSPs are only moral guidelines, not laws.
- **Easily influenced** Non-enforceability of DPSPs can lead to pressure from powerful groups.
- **Creates conflicts** Implementation of DPSPs create problems in centre-state relations and state-level governance.

Fundamental Rights Vs DPSPs

- DPSPs have a broader, limitless scope and they are non-enforceable by law, while Fundamental Rights are specific and enforceable.
- DPSPs provide broad guidelines for the welfare of entire society, whereas Fundamental Rights protect individual freedom.
- DPSPs are positive guidelines, whereas Fundamental Rights are negative and limit the government's power.
- DPSPs are not subordinate to Fundamental Rights; they are separate but work together.

Welfare State

- A welfare state is a state which seeks to ensure the maximum happiness of the maximum number of people living within its territory.
- The Constitution of India seeks to establish India as a Welfare State.
- The words 'Welfare State' are not specifically mentioned in the Constitution, however the aims and objectives of a Welfare State are clearly pointed out in the Directive Principles of State Policy.

EXAM ORIENTED QUESTIONS

TYPE - 1 1 Mark

Multiple Choice Questions

Q.1 The Directive Principles of State Policy has been adopted from which Constitution?
(a) US Constitution (b) British Constitution
(c) Irish Constitution (d) French Constitution

Ans. (c) Irish Constitution

Q.2 Which of the following formed the sources for drafting the Directive Principles of State Policy?
(a) Irish Constitution
(b) UN Human Rights Charter
(c) Mahatma Gandhi's ideas
(d) All of the above

Ans. (d) All of the above

Q.3 Complete the given analogy.
Directive Principles : ? :: Fundamental Rights : Justiciable
(a) Enforceable by courts (b) Not Justiciable
(c) Obligatory (d) Mandatory

Ans. (b) Not Justiciable

Q.4 Which Directive Principle of State Policy aims to reduce the gap between the rich and the poor?
(a) Social Equality (b) Economic Equality
(c) Political Equality (d) Religious Equality

Ans. (b) Economic Equality

Exp. Economic Equality is aimed at reducing the difference between the rich and the poor by promoting fair distribution of wealth and resources. It ensures that everyone has equal opportunities to improve their living standards and well-being.

Q.5 Directive Principles are not enforceable in any court of law. It basically states the principles of policy that the state should follow. It states the uniform civil code for citizens. It follows the duty of the state to improve public health, raise the standard of living, and increase nutrition levels.

Which of the following Articles of the Directive Principles is not likely to have the explanation in the above paragraph?
(a) Article 37 (b) Article 39
(c) Article 44 (d) Article 48

Ans. (d) Article 48

Exp. Article 37 explains that the Directive Principles are not enforceable in any court of law.

The other articles such as

Article 39 focuses on to raise the standard of livelihood, Article 44 advocates for Uniform Civil Code and Article 48 focuses on to protect and improve the environment.

Q.6 Read the description and identify the Article related to it.

The Uniform Civil Code (UCC) calls for the formation of one law of India.
(a) Article 38 (b) Article 41
(c) Article 44 (d) Article 50

Ans. (c) Article 44

Exp. Article 44 of the Indian Constitution says that the government should try to create one common law for all citizens in India for personal matters like marriage, divorce, and inheritance. This is called the Uniform Civil Code.

Q.7 Given below are details of few Directive Principles.

Code	Article	Description
W	Article 41	The state should ensure that all citizens have an adequate means of livelihood, and that wealth is not concentrated in a few hands.
X	Article 45	The state should ensure that workers have just and humane conditions of work, including maternity relief.
Y	Article 48A	The state should ensure that the environment is protected and improved, and that forests and wildlife are safeguarded.
Z	Article 40	The state should ensure that children under six years old receive early childhood care and education.

Identify which article is correct with its description.
(a) W (b) X (c) Y (d) Z

Ans. (c) Y

Q.8 Identify the odd one out of the following objectives of the Directive Principles.

(a) To establish a welfare state where citizens have basic rights and are not exploited.

(b) To promote social justice, economic welfare and equality.

(c) To enforce the Fundamental Rights granted to the citizens.

(d) To focus on improving the living conditions of the poor and marginalised sections of society.

Ans. (c) To enforce the Fundamental Rights granted to the citizens.

Q.9 Which of the following statements are correct about Directive Principles.

P : They are provided in Part III of the Constitution

Q : They are not enforceable by courts

R : They are the guidelines to be followed by the Government

S : They are enlisted from Article 38 to 51 in the Indian Constitution

(a) P and Q (b) P and S (c) R and S (d) Q and R

Ans. (d) Q and R

Q.10 Complete the given analogy.

Land Reforms : Economic Welfare :: Right to Education : ?

(a) Welfare State (b) Social Equality and Justice

(c) Political Justice (d) Legal Reforms

Ans. (b) Social Equality and Justice

Q.11 Complete the given analogy.

Pradhan Mantri Gramin Awaas Yojana : Housing :: Ayushman Bharat : ?

(a) Employment (b) Health

(c) Insurance (d) None of these

Ans. (b) Health

Q.12 Justice Bhushan R Gavai, Judge of the Supreme Court and executive Chairman, National Legal Services Authority (NLSA) elaborated the "critical role of legal services in empowering marginalised communities and ensuring social justice of all citizens of India". *The Times of India, 18th November, 2024*

What information about free legal justice can we obtain from the above passage?

(a) Article 39A imposes an obligation on the state to provide free legal aid to ensure access to justice for all citizens.

(b) Denial of effective legal aid to accused violates Article 15

(c) 'Equal justice and free legal aid' were inserted by the Constitution (44th Amendment) Act, 1976.

(d) It is not a part of the Directive Principles of State Policy (DPSPs).

Ans. (a) Article 39A imposes an obligation on the state to provide free legal aid to ensure access to justice for all citizens.

Exp. Article 39A of the Indian Constitution directs the state to provide free legal aid to ensure justice for all, particularly marginalised communities. This reflects the importance of legal services in empowering citizens and ensuring social justice.

Q.13 Which of the following measures show the implementation of Directive Principles by the government?

(a) Untouchability made a punishable offence

(b) The Right to Education Act

(c) Reservation for Economically Weaker Sections (EWS)

(d) All of the above

Ans. (d) All of the above

TYPE - 2 — 1 Mark

Assertion-Reason Questions

Q.1 Read the two statements given below about the Directive Principles of State Policy and select the option that shows the correct relationship between (A) and (R).

Assertion (A) The Directive Principles are relevant for determining the reasonableness of restrictions under Article 19.

Reason (R) The Directive Principles have been declared superior to Fundamental Rights.

(a) R contradicts A

(b) R is the reason for A

(c) A is true but R is false

(d) A and R are independent of each other

Ans. (c) A is true but R is false

Q.2 Read the two statements given below about the Directive Principles of State Policy and select the option that shows the correct relationship between (A) and (R).

Assertion (A) The Directive Principles contained in Part IV shall not be enforceable by any court.

Reason (R) The Directive Principles and Fundamental Rights are both complementary to each other but in case of any controversy, Fundamental Rights will prevail.

(a) R contradicts A

(b) R is the reason for A

(c) A is true but R is false

(d) A and R are independent of each other

Ans. (b) R is the reason for A

Q.3 Read the statements given below about the Welfare state and select the option that shows the correct relationship between (A) and (R)

Assertion (A) The Directive Principles of State Policy aim to establish a welfare state in India.

Reason (R) The term 'welfare state' is explicitly mentioned in the Constitution.

(a) R contradicts A
(b) R is the reason for A
(c) A is true but R is false
(d) A and R are independent of each other

Ans. (c) A is true but R is false

Q.4 Read the statements given below about the social equality and select the option that shows the correct relationship between (A) and (R)

Assertion (A) The Directive Principles of State Policy are responsible for promoting social equality and justice in India.

Reason (R) The Right to Education Act and reservations for SC/STs in education and jobs are examples of implementing the Directive Principles.

(a) R contradicts A
(b) R is the reason for A
(c) A is true but R is false
(d) A and R are independent of each other

Ans. (b) R is the reason for A

TYPE - 3 　　2 Marks

Very Short Answer Type Questions

Q.1 What are Directive Principles of State Policy? In which part of the Constitution are Directive Principles incorporated?

Ans. The Directive Principles are guidelines that help to manage the governance of India and establish a welfare state.

The Directive Principles of State Policy (DPSP) are incorporated in Part IV of the Constitution of India, in Articles 36-51.

Q.2 Explain briefly any two Articles that are enlisted in the Directive Principles of the Indian Constitution.

Ans. Two Articles enlisted in the Directive Principle of the Indian Consitution are

(i) **Article 49** This aims to protect the country's cultural heritage by ensuring the preservation of monuments, places and objects of national importance. They enable people to study and understand various aspects of history, architecture, art and culture.

(ii) **Article 51** This is based on Liberal-Intellectual principles. It states that the State should advance global harmony and security. It has significant implications for India's foreign policy.

Q.3 Mention any two objectives of Directive Principles of State Policy (DPSP).

Ans. Two objectives of the Directive Principles of State Policy (DPSP) are

(i) **Promote the welfare of the people** The DPSP aims to ensure that the state promotes the welfare of its citizens by securing a social order that is based on justice, equality, and fraternity.

(ii) **Establish a just society** The DPSP aims to establish a just society by ensuring that the state strives to eliminate inequalities in income, status, facilities and opportunities.

Q.4 Give two reasons why Directive Principles of State Policy are non-justiciable.

Ans. Directive Principles of State Policy are non-justiciable because of the following reasons

(i) Implementing DPSPs often requires significant financial resources and making them enforceable would impose legal liabilities on the state.

(ii) The presence of immense diversity and socio-economic backwardness across the country posed significant challenges to their effective implementation.

Q.5 What inputs from the DPSPs can the government consider to improve governance in the following areas?

(i) Economic Development (ii) Labour rights

Ans. (i) **Economic Development** The government can implement policies to prevent the concentration of wealth and means of production. It can also secure the right to adequate means of livelihood for all citizens, promote employment generation and skill development programs.

(ii) **Labour Rights** The government can establish labour rights frameworks to ensure fair wages, safe working conditions and job security. It can also mandate Corporate Social Responsibility (CSR) policies that require businesses to invest in community welfare, environmental sustainability and social justice.

Q.6 Read the extract given below and answer the question which follows.

The Supreme Court has decreed that Article 48A of the Constitution is intricately linked to the citizens' Right to Life. *The Times of India, 20th April, 2024*

What does this Article 48A relate to? What is its importance in the social sphere?

Ans. Article 48A lays down the directive principle for protection and improvement of environment and safeguarding of forests and wildlife. It is important because it protects the environment, improves public health and raises awareness among the people.

Q.7 Mention any two differences between the Fundamental Rights and the Directive Principles of State Policy.

Ans. The differences between the Fundamental Rights and the Directive Principles of State Policy are as follows

Fundamental Rights (FRs)	Directive Principles of State Policy (DPSPs)
Fundamental Rights are justiciable and enforceable in a court of law.	DPSPs are non-justiciable and cannot be enforced by courts.
Fundamental Rights are individual rights that protect citizens from state actions.	DPSPs are guidelines for the government to promote social and economic welfare.

Q.8 When was the Right to Fair Compensation and Transparency in Land Acquisition, Rehabilitation and Resettlement Bill passed? What were its basic objectives?

Ans. The Right to Fair Compensation and Transparency in Land Acquisition, Rehabilitation and Resettlement (RFCTLARR) Act was passed on 26th September, 2013.

Its basic objectives were to ensure that the process of land acquisition is done in a just and transparent manner and that the landowners receive fair compensation and rehabilitation and resettlement measures.

TYPE - 4 — 3 Marks

Short Answer Type Questions

Q.1 The Directive Principles of State Policy are generally categorised into three types based on their content and direction. Mention the three categories of DPSPs.

Ans. The three categories of Directive Principles of State Policy (DPSP) are

(i) **Socialist** These principles promote social and economic justice, and ensure that everyone has a fair chance to succeed. The state should work for the common good and distribute resources equitably.

(ii) **Gandhian** These principles promotes social justice, rural development and the upliftment of the marginalised. For example, the state should organise village panchayats as units of self-government.

(iii) **Liberal-intellectual** These principles are based on the core beliefs of liberalism, which is a political and moral philosophy that emphasises individual liberty, political equality, and the rule of law. For example, the state should ensure a standard civil code for all people and separate the judiciary from the executive.

Q.2 The Government has taken many measures towards implementation of the Directive Principles of State Policy. Mention any three such measures.

Ans. The three measures taken by the government towards implementation of the Directive Principles of State Policy include

(i) **Education** The government passed the Right to Education Act in 2009 to ensure free and compulsory education for children between the ages of 6 and 14.

(ii) **Protection of Weaker Sections** The government has reserved seats in educational institutions for students from Scheduled Castes, Scheduled Tribes and Other Backward Classes (OBCs).

(iii) **Heritage Preservation** The government enacted the Ancient and Historical Monument and Archaeological Sites and Remains Act in 1958 to protect monuments, places, and objects of national importance.

Q.3 Write a short note on the following Government schemes.

(i) Ayushman Bharat Yojana (ABY)

(ii) Pradhan Mantri Gramin Awaas Yojana (PMGAY)

(iii) Pradhan Mantri Fasal Bima Yojana (PMFBY)

Ans. (i) **Ayushman Bharat Yojana** (ABY) It is a government health scheme started on 23rd September, 2018. It provides a health coverage of ₹ 5 lakhs per family per year for secondary and tertiary care hospitalisation across public and private impanelled hospitals in India.

(ii) **Pradhan Mantri Gramin Awaas Yojana** (PMGAY) This scheme was launched in the year 2016 to provide financial assistance for construction of 'pucca house' to all houseless and those who are living in old and broken houses.

(iii) **Pradhan Mantri Fasal Bima Yojana** (PMFBY) It was launched on 13th February, 2016. Under this scheme, farmers will have to pay a uniform premium of 2 per cent for all Kharif crops and 1.5 per cent for all Rabi crops.

Q.4 What happens in case of any conflict between the Directive Principles and Fundamental Rights?

Ans. In case of a conflict between Directive Principles (DPSPs) and Fundamental Rights, the following applies

Fundamental Rights Prevail Courts prioritise Fundamental Rights as they are enforceable and protect individual freedoms.

Amendments Allowed Parliament can amend Fundamental Rights to align with Directive Principles, as seen in cases like the 42nd Amendment.

Harmonious Interpretation Courts aim to balance both by interpreting laws harmoniously, ensuring individual rights and societal welfare coexist.

Q.5 How do the Directive Principles of State Policy reflect India's goal of being a welfare state?

Ans. The Directive Principles of State Policy reflect India's goal of being a welfare state in the following ways

- The DPSPs guide the government to promote policies that reduce inequalities in income, wealth and opportunities, ensuring that all citizens, especially the disadvantaged, have access to basic necessities.
- DPSPs emphasise the importance of providing essential services like education, healthcare, housing, and employment to ensure a decent standard of living for all citizens.
- They encourage the government to establish social security systems, including welfare programmes for the poor, marginalised communities and workers.

TYPE - 5

4 Marks

Long Answer Type Questions

Q.1 Describe the four major importance of Directive Principles of State Policy.

Ans. The four major importance of Directive Principles of State Policy include

(i) **Policy Framework** The DPSP provides guidance to policymakers to frame the policies for the betterment of the nation.

(ii) **Equal Opportunity** The DPSP ensures that all citizens have equal opportunities, regardless of class, gender, or religion. It aims to access to basic rights and opportunities which fosters social justice.

(iii) **Socio-economic Development** Directive Principles focus on improving the living standards through initiatives like education, health care and reducing poverty.

(iv) **Reflects the Country's Vision** They embody India's dream of democratic and inclusive society which guides the nation towards growth and harmony.

Q.2 The implementation of Directive Principles helps in social equality and justice? Analyse this statement with any four points.

Ans. The implementation of Directive Principles helps in social equality and justice in the following ways

(i) The Right to Education Act makes it mandatory for every child between the ages 6-14 to be provided with free education in all government and government aided schools.

(ii) Socially and economically weaker sections of the society are provided special scholarship. The 103rd Constitution Amendment, which came into force on 14th January, 2019, permits 10% reservations to the Economically Weaker Section (EWS) category.

(iii) Scheduled Castes and Scheduled Tribes are provided with reserved seats in jobs and educational institutions.

(iv) A major objective of our national policy according to the Five-Year Plan is the upliftment of weaker sections of the society. 'Garibi Hatao' (The Fifth Five-Year Plan) was focused on removing poverty and providing a minimum income for the poor.

Q.3 Explain the following schemes.

(i) Pradhan Mantri Kisan Samman Nidhi Yojana (PMKSNY)

(ii) Pradhan Mantri Ujjwala Yojana (PMUY)

Ans. (i) **Pradhan Mantri Kisan Samman Nidhi Yojana (PMKSNY)** The scheme was launched in the year 2019. Under this scheme, small and marginalised farmers (SMFs) are given ₹ 6000 per year in three equal installments of ₹ 2000 each, which is transferred directly to the bank accounts of beneficiaries through Direct Benefit Transfer (DBT) scheme.

(ii) **Pradhan Mantri Ujjwala Yojana (PMUY)** It was launched on 1st May, 2016. Under this scheme, 5 crore LPG connections will be provided to Below Poverty Line (BPL) families with a support of ₹ 1600 per connection in the next 3 years. Ensuring women's empowerment, especially in rural India, the connections will be issued in the name of women of the households.

Q.4 **Some scholars have criticised the Directive Principles of State Policy for being non-enforceable. Give any four reasons that justify this statement.**

Ans. The Directive Principles of State Policy (DPSPs) are often criticised for being non-enforceable. Four reasons to justify this are as follows

- **Lack of Legal Obligation** DPSPs are not legally binding, meaning citizens cannot challenge their non-implementation in a court of law, reducing their impact compared to enforceable Fundamental Rights.
- **Reliance on Government Priorities** The execution of DPSPs depends on the political will of the government. Some governments may prioritise these principles, while others may neglect them.
- **Economic Limitations** Many DPSPs, such as those advocating free education or public health, require substantial financial resources. In a developing country like India, limited resources can hinder their implementation.
- **Potential Conflicts** Certain DPSPs may clash with enforceable Fundamental Rights, creating challenges in striking a balance without court intervention.

Q.5 **The Directive Principles of State Policy contribute to India's commitment to international peace and security. Justify the statement.**

Ans. The Directive Principles of State Policy contribute to India's commitment to international peace and security in the following ways

- The DPSPs emphasise the importance of maintaining peaceful and friendly relations with other countries. They urge the state to foster international cooperation based on mutual respect and peaceful coexistence, aligning with India's broader foreign policy objective of peace-building.
- The DPSPs advocate for the peaceful resolution of international disputes. They encourage India to resolve conflicts through diplomacy, negotiation, and arbitration rather than through force or military means, which reinforces India's commitment to non-violence and peaceful dispute settlement.
- India's DPSPs urge the state to respect international law and work towards its observance by all nations. This aligns with India's stance on abiding by international treaties, conventions, and agreements, promoting a rule-based global order that underpins global peace and security.
- The DPSPs express India's commitment to nuclear disarmament and the peaceful use of nuclear energy. India has been a proponent of global nuclear disarmament, urging all nations, including the nuclear powers, to work toward reducing and eventually eliminating nuclear weapons for the safety and security of all nations.

TYPE - 6

10 Marks

Structured Questions

Q.1 **Read the excerpt given below and answer the questions that follow.**

On 19th November, 1948, Dr Ambedkar, speaking in the Constituent Assembly debate during the drafting of the Constitution, said about the Directive Principles of State Policy (DPSPs) contained in Part IV of the Constitution: "It is the intention of this Assembly that in future both the legislature and the executive should not merely pay lip service to these principles enacted in this part, but that they should be made the basis of all executive and legislative action that may be taken hereafter in the matter of the governance of the country."

The Hindu, 23rd August, 2022

(i) Mention the sources of Directive Principles of State Policy in India. **(3)**

(ii) The Directive Principles of State Policy (DPSP) in the Indian Constitution play a crucial role in guiding the government's actions in the legislative and executive branches. Mention any three of its important roles. **(3)**

(iii) The scopes of Fundamental Rights and DPSPs differ. Give any four reasons that justify the statement. **(4)**

Ans. (i) The sources of Directive Principles of State Policy in India include

(a) The Constitution of the Irish Republic.

(b) The Ideas of Mahatma Gandhi.

(c) The Charter of Human Rights framed by the United Nations.

(d) The declaration of the Rights of Man and Citizens of revolutionary France.

(e) The Universal Declaration of Human Rights that was adopted by the United Nations.

(ii) The three of its important roles of DPSPs include.

(a) **Shaping Laws and Policies** The DPSPs help the government create laws and policies that promote social and economic democracy, environmental protection and fair wages.

(b) **Establishing a Welfare State** The DPSPs aim to create a welfare state by promoting social and economic justice and ensuring social equality for all citizens.

(c) **Serving as a Moral Compass** The DPSPs are not legally enforceable, but they serve as a moral compass for the government. They are intended to be a guide for the ruling party in legislative and executive acts.

(iii) The scopes of Fundamental Rights and DPSPs differ in the following ways

- Fundamental Rights are specific and individual-based, protecting the personal freedoms and rights of citizens. On the other hand, DPSPs are broader, aiming at promoting social and economic welfare and guiding the government in formulating policies for the betterment of society.
- Fundamental Rights are enforceable by law in the courts, meaning individuals can approach the judiciary if their rights are violated. DPSPs, however, are non-enforceable, and citizens cannot take legal action if these principles are not implemented by the government.
- Fundamental Rights set limitations on government powers to protect individual freedoms, while DPSPs set out ideals for the government to follow when framing laws, focusing on societal welfare, equality and justice.
- Fundamental Rights address individual liberty, equality and justice, whereas DPSPs deal with broader issues such as economic development, social justice and the establishment of a welfare state.

Q.2 With reference to the image below, answer the following questions.

(i) Mention any three points to analyse how land reforms align with the objectives of Article 38 of the DPSP. (3)

(ii) What challenges in implementing land reforms hindered the fulfillment of DPSP goals? (3)

(iii) Land reforms were included under the DPSPs in India to address the long-standing inequalities in land ownership and exploitation within the agrarian economy. Mention any four Articles from the DPSPs that support the objectives of land reforms. (4)

Ans. (i) Land reforms align with the objectives of Article 38 of the DPSP in the following ways

(a) Land reforms, such as the abolition of the zamindari system and redistribution of surplus land, minimised inequalities in land ownership, reducing the socio-economic gap between landlords and landless farmers.

(b) By granting land ownership to actual cultivators and eliminating exploitative tenancy systems, land reforms protected vulnerable rural populations from economic and social exploitation.

(c) Providing land to marginalised and landless labourers improved their socio-economic status, enabling them to participate more equitably in the economic and social fabric of the country.

(ii) The challenges in implementing land reforms that hindered the fulfillment of DPSP goals are as follows

- Wealthy landlords exploited gaps in land reform laws by transferring land to family members or manipulating land records.
- Poor record-keeping, lack of enforcement, and insufficient government capacity delayed or obstructed the proper implementation of land reforms.
- Politically influential landlords resisted reforms, leading to delays, non-compliance, and weakening of the intended impact.

(iii) Four key articles from the Directive Principles of State Policy (DPSPs) that support the objectives of land reforms are

(a) **Article 38** It promotes social and economic justice by reducing inequality. It encourages the redistribution of land to landless farmers.

(b) **Article 39(b)** It aims to ensure that resources like land are distributed fairly.

(c) **Article 39(c)** It aims to prevent the concentration of wealth and ensures fairness in land ownership.

(d) **Article 43** It promotes worker participation in the management of industries, which can be crucial in ensuring fair treatment of agricultural labourers and pushing for land reforms.

4

ELECTIONS

Meaning of Elections

- An election is a process where people vote to choose representatives to run the government. Different candidates compete in elections for the same position. Thus, in the elections, there are winners and losers.
- In modern societies, elections are usually held along party lines. A political party is a group of people holding similar views or beliefs.
- Any political party or a combination of parties getting the largest number of votes to form the government.

Importance of Elections

(a) They help people to choose their representatives.

(b) They give voters a wider choice of candidates.

(c) They allow people to learn about the ideologies of different political parties through their manifestos.

(d) They help candidates to improve their leadership skills.

(e) They give people the power to decide who should rule and who should be removed, encouraging interest in the country's well-being.

(f) In democracies, elections ensure that the government prioritises the welfare of the people.

Election Commission

- Part XV of the Constitution under Articles 324 to 329, provides detailed guidelines to ensure free and fair conduct of elections.
- The Election Commission of India is an autonomous constitutional authority responsible for administering election processes in India.

Composition of the Election Commission

- The Election Commission of India is a three-member body. It consists of a Chief Election Commissioner (CEC) and two other Election Commissioners (EC).
- They are appointed by the President of India.

Terms and Conditions of Office

- The term of the members of the commission is 6 years or up to the age of 65 years, whichever is earlier.
- The salary of the Chief Election Commissioner and all other such commissioners shall be equal to that of a Supreme Court Judge.
- If there is a disagreement between the Chief Election Commissioner and the other members, the decision is made based on a majority vote.

Powers and Functions

- **Preparation of Electoral Rolls** The Election Commission prepares one electoral roll for every constituency. An electoral roll is a voter's list containing the name, father's name, age and sex of the voter.
- **Recognition of Political Parties** The Election Commission grants recognition to political parties. A political party can be recognised as a national party or a regional party.

REVISION NOTES

- **Allotment of Symbols** The Election Commission allots symbols to the recognised political parties and the candidates for election.
- **Scrutiny of Nomination Papers** The Election Commission examines the nomination papers of the candidates and can accept and reject them.
- **Conduct of Elections** The Election Commission conducts all the elections to the Parliament (Lok Sabha and Rajya Sabha) and State Assemblies. It also supervises the elections to the office of the President and Vice President of India.
- **Advisory Functions** The Election Commission advises the President or the Governors of the state in respect of electoral matters, disqualification of members, election disputes, petitions, etc.

Types of Elections

Direct Elections

- In direct elections, the people of India directly choose their representatives for the Lok Sabha and State Legislative Assemblies.
- Members of the State Legislative Assemblies (MLAs) and members of the Lok Sabha (MPs) are elected directly by the people of the state.
- The party (or combination of parties) having the largest number of legislators elect their leader from among themselves. This leader in the state is elected as the Chief Minister and in the centre as the Prime Minister.

Indirect Elections

- In indirect elections, voters do not vote directly for the candidate. Instead, they elect representatives (like MPs or MLAs) who then vote on their behalf to elect the higher officials.
- The President, the Vice President, Members of Rajya Sabha and State Legislative Councils (Vidhan Parishads) are elected by the method of indirect election.
- In Legislative Councils (Vidhan Parishads), members are elected through a combination of indirect elections and nominations, with 1/3rd elected by the Legislative Assembly, 1/3rd by local authorities and 1/12th each by graduates and teachers.
- The President is elected by an Electoral College, which consists of elected MPs of Lok Sabha and Rajya Sabha, MLAs of States and Union Territories.
- The Vice President is elected indirectly by the members of the Lok Sabha and Rajya Sabha.

System of Elections in India

General Elections

- The elections held to elect the members of the Lok Sabha and State Assemblies after expiry of the normal term of five years are called the 'General Elections'.
- Until 1957, simultaneous elections were held for both the Lok Sabha and the State Assemblies.

Mid-term Elections

- This type of election is held when a State Legislative Assembly or the Lok Sabha is dissolved before the completion of its full term (5 years).
- The new house normally have a full 5-year term.

By-Elections

- When a seat in the Legislative Assembly at the Centre or State becomes vacant due to resignation, death or other reasons, a special election called a 'By-Election' is held to fill the vacancy.
- The person elected in a by-election serves as a member for the remaining time of the house's term.

EXAM ORIENTED QUESTIONS

TYPE - 1 — 1 Mark

Multiple Choice Questions

Q.1 Which of the following helps the Election Commission to ensure free and fair elections?
(a) Code of conduct
(b) Severe punishment for booth capturing
(c) Central observers
(d) All of the above

Ans. (d) All of the above

Q.2 Identify the odd one out based on the composition of the Election Commission.
(a) Chief Election Commissioner
(b) Election Commissioner
(c) President
(d) Regional Election Commissioner

Ans. (c) President

Q.3 Who among the following appoints the Election Commissioners?
(a) President of India
(b) Prime Minister of India
(c) Chief Justice of India
(d) Act of Parliament

Ans. (a) President of India

Q.4 Which of the following is not a function of the Election Commission of India?
(a) Supervision of elections to Parliament, State Legislatures and offices of the President and Vice President
(b) Preparation and revision of electoral rolls
(c) Recognise the Political parties.
(d) Conduct of elections to local bodies such as Municipalities and Panchayats

Ans. (d) Conduct of elections to local bodies such as Municipalities and Panchayats

Exp. The State Election Commission is responsible to conduct the elections for the Panchayats and as well as for the Municipalities.

Q.5 Aryan and Priya were reading about elections in their civics book. Aryan asked, "What makes elections in India so special?" Priya replied, "I think it's because every citizen can vote, no matter what." Their teacher, Mr. Singh, overheard them and said, "That's true, but let's see if you can identify what is most likely a key feature of Elections in a Democracy."
Which of the following is most likely a key feature of elections in a democracy?
(a) Only the rich people can vote
(b) Voters choose their representatives freely
(c) Only government officials are allowed to vote
(d) Elections are conducted in every 10 years

Ans. (b) Voters choose their representatives freely

Exp. In a democracy, the citizens have the freedom to choose their representatives through voting, without any restrictions or influences.

Q.6 Given below are some details regarding Election Commission.

Code	Position	Tenure
W	Chief Election Commissioner	6 years or till the age of 65 years
X	Election Commissioner	6 years or till the age of 62 years
Y	Deputy Election Commissioner	2 years or till the age of 62 years
Z	Additional Election Commissioner	2 years or till the age of 65 years

The information given in the table above is correct for which position?
(a) W (b) X (c) Y (d) Z

Ans. (a) W

Q.7 Who allocates symbols to the political parties in India as shown in the image below?

(a) The Law Commission
(b) The Supreme Court
(c) The Election Commission of India
(d) The Central Vigilance Commission

Ans. (c) The Election Commission of India

Q.8 If a person stands for election as the President of India, he/she requires the votes of

P : Elected members of both Houses of Parliament.

Q : Elected members of the Legislative Assemblies of the States.

R : Elected members of Legislative Councils.

S : Nominated members of Rajya Sabha.

(a) P and Q (b) R and S (c) P and R (d) Q and R

Ans. (a) P and Q

Q.9 Every registered political party is allotted a symbol. Which of the following statements is correct about the allotment of a symbol to a political registered party?

(a) A registered political party is allotted a symbol from its list of 'reserved symbols'.

(b) A registered political party selects a symbol of its choice from the list of 'free symbols'.

(c) A registered political party selects a symbol of its choice from a list of 'reserved symbols'.

(d) A registered political party can take any symbol of its choice.

Ans. (a) A registered political party is allotted a symbol from its list of 'reserved symbols'.

Q.10 Complete the given analogy.

Article 82 :Delimitation Commission : : Article 324 (1): ?

(a) Election Commission (b) Gram Panchayat

(c) UPSC (d) Finance Commission

Ans. (a) Election Commission

Q.11 The Bhartiya Janata Party (BJP), led by Prime Minister Narendra Modi, secured 240 seats, a reduction from the 303 seats won in 2019, resulting in the loss of its outright majority in the Lok Sabha. The National Democratic Alliance (NDA), the BJP's coalition, obtained 293 out of 543 seats. *The Wire, 5th June, 2024*

What is the minimum number of seats required by a party or coalition to form the government in the Lok Sabha in India?

(a) 250 seats (b) 272 seats (c) 300 seats (d) 282 seats

Ans. (b) 272 seats

Q.12 Read the description and answer the following question.

"Elections in India are held at different levels and for different purposes. Some of the key types of elections include: General Elections, State Legislative Elections, Presidential Elections and Local Body Elections. Each type plays a crucial role in shaping the democratic structure of the nation."

Which of the following is the primary purpose of the General Elections in India?

(a) To elect members of the Panchayat

(b) To elect the President of India

(c) To elect members of the Lok Sabha

(d) To elect members of the Rajya Sabha

Ans. (c) To elect members of the Lok Sabha

Q.13 Country 'Y' has decided to adopt a system of direct elections for certain positions in its government. Who will be most impacted by this change?

(a) Members of Rajya Sabha (b) Members of Lok Sabha

(c) The President (d) The Vice-President

Ans. (b) Members of Lok Sabha

Exp. Members of Lok Sabha are elected through direct elections, while the others are elected indirectly.

Q.14 Ravi and Meera were discussing the upcoming elections in their school's civics class. Their teacher, Mr. Sharma, explained how elections are the backbone of democracy and encouraged everyone to explore the process. Ravi was curious and asked, "Sir, what if political parties were not allowed to campaign during elections? Wouldn't that make the process unfair?" Mr. Sharma smiled and replied, "That's an interesting question. Let's test your understanding."

Which of the following is not likely to happen in a democratic election process?

(a) Every adult citizen has the right to vote.

(b) Votes are counted transparently and fairly.

(c) Political parties are banned from campaigning.

(d) The Election Commission ensures the code of conduct is followed.

Ans. (c) Political parties are banned from campaigning.

Exp. In a democracy, political parties are allowed to campaign to inform voters about their plans. Banning political parties from campaigning would make the election unfair and less transparent.

Q.15 Which of the following is <u>not likely</u> interpretation of the cartoon?

(a) The man is unsure about whom to vote for.

(b) The cartoon criticises the complexity of the voting process.

(c) The man is happy with the choices provided.

(d) The cartoon highlights the importance of voter education.

Ans. (c) The man is happy with the choices provided.

TYPE - 2   1 Mark

Assertion-Reason Questions

Q.1 Read the two statements given below about the elections in India and select the option that shows the correct relationship between (A) and (R).

Assertion (A) In a democracy, elections are held at regular intervals to allow citizens to choose their representatives.

Reason (R) Regular elections ensure accountability of the government to the people.

(a) R contradicts A
(b) R is the reason for A
(c) A is true but R is false
(d) A and R are independent of each other

Ans. (b) R is the reason for A

Q.2 Read the two statements given below about the elections in India and select the option that shows the correct relationship between (A) and (R).

Assertion (A) Direct elections are held when people vote for their representatives directly.

Reason (R) In indirect elections, people vote for a political party rather than individual candidates.

(a) R contradicts A
(b) R is the reason for A
(c) A is true but R is false
(d) A and R are independent of each other

Ans. (c) A is true but R is false

Q.3 Read the two statements given below about the Composition of Election Commission in India and select the option that shows the correct relationship between (A) and (R).

Assertion (A) The Election Commission of India is a multi-member body responsible for conducting elections in the country.

Reason (R) The Election Commission consists of three members: the Chief Election Commissioner and two Election Commissioners, appointed by the President of India.

(a) R contradicts A
(b) R is the reason for A
(c) A is true but R is false
(d) A and R are independent of each other

Ans. (b) R is the reason for A

Q.4 Read the two statements given below about the Delimitation Commission and select the option that shows the correct relationship between (A) and (R).

Assertion (A) Delimitation is the process of redrawing the boundaries of constituencies to ensure equal representation in elections.

Reason (R) The Delimitation Commission is a body that is set up by the President of India and consists of members from the Parliament and the Election Commission.

(a) R contradicts A
(b) R is the reason for A
(c) A is true but R is false
(d) A and R are independent of each other

Ans. (c) A is true but R is false

Q.5 Read the two statements given below about the constituency and select the option that shows the correct relationship between (A) and (R).

Assertion (A) A constituency is a designated geographical area represented by an elected member in the legislative body.

Reason (R) Each constituency in India is based on population size, and the number of constituencies is fixed for all states.

(a) R contradicts A
(b) R is the reason for A
(c) A is true but R is false
(d) A and R are independent of each other

Ans. (c) A is true but R is false

TYPE - 3   2 Marks

Very Short Answer Type Questions

Q.1 Give two reasons why regular elections are important in a democracy.

Ans. Regular elections are important in a democracy because

(i) It ensures that the government remains accountable to the people.

(ii) It provides an opportunity for citizens to exercise their right to vote, ensuring that the government reflects the will of the people.

Q.2 Mention the names of the methods of elections held for the Lok Sabha and for the office of the President of India.

Ans. The Lok Sabha elections are held by direct election method. People of India directly elect their representatives to the Lok Sabha. The system of election to the office of the President of India is indirect elections.

Q.3 Imagine you were to bring certain reforms in the system of elections to Lok Sabha and Vidhan Sabha in states, which reforms would you introduce and why?

Ans. If I were to bring reforms in elections to the Lok Sabha and Vidhan Sabha, I would introduce state funding of elections to reduce the influence of black money and ensure fair competition, and implement Right to Recall representatives to hold leaders accountable for non-performance or corruption.

These reforms would promote transparency, equality and accountability in the electoral process.

Q.4 Which political party uses the 'Lotus' as its symbol? What role do election symbols play in an election?

Ans. Bharatiya Janata Party (BJP) uses the 'Lotus' as its symbol.

The election symbols give identification to the political parties on ballot paper/Electronic Voting Machines (EVMs). It helps illiterate voters to identify the party they want to vote for.

Q.5 What is known as the voters list? Who prepares the voters list?

Ans. The Election Commission identifies eligible voters in each constituency and prepares the list of all eligible voters. This is called the voters list.

The Election Commission of India is responsible for preparing and maintaining the voters list.

Q.6 What are constituencies? How many types of constituencies exist?

Ans. For ease in elections, the entire country is divided into fixed electoral areas with specific bodies of registered voters. These areas are called constituencies.

Three types of constituencies exist i.e. single member constituency, multi-member constituency and reserved constituency.

Q.7 Read the extract given below and answer the question which follows.

"Delimitation is the process of redrawing the boundaries of constituencies to ensure that each constituency has an equal representation based on population. This process is carried out by the Delimitation Commission, which is appointed by the President of India."

What is the purpose of delimitation, and who carries out the process in India?

Ans. The purpose of delimitation is to redraw the boundaries of constituencies to ensure equal representation based on population.

This process is carried out by the Delimitation Commission, which is appointed by the President of India.

Q.8 Mention any two important components of an Electronic Voting Machine (EVM).

Ans. The two important components of an Electronic Voting Machine (EVM) include

(i) **Control Unit** This is the main unit operated by the election officials to supervise the voting process and ensure proper functioning of the machine.

(ii) **Ballot Unit** This unit is used by the voters to cast their votes by pressing the buttons corresponding to their chosen candidates.

Q.9 Explain the concept of proportional representation in elections in India.

Ans. Proportional representation is an electoral system where the number of seats a political party receives in a legislature is directly proportional to the number of votes it gains in an election. This system ensures that smaller parties are also represented in proportion to their support, leading to a more inclusive and balanced representation.

Q.10 Mention any two features which make the election commission independent.

Ans. Two features that make the Election Commission independent are as follows

(i) The Election Commission is established under Article 324 of the Constitution, granting it autonomous powers to conduct free and fair elections without interference from the government.

(ii) The Chief Election Commissioner and Election Commissioners have a fixed tenure and can only be removed through a process similar to the removal of a Supreme Court Judge, ensuring protection from arbitrary dismissal.

Q.11 Who constitutes the Election Commission of India, and who is the head of the Commission?

Ans. The Election Commission of India consists of the Chief Election Commissioner (CEC) and two Election Commissioners (ECs).

The Chief Election Commissioner is the head of the Election Commission and is appointed by the President of India.

Q.12 How are members of the State Legislative Assemblies (MLAs) elected, and what is their role in the formation of the State Government?

Ans. Members of the State Legislative Assemblies (MLAs) are directly elected by the people of the state. After elections, the party with the most seats select a leader who becomes the Chief Minister and forms the State Government.

Q.13 How does the system of indirect elections work, and which key political positions are chosen through this method?

Ans. In indirect elections, voters choose representatives (like MPs or MLAs), who then vote for the candidate on their behalf.

Key positions chosen in this way include the President, Vice-President, Rajya Sabha members, and State Legislative Council members.

Q.14 Define the following terms

(i) By-Election (ii) Mid-term Election

Ans. (i) **By-Elections** When a seat held by any member of the Legislative Assembly in the Centre or State falls vacant on account of death or resignation of the member before completion of his/her term, to fill up this vacancy the election which is held is called By-Election.

(ii) **Mid-term Election** This type of election is held when a State Legislative Assembly or the Lok Sabha is dissolved before the completion of its full term (5 years).

Q.15 What are General Elections, and when are they held in India?

Ans. General Elections in India are held to elect members of the Lok Sabha and State Legislative Assemblies, after every five years.

They are conducted when the current term of the Lok Sabha or State Legislative Assemblies ends and all eligible citizens vote to choose their representatives.

TYPE - 4 3 Marks

Short Answer Type Questions

Q.1 Mention any three important powers and functions of the Election Commission of India.

Ans. The three of the important powers and functions of the Election Commission of India include

(i) **Conducting Elections** The Election Commission is responsible for organising and overseeing elections for the Lok Sabha, Rajya Sabha and State Legislative Assemblies, ensuring they are free and fair.

(ii) **Supervising Electoral Rolls** It ensures the maintenance and updating of accurate voters' lists and ensures that only eligible citizens are included.

(iii) **Regulating Political Parties and Candidates** The Election Commission monitors political parties, their election campaigns, and the conduct of candidates, ensuring compliance with the election code of conduct.

Q.2 In the context of elections in India, describe the roles and responsibilities of a Polling Officer and a Presiding Officer as outlined by the Election Commission.

Ans. The roles and responsibilities of a Polling Officer and a Presiding Officer are stated below

Polling Officer	Presiding Officer
Assists in the polling process under the Presiding Officer's supervision.	In-charge of the entire polling station, ensuring smooth conduct of polling.
Reports to the Presiding Officer and works as per instructions.	Supervises all polling officers and activities at the polling station.
Verifies voter identity using the electoral roll and voter ID documents.	Oversees the entire voter verification process to ensure accuracy.

Q.3 In order to maintain the integrity and fairness of the election process, the Election Commission of India ensures that election expenses are strictly regulated. Mention any three points on the importance of the scrutiny of election expenses by the Election Commission of India.

Ans. The importance of the scrutiny of election expenses include

(i) **Ensuring Transparency** The scrutiny of election expenses ensures that political parties and candidates adhere to the legal limits set for election spending. This promotes transparency in the electoral process and prevents unfair advantage through excessive spending.

(ii) **Preventing Corruption** By monitoring and reviewing the expenses, the Election Commission helps in preventing the misuse of money, such as bribing voters or indulging in illegal campaign practices, ensuring that the elections remain free and fair.

(iii) **Maintaining Equal Opportunity** The scrutiny ensures that all candidates, regardless of their financial resources, have equal opportunities to campaign, which supports the democratic principle of fair competition in elections.

TYPE - 5 4 Marks

Long Answer Type Questions

Q.1 'Indirect elections are used for certain offices like the President, Vice President and Rajya Sabha members in India.' Give any four reasons that justify this statement.

Ans. Four reasons that justify the given statement are

(i) Indirect elections ensure that the President, Vice President and Rajya Sabha members represent both the states and the union, maintaining a balance between the central and state governments.

(ii) These positions require the elected representatives (MPs and MLAs) to act collectively, ensuring the candidate has widespread acceptance across the country or states.

(iii) Indirect elections for bodies like the Rajya Sabha allow experienced individuals, who might not contest direct elections, to contribute to governance and policy making.

(iv) Indirect elections for offices like the President and Vice President help avoid excessive politisation and populism, ensuring the process focuses more on merit and broad consensus.

Q.2 **'The Election Commission of India plays a crucial role not only in conducting elections but also in advising the government on various electoral matters'. Explain any four advisory functions of the Election Commission of India.**

Ans. The four advisory functions of the Election Commission of India include

(i) **Advising the President on Elections** The Election Commission advises the President of India on the decision regarding the dates of elections for the Lok Sabha, Rajya Sabha and State Legislative Assemblies.

(ii) **Advising on Election Schedules** The commission suggests suitable dates and timelines for conducting elections to ensure they are organised and efficient.

(iii) **Advising on Electoral Reforms** The Election Commission offers recommendations on necessary electoral reforms, such as changes to the voting system, campaign finance regulations and other matters related to the electoral process.

(iv) **Advising on Electoral Roll Issues** The commission helps address discrepancies or problems with electoral rolls, making sure that eligible voters are included and any errors are corrected.

Q.3 **"Constituencies form the basis of representation in the Indian Parliament and State Assemblies". Discuss the concept of constituencies in India and their significance in the election process.**

Ans. In India, a constituency is a defined geographical area from which voters elect their representatives for the Parliament or State Legislative Assemblies. The country is divided into numerous constituencies to ensure fair and balanced representation based on population.

Each constituency elects one representative in a single-member constituency system, which is common in India. There are also reserved constituencies for Scheduled Castes and Scheduled Tribes to promote inclusivity and provide a voice to marginalised communities.

- The significance of constituencies lies in enabling democratic representation.
- They allow people to choose leaders who address their specific regional concerns.
- The process of delimitation ensures that constituencies are revised periodically based on population changes, promoting equitable representation.

Thus, the Constituencies form the backbone of the election process, ensuring that citizens across the country have an opportunity to participate in decision-making through their elected representatives.

TYPE - 6 — 10 Marks

Structured Questions

Q.1 **In a democracy, elections serve as a vital tool for citizens to choose their representatives, ensuring their participation in governance. Free and fair elections guarantee that the voice of the people is heard and that leaders are accountable to the public.**

With reference to democracy and elections, answer the following questions.

(i) "Elections held in India are of different nature for different purposes". Distinguish between any two types of elections. (3)

(ii) Democracy is a system where the people elect their representatives to make decisions on their behalf. Discuss any three ways of conducting free and fair elections in India. (3)

(iii) How are the elections to the President and the Vice President of India held? (4)

Ans. (i) The differences between direct and indirect elections are

Direct Election	Indirect Election
People directly vote for their representatives.	The elected representative vote on the behalf of the voters.
Members of Lok Sabha (MPs) and Members of Legislative Assemblies (MLAs) are directly elected.	The President of India is indirectly elected by an electoral college.

(ii) Three ways of conducting free and fair elections in India are as follows

(a) An independent body, such as the Election Commission of India, oversees the electoral process to ensure neutrality and fairness. This body ensures that elections are conducted without political interference.

(b) Every citizen, regardless of their social or economic status, must have an equal vote. The principle of 'one person, one vote' ensures that all votes carry the same weight.

(c) Voters must be allowed to vote in secrecy, free from intimidation or coercion. This ensures that individuals can make their choices without fear of manipulation.

(iii) For answer, refer to Q.1 of Long Answer Type Questions.

Q.2 In India, constituencies are the basic units of elections, and they ensure the representation of people in both the Parliament and State legislatures. There are different types of constituencies based on the electorate and specific needs. With reference to the constituencies, answer the following questions.

(i) Explain the different types of constituencies in India and the role they play in the electoral process. (3)

(ii) Discuss how these constituencies ensure representation of all sections of society in the Parliament and State Legislatures. (3)

(iii) "Reserved constituencies play a crucial role in ensuring political representation and social justice for historically marginalised communities, fostering inclusivity and empowering underrepresented sections of society in India's democratic framework". What is the significance of reserved constituencies in India? Discuss their purpose and importance in promoting social justice. (4)

Ans. (i) In India, there are different types of constituencies, each serving a distinct purpose to ensure fair and diverse representation

- **General Constituencies** These constituencies are open to all citizens, where any eligible voter can elect a representative regardless of their social or economic background. General constituencies form the majority of the electoral divisions in India and ensure representation from all sections of the population.
- **Reserved Constituencies** Reserved constituencies are specifically set aside for candidates from the Scheduled Castes (SCs) and Scheduled Tribes (STs). This system is aimed at ensuring political empowerment for historically marginalised communities, promoting social justice, and giving them a platform for active participation in governance.
- **Nominated Constituencies** Though this provision has been discontinued after the 104th Constitutional Amendment, nominated constituencies were once created to give representation to the Anglo-Indian community in the Lok Sabha and State Assemblies. These seats were filled by appointments made by the President, ensuring that the community had a voice in the legislature.

(ii) The different types of constituencies in India ensure representation of all sections of society in the Parliament and State Legislatures by creating a more inclusive and equitable electoral system in the following ways

- General constituencies are open to all voters and elect representatives from the general population. These constituencies ensure that the diverse voices of the Indian electorate, regardless of caste, creed, or social background, are heard.
- Reserved constituencies guarantee that members from Scheduled Castes (SCs) and Scheduled Tribes (STs) are given the opportunity to participate in governance and have their voices heard in the Parliament and State Assemblies.
- Nominated constituencies originally allowed for the representation of the Anglo-Indian community in the Lok Sabha and state assemblies. This ensured that a minority community, whose interests might otherwise be overlooked, had a direct voice in shaping national and state policies.

(iii) Reserved constituencies are significant in India because they give members of weaker sections of society a chance to participate in politics and address historical marginalisation.

Their purpose and importance in promoting social justice are as follows

- **Promote Political Inclusivity** They ensure that underrepresented groups have a voice in legislative processes.
- **Address Historical Inequalities** They help to address the historical marginalisation of communities like Scheduled Castes (SC), Scheduled Tribes (ST), and Other Backward Classes (OBC).
- **Provide Opportunities to Influence Policy** They give these communities the opportunity to influence policy and decision-making.
- **Give a Platform to Participate in Politics** They give weaker sections of society a platform to participate in politics.
- **Ensure Adequate Representation** They ensure that members from these communities are elected to legislatures.

THE STATE LEGISLATURES

- State Legislatures are the law-making bodies at the state level, which are responsible for enacting laws and representing the interests of the people within their respective states.
- In India, a State Legislature can be unicameral or bicameral and in either case, the Governor is also part of the legislature.
- Articles 168 to 212 in Part VI of the Constitution deals with the organisation, composition, duration, officers, procedures, privileges, powers etc. of the State Legislature.
- Each state in India has a legislature, which may have either one or two houses.
  (i) **Legislative Assembly** (Vidhan Sabha) The Legislative Assembly is the Lower House. Its members are directly elected by the people in their constituencies.
  (ii) **Legislative Council** (Vidhan Parishad) The Legislative Council is the Upper House, present in states with bicameral legislatures. Its members are elected indirectly by specific groups such as teachers, graduates and local leaders.

Meaning of Unicameral and Bicameral Legislature

- **Unicameral Legislature** States with only one house, the Legislative Assembly, are called unicameral. Examples include Kerala and Uttarakhand.
- **Bicameral Legislature** States with two houses, the Legislative Assembly and the Legislative Council, are called bicameral. In India, six states have bicameral legislatures: Andhra Pradesh, Bihar, Karnataka, Maharashtra, Telangana and Uttar Pradesh.

Term and Composition of the Legislatures

- Article 170 of the Constitution of India deals with the composition of the legislative assemblies in the states and Article 171 deals with the legislative council.
- Article 172 of the Constitution outlines the duration of state legislative assemblies and councils.

Legislative Assembly

- **Term** The Legislative Assembly's term is five years. However, it may be dissolved earlier than that by the Governor at the reavest of the Chief Minister, when the Chief Minister has actual majority support in the Assembly.
- **Composition** The number of members in the Legislative Assembly varies from state to state, depending on the population. The number of members cannot be fewer than 60 or more than 500.

Legislative Council

- **Term** The Legislative Council members have a term of six years, but 1/3rd of the members retire every two years.
- **Composition** Under Article 171 of the Constitution the Legislative Council of a State is compassed of a maximum of one-third of the total strength of the State Assembly, with a minimum requirement of 40 members.

Qualification for Membership

Qualifications required to become a member of the Legislative Assembly and the Legislative Council are

- He/She must be a citizen of India.
- He/She must be at least 25 years old for the Legislative Assembly.
- He/She must be at least 30 years old for the Legislative Council.
- He/She must an enrolled voter of the state.
- He/She must not hold any office of profit under the Government of India or any state.

Powers and Functions

- **Making Laws** The State Legislature has the authority to make laws on matters mentioned in the State List and concurrent list of the Seventh Schedule of the Constitution. For example: police, healthcare and education.
- **Budget Approval** The State Legislature approves the state's budget, which includes the spending and revenue plan for the state.
- **Control over the Executive** The State Legislature can examine the actions of the State Government. Members can ask questions, debate on issues pertaining to the functioning and performance of the government to ensure transparency and accountability.
- **Approval of Bills** A bill must be approved by the State Legislature and receive the Governor's approval before it becomes a law.
- **Policy Discussion** Members discuss and debate policies to improve the state's development and address issues like agriculture, education, infrastructure etc.

EXAM ORIENTED QUESTIONS

TYPE - 1 1 Mark

Multiple Choice Questions

Q.1 Which part of the Indian Constitution deals with the State Legislature?
(a) Part IV (b) Part V (c) Part VI (d) Part VII

Ans. (c) Part VI

Q.2 The Central Legislature was expanded and provincial legislatures were also established. Under the Montague Chelmsford report, the Government of India Act of 1919 provided for a bicameral legislature or the Centre as well as the provinces became bicameral. *Source: Deccan Herald, 18th May, 2024*

Which two houses were created in the provinces under the Government of India Act, 1919?
(a) Legislative Assembly and Legislative Council
(b) Legislative Council and Executive Council
(c) House of Commons and House of Lords
(d) Lok Sabha and Rajya Sabha

Ans. (a) Legislative Assembly and Legislative Council

Q.3 Which of the following statements is true based on the structure of the State Legislature?

(a) The Legislative Assembly is the Lower House and the Legislative Council is the Upper House in the bicameral legislature.
(b) The Legislative Assembly's term is four years, while the Legislative Council's term is six years.
(c) The members of the Legislative Councils are elected directly, while the members of the Legislative Assemblies are elected indirectly.
(d) The qualifications for membership in the Legislative Assembly are higher than those for the Legislative Council.

Ans. (a) The Legislative Assembly is the Lower House and the Legislative Council is the Upper House in the bicameral legislature.

Q.4 Identify the composition and term of the Legislative Assembly and the Legislative Council.
P : The Legislative Assembly's term is five years and the number of members varies between 60 to 500.
Q : The Legislative Council's term is five years, with one-fourth of the members retiring every two years.
R : The Legislative Council's term is six years, with one-third of the members retiring every two years.
S : The Legislative Assembly's term is six years, and the number of members varies between 50 to 600.
(a) P and Q (b) R and S
(c) P and R (d) Q and S

Ans. (c) P and R

Q.5 If a state has a Legislative Assembly with 400 members, what is the maximum number of members the state can have in its Legislative Council?
(a) 123 (b) 133 (c) 143 (d) 153

Ans. (b) 133

Exp. The Legislative Council can have a maximum of one-third of the assembly members. For a 400-member assembly, the maximum council members would be 133.

Q.6 Given below are the details of the qualifications for membership in the Legislative Assembly of state.

Person	Age	Description
W	22	He is a Scientist.
X	20	He is a Lawyer.
Y	25	He have a citizenship of India.
Z	26	He have a citizenship of China.

Select the person who meets the correct qualifications for membership in the Legislative Assembly of the state.
(a) W (b) X (c) Y (d) Z

Ans. (c) Y

Q.7 Who creates the budget in the state which resulted in the below headline?

Fourth budget of Yogi 2.0 today, focus on infrastructure push likely

(a) Chief Minister (b) Finance Minister
(c) Home Minister (d) Education Minister

Ans. (b) Finance Minister

Exp. The Finance Minister of a state has the power to create the budget, which is known as the 'Annual Financial Statement', under Article 202 of the Indian Constitution.

Q.8 **The Himachal Pradesh Legislative Assembly discusses a new bill aimed at improving healthcare facilities. After a series of debates and amendments, the bill is passed and sent to the Governor for approval. In this context, which of the following roles best describes the function of the Legislative Assembly?**

(a) To determine the allocation of funds for healthcare initiatives
(b) To review and suggest changes to the state constitution
(c) To pass legislation after thorough discussions and amendments
(d) To oversee the operational aspects of healthcare programs in the state

Ans. (c) To pass legislation after thorough discussions and amendments

Q.9 Legislative council : Permanent body :: Legislative Assembly : ?

(a) Temporary body (b) Dissolved after 10 years
(c) Dissolvable after 5 years (d) Cannot be dissolved

Ans. (c) Dissolvable after 5 years

Q.10 The Legislative Assembly of Kerala is discussing a new bill on agricultural reforms. Members are raising concerns about the funding and the timeline for its implementation. This process is an example of which of the following functions of the State Legislature?

(a) Making Laws (b) Budget Approval
(c) Control over the Executive (d) Policy Discussion

Ans. (d) Policy Discussion

Q.11 Identify the odd one out of the following functions of the State Legislature.

(a) Making laws on matters mentioned in the State List and Concurrent List.
(b) Approving the state's budget, which includes the spending and revenue plan.
(c) Scrutinising the actions of the Central Government.
(d) Discussing and debating policies to improve the state's development.

Ans. (c) Scrutinising the actions of the Central Government.

Q.12 Which of the following statements best reflects the role of the State Legislature in approving the state's budget?

(a) It only approves the budget prepared by the Central Government.
(b) It reviews the revenue and spending plan for the state.
(c) It creates the budget for the Central Government
(d) It allows the Central Government to approve the state's budget.

Ans. (b) It reviews the revenue and spending plan for the state.

TYPE - 2
1 Mark

Assertion-Reason Questions

Q.1 **Assertion** (A) A state legislature with one house is called a unicameral legislature.

Reason (R) States like Andhra Pradesh and Telangana have only one house in their legislature.

(a) R contradicts A
(b) R is the reason for A
(c) A is true but R is false
(d) A and R contradict each other

Ans. (c) A is true but R is false

Q.2. **Assertion** (A) The state legislature has the power to make laws on matters mentioned in the state list and the concurrent list.

Reason (R) The state legislature can make laws on matters like- police, public health care, agriculture, state public services etc.

(a) R contradicts A
(b) R is the reason for A
(c) A is true but R is false
(d) A and R contradict each other

Ans. (b) R is the reason for A

TYPE - 3 2 Marks

Very Short Answer Type Questions

Q.1 With reference to the State Legislature, answer the following questions

(i) What is the State Legislature?

(ii) Which articles of the Indian Constitution deals with the State Legislatures?

Ans. (i) The State Legislature is the law-making body at the state level in India. It is responsible for making laws and representing the interests of the people within the state.

(ii) Articles 168 to 212 of the Constitution define the state legislatures.

Q.2 Name any two states which have bicameral legislature?

Ans. The two states which have bicameral legislature are Maharashtra and Karnataka.

Q.3 Give two reasons why the Legislative Council has a term of six years with one-third retiring every two years?

Ans. The Legislative Council has a term of six years with one-third retiring every two years because of

- **Continuity** It ensures that the Legislative Council always has experienced members, avoiding a complete overhaul at once.
- **Efficiency** Gradual member replacement allows smoother functioning without disrupting legislative processes entirely.

Q.4 'The Legislative Assembly and Legislative Council have different functions.' Explain this statement.

Ans. The Legislative Assembly focuses on making laws, discussing policies and representing the public. On the other hand, the Legislative Council acts as a revising body, reviewing and suggesting changes to laws passed by the Assembly. Both ensure checks and balances in state governance.

Q.5 Mention any two powers of the State Legislature in India.

Ans. The two powers of the State Legislature are

- **Law-Making Powers** The State Legislature makes laws on subjects listed in the State List and Concurrent List such as police, public health and agriculture.
- **Financial Powers** It passes the state budget and approves bills related to state taxes and financial expenditures.

Q.6 'The State Legislature plays a key role in law-making'. Explain this statement.

Ans. The State Legislature is crucial in law-making as it debates, proposes and passes laws on state matters. It consists of elected representatives who discuss, amend and approve bills, ensuring laws are created to address the needs and issues of the state.

Q.7 Imagine you are a member of a State Legislature. What are two key functions of the legislature that directly impact the development of the state?

Ans. As a member, the legislature's key functions that directly impact the development of the state include

- **Making Laws** The legislature creates laws that address issues like education, healthcare and infrastructure, which directly affect the state's development and the well-being of its people.
- **Approving the Budget** The legislature approves the state budget, deciding how resources are allocated for development projects, public services and economic growth.

Q.8 Read the extract given below and answer the question

'Governors can't stay silent'. SC says Raj Bhawan must give reasons for blocking Bills'.

Source: The Indian Express, 11the Feb., 2025

(i) Which article of the Indian Constitution defines the executive powers of the Governor?

(ii) What is the role of the Governor in the State Legislature?

Ans. (i) Article 162 defines the executive power of the Governor.

(ii) The Governor is a part of the State Legislature and plays a key role in giving assent to bills, summoning or dissolving the legislature, and ensuring the implementation of laws.

TYPE - 4

3 Marks

Short Answer Type Questions

Q.1 Mention three differences between unicameral and bicameral legislature.

Ans. The three differences between the unicameral and bicameral legislature are

Unicameral Legislature	Bicameral Legislature
A unicameral legislature has only one house, the Legislative Assembly (Vidhan Sabha).	The bicameral legislature has two houses - the Legislative Assembly (Vidhan Sabha) and the Legislative Council (Vidhan Parishad).
In a unicameral system, all legislative work is done by one house.	In a bicameral system, the two houses share the responsibilities. The Upper House reviewing and revising legislation passed by the Lower House.
22 states have a unicameral legislature. For example: Kerala, Gujarat, Odisha etc.	Six states have bicameral legislatures. For example: Uttar Pradesh, Bihar, Maharashtra etc.

Q.2 'Any State Assembly is dissolved before completing its full term, mid-term elections will be held only for the remainder of the five-year term'. Justify the above given statement. *Source: The Hindu, 17th Dec, 2024*

Ans. If a State Assembly is dissolved before completing its full five-year term, elections will be held only for the remaining period because

- This system ensures that the new government is elected for the remaining time and doesn't cause unnecessary disruption. Holding elections for the entire term would be costly and time-consuming.
- This approach prevents frequent political instability and allows for smooth governance.
- This approach provides continuity in administration and development work. By conducting elections only for the remainder of the term, the electoral process remains efficient, saving resources while maintaining democratic processes.

Q.3 What qualifications are required to become a member of the Legislative Assembly and Council?

Ans. To become a member of the Legislative Assembly (MLA), a person must be at least 25 years old, he/she should be an Indian citizen and should not be disqualified under any law. For the Legislative Council (MLC), a person must be at least 30 years old, he/she should be an Indian citizen and meet similar criteria.

Both must be mentally sound and not convicted of serious crimes. These qualifications ensure that members are mature and capable of representing the people effectively.

Q.4 'The State Legislature plays a crucial role in governance'. Justify the statement by citing three functions with examples.

Ans. The State Legislature plays a crucial role in governance by performing several important functions which are

- **Law-making** The legislature passes laws that guide the state's functioning. For example, the law regulating traffic safety ensures public order on the roads.
- **Budget Approval** It approves the state's budget which determines how funds are allocated for various sectors like health, education and infrastructure. This impacts the state's development.
- **Oversight of the Executive** The legislature checks the actions of the executive branch which ensures accountability. For example, during a session the lawmakers can question government officials on policies or spending.

TYPE - 5

4 Marks

Long Answer Type Questions

Q.1 Explain the following terms

(i) Legislative Assembly (ii) Legislative Council

Ans. The explanation of the terms are

(i) **Legislative Assembly** The Legislative Assembly (Vidhan Sabha) is the Lower House of the State Legislature in India. Members of the Legislative Assembly are directly elected by the people of the state through elections held every five years. The size of the assembly varies, depending on the population of the state, with a minimum of 60 and a maximum of 500 members.

(ii) **Legislative Council** The Legislative Council (Vidhan Parishad) is the Upper House in states with a bicameral legislature. Members of the Legislative Council are indirectly elected by specific groups, such as graduates, teachers and local leaders and they serve a six-year term, with one-third of the members retiring every two years. The council's size is smaller than the Legislative Assembly and cannot exceed one-third of its size.

Q.2 **How can the State Legislature effectively influence the approval and implementation of a new policy in India?**

Ans. The State Legislature can influence the approval and implementation of new policies by actively engaging in the debate and scrutiny of bills presented by the government. Through committee discussions, proposed policies can be modified or rejected based on the concerns raised by legislators. For example, if a policy affects a particular region or group, members from that area can highlight issues, ensuring the policy is more equitable.

The Legislature's power to pass or reject the budget ensures that financial aspects of policies are aligned with the state's priorities. This democratic process strengthens governance and ensures policies reflect public interests.

Q.3 **Mention any four points on how the State Legislature ensures accountability of the Executive.**

Ans. The State Legislature ensures accountability of the Executive through the following

- **Question Hour** During the legislative sessions members can ask questions to ministers regarding the functioning of the government. The ministers are required to answer, making them accountable for their actions.
- **Debates and Discussions** The legislature holds debates on various policies and decisions taken by the Executive. These discussions allow lawmakers to scrutinise the actions and policies of the government.
- **Approval of Budget** The Executive requires the approval of the State Legislature for the budget. Legislators review and analyse government spending and policies, ensuring that public funds are used properly.
- **Committees** The legislature forms committees to investigate the administration's actions in detail. These committees examine the functioning of government departments and hold the Executive accountable for any misconduct or inefficiency.

TYPE - 6

10 Marks

Structured Questions

Q.1 **The State Legislature has several important powers and functions. It is responsible for making laws on matters in the State List and Concurrent List, which include areas like healthcare, education and law enforcement. With reference to State Legislature, answer the following questions**

(i) Describe the process for a bill to become a law in the State Legislature. **(3)**

(ii) The State Legislature is responsible for making laws related to public issues. Mention three reasons to justify the statement. **(3)**

(iii) Explain the two lists on which the State Legislature can make laws. **(4)**

Ans (i) The process for a bill to become a law in the State Legislature begins with its introduction in either the Legislative Assembly or the Legislative Council. The bill is then debated and discussed by members of the legislature and changes may be made through amendments.If the bill is approved by a majority of members, it moves to the other house (if a bicameral legislature) for further debate and approval.

After both houses (if a bicameral legislature) pass the bill, it is sent to the Governor for approval. If the Governor gives their assent the bill becomes a law. The whole process ensures that the bill is thoroughly examined before it becomes part of the state's legal framework.

(ii) The State Legislature is responsible for making laws related to public issues

- **Addressing Local Concerns** State Legislatures can make laws on matters specific to the state's needs and its citizens.
- **Improving Public Welfare** It ensures that laws are passed to improve education, health services and welfare in the state.
- **Regional Issues** The legislature handles issues like law and order, infrastructure and agriculture that directly affect the state's public.

(iii) The State Legislature can make laws based on two lists

- **State List** This list contains subjects on which only the state can make laws, such as police, public health, agriculture and local governance.

- **Concurrent List** This list includes subjects on which both the State and Central Governments can make laws, like education, marriage and criminal law. If there is a conflict, the central law prevails.

Q.2 Look at the picture given below and answer the following questions.

(i) Describe the incident depicted in the cartoon. **(3)**

(ii) Mention any three functions of the State Legislature related to the state's budget. **(3)**

(iii) 'The policy discussion is a key function of the State Legislature'. Give any four reasons that justify the statement. **(4)**

Ans (i) The cartoon clearly depicts that in a State Legislature, members of the State Legislature gather to discuss and debate on important issues. They raise questions, present opinions and debate policies to ensure effective governance and make decisions for the welfare of the state's people.

(ii) Functions of the State Legislature related to the State's budget

- **Approval of the Budget** The State Legislature must approve the state's annual budget, which outlines government spending and revenue.
- **Scrutiny of Financial Proposals** The legislature examines various financial proposals and ensures that public funds are used efficiently.
- **Allocation of Funds** It decides how funds should be distributed among different sectors such as education, healthcare and infrastructure and ensures proper resource management.

(iii) The reasons that justify the policy discussion is a key function of the State Legislature are

- **Debating Key Issues** The State Legislature provides a platform where legislators discuss important policies affecting the state's development and welfare.
- **Shaping Laws** Through policy discussions the lawmakers can propose new laws or amend existing ones to address emerging challenges in the state.
- **Public Accountability** These discussions keep the government accountable, which allow the public to understand the rationale behind decisions and policies.
- **Reflecting Public Opinion** Legislators voice the concerns and needs of their constituencies and ensure that state policies reflect the people's priorities.

History

1

THE HARAPPAN CIVILISATION

A Civilisation is a society that is well-developed and organised. Around 2500 BCE, four major Bronze Age Civilisations emerged, due to the use of bronze, which is an important metal alloy. These Civilisations are known as the Bronze Age Civilisations. These civilisations were

- The Harappan or Indus Valley Civilisation in Northern and Western parts of India and Pakistan
- The Mesopotamian Civilisation on the banks of river Euphrates and Tigris in modern Iraq
- The Chinese Civilisation in the valley of Hwang Ho and Yangtze rivers
- The Egyptian Civilisation on the banks of Nile River in Egypt

The Harappan Civilisation

- The Harappan Civilisation (also called the Indus Valley Civilisation) is the first civilisation that developed in the North-Western part of the Indian subcontinent.
- The Harappan Civilisation is believed to have originated around 2500 BCE.
- It is named after Harappa, the first major site of the civilisation, discovered in 1921 in West Punjab, Pakistan.

Sources of Harappan Civilisation

Our understanding of the Harappan Civilisation is primarily based on archaeological evidences, such as buildings, pottery, sculpture, seals and cemeteries, as there are no written records.

The major sources of Harappan Civilisation are

1. The Great Bath

The Great Bath

- The Great Bath is one of the largest public buildings found among the ruins of the ancient Indus Valley Civilisation at Mohenjodaro in Sindh, Pakistan.
- It has a large rectangular tank in a courtyard surrounded by a corridor on all four sides.
- There are two flights of steps, one in the North and the other in the South leading into the tank.
- To make the pool watertight, burnt bricks and mortar lined with 'bitumen' and 'gypsum' were used for construction.
- The water for the bath was provided by a well in an adjacent room.
- It is believed that this structure, with its unique features, was used for a type of 'ritual bath'.
- It provides insights into Indus Valley culture, showing advanced building skills, the importance of ceremonial bathing and efficient water supply and sewage planning.

2. The Citadel

- The raised area of each city was called the Citadel. It was elevated by buildings constructed on mud brick platforms. It includes important civic and religious public buildings.
- It housed the ruling class and important buildings like the Great Bath, Granary, Assembly Hall and Workshops.
- The elaborated planning of the citadel justifies that the Harappan Civilisation was an urban civilisation.
- The presence of specific buildings indicates that it had some sort of political organisation and social classification.

3. Seals

- About 2,000 seals have been discovered from various sites of the Indus Valley Civilisation. Most of them feature short inscriptions and images of animals like the one-horned bull, buffalo, tiger, goat, elephant and rhinoceros.
- Material used in making the seals comprise terracotta, steatite, agate, etc.
- Most of the seals are rectangular or square but some of them are circular in shape.
- Harappan seals provide useful information about the script, social life, trade, religion and beliefs of the Harrapans.
- Some of the famous seals include the Pashupati seal and Unicorn seal.
- The seals of Pashupati depicts a three-faced male god, sitting in a yogic posture and resembles Shiva.
- The seal of unicorn shows their mythical beliefs.
- The seals were mainly used for trade, stamped on goods by traders. They were also worn as amulets, like modern identity cards.

Pashupati Seal

Unicorn Seal

4. Bearded Man

- The stone sculpture of a man with a beard was discovered from Mohenjo-daro. Some scholars believe that this is the statue of a yogi or a priest.
- The statue has a shawl worn over the left shoulder and the eyes are half-closed as if in a state of meditation.
- This sculpture is artistically valuable, which shows the existence of skilled artisans in the Harappan Civilisation.

Bearded Man

5. Dockyard

- A rectangular dockyard found at Lothal in Gujarat is believed to be one of the oldest in the world. It is 223 m long and 35 m in width and 8 m in depth.
- It was surrounded by a massive brick wall, probably as a protection against floods.
- The dockyard was made of baked bricks and it was connected by channels to the Gulf of Cambay.
- The dockyard indicates the existence of both internal and external trade.

6. Dancing Girl

- The bronze statue of a dancing girl from Mohenjo-daro is a stunning work of art, showcasing advanced metallurgy and artistic skills. It was made by the lost wax technique.
- Her right arm rests on her hip, while her left arm is adorned with bangles and holding a small bowl.

Dancing Girl

7. Script

- The Harappans used a pictographic script with 375 to 400 signs, representing birds, fish and human figures.
- The script is found on seals, copper tools, jar rims, copper and terracotta tablets, jewellery, and an ancient sign board.
- The Harappan script was not alphabetical but it was likely a logo-syllabic system, means signs represent words. It was written from right to left.
- The availability of the script on a wide variety of objects indicates that probably many people were literate.

8. Granaries

- Granaries were used to store food grains. Granaries have been found at several sites like Mohenjadaro, Harappa, Lothal and Kalibangan.
- It was built on raised platform to protect from floods. The granary had ventilation to prevent the food grains from becoming mildewed.
- The granaries are the evidence of surplus agriculture production, suggests a well-organised society.

Origin theory of the Civilisation

Foreign Influence

- Some scholars believed the Harappan Civilisation resulted from a migration of people with urban culture to the Indus basin and was influenced by Mesopotamian Civilisation.
- However, this theory was rejected due to a lack of evidence for trade with Mesopotamia during the early Harappan period.

Indigenous Development

- The Harappan Civilisation originated in India, near the Indus river, and evolved over time.
- Its urban culture was an extension of local village culture, influenced by trade with Mesopotamia.
- Historians have noted similarities between pre-Harappan and proto-Harappan cultures including pottery, seals, figurines and ornaments, which suggests a connection and possible evolution from the earlier to later phrase at sites like Kot Diji, Amri and Kalibangan.

Discovery of Harappan Sites

Site	Year of Excavation	Leader of Excavation
Harappa	1921	Daya Ram Sahni
Mohenjo-daro	1922	R.D. Banerjee
Chanhudaro	1931	N.G. Mazumdar
Kalibangan	1953	B.B. Lal and A.N. Ghosh
Kot Diji	1955	Fazal Ahmad Khan
Lothal	1955	S.R. Rao
Surkotada	1964	J.P. Joshi
Dholavira	1990	R.S. Bisht

Extent of the Harappan Civilisation

- The Harappan Civilisation was the largest of all ancient civilisations covering a triangular area of 1.3 million sq. km.
- It extended from Suktagendor (on the sea-coast of South Baluchistan) in the West to Alamgirpur (in the Upper Ganga-Yamuna Doab in Western U.P.) in the East and from Manda (Jammu) in the North to Bhagatrav (Narmada Estuary) in the South.

- It included regions like Punjab, Haryana, Sindh, Baluchistan, Gujarat, Rajasthan and Western Uttar Pradesh.
- Key sites include Manda, Banawali, Kalibangan, Alamgirpur, Lothal, Rupar, Rangpur and Dholavira.
- The largest sites of the Harappan Civilisation are Mohenjo-daro, Harappa, Kalibangan and Lothal. The ruins of Mohenjo-daro were designated a UNESCO World Heritage Site in 1980.

Urban Planning of the Harappan Civilisation

Town Planning

- The town planning of the Harappan Civilisation was based on grid pattern or chess board pattern.
- Each city was divided into two parts-the raised area called the citadel and the 'Lower town'.
- The main streets followed a grid pattern running from North to South or from East to West.
- The street corners were round in shape to allow the carts to pass easily.
- House drains emptied all waste water into the street drains.
- The streets crossed the main road at right angles, dividing the city into square or rectangular blocks.

Drainage system

- The Indus Valley Civilisation had an advanced drainage system, made of bricks with lime mortar, featuring underground drains, street drains and effective wastewater management.
- Houses were connected to the main drain equipped with manholes.
- The drains were covered with bricks or stones.
- The floor of the kitchen and bathroom had a slight slope, so that the water could drain into the narrow drain.

Houses

The main characteristics of houses were the following

- The houses or residential buildings were built on a high mound to protect them from floods.
- Houses were made of brick and wood. Each house had doors, windows and ventilators opening onto the streets and not on the main roads.
- There were variations in the size of houses from single room houses to bigger houses with courtyards, up to twelve rooms, private wells and toilets.
- Each house had covered drains connected with street drains.

Trade in the Harappan Civilisation

Internal Trade

- The cities like Mohenjo-daro, Harappa and Lothal were key centres for metallurgy, producing tools, weapons, as well as kitchenware and other objects for wide distribution.
- They, however, did not use metal money but carried on all exchanges through barter system.
- Rice seems to have been imported to Punjab from Gujarat.
- Chanhudaro and Balakot were centres for bangle-making. While Lothal and Chanhudaro were centres for the manufacturing of beads.

External Trade

- Lothal, Surkotada and Balakot were some of the important trading coastal towns which carried on trade with Mesopotamia and other West Asian sites.
- They had also set up a trading colony in Northern Afghanistan which facilitated trade with Central Asia.
- The Mesopotamian records of about 2350 BC onwards refer to the trade relations with Meluha (the ancient name given to the Indus region).
- Gold was imported from North Karnataka and Afghanistan; Copper from Rajasthan, South India, Baluchistan and Arabia; Lead from either East or South India. Lapiz Lazuli (a bright blue stone) from Afghanistan.

Weights and Measures

- The Indus people used sets of cubical stone weights. The basic unit was 16 (equal to modern 14 grams).
- The larger weights were multiples of 16 like 32, 48, 64, 128 and so on. The smaller ones were all fractions of 16.
- A number of stone weights were discovered from the excavations.

Art and Craft of the Harappan Civilisation

- **Sculpture** A large number of stone sculptures have been found in Mohenjo-daro. Stone statues like the Bearded Man and Male Torso are fine examples of Harappan art.
- **Bronze Casting** The bronze casting in the Indus Valley included human and animal figures was highly realistic in nature with detailed anatomical details. The best example is the 'dancing girl' from Mohenjo-daro.
- **Pottery** Pottery found at Harappan sites features depictions of birds, animals, trees and geometric patterns. Notable examples include large jars with narrow necks and red pots with black decorations.
- **Terracotta Figures** Terracotta figures in the Indus Valley were more less detailed compared to stone and bronze statues. However, they were more realistic in Gujarat and Kalibangan. The most important terracotta figure is the mother goddess.
- **Beads and Ornaments** Lothal and Chanhudaro had a well-developed bead industry. Ornaments were worn by both men and women. Jewellery found at Mohenjo-daro and Lothal included gold and semi-precious metal necklaces, copper bracelets, gold earrings and head ornaments.

Harappan Pottery

Mother Goddess

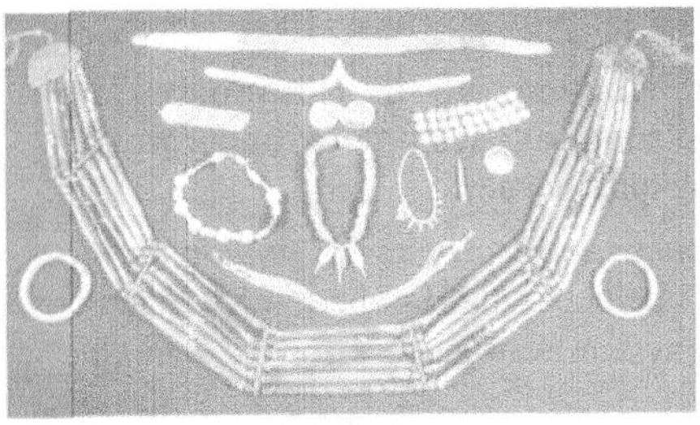

Ornaments

Decline of the Civilisation

The Harappan Civilisation declined around 1800 BCE. The causes for the decline of Harappan civilisation are

- **Floods and Earthquakes** Floods in Mohenjo-daro and earthquakes may have changed the course of the Indus river, damaging the cities.
- **Increased Aridity** The drying up of the river Ghaggar, caused by tectonic changes, led to a lack of water supply, contributing to the decline of the Harappan Civilisation.
- **Deforestation** Overuse of wood for construction, pottery and other purposes may have caused deforestation leading to climate changes, thereby causing the decline of civilisation.
- **Invasion** Some historians like Mortimer Wheeler believed that the Aryans destroyed the Indus settlements. This is supported by evidence of human skeletons found lying in a room.

EXAM ORIENTED QUESTIONS

TYPE - 1   1 Mark

Multiple Choice Questions

Q.1 Identify the odd one out regarding Bronze Age civilisation

(a) Harappan Civilisation (b) Chinese Civilisation
(c) Egyptian Civilisation (d) Maya Civilisation

Ans. (d) Maya Civilisation

Q.2 Which of the following terms archaeologists used for a group of objects, distinctive in style, usually found together within a specific geographic area and period of time?

(a) Civilisation (b) Culture (c) Period (d) History

Ans. (b) Culture

Q.3 Archaeologists working at a Harappan site discovered an elaborated system of underground drains made of baked bricks.

Based on the case above, which of the following statements is not true about the Harappan Civilisation?

(a) The drainage system was made of bricks with lime mortar.
(b) The drains were covered with bricks or stones slabs.
(c) The drains were covered with wooden slabs.
(d) The floors of the kitchen and bathroom were water-tight.

Ans. (c) The drains were covered with wooden slabs.

Exp. The drains were covered with bricks or stones slabs, which demonstrates advanced sanitation practices of the Harappans.

Q.4 Read the following statements about the Harappan Civilisation and choose the correct option.

P : The Harappan Civilisation was one of the earliest urban civilisations in the world.
Q : The Harappans used a script that has been fully deciphered and understood.
R : Harappan cities had well-planned streets, drainage systems, and public baths.
S : The Harappan economy was merely dependent on agriculture, trade and craft production.

Codes

(a) P and Q (b) P and R (c) P and S (d) Q and S

Ans. (b) P and R

Q.5 Which of the following statements about the extent of the Harappan Civilisation is incorrect?

(a) The civilisation extended across parts of modern-day Pakistan and North-Western India.
(b) The civilisation was confined to the Indus Valley region.
(c) The Harappan sites have been found as far as Afghanistan and Iran.
(d) The civilisation had trade links with regions as far as Mesopotamia.

Ans. (b) The civilisation was confined to the Indus Valley region.

Exp. The Harappan Civilisation was not confined to the Indus river valley. It was extended beyond the region and encompasses areas of present day Pakistan and even North-East Afghanistan.

Q.6 What does this structure tell us about the Harappan Civilisation?

(a) The Harappans were skilled in building large-scale irrigation canals.
(b) It was a ceremonial structure used for religious or social gatherings.
(c) It was the large granary, primarily used for grain storage.
(d) The Harappans lacked advanced construction techniques.

Ans. (b) It was a ceremonial structure used for religious or social gatherings.

Q.7 What made the pool at the Great Bath watertight?

(a) Burnt bricks
(b) Mortar lined with bitumen and gypsum
(c) Mud brick platforms
(d) Both (a) and (b)

Ans. (d) Both (a) and (b)

Exp. The pool at the Great Bath was made watertight using mortar lined with bitumen and gypsum. This helped prevent water from leaking and kept the pool filled. Burnt bricks were also used to construct the structure.

Q.8 Which of the following is a feature of the Great Bath?
(a) Tank in a courtyard
(b) Tank surrounded by corridors
(c) Terrace and rooms
(d) All of the above

Ans. (d) All of the above

Q.9 Which of the following insights about the Harappan Civilisation was provided by the Citadel?
(a) There were public buildings for specific purposes.
(b) There was beads making machines.
(c) There were no windows on ground level.
(d) There was overseas trade.

Ans. (a) There were public buildings for specific purposes.

Q.10 Identify the correct statements regarding seals.
(a) Pashupati seal has been found at Mohenjo-daro.
(b) It serves as an authentic source of information.
(c) Some seals were also been found in gold and ivory
(d) All of the above

Ans. (d) All of the above

Q.11 The 'dancing girl' has which of the following features?
(a) Stone sculpture
(b) Heavily-bangled left arm
(c) Half-closed eyes
(d) Seated cross-legged

Ans. (b) Heavily-bangled left arm

Q.12 Bronze statues were made by a special process called
(a) moulded clay process (b) lost wax process
(c) clay wax process (d) lost clay process

Ans. (b) lost wax process

Exp. This method involves creating a model of the statue with wax, covering it with a clay shell, and then heating it. The wax melts away, leaving a mold to pour in molten metal, creating the statue.

Q.13 Which of the following is not a feature of the Dockyard at Lothal?
(a) World's oldest dockyard
(b) Presence of mud brick platform
(c) Surrounded by wall of baked bricks
(d) Connected by channels to the Gulf of Cambay

Ans. (b) Presence of mud brick platform

Q.14 Which of the following was true about the earliest specimen of Harappan script?
(a) It was noticed in 1953
(b) The Harappan script was pictographic
(c) It was written from left to right
(d) It was found on dockyard

Ans. (b)The Harappan script was pictographic

Q.15 Which of the following was the limits of Southernmost site of Harappan Civilisation?
(a) Manda
(b) Bhagatrav
(c) Sutkagandor
(d) Alamgirpur

Ans. (b) Bhagatrav

Exp. The site of Bhagatrav is located in Jetpur village, near Hansot, Baruch district of Gujarat. It is situated on the South of the Narmada river.

Q.16 Which of the following is most likely to provide evidence of Harappan craftsmanship?
(a) The Great Bath at Mohenjo-Daro
(b) Terracotta figurines and pottery
(c) Inscriptions on stone tablets
(d) Trade goods found in Mesopotamia

Ans. (b) Terracotta figurines and pottery

TYPE - 2 — 1 Mark

Assertion-Reason Questions

Q.1 Read the two statements given below about the Harappan Civilisation and select the option that shows the correct relationship between (A) and (R).

Assertion (A) The Harappan Civilisation is considered as the first civilisation that arose in the North-Western regions of the Indian subcontinent.

Reason (R) The Harappan civilisation is also known as the Indus Valley Civilisation.

Codes
(a) R contradicts A
(b) R is the reason for A
(c) A is true but R is false
(d) A and R are independent of each other

Ans. (d) A and R are independent of each other

Q.2 Read the two statements given below about the Great Bath and select the option that shows the correct relationship between (A) and (R).

Assertion (A) The Great Bath has a large rectangular tank in a courtyard surrounded by a corridor on all four sides.

Reason (R) The water for the Great Bath was directly provided by the Indus River.
(a) R contradicts A
(b) R is the reason for A
(c) A is true but R is false
(d) A and R are independent of each other

Ans. (c) A is true but R is false

Q.3 Read the two statements given below about the bearded man and select the option that shows the correct relationship between (A) and (R).

Assertion (A) The bearded man is a three-dimensional stone sculpture discovered from Mohenjo-daro.

Reason (R) According to some scholars, it is a statue of a yogi or a priest.

(a) R contradicts A
(b) R is the reason for A
(c) A is true but R is false
(d) A and R are independent of each other

Ans. (d) A and R are independent of each other

Q.4 Read the two statements given below about the Seals and select the option that shows the correct relationship between (A) and (R).

Assertion (A) One of the important sources of information about the Harappan Civilisation are the seals.

Reason (R) The script used for the letters engraved on seals has not been deciphered.

(a) R contradicts A
(b) R is the reason for A
(c) A is true but R is false
(d) A and (R) are independent of each other

Ans. (d) A and R are independent of each other

Q.5 Read the two statements given below about the Seals and select the option that shows the correct relationship between (A) and (R).

Assertion (A) About 2,000 Harappan seals have been discovered.

Reason (R) The seals were mainly used for religious purposes.

(a) R contradicts A
(b) R is the reason for A
(c) A is true but R is false
(d) A and R are independent of each other

Ans. (c) A is true but R is false

TYPE - 3 — 2 Marks

Very Short Answer Type Questions

Q.1 Mention two important sources of information about the Harappan Civilisation.

Ans. The two important sources of information about the Harappan Civilisation are

(i) **The Great Bath** It provides insights about Indus valley culture, advanced building skills, importance of ceremonial bathing and water supply.

(ii) **The Citadel** It indicates the social classification, political organisation and planning and development of cities in Harappan civilisation.

Q.2 Give any two characteristic features of the Citadel.

Ans. Two important characteristic features of the Citadel are

(i) Citadel was built on a mud brick platform and hence it was a raised area.

(ii) Citadel had important buildings like the houses of the ruling class, the great bath, the granary and the assembly hall.

Q.3 Mention any two features of the Great Bath at Mohenjo-daro.

Ans. Two features of the Great Bath at Mohenjo-daro are

(i) It was a large, rectangular structure with a complex drainage system.

(ii) It was made of burnt bricks and mortar lined with bitumen for water tightness.

Q.4 Mention any two materials used for making Harappan seals.

Ans. Two materials used for making Harappan seals are

(i) Steatite (ii) Terracotta

Q.5 What does seals indicate? Which animals were depicted on the seals apart from unicorn?

Ans. Seals indicate dresses, ornaments, religious beliefs, script of Harappan people, etc.

Other animals depicted on seals apart from unicorn are elephant, tiger, rhinoceros, buffalo, goat and one-horned bull.

Q.6 How were seals used? What information do they give about Harappan trade?

Ans. The seals were used by the traders to stamp their goods. The goods were packed and tied and the knot was covered with wet clay and the seal was pressed on it.

The seals indicate that the Harappan trade had spread over a vast area. It indicates extensive maritime and land based commerce with regions like Mesopotamia.

Q.7 Mention any two places where Harappan seals have been discovered.

Ans. Two places where Harappan seals have been discovered are

(i) Mohenjo-Daro (ii) Harappa

Q.8 Name and briefly describe the process by which sculpture in metal was done.

Ans. The bronze statues were made by using the special lost wax process. In this process wax figures were covered with a coating of clay. Then the wax was melted by heating and the hollow mould thus created was filled with molten metal which took the original shape of the object.

Q.9 Mention any two ways to show the value of Indus script as a source of historical information.

Ans. The ways which shows the values of Indus script as a source of historical information are

(i) **Insights into Language and Culture** Its existence suggests a complex language and culture within the Indus Valley Civilisation. The script's logo-syllabic nature provides a glimpse into their communication system.

(ii) **Distribution of Sites** The distribution of seals and inscribed objects across various sites in the Indus Valley region, indicates the extent and interconnectedness of the civilisation.

Q.10 Explain the evidence that suggests Lothal was an important port city.

Ans. Lothal is believed to be an important port city because archaeologists have found a well-planned dockyard there. The dockyard, connected to the sea, suggests that it was used for external trade and transportation.

Q.11 State two features of the internal trade in the Indus Valley Civilisation.

Ans. The two features of the internal trade in the Indus Valley Civilisation were

(i) All exchanges were carried through barter system.

(ii) There were important centres of different products, for example, Lothal, Harappa and Mohenjo-daro were centres for metallurgy; Balakot and Chanhudaro were centres for bangle-making.

Q.12 State any two pieces of evidence that show the Harappans also had trade relations with foreign countries.

Ans. The evidences that show the Harappans also had trade relations with foreign countries are

(i) The Mesopotamian records from about 2350 BC onwards refer to trade relations with Meluha, which is the ancient name given to the Indus region.

(ii) The depictions of ships and boats on seals also indicate foreign trade. Mesopotamian texts refer to Meluha as a land of seafarers.

Q.13 Mention the types of dress worn by the Indus Valley people.

Ans. The people of the Indus Valley Civilisation wore clothes made up of cotton. Men typically wearning a draped lower garment similar to a dhoti and a shawl was used to cover the upper part of the body. The women wore a skirt and used a cloak to cover their arms and shoulders.

Q.14 How did Indus pottery reflect the potter's artistic skill?

Ans. Indus pottery reflects the potter's artistic skill through its fine craftsmanship, intricate designs, and smooth finishes. The pottery often featured geometric patterns, floral motifs, and animal figures painted with precision. The use of a potter's wheel to create symmetrical shapes and the ability to produce both functional and decorative items showcase the creativity and expertise of the potters.

Q.15 Briefly describe the ornaments worn by the Harappans.

Ans. Ornaments were worn by both men and women. The ornaments were made up of gold, silver, precious stones such as carnelian, lapis lazuli and jasper and ivory. Some common ornaments were necklaces, finger-rings, bangles, armlets, anklets, fan-shaped head dress and earrings.

Q.16 State any two causes that led to the decline of the Harappan Civilisation.

Ans. Two causes that led to the decline of the Harappan Civilisation were

(i) Floods and Earthquakes (ii) Deforestation

Q.17 Imagine that you read a news regarding Harappan Civilisation. You enquired about the characteristic features of society prevalent during that era. From the reply received by you, which features of society during the Indus Valley Civilisation do you think have continued till today?

Ans. I think the Harappan Civilisation had many characteristic features that have been continued till today, including

- Grid-patterned cities and sophisticated drainage system continues to inflame modern urban design and infrastructure, which shows their remarkable ingineering skills.
- The Harappans were skilled in craftsmanship and they also had advanced knowledge of metallurgy. These skills continue to inspire artisans today.

TYPE - 4 — 3 Marks

Short Answer Type Questions

Q.1 Discuss briefly the Indigenous origin of the Harappan Civilisation.

Ans. The Harappan Civilisation had its roots in Indian soil.The civilisation evolved in areas near the Indus river and expanded over the time.The urban culture which has been observed was just the extension of local village culture along with effect of trade relations with Mesopotamia.

The historians found some marked similarities between the pre-Harappan and proto-Harappan culture at Kot Diji, Amri and Kalibangan in terms of granary, defensive walls and long-distance trade in these settlements, which suggests a connection and possible evolution from the earlier to later phase.

Q.2 Briefly describe the social classification of Harappans which shows in their pattern of cities.

Ans. The cities of Harappans were divided into two parts - the raised area called Citadel and the lower town.

The Citadel had the houses of the ruling class and all the important buildings like the Great Bath, the granary and the assembly hall.

The lower town had the residential buildings where the common people lived and worked. It included industrial areas and workshops. This shows some sort of political organisation and social classification of Harappans.

Q.3 Mention any three important features of Pashupati seal.

Ans. The three important features of Pashupati seal are as follows

- It is shown as the three-faced deity wearing a buffalo-horned head-dress, seated cross-legged on a throne and surrounded by an elephant, a tiger, a buffalo and a rhinoceros, with two deer at his feet.
- This deity has been identified as Pashupati Mahadeva.
- The seal is carved in steatite, a soft stone and it was excavated from the Mohenjo-daro, in the Sindh province of present-day Pakistan.

Q.4 From where do we get the evidence of a dockyard? What was it made of? What does it indicate?

Ans. A dockyard has been found from Lothal, situated in Gujarat. It was built of burnt bricks and was rectangular in shape and was connected by channels to the Gulf of Cambay.

It indicates that Lothal was an important trading and manufacturing centre and was used for carrying out overseas trade.

Q.5 Explain briefly the characteristic features of the bearded man in the Harappan Civilisation.

Ans. The stone sculpture of a man with a beard was discovered from Mohenjo-daro. The characteristic features of the bearded man are

- The statue has a shawl worn over the left shoulder and the eyes are half-closed as if he is in a state of meditation.
- Some scholars believe that this is the statue of a yogi or a priest.
- This sculpture is of high artistic value and points to the existence of skilled artisans in the Harappan Civilisation who could make beautiful three-dimensional figures.

Q.6 What does the Dancing Girl statue reveal about Harappan artistry?

Ans. The Dancing Girl statue, found in Mohenjo-daro, shows the advanced skills of Harappan artists

- It depicts a young girl with one hand on her hip and the other hanging freely, suggesting movement as if she is dancing.
- The statue is made of bronze, and the detailed craftsmanship shows how the Harappans were skilled in metalworking.
- The girl's jewellery and body posture also indicate that they appreciated beauty and had a sense of style.

Thus, this statue gives us a glimpse into their culture, showing that art, dance, and fashion were important aspects of Harappan life.

Q.7 State any three aspects about how Harappan civilisation is our greatest heritage.

Ans. Harappan Civilisation is our greatest heritage as

(i) The Harappan way of making baked pottery, standard size of bricks, beads, jewellery, textiles, etc. was adopted by the later civilisations.

(ii) Cultivation of cotton was the biggest achievement of Harappan civilisation which was adopted by Egyptians after several centuries.The Harappan Civilisation also made major advancements in transportation.

(iii) In the religious sphere, the worship of Pashupati Shiva, the female deity as Mother Goddess, sacred trees, animals, serpents, religious symbols, etc. which were prevalent during the Harappan period, some of them have continued to this day.

As, Harappan sites represent the advanced urban planning, engineering and cultural achievement, so, some of its sites such as Dholavira, Mohenjodaro designated as World Heritage site by UNESCO.

Q.8. What does the discovery of granaries in the Harappan Civilisation tell us about their agricultural practices and economy? Explain.

Ans. The discovery of granaries in the Harappan Civilisation shows that they had advanced agricultural practices.

- These large storage structures were used to store surplus grain, which suggests that the Harappans grew more food than they needed.

- This surplus was important for trade and helped support their urban centers.
- The granaries also reflect the organised planning of Harappan society, as they were carefully designed and placed in central locations.

  This indicates that the Harappans had a strong economy based on agriculture, trade, and a structured system for managing resources.

Q.9 **Discuss any three form of arts produced during the Harappan Civilisation.**

Ans. The Harappan Civilisation produced many forms of art, including.

(i) **Sculptures** Three-dimensional stone statues were found at Harappa and Mohenjo-Daro. Such as Bearded men and Male Torso.

(ii) **Seals** Seals were used for stamping and could also be worn around the neck or arm. The seal of Pashupati Mahadeva depicts a seated figure of a Yogi surrounded by animals.

(iii) **Jewellery** The Harappans made jewellery from gold, silver, copper, bronze and stones such as Lapis Lazuli.

TYPE - 5 4 Marks

Long Answer Type Questions

Q.1 **The Great Bath is considered to be one of the most important sources of information that shows the life, art and culture of the Harappan Civilisation. Justify this statement.**

Ans. The Great Bath provides insights into the lives, culture and art of the people who lived there in the following ways

(i) **Evidence of a ruling class** The structure suggests the existence of a ruling class that governed the civilisation.

(ii) **Ritual bathing** The **Great Bath** was used for ritual bathing where water was used to purify and renew the well-being of the bathers.

(iii) **Scientific developments** The Great Bath reveals scientific developments in sanitation and water management techniques.

(iv) **Well-engineered** The Great Bath was a well-engineered pool with burnt brickwork on the floor and side walls that was fitted together so finely that the tank was watertight. It shows advanced engineering skills of the Harappans.

Q.2. **Discuss the significance of the Harappan or Indus Valley Civilisation, highlighting the archaeological sources of information like seals, pottery, and buildings.**

Ans. The Harappan or Indus Valley Civilisation is important because it was one of the earliest urban societies, known for its advanced planning and culture.

Archaeological sources like seals, pottery, and buildings help us to understand the Indus Valley Civilisation.

- **Seals** Seals, often with animals or symbols, show their trade networks and possibly their beliefs.
- **Pottery** Pottery, found in various shapes and sizes, gives insights about daily life and the food people ate.
- **Buildings** The well-planned cities with straight streets, drainage systems, and large buildings suggest a highly organised society.

These archaeological findings provide valuable insights into the life, art, economy, and technology of the Harappans, helping us understand how advanced they were in their time.

Q.3 **Explain the following terms.**

(i) Granaries at Harappa

(ii) Statue of the Dancing Girl

Ans. (i) **Granaries** The granaries at Harappa were built on raised platforms to protect them from floods. There were two rows of six granaries each. To the South of the granaries there were rows of circular floors which probably were working platforms for threshing.

The granaries also had two-roomed barracks which possibly accommodated labourers. The granary had ventilation to prevent grains from becoming waste.

(b) **Statue of the Dancing Girl** The statue of a dancing girl, made up of bronze, was found at Mohenjo-daro. The statue is a masterpiece of art and shows the high degree of development in the field of art of sculpture.

The right hand of the dancing girl rests on the hip and the heavily bangled left arm holding a small bowl. The figurine shows that Harappans were skilled in metal work.

Q.4 **Discuss the features and significance of the script used in the Harappan Civilisation. Explain what information it provides about the Harappans?**

Ans. The Harappans used a script which is regarded as pictographic since its signs represent birds, fish and varieties of the human form. The number of signs of Harappan script is known to be between 375 and 400. The script is found inscribed on a number of seals, copper tools, rims of jars, copper and terracotta tables, jewellery and on an ancient signboard.

The script's significance lies in its potential to reveal details about Harappan society, trade, and administration.

- Seals with inscriptions were likely used for identification and trade, suggesting a well-organised economic system.
- The presence of writing on various materials indicates literacy among the Harappans.
- Although the script is not deciphered yet, but it reflects the advanced cultural and intellectual achievements of the civilisation, highlighting their ability to develop a unique system of communication.

Q. 5 How were houses and town planning organised in the urban planning of the Harappan Civilisation?

Ans. House were organised in the urban planing of the Harappan civilisation in the following ways

- The houses or residential buildings were built according to a set plan on a high mound in order to protect them from floods.
- There were variations in the size of houses from single room houses to bigger houses with courtyards, up to twelve rooms, private wells and toilets. Each house had covered drains connected with street drains.
- The houses were made of brick and wood. Each house had doors, windows and ventilators. Doors and windows opened on the side of the streets and not on the main roads.

Town planning was organised in the urban planning of the Harappan Civilisation in the following ways

- Each city was divided into two parts, Citadel and lower town.
- The main streets followed a grid pattern running from North to South or from East to West.
- House drains emptied all waste water into the street drains.

Q.6 Though the definite reason for the decline of Harappan Civilisation is unknown, there are some speculative causes. In contact of this, explain any four such causes.

Ans. The Harappan Civilisation declined sometime around 1800 BCE Some of the key reasons behind this decline include.

(i) **Floods and Earthquakes** It is believed that floods in Mohenjo-daro led to the abandonment of this settlement. The earthquakes might have altered the course of river Indus, causing immense damage to the cities of the Indus Valley.

(ii) **Increased Aridity** Harappan Civilisation declined because of increasing aridity in the area and the drying up the river Ghaggar. Yamuna and Sutlej used to be the tributaries of the river Ghaggar. Due to some tectonics disturbances, the Sutlej streams was captured by the river Indus and Yamuna shifted East to join the Ganges. As a result of this change, the river Ghaggar became waterless.

(iii) **Deforestation** The excessive use of wood in Indus Valley to bake bricks, to produce jewellery, to make pottery, stoneware and manufacture furniture and boats could have caused deforestation leading to climatic changes in the area thereby causing the decline of the civilisation.

(iv) **Invasion** Some historians like Mortimer Wheeler believed that the invading Aryans destroyed the Indus settlements.

Q.7 Ornaments held significant cultural and social value in the Harappan Civilisation. Who wore ornaments in the Harappan civilisation? What materials were used to make beads and other ornaments?

Ans. In the Harappan Civilisation, both men and women wore ornaments, reflecting the importance of personal adornment in their culture. These ornaments were not just for decoration but also symbolised social status and wealth.

Beads were made from lapis lazuli, agate, carnelian, turquoise, and jasper. Shells, ivory, and bones were also used to make beads, particularly for simpler or more rustic designs. Terracotta beads were also used. The Harappans used copper and gold to create ornaments, including bracelets, pendants, and rings.

TYPE - 6 — 10 Marks

Structured Questions

Q.1 With reference to Harappan Culture, answer the following questions.

(i) Discuss briefly about the Harappan Civilisation. (3)

(ii) The Harappan Civilisation spanned a vast area across parts of present day India, Pakistan and beyond. Describe the extent of the civilisation. (3)

(iii) Name any four cities of the Harappan Civilisation and a significant feature of each city. (4)

Ans. (i) The Harappan Civilisation, also known as the Indus Valley Civilisation, flourished around 2500 BCE in present-day Pakistan and North-West India. It is known for its well-planned cities like Harappa and Mohenjo-daro, advanced drainage systems and skilled craftsmanship, including pottery and jewellery making.

The Harappans engaged in trade, had a writing system, and practiced agriculture. Despite its advancements, the reasons for its decline remain unclear

(ii) **Extent of the Harappan Civilisation** The Harappan Civilisation was the largest of all ancient civilisations covering a triangular area of 1.3 million sq. km. It extended from Suktagendor (Baluchistan) in West to Alamgirpur (U.P.) in the East and from Manda (Jammu) in the North to Bhagatrav (Narmada Estuary) in the South.

The Harappan Civilisation covered parts of Punjab, Haryana, Sindh, Baluchistan, Gujarat, Rajasthan and fringes of Western Uttar Pradesh. Mohenjo-daro, Harappa, Chanhudaro and Sutkagendor are now in Pakistan.

The key sites include Manda, Banawali, Kalibangan, Alamgirpur, Lothal, Rupar and Rangpur. Dholavira.

The largest sites of the Harappan Civilisation are Mohenjo-daro, Harappa, Kalibangan and Lothal.

(iii) The four prominent cities of the Harappan civilisation and their significant features are

(a) **Harappa** It is located on the banks of the Ravi river and it is known for its granaries and advanced urban planning. It had a citadel and a lower town, showcasing a well-organised layout.

(b) Mohenjo-daro It is located near the Indus river and it is famous for the Great Bath, a large water tank used for ritualistic purposes. It also had a drainage system.

(c) **Dholavira** It is located in Gujarat and it is notable for its water reservoirs and sophisticated water management system, essential for agriculture in the semi-arid region.

(d) **Lothal** It is located near the Gulf of Cambay and it is recognised for its dockyard, indicating the Harappans expertise in maritime trade and engineering.

Q.2 Look at the picture below and answer the questions that follow

(i) Identify the structure. Mention its important characteristic features. **(3)**

(ii) State the importance of this structure as a source of information about art and culture of Harappan Civilisation. **(3)**

(iii) Name another architectural structure of this period. How does this structure show that Harappan Civilisation was highly developed? **(4)**

Ans. (i) The given structure is the Great Bath. Its important characteristic features include

- It is one of the largest public buildings at Mohenjo-daro. It has a large rectangular tank in a courtyard surrounded by a corridor on all four sides.
- There are two flights of steps one in the North and the other in the South leading into the tank.
- To make the pool watertight, burnt bricks and mortar lined with bitumen and gypsum were used for construction.

(ii) For answer refer to Q. 1 of Long Answer Type Questions.

(iii) The Citadel was the other structure of this period. It shows that Harappan Civilisation was highly developed in the following ways

- It was a raised area of the city on which the important buildings like the Houses of ruling class, the Granary, the Great Bath and the Assembly Hall were made.
- The alignment of the Citadel with the grid layout of the city reflects a high degree of precision and foresight in city planning. Its strategic location on elevated ground might have also protected these structures from flooding, showcasing the Harappan's understanding of geography and environmental challenges.
- The Citadel shows that there was a classification or stratification in Harappan society.
- It also indicates that the Harappans were developed and their civilisation was an urban one.

Thus, The Citadel's prominent buildings suggest the existence of centralised authority that controlled resources, trade, and urban planning.

Q.3 Look at the picture below and answer the questions that follow.

(i) **Identify the animal depicted on the seal. Explain briefly about the seal.** **(3)**

(ii) **Of what material were these seals made? How were the seals used?** **(3)**

(iii) **What do the seals reveal about the Harappans?** **(4)**

Ans. (i) The animal depicted on this seal is a unicorn. The seal shows their mythical beliefs. The seals bear some kind of script which has not yet been deciphered.

The seal typically shows a one-horned animal with a human-like body, standing in a particular posture. Some interpretations suggest it represents a mythical creature, while others believe it depicts a real animal such as a bull or rhinoceros, symbolising power.

(ii) These seals were made up of terracotta, steatite, agate etc.

These seals were used by traders to stamp their goods. Seals were also used as amulets, carried on the persons of their owners, as modern-day identity cards.

Some seals were used in spiritual ceremonies and rituals. For example, the famous Pashupati seal depicts a human or humanoid figure, which may have been a priest or deity. Seals may have been used in administration.

(iii) The seals of the Harappan Civilisation are a rich source of information, revealing significant insights into their script, trade, religion, and beliefs, as follows

(a) **Script and Language** The seals bear inscriptions in the Harappan script, which is yet to be deciphered. These inscriptions suggest a well-developed writing system used for communication and record-keeping.

(b) **Trade and Commerce** Seals were likely used as trademarks or stamps on goods, indicating ownership or authenticity. Their discovery in regions as far as Mesopotamia suggests extensive trade networks. This highlights the Harappans' economic prosperity and their connections with other ancient civilisations.

(c) **Religion and Beliefs** Many seals depict religious symbols, animals, and deities. The famous Pashupati seal, showing a figure surrounded by animals, suggests early beliefs in nature worship and possibly proto-Shiva practices. The frequent use of animal motifs reflects their symbolic and cultural significance.

(d) **Extent of Trade** The seals not only showcase long-distance trade but also highlight the organised nature of Harappan commerce, which contributed to their urban prosperity.

Q.4 With reference to art and craft of the Harappan Civilisation, answer the following questions.

(i) **Give a brief description about Harappan pottery** **(3)**

(ii) **Ornaments held significant cultural and social value in the Harappan Civilisation. Who wore ornaments in the Harappan Civilisation? What materials were used to make beads and other ornaments?** **(3)**

(iii) **The Harappans wore clothing reflecting both practicality and cultural sophistication. Explain briefly about the dresses wore by Harappans.** **(4)**

Ans. (i) Pottery was found in a large number from the sites of Harappan Civilisation. Harappan pottery mostly consisted of finely crafted wheel-made items, only some of them were handmade.

Figures of birds, animals and trees and geometric figure were depicted on the pots. Some of the pottery found from Indus Valley Civilisation were large jars with narrow neck and red pots with black decoration.

(ii) Refer Q.7 of Long Answer Type Question for answer.

(iii) Men of Indus Valley used to wear a drapped lower garment, which is similar to a dhoti and wore a shawl as an upper-garments as shown by the famous figure of the priest from Mohenjo-daro. The women wore a type of skirt and use to cover their upper portion with a cloak.

The primary material for Harappan clothing was cotton, which is believed to have been cultivated in the region. The Harappans were among the earliest people to spin and weave cotton fibres into fabric. Wool was also used, especially for colder regions.

2

THE VEDIC PERIOD

- After the decline of Indus Valley Civilisation, Vedic Civilisation flourished in India. The Vedic culture grew in India around 1500 BCE.
- In order to understand Vedic age, the sources have been divided into two parts as literary sources and archaeological sources.

Literary Sources

- The Vedic text was divided into two broad groups i.e. the Early Vedic texts (1500 - 1000 BCE) when most of the hymns of the Rig Veda were composed and the Later Vedic texts (1000-500 BCE) which belongs to Brahmanas, Upanishads, Aranyaka, etc.
- The Vedic literature was written in Sanskrit. The term 'Veda' has been derived from the Sanskrit word, 'vid' which means knowledge.
- Vedic literature was divided into two parts i.e., Shruti and Smriti.
- Shruti was divine knowledge revealed to the sages by God, who then passed it down orally from one generation to the next. Smriti was composed by the Saints (Rishis).
- The Vedic literature can be classified into four categories: the four Vedas, Brahmanas, Aranyakas and Upanishads.

(i) **The Vedas**

- **The Rig Veda** It is the oldest religious text in the world and is, therefore, known as the first testament of mankind. It is the collection of hymns to be recited at the time of sacrificial rites and other rituals. The priests of Rigveda is known as Hotri.
- **The Sama Veda** It is a collection of 1875 hymns taken from the Rig Veda and set to tunes for the purpose of singing. It is sung by the priest, known as Udgatri.
- **The Yajur Veda** It is a collection of rituals for performing different sacrifices and recited by the priests known as **Adhvaryu**. It deals with hymns recited during the performance of Yajnas.
- **The Atharva Veda** It contains 731 hymns to protect people from evils and demons. It is a collection of charms, magic and spells. Apart from this, the hymns also deal with *Gyan* (knowledge), *Karma* (action) and *Upasana* (invocation). Some hymns also deal with medicines for the treatment of various diseases. The priests of Atharva veda is known as Brahman.

(ii) **The Brahmanas** The Brahmanas elaborated prose texts and are also known as Liturgies. These are texts on sacrificial rituals. They contain explanations of hymns, their origin describe their application. They advocate *Karma Marga* for attainment of salvation.

(iii) **The Aranyakas** The literal meaning of 'Aranyakas' is 'forest'. They are known as 'forest books'. The Aranyakas deal with mysticism, moral values and philosophical doctrines of the Aryans who were ascetics and hermits living in the forests.

(iv) **The Upanishads** The word 'Upanishad' literally means to sit down near someone. They are the philosophical commentaries on the Vedas. The doctrines such as - *Karma*, *Moksha* and *Maya* are explained in detail. The most famous Upanishads are *Chandogya Upanishad*, *Kena Upanishad*, *Aitareya Upanishad* and *Taittiriya Upanishad*.

Allied Vedic Literature

- **The Vedangas** They deal with the ways in which the Vedas ought to be chanted. The six Vedangas deal with Pronunciation, Grammar, Etymology, Metrics, Rituals and Astronomy.
- **The Sutras** The ancient texts are divided into three groups: the Grihyasutras (dealing with family ceremonies), the Srautasutras (focused on yajnas and sacrifices), and the Dharmasutras (providing rules of conduct for different classes and life stages).
- **The Upavedas** They are the subsidiary of the Vedas. There are four Upavedas, namely; the *Dhanurveda* (deals with the art of warfare), *Gandharvaveda* (deals with art of music), *Shilpaveda* (deals with art and architecture) and *Ayurveda* (deals with Indian system of medicine).
- **Darshanas** There are six schools of Indian philosophy known as *Shad-Darshans*. These are *Nyaya, Vaishesika, Sankhya, Yoga, Purva Mimamsa and Uttara Mimamsa*. They all propagate the virtues of life and are opposed to external rituals.
- **The Dharmashastras** The law-books called the Dharmasutras and the Smritis together with their commentaries, are called Dharmashastras. They elaborate the duties of common folk, royal officials and Kings. *Manusmriti* elaborates the Hindu code of law and gives details about the Varnas i.e. the castes and different *Ashramas* of individual life.
- **The Ashtadhyayi** It is a Sanskrit treatise on grammar written by the Indian grammarian Panini. This work set the linguistic standards for classical Sanskrit.

The Epics

The Ramayana written by Maharishi Valmiki and the Mahabharata composed by the great sage Ved Vyasa are the Vedic Epics, which offer insights into dharma, morality and the nature of life.

The Bhagavad Gita is a key Hindu scripture and a part of the Mahabharata. It features a philosophical discourse between Arjuna and Lord Krishna.

Importance of the Epics

- The epics are the main sources of information on the political institutions and the social and cultural organisation of Vedic period.
- They give insights on various Aryan kingdoms, their armies and their weapons.
- The Kshatriyas were entrusted with the defence of their kingdoms and they believed that the death on the battlefield was the noblest act in the life of a warrior.
- They reveal the high ideals of family life of the Aryans.
- The Bhagavad Gita elaborates the Karma and immortality of the soul.

Archaeological Sources

The available archaeological sources that give information about the Vedic Age, include iron artifacts and remains of pottery.

Iron Artefacts

- The Vedic Aryans became aware of iron around 1000 BCE. Evidences of iron tools have been found at **Atranjikhera** in Uttar Pradesh. Arrowheads and spearheads are found most frequently.
- Iron artifacts have also been found from Kaushambi, Allahabad, Jakhera in Etah district (Uttar Pradesh) and Hallur in Karnataka.

Remains of Pottery

- The **Grey Ware** (GW) and Painted Grey Ware (PGW) pottery has been discovered at different sites of Punjab and Haryana. It is believed that they to belonged to the Rig Vedic Aryans.
- Important sites from where pottery was found are Bhagwanpura (Kurukshetra), Dadheri (Ludhiana), Katpalan and Nagar (Jalandhar).
- The PGW culture was followed by Northern Black Polished Ware (NBPW) culture which began around 700 BC.

Early Vedic Period

The early Vedic period was the period between 1500 and 1000 BC when the Aryans came and settled in India.

Social Organisation

The early Vedic society was a predominantly pastoral and agricultural society organised into tribes and governed by tribal chiefs.

Family

- There was a joint family system prevalent in the early Vedic period. The family was the fundamental unit of society and it was patriarchal. The head of the family was the eldest male member known as Grihapati.
- The early Vedic Aryans lived in villages. A group of villages is called the Visha. Many Vishas formed a Jana.
- The head of the village was called Gramini, the head of the Visha was called Vishapati and the head of Jana was called Rajan.

Position of the King

- In the early Vedic period the Rajan (king) was primarily a tribal chief, not an absolute monarch.
- He had limited power and he governed with the help of the ministers.
- The three key assemblies i.e. Sabha, Samiti and Vidatha gave advice to the king.
- Officers included the Senani (the Commander of the Army) and the Purohita (who performed religious ceremonies) help and assist the King.

Rig Vedic Assemblies

- **Sabha** It primarily focused on Judicial, administrative and religious decisions.
- **Samiti** It primarily focused on folk assembly discussions, religious ceremonies and philosophical debates. The Rajan could be elected or re-elected by the Samiti, which had a more democratic role.
- **Vidhatha** It was the earliest assembly handling economic, religious, social and military functions.

Position of Women and Class Divisions in Early Vedic Period

- Women were respected and enjoyed equal status as men. Women could participate in various assemblies.
- The daughters were given the freedom to choose their husbands and also the system of widow remarriage was prevalent.
- The early Vedic society was equitable and lacked the rigid caste system.
- The society had professional mobility and occupution was not based on birth and people could adopt any profession of their choice, but with the time the profession became hereditary. This resulted in division of society on the basis of occupation.

Food, Dresses and Amusements in Early Vedic Period

- The diet of Rig Vedic Aryans was both balanced and enriching which included both, vegetarian and non-vegetarian dishes.
- The Aryans wore dresses made from cotton, wool and deer skin.
- The garments consisted of three parts i.e. an undergarment called Nivi, lower garment called Vasa or Paridhan and upper garment known as Adhivasa.

- Both men and women wore gold ornaments.
- The main sources of amusements in the early Vedic period were horse races, hunting, singing, dancing, chariot races, gambling, etc.

Education and Religious Belief in Early Vedic Period

- Education was imparted through Gurukuls in the early Vedic period. The residence of the Guru or the teacher was called Gurukul (family of the guru) and was considered the most sacred institution.
- Vedas, Grammar, Puranas, Mathematics, Ethics, Logic and Military Science were the subjects in the early Vedic period.
- Two women teachers; Maitreyi and Gargi were prominent and considered gifted.
- Rig Vedic Aryans worshipped and personified the natural forces into many gods such as Prithvi (Earth), Agni (Fire), Vayu (Wind), Varuna (Rain) and Indra (Thunder) also known as Purandara.
- There were also female gods like Aditi and Usha.
- There were no temples or idol worship. Prayers were offered to gods for rewards, with offerings like ghee, milk, and grain.
- Animals like - horses, buffaloes, rams, bulls and even cows were also sometimes sacrificed.
- The Rig Vedic hymns had no consistent theory regarding life after death.

Economy during Early Vedic Period

- **Agriculture** The Rig Vedic economy was primarily rural in nature. People had knowledge of agriculture and practiced it to supplement their food requirements. There are references of producing Yava (Jau or barley), during that period.
- **Cattle Rearing** The main occupation of the Rig Vedic Aryans was cattle rearing. Cows were the principal wealth, often gifted to priest for performing sacrifices. A wealthy person was known as Gomat and his wealth was measured by the number of cows he owned. Prayers were offered for increasing cattle. King was referred to as Gopa and Gopati.
- **Other Activities** It included hunting, carpentry, tanning, pottery weaving, chariot making, fishery, etc. Women were also engaged in crafts.
- **Trade** The products were exchanged through barter system. Cow and Nishka (gold ornaments) were used as medium of exchange.

Later Vedic Period

The period between 1000 and 600 BCE when the Aryans started setting in new places is called the later vedic period.

Social Organisation

- The later Vedic period saw a shift in the structure of society.
- The social structure became complex and it includes the four varnas, the development of powerful kingdoms and the codification of rituals.

The Four Ashramas

Ashrama system came into existence in later Vedic period which means four stages in the long journey of life of a man. These were

(i) **Brahmacharya Ashrama** (from birth to 25 years of age) The student went to a Gurukul and typically would live with a Guru to acquire knowledge.

(ii) **Grihastha Ashrama** (the age of 25 to 50 years) A man was supposed to marry and lead a family life following a set of customs and traditions.

(iii) **Vanaprastha Ashrama** (the age of 50 to 75) In this stage, a person withdrew from worldly duties, took on an advisory role, and focused on detachment, study and meditation, with the belief that death during this stage led to *moksha*.

(iv) **Sanyasa Ashrama** (the age of 75 to 100) A man had to abandon his complete social life and devote all his time in the service of God to attain salvation or *moksha*.

Position of Women

- Women lost the right to the Upanayana ceremony. They were not allowed to take part in Sabha and Samiti.
- Birth of a daughter came to be regarded as a source of misery.
- Women were not allowed to own property and widow marriage was not allowed.

The Four Class Division

- The caste system is not mentioned in Rig Veda but due to social inequalities, the tribal society was divided and the caste system emerged and became rigid.
- The word Shudra was added in the Tenth Mandala of Rig Veda during the Later Vedic period.
- The four-fold Varna system came to be firmly established during the later Vedic period. This include
  (i) **Brahmins** They learnt the Vedas and performed religious ceremonies and taught the people.
  (ii) **Kshatriyas** They were rulers and warriors, responsible for defense and governance.
  (iii) **Vaishyas** They were engaged in trade, industry and agriculture and animal husbandry. They didn't have any privileges that the Brahmanas and Kshatriyas enjoyed.
  (iv) **Shudras** They had to serve the other three castes. They were considered as untouchables. They had no right to approach the sacred fire, i.e. perform sacrifice or to read the sacred texts.

The Education System

- At the age of seven the student was sent to a Gurukul, which was the house of the teacher. He was supposed to live there until he completed his education.
- Most of the teaching was done orally and the students were required to learn everything.
- The students were taught Vedic literature, grammar, astronomy, medicine, music, architecture and the art of warfare.
- After completing the education, the students paid Guru Dakshina or a fee to the teacher according to their means.

Food and Dresses and Religious Belief in Later Vedic Period

- Rice became the staple food of the later Vedic Aryans.
- The practice of eating meat declined. Slaughter of cow became crime.
- Drinking of *Sura* or wine was still favoured.
- Wool and silk were increasingly used for dress in addition to cotton.
- Varun and Indra, the most important Gods of Rig Vedic age, lost prominence in later Vedic period.
- Prajapati or Adipurush became the Supreme God in later Vedic phase.
- Rituals, sacrifices and requirement of supervising priest (Purohita) made religious life complex.
- Magic and omen entered the socio-religious life.
- Few Kshatriyas, like Janak and Vishswamitra succeeded in knowing the supreme i.e. Brahma.
- New doctrines were included by the Brahmanas which were *karma* (action), *dharma* (duty) and *moksha* (salvation). There was an emergence in the belief of rebirth.

Economy during Later Vedic Period

- The Aryans transitioned from a nomadic to a settled, agrarian life in the Gangetic plains. With fertile soil, they grew crops like rice, wheat, barley, and sugarcane. The knowledge of iron technology revolutionised agriculture, leading to significant economic changes.
- Uses of metal and leather work, carpentry and pottery grew, which gave rise to trade and enabled exchange of goods in the market.
- Coins were not used, but Nishka and Satamana which were gold ornaments during Rig Veda age came to be used for trade and commerce.
- Beginning of regular taxation system, Bali became a compulsory tax. In addition to internal trade, foreign trade also became extensive.
- A class of hereditary merchants (Vaniya) also came into existence. They also carried on trade and commerce.

Comparative Study of the Position of Women in Early and Later Vedic Society

The comparison of the positions of Women between Early and Later Vedic society are

Position of Women in Early Vedic Society	Position of Women in Later Vedic Society
Women were respected and actively participated in assemblies like Sabha and Samiti.	Women lost this right and were excluded from gatherings in assemblies.
Women had the freedom to choose their husbands and had the right to remarry if widowed.	Women were discouraged from remarrying and their marital freedoms were restricted.
Women like Gargi and Maitreyi were celebrated scholars.	Women were denied the right to Upanayana (a ceremony marking formal education).
Daughters were welcomed.	Birth of daughters was seen as less desirable.

Comparison between the Economy of Early and Later Vedic Period

Comparison between the economy of Early and Later Vedic Period are:

Economy of in Early Vedic Society	Economy of Later Vedic Society
In the beginning, the main occupation was domestication of animals and agriculture was secondary.	Agriculture became the chief occupation and domestication of cattle also continued.
Cattle was the important source of wealth.	Land was the important source of wealth.
Many people were engaged in trade and commerce.	Trade continued in barter and currency mode of exchange was in silver coins.
Barter system prevailed and was carried out in terms of bullocks and horses.	Traders guilds had come up and vaisyas also carried on trade and commerce.
Dyeing, embroidery, hunting, carpenting, tanning, pottery, weaving, chariot making, fishery, crafts in gold and iron were important occupations.	Besides occupations of earlier period, many new occupations like physicians, musicians and many other professions emerged. Metal work, leather work, jewellery making, carpentry and pottery made great improvement.

EXAM ORIENTED QUESTIONS

TYPE - 1 1 Mark

Multiple-Choice Questions

Q.1 The Vedas were composed in a language that was considered ancient and sacred in Indian culture. Which language was primarily used in the composition of Vedas?

(a) Sanskrit (b) Hindi (c) Tamil (d) Pali

Ans. (a) Sanskrit

Q.2 Which of the following is not a category of the Vedic literature?

(a) The Aranyakas (b) The Upanishads
(c) The Early Vedic Texts (d) The Brahmanas

Ans. (c) The Early Vedic Texts

Exp. The Early Vedic Texts is a reference to a time period in Vedic literature and it is not considered a specific category.

Q.3 Read the description and identify the person.
He was Arjuna's guide and charioteer.

(a) Varuna (b) Indra (c) Krishna (d) Rama

Ans. (c) Krishna

Q.4 Complete the given analogy.
Ramayana : Valmiki :: Mahabharata : ?

(a) Ved Vyasa (b) Panini
(c) Tulsidas (d) Kalidas

Ans. (a) Ved Vyasa

Q.5 Identify the appropriate use of iron by Vedic Aryans.

P : Iron tools were used for cleaning forest.
Q : It was used for weapons.
R : It was used for making ornaments.
S : It was used for making houses.

Codes

(a) P and Q (b) R and S (c) P and S (d) Q and R

Ans. (a) P and Q

Q.6 What is referred to as PGW or Painted Grey Ware pottery?

(a) Rugged grey pottery
(b) Very fine, smooth and even-coloured pottery
(c) Bead-encrusted black pottery
(d) All of the above

Ans. (b) Very fine, smooth and even-coloured pottery

Exp. PGW was very fine, smooth and even coloured pottery made of high quality clay. It had geometrical designs.

Q.7 Which of the following statement is true about the position of women during early Vedic age?

(a) Women were respected and enjoyed equal status as men.
(b) Women couldn't participate in assemblies.
(c) Women were not given the freedom to choose their husband.
(d) System of widow re-marriage was not prevalent.

Ans. (a) Women were respected and enjoyed equal status as men.

Q.8 Read the following statements about the education during the Vedic period and choose the correct option.

P : The Gurukul system was prevalent.
Q : Education was free and accessible to everyone.
R : The Vedas and Vedangas were the main subjects taught.
S : Women were completely excluded from education.

Options

(a) P and Q (b) P and R
(c) P and S (d) Q and S

Ans. (b) P and R

Q.9 Read the description and identify the correct answer to the following question.

"During early Vedic period products were exchanged through barter system". What were used as medium of exchange?

(a) Ox and Sheep (b) Camel and Buffalo
(c) Goat and Cow (d) Cow and Niksh

Ans. (d) Cow and Niksh

Q.10 The stage in which a man had to abandon his complete social life and devote all his time in the service of God to attain salvation was called

(a) Grihastha Ashrama
(b) Vanaprastha Ashrama
(c) Sanyasa Ashrama
(d) Brahmacharya Ashrama

Ans. (c) Sanyasa Ashrama

Q.11 Complete the given analogy.

Brahmanas : Vedas religious ceremonies ::Vaishyas : ?

(a) Fighting (b) Trade

(c) Serve others (d) All of these

Ans. (b) Trade

Q.12 Identify the odd one out with reference to the Vedic economy.

(a) Barter system (b) Use of coins

(c) Cattle wealth (d) Agriculture

Ans. (b) Use of coins

Exp. In the Vedic economy, barter system, cattle wealth, and agriculture were common, but coins were not widely used during that period.

TYPE - 2 1 Mark

Assertion-Reasons Questions

Q.1 Read the two statements given below about the Vedic age and select the option that shows the correct relationship between (A) and (R).

Assertion (A) During the early Vedic period, the society was divided into different classes based on their profession.

Reason (R) During the later Vedic age, the caste system became quite rigid.

(a) R contradicts A

(b) R is the reason for A

(c) A is true but R is false

(d) A and R are independent of each other

Ans. (d) A and R are independent of each other

Q.2 Read the two statements given below about the early Vedic period and select the option that shows the correct relationship between (A) and (R).

Assertion (A) The period between 1500-1000 BCE when the Aryans settled in India is known as the early Vedic period.

Reason (R) During this period, following the course of rivers, the Aryans settled in the Gangetic Valley.

(a) R contradicts A

(b) R is the reason for A

(c) A is true but R is false

(d) A and R are independent of each other

Ans. (c) A is true but R is false

Q.3 Read the two statements given below about the early Vedic age and select the option that shows the correct relationship between (A) and (R).

Assertion (A) In the early Vedic age, the King did not maintain any regular army.

Reason (R) In times of war, he used to organise tribal groups to perform military functions.

(a) R contradicts A

(b) R is the reason for A

(c) A is true but R is false

(d) A and R are independent of each other

Ans. (b) R is the reason for A

Q.4 Read the two statements given below about the later Vedic period and select the option that shows the correct relationship between (A) and (R).

Assertion (A) Iron began to be used in India during the period of later Vedic age.

Reason (R) Iron was a harder metal than copper and bronze.

(a) R contradicts A

(b) R is the reason for A

(c) A is true but R is false

(d) A and R are independent of each other

Ans. (b) R is the reason for A

TYPE - 3 2 Marks

Very Short Answer Type Questions

Q.1 Explain the term 'Veda'. Give its importance.

Ans. The term 'Veda' comes from the Sanskrit word vid, meaning knowledge.

They are important because they provide valuable insights about ancient Indian life, thoughts, spirituality and culture.

Q.2 Name any two literary sources of the Vedic period.

Ans. The two literary sources of the Vedic period are

(i) Vedas (ii) Epic

Q.3 Name the two categories of early Vedic literature. Why was the early Vedic literature known as Shruti?

Ans. The early Vedic literature was classified into two categories - Shruti and Smriti.

The early Vedic literature was known as Shruti because it was revealed to the sages by God and they passed on the knowledge orally from generation to generation.

Q.4 Explain any two key characteristics of Vedic literature.

Ans. Two key characteristics of Vedic literature are

(i) It mainly deals with hymns, prayers and rituals for gods, reflecting the spiritual life of the Vedic people.

(ii) The texts were passed down orally, with careful memorisation and recitation by priests and scholars.

Q.5 Why are Aranyakas known as forest books?

Ans. The literal meaning of Aranyakas is 'forest'. They were meant for the ascetics and hermits living in the forest. So, they are known as forest books.

These texts provided guidance on rituals and meditation practices suited to the secluded lifestyle of those dwelling in the forests.

Q.6. What are the Upanishads? Mention any two Upanishads.

Ans. The Upanishads are philosophical commentaries on the Vedas that include the doctrines such as Karma, Moksha and Maya. The two Upanishads are

(i) Chandogya Upanishad

(ii) Kena Upanishad

Q.7 What are sutras? How many groups of sutras are there?

Ans. Sutras explain the customs and rituals of the later Vedic period, especially with the rituals relating to soma (yajna) sacrifice.

There are three group of Sutras : the Grihyasutras, the Srautasutras and the Dharmasutras.

Q.8 What are the Dharmashastras and what do they elaborate?

Ans. The law-books called the Dharmasutras and the Smritis together with their commentaries, are called Dharmashastras.

They elaborate the duties of common folk, royal officials and Kings.

Q.9 Explain briefly the following terms.

(i) Ramayana (ii) Mahabharata

Ans. (i) **Ramayana** It is an ancient Indian epic written by Sage Valmiki. It tells the story of Lord Rama, his exile and his battle to rescue his wife Sita from the demon king Ravana.

(ii) **Mahabharata** The Mahabharata is an ancient Indian epic composed by the Sage Ved Vyasa. In this epic the main story revolves around two branches of a family - the Pandavas and Kauravas - who, in the Kurukshetra War, battle for the throne of Hastinapura.

Q.10 Explain the structure of the family in the early Vedic period?

Ans. The joint family system was prevalent in the early Vedic period. The family was the fundamental unity of society and it was patriarchal. The head of the family was the eldest male member known as Grihapati.

Q.11 Write any two features of later Vedic religious life.

Ans. Two features of later Vedic religious life are

(i) There was a rise of new Gods into prominence Vishnu, Rudra and Prajapati. Gods like Indra, Varuna and Agni lost their supreme position.

(ii) The sacrifices became more elaborate and complex and gained pre-eminence over prayers.

Q.12 Explain the role of rituals and sacrifices in the religious life of the early Vedic people.

Ans. Rituals and sacrifices were central to the religious life of early Vedic people. They believed these practices pleased gods and ensured prosperity. Sacrifices, like 'yajnas', were performed by priests to bring good harvests, wealth and protection from enemies.

Q.13 Name two important deities worshipped during the Vedic period.

Ans. The two important deities worshipped during the Vedic period are

(i) Indra, the god of thunder and war.

(ii) Agni, the god of fire.

Q.14 State two important changes that took place in the society in the process of its transition from the early Vedic period to the later Vedic period.

Ans. The two important changes that took place in the society in the process of its transition from the early Vedic period to the later Vedic period were

(i) Women enjoyed equal rights in early Vedic period but their status in the society gradually declined during the later Vedic period.

(ii) Caste system which was based on occupation earlier became hereditary and rigid with course of time.

Q.15 Give two reasons why cattle were important to the Vedic people.

Ans. Cattle were important to the Vedic people due to the following reasons

(i) Cattle were used for food, milk and as a form of wealth.

(ii) They were also used for agricultural work and played an important role in religious sacrifices.

TYPE - 4 3 Marks

Short Answer Type Questions

Q.1 List the four Vedas and briefly describe the subject matter of each.

Ans. The four Vedas are

(i) **The Rig Veda** The Rig Veda is composed of 10 mandalas. It has hymns that are dedicated to Gods by sages. They also give insight about life of people during that time.

(ii) **The Sama Veda** The hymns of Sama Veda were meant to be sung at the time of the sacrifice by priests.

(iii) **The Yajur Veda** It deals with hymns recited during the performance of yagnas.

(iv) **The Atharva Veda** The hymns of the Atharva Veda deal with magic and charm. The hymns also deal with *Gyan* (knowledge), *Karma* (action), *Upasana* (invocation) and some with medicine and treatment.

Q.2 State the significance of iron in the development of agriculture during the Vedic Age.

Ans. The discovery of iron provided the Aryans with new tools, such as axes, which facilitated clearing forests and cultivating land. Iron plough-heads, sickles and hoes made farming more efficient, enabling the cultivation of extensive areas. As a result, agriculture emerged as their primary occupation.

The surplus production of crops like rice, wheat, barley, along with vegetables and fruits, significantly enhanced their standard of living.

Q.3 How did the discovery of iron during the later Vedic period impact agriculture, trade and the growth of towns and cities?

Ans. The discovery of iron during the Later Vedic period significantly advanced agriculture, leading to surplus production. This agricultural surplus facilitated trade, which in turn gave rise to markets and contributed to the growth of towns and cities. As a result, trade became the central focus of people's lives during this period.

Q.4 Mention the importance of the Epics as a source of information about the Aryans.

Ans. The Epics are a vital source of information about the political systems, social structure, and cultural practices of the Aryans.

- They describe various Aryan kingdoms, their military forces and the weapons they used.
- The defense of their kingdoms was the responsibility of the Kshatriyas.
- The Epics also highlight the Aryans' lofty ideals of family life. The heroic figures portrayed in these texts embody noble moral values and have left a lasting impression on generations to come.

Q.5 "The early Vedic age can be defined as a period when women were given equal rights with men". Justify this statement with any two examples.

Ans. The statement "The early Vedic age can be defined as a period when women were given equal rights with men" can be justified through two key examples as follows

- First, during this period, women had the freedom to choose their husbands, highlighting their rights in marital decisions.
- Second, widow remarriage was accepted, providing women with the right to remarry and continue their lives independently. Additionally, women were actively involved in Yajnas, a religious practice, emphasising their significant role in spiritual and social life.

Q.6 The role of the priestly class (Brahmins) was pivotal in Vedic society. Justify the statement by mentioning any three points.

Ans. The role of the Brahmins (priestly class) was crucial in Vedic society for the following reasons

(i) **Religious Duties** Brahmins were responsible for performing rituals, sacrifices and prayers to the gods. These rituals were believed to ensure prosperity, peace and the well-being of society.

(ii) **Preserving Knowledge** Brahmins were the keepers of sacred knowledge, especially the Vedas, which they memorised and passed down orally. This made them the main educators and intellectuals in society.

(iii) **Advisors to Kings** Brahmins often acted as advisors to kings, guiding them in both spiritual and political matters. Their counsel was highly valued in maintaining the harmony and order of society.

Q.7 Compare and contrast the roles of kings and priests in the Vedic society.

Ans. In Vedic society, kings and priests had different roles but their important roles were as follows

- Kings were political leaders who ruled over tribes and protected their people. They managed resources, organised battles and ensured justice. Priests, on the other hand, were spiritual leaders who performed rituals and sacrifices to please the gods.
- The kings focused on earthly matters, priests handled religious practices.

- Both were respected, but priests had more authority in religious matters, while kings held power in governance and military affairs.

Together, they maintained harmony in Vedic society.

TYPE - 5 — 4 Marks

Long Answer Type Questions

Q.1 Discuss the significance of the Rig Veda in understanding their early life, culture and social organisation. Also, analyse the impact of the Aryans on the development of Indian civilisation during the Vedic period.

Ans. The Rig Veda provides valuable insights into the early life, culture and social organisation of the Aryans. It reveals that the Aryans were a nomadic and pastoral people who initially settled along the rivers of the Indian subcontinent, especially the 'Sapta Sindhu' region (the area of the seven rivers). The Rig Veda highlights their devotion to nature, particularly to deities like Indra (the god of thunder) and Agni (the fire god).

During the Vedic period, the Aryans significantly influenced the development of Indian civilisation. Their religious texts, including the Vedas, laid the foundation for Hinduism, shaping the concepts of Dharma (righteousness) and Karma (action and its consequences).

The Aryans also introduced the caste system, which structured society into distinct social groups, and they contributed to advancements in language, literature and rituals.

Q.2 Explain the following terms.

(i) Rig Vedic Assemblies.

(ii) Education in Early Vedic society.

Ans. (i) In early Vedic period, there were three Rig Vedic assemblies which are

- **Sabha** It primarily focused on Judicial, administrative, and religious decisions.
- **Samiti** It primarily focused on folk assembly discussions, religious ceremonies and philosophical debates. The Rajan could be elected or re-elected by the Samiti, which had a more democratic role.
- **Vidhatha:** It was the earliest assembly handling economic, religious, social and military functions.

(ii) Education was imparted through Gurukuls in the early Vedic period. The residence of the Guru was called Gurukul and was considered the most sacred institution. Vedas, Grammar, Puranas, Mathematics, Ethics, Logic and Military Science were the subjects in the early Vedic period.

Q.3 Compare and contrast the food, dress, and amusements of the early Vedic period with those of the later Vedic period.

Ans. The comparison between the food, dress and amusements of the early Vedic period and the later Vedic period is as follows

Basis	Early Vedic Period	Later Vedic Period
Food	Mainly barley, wheat, and milk products. Occasional meat consumption, especially by Kshatriyas.	More diverse foods like rice, vegetables, and fruits. More elaborate food preparations for religious rituals.
Dress	Simple clothing made of bark cloth, wool, and hides. Loose, unstitched garments, women wore anklets and jewellery.	Refined clothing made of cotton and silk. Stitched garments, turban, and headgear for men, draped garments for women.
Amusements	Focused on outdoor activities like horse riding and chariot racing. Enjoyed musical performances with instruments like vina and drums.	More elaborate entertainment like royal feasts and musical performances. Board games like dice was popular in later Vedic period.

Q.4 Distinguish between economy of early Vedic period and later Vedic period.

Ans. The differences between the economy of early and later Vedic period are

Economy of Early Vedic Period	Economy of Later Vedic Period
In the beginning, the main occupation was domestication of animals and agriculture was secondary.	Agriculture became the chief occupation and domestication of cattle also continued.
Cattle was the important source of wealth.	Land was the important source of wealth.

Economy of Early Vedic Period	Economy of Later Vedic Period
Many people were engaged in trade and commerce.	Trade continued in barter and currency mode of exchange was in silver coins.
Barter system prevailed and was carried out in terms of bullocks and horses.	Traders guilds had come up and vaisyas also carried on trade and commerce.

TYPE - 6

10 Marks

Structured Questions

Q.1. With reference to the sources of information about the Vedic age, answer the following questions.

(i) The Vedas, the oldest sacred texts in Hinduism, hold a central place in shaping the religious, cultural and philosophical framework of ancient Indian society. Explain briefly its important role. (3)

(ii) The epics of ancient India hold a significant role in shaping the moral, cultural and social fabric of Indian society. Explain the importance of Epics in context to Indian society. (3)

(iii) "The role of iron implements in the Vedic period was crucial". Justify this statement with reasons. (4)

Ans. (i) The Vedas serve as a vast reservoir of knowledge about the Vedic age, offering insights into the lives of its people. They provide valuable information on the social, economic, political, and religious aspects of their society.

Comprising four texts - the Rig Veda, the Sama Veda, the Yajur Veda, and the Atharva Veda - each Veda contributes uniquely to our understanding of this ancient era.

The Rig Veda primarily chronicles the early Vedic period, while the other three Vedas shed light on the later Vedic period.

(ii) The ancient Indian epics, Ramayana and Mahabharata are invaluable treasures of wisdom, morality and life lessons.

- The Ramayana written by Maharishi Valmiki teaches ideals of duty, family and virtue.
- The Mahabharata, composed by Sage Ved Vyasa, portrays the battle between good and evil. The Bhagavad Gita guides spiritual growth and the philosophy of karma and immortality of the soul.
- These epics provide detailed accounts of Aryan kingdoms, their military forces, weaponry and also highlight the noble ideals of family life within Aryan society.

Thus, these epics not only reflect the political, social and cultural practices of the Vedic period but also provide deep life lessons, which inspire generations and shape India's moral and cultural fabric.

(iii) The Iron age in India began around 1000 BCE, marking a significant technological advancement. Iron, being abundant, cost-effective, and tougher than copper and bronze, became widely utilised due to its availability in various regions. It played a crucial role in several key areas

(a) **Agriculture** Iron tools such as axes enabled the Aryans to clear forests and cultivate land efficiently. The introduction of iron plough-heads, sickles, and hoes allowed them to expand agriculture, leading to the production of larger quantities of rice, wheat, barley, fruits, and vegetables, thereby improving their standard of living.

(b) **Occupation** The durability of iron tools like saws, chisels, hammers, nails, and tongs supported the growth of various professions, including weaving, spinning, carpentry, tanning, and tool-making.

(c) **Defence** Iron was also vital for the production of weapons, including swords, armours, and shields, enhancing the military capabilities of the time.

Q.2 With reference to the society during the Vedic Age, answer the following questions.

(i) Explain briefly the class divisions that existed in the society. (3)

(ii) State the position of women in the Vedic period. (3)

(iii) "Ashrama system came into existence which means a stage in the long journey of life of a man". Explain the four stages in the life of an Aryan. (4)

Ans. (i) In the early Vedic period, society was structured into various classes based on professions, which eventually became hereditary. By the later Vedic period, these occupational division evolved into the caste system and the society was organised into four main Varnas: Brahmins, Kshatriyas, Vaishyas and Shudras.

The Brahmins were responsible for conducting religious rituals, while the Kshatriyas, as warriors, emerged as the ruling class. The Vaishyas were engaged in trade, agriculture and industry, and the Shudras primarily served the higher classes.

(ii) In the early Vedic period, women were highly respected and enjoyed significant rights.

- They had the freedom to choose their husbands and actively participated in rituals.
- Widow remarriage was common, and child marriage was not practiced.
- The marriageable age, as mentioned in the Rig Veda, appears to have been around 16 to 17 years. However, during the later Vedic period, there was a marked decline in the status of women.
- Their role in Yajnas became less important.
- They lost their right to choose a husband and control over property.

(iii) The life of an Aryan was traditionally divided into four stages, known as the four Ashramas. These stages were

(a) **Brahmacharya Ashrama** This stage lasted until the age of 25, during which the individual was expected to live a life of discipline and focus on acquiring knowledge in a Gurukul.

(b) **Grihastha Ashrama** Spanning from ages 25 to 50, this phase marked the period when an individual was expected to marry, raise a family and support his household.

(c) **Vanaprastha Ashrama** Lasting from 50 to 75 years, this stage involved a gradual withdrawal from worldly life, with an emphasis on seeking spiritual knowledge.

(d) **Sanyasa Ashrama** From 75 to 100 years, this final stage was one of renunciation, where the individual abandoned all attachments and devoted himself to meditation in pursuit of moksha or salvation.

Q.3 With reference to economic organisation of the people in the Vedic period, answer the following questions.

(i) State the methods used by the Aryans in agriculture during early and later Vedic period. (3)

(ii) Why was the domestication of animals important to the Aryans? (3)

(iii) How was trade managed during later Vedic period? (4)

Ans. (i) In the early Vedic period the Rig Veda mentions little about agriculture activities. However, it mentions the use of fire for clearing forests and the practice of shifting cultivation. In contrast, during the Later Vedic Period, agriculture gained greater significance due to the availability of fertile alluvial lands in regions like the Ganga-Yamuna doab and the middle Ganga valley.

Later Vedic texts indicate the use of oxen fasten to ploughs, suggesting the widespread use of plough cultivation. The introduction of iron ploughshares and metal tools further advanced agricultural practices, and by the end of this period, a diverse range of crops was being cultivated.

(ii) Animal domestication played a crucial role for the Aryans, especially during the early Vedic period, as cattle were their primary source of wealth. For them, cattle symbolises prosperity, and the cow held religious significance.

In addition, animals like sheep were domesticated for their wool, and Vedic texts also mention leather workers, indicating the use of animal products.

The region's low rainfall and the shifting courses of major rivers made it challenging to cultivate the fertile alluvial lands permanently, which in turn increased the reliance on animal husbandry as an essential part of their economy and lifestyle.

(iii) In the later Vedic period, the agricultural surplus created a foundation for thriving trade, leading to the development of markets and the gradual growth of towns and cities. This urbanisation was closely linked to the need for distribution of surplus produce, along with the exchange of goods and services.

- **Barter System and Coins** Although the introduction of coins provided a more standardised form of currency, the barter system remained the primary mode of trade. This system involved direct exchange of goods like grains, cattle, textiles, and crafts, highlighting the continued reliance on tangible assets rather than monetary transactions.
- **Trade Centers** Places like Kosambhi, Hastinapur, Kashi and Videha became known as trade hubs, suggesting organised trade routes and markets.
- **Transportation** Bullock carts were used for land transport, while boats and ships facilitated trade along rivers and potentially overseas.
- **Specialized Traders** The emergence of proto-guilds or early trading organisations as well as caravan traders indicates a growing specialisation in trade.

As trade expanded, it not only facilitated economic growth but also fostered cultural interactions and the spread of ideas across regions.

Q.4 With reference to the picture given, answer the following questions.

(i) Identify this ancient education system. Persons belonging to which ashrama of life attended this system? **(3)**

(ii) Describe briefly the ancient education institution. **(3)**

(iii) Mention the advantages and disadvantages of studying in this educational setup? **(4)**

Ans. (i) The given picture shows the Gurukul system of education in which the students used to live with their teacher called Guru.

Persons belonging to Brahmacharya ashrama of life attended the Gurukul.

(ii) The Gurukul, the residence of the Guru, was considered one of the most sacred institutions in ancient Vedic society. The Guru treated his students as his own children, and in return, students were expected to assist with household chores as part of their education. Daily routines began early with a bath, followed by the chanting of Vedic mantras.

The majority of teachings were passed down orally. Upon completing their studies, students would offer Guru Dakshina-a token of gratitude, typically in the form of a gift, to their teacher.

The primary aim of education was the overall development of students-physically, mentally, and spiritually.

The curriculum included a wide range of subjects, such as the Vedas, Puranas, Grammar, Mathematics, Ethics, Logic, and Military Science.

(iii) **Advantages of the Gurukul System of Education are**

- The Gurukul system promoted equality among students, as children from both royal families and common households were educated under the same conditions and rules.
- It fostered the physical, mental, and spiritual growth of the students, offering a well-rounded education that nurtured all aspects of their development.

Disadvantages of the Gurukul System of Education are

- The education was primarily oral, limiting the scope for written learning and documentation.
- Students had to live away from their families, often enduring a rigorous and disciplined lifestyle with little room for personal choice.
- Moreover, there was no standardised curriculum or formal methods of assessment, leading to variations in the learning experience and outcomes.

Q.5 In the context of the economy of the early Vedic age, answer the following questions.

(i) How did the barter system in the Vedic period work, and what role did cows and Nishka play in trade? How did the growth of towns and cities affect trade during this time? **(3)**

(ii) Discuss the various economic activities during the Vedic period, highlighting the roles of chariot makers, women in crafts, and the use of wool as a raw material. **(3)**

(iii) How did cattle rearing influence the economy, religious practices, and social status of the Rig Vedic Aryans? Discuss the significance of cows in their daily life and society. **(4)**

Ans. (i) The barter system in the Vedic period involved the exchange of goods without the use of money to fulfil the basic needs of people.

Cows, being valuable possessions, and Nishka (gold ornaments), served as common mediums of exchange. This system allowed people to trade goods such as grain, cattle and clothes for items they did not produce themselves.

The growth of towns and cities provided additional opportunities for trade, as these urban centres became hubs where merchants and traders gathered, further stimulating economic activity. This led to the development of a more organised form of trade and a shift towards more complex economic exchanges.

(ii) During the Vedic period, people were involved in many economic activities like hunting, fishing and carpentry.

Chariot makers held an important position as chariots were essential for battles and transport and it reflects advanced craftsmanship.

Women played a key role in crafts such as weaving, dyeing, spinning, and knitting. They used wool, especially from sheep, as the main material for making clothes and textiles.

These activities helped the Vedic society to thrive and create a strong economy based on both agriculture and handicrafts.

(iii) Cattle rearing was indeed the primary occupation of the Rig Vedic Aryans, forming the backbone of their economy. Cows, in particular, were considered a symbol of wealth and prosperity, and their importance is reflected in the fact that they were used as a form of payment for various services, including sacrificial rituals.

The Aryans believed that the well-being of their herds directly influenced their prosperity, so prayers were often offered to deities like Indra and Agni for an increase in cattle.

Cows were gifted to priests as offerings for performing yajnas (sacrificial rituals), highlighting their significant role in religious practices. The exchange of cattle also facilitated trade and social status within the community, making them a central part of Vedic society.

Q.6. **In context of the available archaeological sources about Vedic age, answer the following questions**

(i) How did the rise in agricultural practices contribute to the development of pottery during the later Vedic period? Mention the types of pottery associated with this period and important sites where they have been discovered. (3)

(ii) What are some of the features of Painted Grey Ware (PGW) pottery? Mention at least three characteristics and their significance. (3)

(iii) How did the discovery and use of iron during the Vedic period impact agriculture and trade? Explain with at least four points. (4)

Ans. (i) The rise in agricultural practices during the later Vedic period led to the development of pottery as it became essential for storing surplus grains and other agricultural products. Pottery was needed to store, cook and transport food.

During this period, the Aryans advanced their pottery skills, creating types such as Grey Ware (GW) and Painted Grey Ware (PGW). These types of pottery are linked to the Rig Vedic culture because they were used in the regions and time frame mentioned in the Rig Veda.

Important sites where these pottery were discovered include Bhagwanpura (Kurukshetra), Dadheri (Ludhiana), Katpalan, and Nagar (Jalandhar), highlighting the connection between agriculture and the growth of pottery.

(ii) Painted Grey Ware (PGW) pottery is known for its distinct features, such as

(a) It has a grey colour, which is due to the unique firing technique.

(b) It is often decorated with geometric patterns or lines, adding to its aesthetic appeal.

(c) The pottery is made using a fine clay that makes it durable.

These features signify the progress in pottery techniques and are linked to the cultural and technological advancements of the later Vedic Aryans. PGW pottery provides insights into their daily life and art.

(iii) The discovery and use of iron during the Vedic period had a significant impact on both agriculture and trade in the following ways

(a) **Agriculture Expansion** Iron tools, especially ploughshares, allowed for deeper ploughing, which led to the development of wet paddy cultivation, improving agricultural productivity.

(b) **Clearing Forests** Iron was used in tools that helped clear forests, enabling the expansion of agricultural land for farming.

(c) **New Trades** Iron also enabled the creation of various tools like saws, chisels, and hammers, which led to the growth of new trades and industries.

(d) **Improved Weapons** The use of iron for making stronger weapons, such as swords and shields, enhanced military strength and security, indirectly promoting trade by stabilising regions.

JAINISM AND BUDDHISM

- The sixth century BCE is regarded as an important era in the world history which saw the emergence of thinkers like Confucius in China, Zoroaster in Persia and Vardhamana Mahavira and Gautama Buddha in India.
- In India, it was the phase when orthodox religious beliefs and practices were challenged and rejected by the new sects.
- Jainism founded by Mahavira and Buddhism founded by Gautama Buddha, emerged as the most influential religious reform movements.

Causes for the Rise of Jainism and Buddhism in the 6th Century BCE

- **Reaction against Ritualism** Religious ceremonies had become very expensive and were beyond the means of ordinary people. This gave rise to faiths that were simple and inexpensive.
- **Corruption in Religion** The Priests used to extract money from people on the name of yajnas, rites and rituals. Kshatriya rulers protested against such practices. Both Jainism and Buddhism were founded by two Kshatriya princes.
- **Rigid Caste System** The division of society into Brahmans, Kshatriyas, Vaishyas and Shudras had become rigid. The caste system did not even allow any social mobility. Interchange of caste was impossible. Jainism and Buddhism gave a simple and liberal society to the people of that period.
- **Difficult Language** Sanskrit was considered a sacred language. Most of the Vedic literature was composed in Sanskrit. The priestly class gave discourses and chanted mantras in this language, which the common people found difficult to understand. Therefore, many people began to look for an alternative religion that they could understand better.
- **Political Condition** During sixth Century BCE, Magadha was ruled by Bimbisara and later by condemned Ajatashatru. Both these rulers were liberal and tolerant. They were free from Brahmanic influence and condemned certain social evils in their kingdoms. When the opportunity came, they patronised both Jainism and Buddhism.
- **Agricultural Economy** The use of iron had made the animal-drawn plough popular. The farmers needed a religion that would give protection to animals. Both Jainism and Buddhism preached non-violence and were against sacrifices.

Jainism

The doctrines of the Jains were preached by saints or acharyas called - Tirthankaras (literally meaning, those who guide men and women in crossing over life's stream of rebirths). Rishabhadev was the first Tirthankara and Mahavira was the 24th (last) Tirthankara in Jainism.

Sources of Jainism

Angas

- The Angas, also known as Dwadashangi, are the 12 primary texts of Jainism. These texts are based on the teachings of the Tirthankaras.

- These texts were written in Prakrit language.
- These discourses were recorded by the Gandharas (disciples) and provide key insights into Jain philosophy and practices.
- Among them, two of the most significant texts are the Aacharang Sutra, which outlines the ethical code for Jain monks, and the Vyakhya Pragnapti (or Bhagavati Sutra), which offers an extensive overview of Jain philosophy.
- The Angas cover a wide range of topics, including religious rituals, the various stages of a householder's life, vows of chastity, rules of conduct, and the broader philosophical principal of Jainism.
- The Upangas are a group of 12 texts that were written to explain and expand upon the ideas found in the Angas. It helps to provide a deeper understanding of Jain teachings.

Vardhamana Mahavira

Vardhamana Mahavira

- Mahavira was born in Kundagrama near Vaishali in Bihar in the second half of 6th century BCE.
- At the age of 30, Mahavira left his home and family and became an ascetic (monk).
- He wandered from place to place in search of truth for 12 years. At the age of 42, he conquered his senses. He was now called Jina (the conqueror).
- His followers came to be called Jinas or Jains (those who have conquered their desires).
- Mahavira taught his religion for the next 30 years in places such as Kosala, Magadha, Vaishali, Mithila and Champa.
- He gave his first sermon at Mount Vipul in Rajgriha, the capital of Magadha. He attained salvation at the age of 72 at a place called Pavapuri in Bihar.

Teachings of Jainism

- **The Five Vows** A Jain householder has to take the following five vows i.e., Ahimsa (non-violence), Achaurya or Asteya (not stealing), Satya (not telling a lie), Aparigraha (not possessing property), and Brahmacharya (practicing chastity).
- **Nine Truths** The nine truths are - Jiva (living things), Ajiva (non-living things), Punya (results of good deeds), Pap (sin), Ashrav (good deeds), Sanvar (hindrances in the way of karma), Bandha (bondage), Nirjara (destruction of karmas), and Moksha (salvation).

Doctrines of Jainism

- **Tri-ratnas** It teaches that following the tri-ratnas or three jewels of right faith, right knowledge and right conduct is essential to attain spiritual liberation.
- **Karma** It is seen as the result of one's actions. Good deeds accumulate positive karma, which leads to Moksha (liberation from the cycle of birth and death).
- **Equality** It promotes the idea of equality, emphasising universal brotherhood and compassion for all living beings, regardless of their form or nature.
- **Eternal soul** It teaches that the soul (jiva) is eternal and immortal. It undergoes cycles of birth and rebirth until it attains liberation (Moksha).
- **Belief in Penance** It believes in the importance of penance (tapas), which involves self-discipline, fasting and renouncing physical desires to purify the soul.
- **Moksha** (Nirvana) It signifies the ultimate liberation of the soul from the cycle of birth and death and it is achieved through the destruction of all karmic bonds and the attainment of a blissful state.

Spread of Jainism

- Jainism had royal patronage. Therefore, it spread easily around Kosala, Magadha, Mithila, Champa and other parts of the country.
- Mahavira founded monasteries headed by learned munis (sages).
- In the Western parts of India, Jainism was patronised by the business community.

Causes of the Spread of Jainism

- **Local Dialect** Mahavira adopted the language of common people i.e., Prakrit instead of Sanskrit to preach his doctrines.
- **Royal Patronage** Jainism received royal patronage of Chalukyas and Rashtrakutas. Chandragupta Maurya is also believed to have converted to Jainism. Kharavela, the ruler of Kalinga (Odisha) helped in spread of Jainism in Eastern India.
- **Saints** There were many devout Jain saints like Kalkacharya who lived in Ujjain and made it a centre of Jainism. Another Jain saint Bhadrabahu, took Jainism to Karnataka.
- **Appeal to People** People found the religion attractive as it was based on self-denial, simplicity and spirituality. There were neither animal sacrifices nor there was any class distinction.

Two Sects of Jainism

- **Shvetambaras or the white clad** They wore white clothes and covered their faces with a small white cloth to avoid killing the tiniest of insects or germs that might enter the nose while breathing. They fasted but did not believe in extreme penance and strictness.
- **Digambaras or sky-clad** They followed Bhadrabahu. According to Digambaras, living without clothes signified detachment from worldly pleasures. They were orthodox followers of Mahavira. They kept long fasts and lived an austere life.

Impact of Jainism

Dilwara Temple, Mount Ab

- Mahavira preached in the common languages like Ardha-Magadhi, so that his teaching could be easily understood by everyone. Jain texts were written in Prakrit and Sanskrit, enriching regional languages and literature.
- Mahavira's principle of non-violence influenced Indian history by making the kshatriyas kinder and more tolerant. However, this also caused a decrease in their military strength.
- Jainism promoted peaceful living, but Jains did not establish a political empire due to their non-violent stance.
- Jainism became popular among traders and merchants, fostering unity and leading to the rise of a prosperous trading community.
- Mahavira opposed the caste system, promoting equality and reducing societal divisions between higher and lower castes.
- Kings patronised Jain culture, which influenced the Jain art and architecture. Notable Jain sculptures include the statue of Bahubali at Shravanabelgola and cave art at Udayagiri and Ellora. The Dilwara Jain temples at Mount Abu are a fine example of Jain architecture.

Decline of Jainism

- Jainism required severe penance, meditation, fasting and restraint, which was difficult for people to follow.
- Some early rulers like Bimbisara, Ajatshatru, Udayin and Kharavela supported Jainism. However, later rulers like Ashoka, Kanishka, and Harshavardhana favoured Buddhism, which led to less support for Jainism from the kings.
- Jain followers were not enthusiastic about spreading the religion in villages and towns and foreign countries.
- Although Jainism promoted equality among people, it did not completely remove the differences between high and low positions in society.
- During the Gupta period and in later years, Hinduism once again became popular. Therefore, Jainism remained restricted to a few areas in the country.

Buddhism

The word 'Buddhism' comes from 'budhi' meaning 'to awaken'. Buddhism has its origins about 2500 years ago when Siddhartha, known as the Buddha, was himself enlightened at the age of 35.

Sources of Buddhism

Tripitakas

- The Tripitakas are regarded as the foundational literary works of Buddhism, comprising three essential collections as follows
  (i) **Vinaya Pitaka** This text outlines the rules and regulations governing the lives of monks and nuns. It also provides valuable insights into the life and teachings of the Buddha, alongside details about the customs, arts, and historical context of ancient times.
  (ii) **Sutta Pitaka** It contains the teachings of the Buddha and his prominent disciples, such as Sariputta and Ananda. It presents teachings that form the core of Buddhist doctrine. One of its key components is the Dhammapada, a guide to the path of truth.
  (iii) **Abhidhamma Pitaka** It is a collection of Buddhist texts that describes Buddhist philosophy. It is the third part of the Pali Tripitaka, the sacred scripture of Theravada Buddhism. It contains commentaries, analyses and debates about the Buddha's teachings.

Jatakas

- The Jatakas is a collection of stories that recount the past lives of the Buddha, in which he takes various forms, including those of animals and humans.
- While the Jatakas offer limited biographical details about Gautama Buddha's life, they provide valuable insights into the political, economic, and social conditions of the people during the 5th to 2nd centuries BCE.
- Jataka tales reflect the core morals, ethics and principles of Buddhism.

Gautama Buddha

- Gautama Buddha was born in 563 BCE at Lumbini near Kapilavastu, in Nepal. He belonged to the Kshatriya clan of Sakya.
- At the age of 29, he asked his charioteer, Channa, to take him outside the palace grounds to the neighbouring villages. There, he saw an old man, a sick man, a corpse being carried in a funeral procession and a holy (ascetic) man. These sights are known as 'Four Great Sights'.
- These four sights had a great effect on Gautama as he could not forget these experiences. As a result, he became restless and decided to leave home to seek religious enlightenment. This event is known as Mahabhiskramana (Great renunciation).

Gautama Buddha

- At the age of 35, Gautama attained enlightenment at Bodh Gaya in Bihar. From then onwards, he began to be called as the Buddha or the Enlightened One.
- Buddha did not profess the non-existence of God, unlike Mahavira. Rather, he believed that the entire universe works according to the Dharma (universal law).

Teachings of Buddhism

- **Four Noble Truths** The essence of Buddhism lies in Four noble truths. They are
  - (i) The world is full of suffering.
  - (ii) The suffering has a cause.
  - (iii) Desire is the cause of suffering.
  - (iv) If desire is stopped, suffering can also be stopped.
- **Eightfold Path** The way to nirvana in Buddhism, or the path that leads to removal of suffering, is known as the Eightfold Path (Ashtangika Marg) or the middle path. It includes
  - (i) **Right Action** To remain away from theft, luxuries and violence.
  - (ii) **Right Thought** To remain away from empty rituals and worldly evils.
  - (iii) **Right Belief** To give up desire.
  - (iv) **Right Living** To remain honest, when dealing with others.
  - (v) **Right Speech** To speak the truth and do not think of ill for others.
  - (vi) **Right Effort** To focus on freeing yourself from negativity and working for the well-being of others.
  - (vii) **Right Recollection** To think about right or pious things.
  - (viii) **Right Meditation** To concentrate only on right things.

Doctrines of Buddism

- **Code of Conduct** The Buddha formulated a code of conduct for his disciples or followers. It included the following
  - (i) Not to tell a lie
  - (ii) Not to own property
  - (iii) Not to consume alcoholic drinks
  - (iv) Not to commit violence
  - (v) Not to indulge in corrupt practices
- **Karma** Gautama Buddha had faith in the theory of karma. It means that the condition in which a man lives his present life and the deeds. The Karma decides the course of the life in the next birth and the person has to face the consequence of their actions.
- **Stress on Morality** Buddha insisted on a life based on good actions. His followers were instructed to practice non-violence and to lead an upright life.
- **Nirvana** The ultimate goal of life is to attain Nirvana or Salvation. It is a peaceful state of mind which conquers all diseases and makes the person free from the cycle of birth and death (Moksha).
- **Ahimsa** Buddha attached great importance to ahimsa or non-violence and strongly opposed any kind of violence against others.
- **No Faith in Rituals and Sacrifices** Buddha believed that yajnas cannot change a man's destiny. Sacrifices and rituals are meaningless ceremonies.

The Sangh

The organisation for teaching of Buddhism is known as Sangha. It was a monastic order established to spread Buddhism.

- **Membership** The members of this organisation were called Bhikshus (monks) and Bhikkhunis (nuns). The followers had to undergo training for 10 years. The minimum age to join the Sangha at the time of Buddha was 15 years.
- **Ten Commandments** The members had to lead a disciplined life and follow the ten commandments (Paramita)
  - (i) To speak the truth
  - (ii) Not to harm creatures
  - (iii) Not to use intoxicants
  - (iv) To abide by Brahmacharya

(v) To avoid music and dancing
(vi) Not to use scented goods
(vii) Not to sleep on cushions
(viii) Not to keep money
(ix) To take meals only at fixed times
(x) Not to own property

- **Viharas** This was a place where the monks and nuns spend their time during training. In the Viharas, the members led a life of chastity (Brahmacharya), austerity (strictness), devotion and purity.

Sects of Buddhism

During the deliberations of the 4th Buddhist Council, in the reign of Kanishka, Buddhism split into two sects - the Hinayana and the Mahayana.

(i) Hinayana

- This sect views Gautama Buddha as a human who achieved nirvana through the noble eight-fold path.
- They rejected idol worship and emphasised individual effort to attain nirvana. They used Pali language.
- They are found in India, Sri Lanka, Myanmar, Cambodia and Laos.

(ii) Mahayana

- Mahayana, meaning the Greater Vehicle, of salvation. It is a combination of Buddhism and Hinduism. Mahayanists view Buddha as an incarnation of God.
- They believe in the collective salvation through faith and commitment to Buddha.
- They used Sanskrit language.
- They worship Buddha and Bodhisattva idols and believe in helping others to attain enlightenment. Mahayanists are found in China and Japan.

Impact of Buddhism

- The rise of Buddhism led to the idea of ahimsa, which became a weapon against society's ill practices. Animal protection became a new culture.
- Buddhism promoted intellectual growth and rejected caste distinctions, giving the weaker sections a chance to take part in political and social matters.
- Buddhism also challenged Hinduism by ending yajnas and sacrifices.
- Buddhism spread to other countries also apart from India. This led to close cultural contacts between different countries.

Decline of Buddhism

- The important cause of the decline and fall of Buddhism was the Sangha. It became centers of corruption and money.
- The division of Buddhism into a number of groups like 'Hinayana', 'Mahayana' and other sects led to the decline of Buddhism.
- Pali and Prakrit, the spoken language of most people of India, was the medium for the spread of the message of Buddhism. But Sanskrit replaced these at the Fourth Buddhist Council during the reign of Kaniska.
- The revival of Brahmanical Hinduism also served as a cause for the decline of Buddhism. The rights and rituals of Hinduism were simplified and it incorporated the positive aspects of Buddhism.
- The Muslim invasion of India almost wiped-out Buddhism. Their invasions of India became regular and repeated. The invaders destroyed the monasteries and looted the wealth. Many Buddhist monks were killed, some of them were converted to Islam and others fled to Nepal and Tibet and took shelter there.
- Buddhism lost the royal patronage, which they received during the period of Ashoka, Kanishka and Harshavardhana. Rajput rulers were warlike and could not follow the policy of Ahimsa. Besides, the Gupta kings patronised temples.

EXAM ORIENTED QUESTIONS

TYPE - 1 1 Mark

Multiple Choice Questions

Q.1 Read the description and identify the person
He is the first Tirthankara.
(a) Rishabhadev
(b) Parshvanath.
(c) Mahavira
(d) Siddharth Gautma

Ans. (a) Rishabhadev

Q.2 Consider the following statements about Jainism and choose the correct option.

P : Jainism was founded by Mahavira in the 6th century BCE.

Q : Jainism teaches that all living beings, including plants, have souls.

R : Jainism rejects the importance of ascetic practices and rituals.

S : Mahavira wandered from place to place in search of truth for 20 years.

(a) P and Q (b) R and S
(c) P and R (d) Q and R

Ans. (a) P and Q

Q.3. Which of these practices is most likely to be followed by a Jain monk?
(a) Regular meditation and self-discipline
(b) Offering sacrifices to gods
(c) Celebrating festivals with animal sacrifices
(d) Worshiping a supreme deity

Ans. (a) Regular meditation and self-discipline

Exp. Jain monks focused on meditation, self-control and non-violence. They avoided sacrifices, deities or festivals which involves harm to living beings.

Q.4 Complete the given analogy.
Digambaras : Bhadrabahu :: Swetambaras : ?
(a) Sthulabhadra
(b) Suddhodana
(c) Uddaka Ramaputra
(d) Alara Kalma

Ans. (a) Sthulabhadra

Q.5 Consider the following statements about the founder of Buddhism.

P : Siddhartha Gautama, the founder of Buddhism, is known as the Buddha.

Q : Siddhartha Gautama was married at young age to princess Yashoda.

R : The Buddha achieved enlightenment after a long period of asceticism.

S : Siddhartha Gautama spread the teachings of the Hindu scriptures after his enlightenment.

(a) P and Q (b) R and S (c) P and R (d) Q and R

Ans. (c) P and R

Q.6 Buddhism focussed on preserving and transmitting the teachings of the Buddha, and commentary there on; and throughout history. *BBC, 15th January, 2020*

What was the central theme of Buddha's teachings?
(a) The importance of wealth and power
(b) To achieve Nirvana by following the Eightfold Path
(c) The importance of idol worship
(d) The need for a strong political system

Ans. (b) To achieve Nirvana by following the Eightfold Path

Q.7 Identify the odd one out in the context of Buddhist teachings?
(a) The Four Noble Truths (b) The Eightfold Path
(c) The Concept of Brahman (d) The Middle Path

Ans. (c) The Concept of Brahman

Q.8 Which of the following means 'Three Baskets' of Buddhist canon?
(a) Jataka (b) Tripitikas (c) Angas (d) Upangas

Ans. (b) Tripitakas

Exp. Tripitakas refers to the three main collections of Buddhist scriptures: the Vinaya Pitaka (rules), Sutta Pitaka (teachings of Buddha) and Abhidhamma Pitaka (philosophy).

Q.9 Jataka tales gives information about
(a) Past lives of Buddha (b) Sects of Jainism
(c) Sects of Buddhism (d) Past lives of Mahavira

Ans. (a) Past lives of Buddha

Exp. Jataka tales gives information about the past lives of Buddha, in which he takes various forms, including those of animals and humans.

Q.10 Which of the following vows means 'practising chastity'?

(a) Asteya (b) Ahimsa
(c) Aparigraha (d) Brahmacharya

Ans. (d) Brahmacharya

Q.11 Which of the following is the reason for the decline of Buddhism?

(a) Division of Buddhism
(b) Use of Sanskrit language
(c) Loss of royal patronage
(d) All of the above

Ans. (d) All of the above

Q.12 Which of the following is not likely to be a common practice in Jainism and Buddhism?

(a) Meditation and mindfulness for spiritual growth
(b) Veneration of idols and deities
(c) Reincarnation and belief in karma
(d) Rejection of material attachments and desires

Ans. (b) Veneration of idols and deities

Exp. Jainism and Buddhism focus on personal spiritual growth, meditation, and ethical living rather than idol worship or belief in deities.

Q.13 Complete the given analogy.

Buddhism : Gautama Buddha : Jainism : ?

(a) Parshvanath (b) Mahavira
(c) Siddartha (d) Rishabhadeva

Ans. (b) Mahavira

Q.14 While Jainism strongly advocates Ahimsa (non-violence) towards all living beings, Buddhism teaches the importance of understanding suffering through the Four Noble Truths and following the Eightfold Path.

What is the common aim of both Jainism and Buddhism?

(a) To achieve worldly success and power.
(b) To attain liberation from the cycle of birth and rebirth.
(c) To strictly follow rituals and prayers to the gods.
(d) To establish a powerful political system in India.

Ans. (b) To attain liberation from the cycle of birth and rebirth.

Q.15 Complete the given analogy.

Jainism : Angas : : Buddhism : ?

(a) Vinaya Pitaka (b) Acharang Sutra
(c) Bhagvati Sutra (d) Upangas

Ans. (a) Vinaya Pitaka

TYPE - 2 1 Mark

Assertion-Reason Questions

Q.1 Read the two statements given below about Jainism and Buddhism and select the option that shows the correct relationship between (A) and (R).

Assertion (A) In the sixth century BCE, orthodox religious beliefs and practices were challenged by the new sects.

Reason (R) During this period, Jainism and Buddhism emerged as important religious reform movements.

(a) R contradicts A
(b) R is the reason for A
(c) A is true but R is false
(d) A and R are independent of each other

Ans. (b) R is the reason for A

Q.2 Read the two statements given below about Jainism and Buddhism and select the option that shows the correct relationship between (A) and (R).

Assertion (A) Jainism and Buddhism grew and spread as a reaction against ritualism prevalent in the existing religious practices.

Reason (R) Most of the Vedic literature was composed in Sanskrit and difficult to be understood by the common people.

(a) R contradicts A
(b) R is the reason for A
(c) A is true but R is false
(d) A and R are independent of each other

Ans. (b) R is the reason for A

Q.3 Read the two statements given below about Jainism and select the option that shows the correct relationship between (A) and (R).

Assertion (A) Angas and Upangas are Jain texts which were orally passed on by religious leaders to their pupils.

Reason (R) Tripitakas are the most important literary works of Jains.

(a) R contradicts A
(b) R is the reason for A
(c) A is true but R is false
(d) A and R are independent of each other

Ans. (c) A is true but R is false

Q.4 Read the two statements given below about Mahavira and select the option that shows the correct relationship between (A) and (R).

Assertion (A) Mahavira attained salvation at Pavapuri in Bihar.

Reason (R) Mahavira gave his first sermon at Deer Park in Sarnath near Varanasi.

(a) R contradicts A
(b) R is the reason for A
(c) A is true but R is false
(d) A and R are independent of each other

Ans. (c) A is true but R is false

Q.5 Read the two statements given below about Jainism and select the option that shows the correct relationship between (A) and (R).

Assertion (A) According to Jainism, good deeds alone liberate a man from the cycle of life and death.

Reason (R) Jains believe in Moksha or freedom from the cycle of births and rebirths.

(a) R contradicts A
(b) R is the reason for A
(c) A is true but R is false
(d) A and R are independent of each other

Ans. (b) R is the reason for A

Q.6 Read the two statements given below and select the option that shows the correct relationship between (A) and (R).

Assertion (A) Mahavira adopted the language of the common people, i.e., Prakrit to preach his doctrines.

Reason (R) Buddhists adopted Pali language in their literature.

(a) R contradicts A
(b) R is the reason for A
(c) A is true but R is false
(d) A and R are independent of each other

Ans. (d) A and R are independent of each other

Q.7 Read the two statements given below about Buddhism and select the option that shows the correct relationship between (A) and (R).

Assertion (A) Hinayana does not believe that Buddha was God.

Reason (R) Mahayana believes that Buddha was an incarnation of God.

(a) R contradicts A
(b) R is the reason for A
(c) A is true but R is false
(d) A and R are independent of each other

Ans. (d) A and R are independent of each other

TYPE - 3 — 2 Marks

Very Short Answer Type Questions

Q.1 Mention any two key reasons why the 6th century BCE is considered a turning point in Indian history.

Ans. The 6th century BCE is a turning point because

(i) Many religious lenders like Buddha and Mahavira challenged orthodox religious practices and offered new paths to spirituality.

(ii) The rise of 16 Mahajanapadas brought significant political and social changes in the society.

Q.2 List any two vows prescribed for the Jains.

Ans. The two vows prescribed for the Jains are

(i) **Ahimsa** Non-violence

(ii) **Achaurya or Asteya** Not stealing

Q.3 What are Angas? What is the subject matter of these Angas?

Ans. Angas are the 12 primary texts of Jainism that were compiled by the disciples of Lord Mahavira after he attained enlightenment.

The subject matter of the Angas includes

- Religious rituals
- The stages of a householder's life
- Vows of chastity
- Rules of conduct
- Other essential principles of Jainism

Q.4 Mention the three Jewels or triratnas.

Ans. The three Jewels or triratnas are the Doctrine of Jainism, it includes right faith, right knowledge and right conduct or action.

Q.5 List any two reasons for Jainism having few followers.

Ans. Two reasons for Jainism having few followers include

(i) Jainism preached rigid austerity. The theory of ahimsa was extended even to the wearing of clothes, which is challenging for many people to follow.

(ii) The Jain concept of Karma, where action create Karmic particle that bind to the soul is challenging to practice in everyday life.

Q.6 Discuss the doctrine of 'Karma' in Jainism and its effect on the soul's liberation.

Ans. In Jainism, the doctrine of Karma teaches that every action, good or bad, affects the soul.

Positive actions lead to spiritual progress, while negative actions create bad karma, binding the soul to the cycle of birth and death. To achieve liberation, one must purify the soul by avoiding negative actions.

Q.7 Mention the two sects of Jainism.

Ans. The two sects of Jainism are

(i) Shvetambaras (white clad)

(ii) Digambaras (sky-clad)

Q.8 How did Buddha attain enlightenment?

Ans. Buddha attained enlightenment after years of meditation and seeking truth. He sat under the Bodhi tree in Bodh Gaya, overcame temptations and achieved a state of perfect understanding at the age of 35 and became 'The Enlightened One'.

Q.9 What are Tripitakas? Name the three Tripitakas.

Ans. The Tripitakas are the most significant literary works of Buddhism, originally written in the Pali language on long, narrow leaves and preserved in baskets. The term 'Tripitakas' translates to 'The Three Baskets', referring to the three main divisions of these sacred texts.

The three Tripitakas are

(i) The Vinaya Pitaka (ii) The Sutta Pitaka

(iii) The Abhidhamma Pitaka

Q.10 What are the 'Four Great Sights' in Gautama Buddha's life, and how did they influence his decision to renounce worldly life?

Ans. The 'Four Great Sights' in Gautama Buddha's life were an old man, a sick person, a dead body, and a peaceful monk.

These sights made him realise the realities of life-aging, illness and death, which inspired him to leave his royal life to find a path beyond suffering and uncertainty.

Q.11 Mention four Noble Truths of Buddhism.

Ans. The four Noble Truths of Buddhism are

(i) The world is full of suffering.

(ii) The suffering has a cause.

(iii) Desire is the cause of suffering.

(iv) If desire is stopped, suffering can also be stopped.

Q.12 Give the meaning of Buddha

Ans. The term 'Buddha' means 'the enlightened one' or 'the awakened one'. It refers to someone who has gained perfect knowledge and wisdom, overcoming ignorance and suffering.

In the context of Gautam Buddha, it signifies the person who achieved enlightenment and shared his teachings with others.

Q.13 Mention any two principles that governed the Sangha.

Ans. The two principles that governed the Sangha are

(i) **Membership** The members were required to renounce the world and take oath before joining sangha.

(ii) **Ten Commandments** Members followed the Ten commandments, which promoted a strict and disciplined lifestyle.

TYPE - 4 — 3 Marks

Short Answer Type Questions

Q.1 Mention any three causes for the spread of Jainism.

Ans. The three causes for the spread of Jainism are

(i) **Local Dialect** Mahavira adopted the language of common people, i.e, Prakrit instead of Sanskrit to preach his doctrines.

(ii) **Royal Patronage** Jainism received royal patronage of Chalukyas and Rashtrakutas.

Chandragupta Maurya is also said to have converted to Jainism. Kharvela helped in the spread of Jainism in Eastern India.

(iii) **Saints** There were many devout Jain saints like Kalkacharya who lived in Ujjain and made it a centre of Jainism. Another Jain saint Bhadrabahu took Jainism to Karnataka.

Q.2 What are the two sects into which Jainism was divided? Explain.

Ans. Jainism was divided into two sects: Digambaras and Svetambaras.

- **The Digambaras** believe in complete renunciation, including wearing no clothes, symbolising detachment. They argue that women must be reborn as men to attain liberation.
- **The Svetambaras**, however, wear white robes and allow women to achieve liberation directly.

This division emerged around 200 BCE due to differences in interpreting ascetic practices and the teachings of Lord Mahavira.

Q.3. Explain the factors responsible for the decline of Jainism in India.

Ans. Factors responsible for the decline of Jainism in India were

- **Strict Practices** Jainism demanded strict discipline, such as severe penance, fasting and meditation which made difficult for people to follow.

- **Reduced Royal Patronage** Later rulers like Ashoka and Harshavardhana favoured Buddhism.
- **Resurgence of Hinduism** Hinduism, with reform movements and simpler rituals regained popularity, which overshadowed Jainism in India.

Q.4 The most important precept of Jainism is ahimsa or non-violence. It was popularised by Mahatma Gandhi during India's freedom struggle. Do you think the philosophy of ahimsa is as relevant today as it was in the era of the Mahavira?

Ans. Ahimsa remains highly relevant today, as the world faces violence, inequality and environmental challenges. Ahimsa means 'non-violence' or 'no injury,' which is a fundamental principle that transcends cultural and religious boundaries. Its core message of peace and compassion resonates with people across the globe, regardless of their background.

Its focus on peace, respect for life, empathy and sustainable living, which are essential for global harmony.

Today, ahimsa inspires social movements and conflict resolution. Gandhi's application during India's freedom struggle proves its timeless power to combat injustice through non-violence.

Q.5 Describe the concept of Nirvana in Buddhism.

Ans. Nirvana is the ultimate goal in Buddhism and signifies the end of suffering and the cycle of birth, death, and rebirth (samsara). It is achieved when an individual extinguishes the three poisons - desire (Tanha), hatred (Dvesha), and ignorance (Moha).

Nirvana is a state of spiritual liberation where one is free from attachments and mental suffering. It is not considered a place but a state of profound peace and enlightenment, where the individual transcends the illusions of worldly existence and attains true wisdom and inner peace.

Q.6 State any three features of Buddhism that attracted people towards it.

Ans. The three features of Buddhism that attracted people towards it are

- **Equality** Buddhism opposed the caste system and promoted universal brotherhood, making it accessible to all.
- **Easy Accessibility** Buddha preached in local languages like Pali, making his teachings understandable to the common man.
- **Non-violence** Buddhism emphasised ahimsa (non-violence), which resonated deeply with people seeking peace and harmony.

Q.7 Mention any three differences between Hinayana and Mahayana Buddhism.

Ans. The differences between Hinayana and Mahayana Buddhism are as follows

Concepts	Hinayana	Mahayana
Belief in God	Rejected the idol worship and denied the existence of God.	A combination of Buddhism and Hinduism with faith in God.
View on Buddha	Buddha is a human being who attained enlightenment and Nirvana through his own efforts.	Buddha is considered an incarnation of God who ensures salvation.
Focus of Practice	Emphasised individual liberation through personal effort and meditation.	Believe in collective Salvation and focused on helping others to attain enlightenment, promoting the ideal of the Bodhisattva.

Q.8 What were the reasons due to which Buddhism could spread beyond the Indian borders in other countries of the world?

Ans. Buddhism spread beyond Indian borders for several key reasons that include

(i) **Missionary Activities and Royal Patronage** Emperor Ashoka of the Mauryan Empire played a significant role in spreading Buddhism beyond India. After his conversion to Buddhism, Ashoka sent missionaries to neighbouring regions such as Sri Lanka, Central Asia, Southeast Asia, and even as far as Greece and Egypt.

(ii) **Trade Routes and Cultural Exchange** The Silk Road and other ancient trade routes acted as channels through which Buddhist teachings, scriptures, and monks were carried to Central Asia, China, and beyond.

(iii) **Adaptability to Local Cultures** Buddhism demonstrated a remarkable ability to adapt to different cultural and societal contexts. For example, it integrated local beliefs and practices, which made it more appealing to diverse populations. In China, it merged with confucianism and Taoism, and in Japan, it integrated with Shinto beliefs.

Q.9 Mention three causes for decline of Buddhism.

Ans. The three causes for decline of Buddhism are

(i) **Split in Buddhism** The popularity and prestige of Buddhism suffered due to its division into Hinayana, Mahayana and sixteen other sects led to the decline of Buddhism.

(ii) **Corruption in Sangha** Buddhist sangha received patronage of royalty and had become very rich. The monks and nuns started leading a luxurious life instead of simple spiritual life.

(iii) **End of Royal Patronage** Buddhism lost the royal patronage which it received during the period of Ashoka, Kanishka and Harshavardhana as the Rajput rulers could not follow the policy of ahimsa.

TYPE - 5 — 4 Marks

Long Answer Type Questions

Q.1 Buddhism which emerged in ancient India against the Brahmanic social order, has gained importance in contemporary India. State your views with examples.

Ans. Buddhism, which emerged in ancient India as a response to the Brahmanic social order, has indeed gained importance in contemporary India.

There are several reasons for this, some of which are

- **Emphasis on non-violence** Buddhism has always emphasised non-violence and compassion towards all living beings, which has become increasingly relevant in contemporary India. With the rise of communal violence, many people have turned to Buddhism as a way of promoting peace and harmony.
- **Influence on modern Indian leaders** Several modern Indian leaders, such as Dr. B.R. Ambedkar were deeply influenced by Buddhism. He converted to Buddhism in 1956, and his followers have continued to promote the religion as a means of empowerment for Dalits, who have historically faced discrimination in India.
- **Interest in meditation and mindfulness** Buddhism has also gained popularity in India due to its emphasis on meditation and mindfulness practices. Many people in contemporary India are turning to these practices as a means of coping with stress and anxiety in their daily lives.
- **Philosophical Influence** Buddhism encourages ethical living and compassion, which shapes moral perspectives across the societies.

Q.2 Buddha delivered his first sermon at Sarnath. What is this event called? What is the literal meaning of the name of the event? Discuss the significance of this event.

Ans. Buddha delivered his first sermon at the Deer Park in Sarnath, near Varanasi, in the presence of five ascetics who had previously been his companions.

This sermon is known as 'Dharmachakraparivartan', which means 'the turning of the Wheel of sacred law'. The term 'Dharmachakraparivartan' symbolises the moment when Buddha set the wheel of Dharma in motion, inviting others to follow the path of liberation and enlightenment.

The significance of this event lies in Buddha's teaching of the Four Noble Truths and the Eightfold Path, which form the foundation of Buddhist philosophy. By delivering this sermon, Buddha began to share his enlightenment with the world, marking the start of his mission to spread the teachings of suffering, its cause, its cessation, and the path to end it.

Q.3 Describe the ten commandments for the Sangha members. How do these commandments reflect the principles and values of Buddhism?

Ans. The ten commandments for the Sangha members, also known as Paramita, reflect the core principles of Buddhism, emphasising discipline, purity, and self-control. These commandments include

(i) Speaking the truth,

(ii) Avoiding harm to living creatures,

(iii) Abstaining from intoxicants,

(iv) Practicing celibacy

(v) Refraining from indulging in music and dancing,

(vi) Not using scented goods,

(vii) Not sleeping on luxurious bedding,

(viii) Not keeping money,

(ix) To take meals at fixed times,

(x) Not owning property.

These rules encourage simplicity, non-violence (Ahimsa), and detachment from materialism, aligning with Buddha's teachings on leading an upright, moral life. By following these rules, sangha members can lead a life dedicated to their spiritual growth and help maintain a supportive and peaceful environment for everyone.

Q.4 Mention any four points of the Eightfold Path of Buddha.

Ans. The way to Nirvana or the path that leads to removal of suffering is known as the Eightfold Path.

The four points of the Eightfold Path of Buddha are

(i) **Right Action** This refers to ethical conduct and involves refraining from harmful actions like theft, killing, or causing harm to others.

(ii) **Right Thought** This is about cultivating the correct mental attitude. It involves thinking free from hatred, greed and delusion.

(iii) **Right Belief** This involves understanding the four Noble Truths of Buddhism: the reality of suffering, its cause, the cessation of suffering, and the path to the cessation of suffering.

(iv) **Right Speech** This refers to abstaining from false, harsh and idle speech and promote truthful, kind and helpful communication.

Q.5 Discuss the key differences between Jainism and Buddhism.

Ans. Jainism and Buddhism are both ancient Indian religions that share some similarities but have distinct differences

Concepts	Jainism	Buddhism
Beliefs about the Soul	Every living being possesses a soul that is eternal, and the soul's liberation (moksha) is achieved through non-violence and ascetic practices.	There is no permanent soul (atman); instead, the concept of anatman (no-self) prevails, and Nirvana is achieved through the cessation of desires and attachment.
The Role of the Gods	It does not believe in God, but acknowledge the existence of deities including the Tirthankaras.	It does not believe in God and focuses on the teachings of Buddha.
Practice of Asceticism	It laid strong emphasis on extreme ascetic practices, such as fasting and renunciation of worldly possessions, to achieve spiritual liberation.	It advocates moderation and the Middle Path, avoiding extreme asceticism or indulgence.
Concept of Karma	Karma is seen as a physical substance that attaches to the soul, affecting its future.	Karma is more related to actions, intentions, and the cycle of samsara.

Q.6 "The use of simple language made Jainism and Buddhism more accessible to common people." Analyse this statement with examples.

Ans. Jainism and Buddhism became popular because they used simple language that common people could understand, unlike the complex Sanskrit used in vedic rituals. Buddha and Mahavira taught in languages like Pali and Prakrit, which were spoken by ordinary people.

For example, Buddha's teachings about the Middle Path and non-violence were easy to grasp and relatable. Similarly, Mahavira's focus on non-violence and truth was taught in everyday language, making it accessible to farmers, traders, and others.

This simplicity helped to spread their teachings widely, as people could easily follow and practice their messages without depending on priests or rituals.

TYPE - 6 — 10 Marks

Structured Questions

Q.1 With reference to Jainism answer the following questions.

(i) Who was Mahavira? Why was he called Jina? (3)

(ii) In Jainism, followers adhere to five core vows, which guide their spiritual practice and ethical conduct. State those five vows which a Jain householder has to take. (3)

(iii) What is the Jain perspective on Karma and the path to Salvation? (4)

Ans. (i) Mahavira was the twenty-fourth and last Tirthankara in Jainism. While Jainism existed before him, Mahavira is regarded as its founder due to his efforts in making the teachings both popular and systematic.

He came to be known as Jina, meaning 'conqueror', because, after attaining supreme knowledge, he overcame all desires and achieved spiritual victory. The term Jina is used to refer to individuals who have triumphed over their desires and attained enlightenment.

(ii) A Jain householder is expected to observe five key vows that include

(a) **Ahimsa** (Non-violence) Avoid causing harm to any living being, whether through thought, speech or action.

(b) **Satya** (Truthfulness) Always speak the truth.

(c) **Asteya** (Non-stealing) Do not take what is not freely given.

(d) **Brahmacharya** (Chastity) Maintain celibacy or self-control in relationships.

(e) **Aparigraha** (Non-possession) Renounce attachment to material possessions and practice detachment.

The ultimate goal of Jainism is to achieve liberation from the cycle of birth and rebirth by following these ethical principles and living a life of self-restraint and non-violence.

(iii) The Jain perspectives of Karma and salvation are

(a) **Karma** Jains believe that individuals are responsible for their own actions (Karma), and that it is through performing good deeds that one can break free from the cycle of birth and rebirth.

(b) **Salvation** Jains view salvation, or Moksha, as the ultimate goal. To achieve Moksha, one must follow the tri-ratnas or the three jewels i.e. Right faith, Right knowledge, and Right action.

These principles guide the path to liberation.

Q.2 With reference to the teachings of Jainism answer the following questions.

(i) Where was Mahavira born and how did his early life influence his teachings? (3)

(ii) What are the Nine Truths according to Jainism? (3)

(iii) What is the core principle of the Buddha's doctrine and how does it guide the path to enlightenment? (4)

Ans. (i) Mahavira was born in Kundagrama, near Vaishali (modern-day Bihar), in a royal family. He grew up in luxury but was deeply moved by the suffering he saw around him. At the age of 30, he left his family to seek spiritual enlightenment.

His early life of privilege made him aware of the importance of detachment, non-violence, and self- discipline, which became core principles of Jainism.

(ii) The Nine Truths in Jainism, known as 'Nav Tattva', which are

(a) **Jiva** (Soul) The living soul, which is eternal.

(b) **Ajiva** (Non-soul) The non-living elements like matter, time, space, etc.

(c) **Asrava** (Influx) The influx of karma into the soul due to actions.

(d) **Bandha** (Bondage) The attachment of karma to the soul.

(e) **Punya** (Merit) Good karma accumulated from virtuous actions.

(f) **Papa** (Demerit) Bad karma accumulated from sinful actions.

(g) **Samvara** (Restraint) Stopping the influx of karma.

(h) **Nirjara** (Shedding) The process of shedding accumulated karma.

(i) **Moksha** (Liberation) The ultimate liberation of the soul from the cycle of birth and death.

(iii) The Four Noble truths are the foundations of Buddhism, which offers profound insights into the nature of human existence and the path to liberation.

- **The First Truth** explain that suffering (dukkha) is a part of life, and it arises due to desire and attachment.
- **The Second Truth** explains the cause of suffering, which is craving.
- **The Third Truth** shows that it's possible to end suffering by eliminating craving.
- **The Fourth Truth** is the Eightfold Path, a guide to ethical living and mental discipline.

By following this path-right understanding, right intention, right speech, right action, right livelihood, right effort, right mindfulness, and right concentration- one can achieve Nirvana, the ultimate freedom from suffering.

Q.3 With reference to Buddhism, answer the following questions.

(i) What is the Eightfold Path? Mention any three points of Eight fold path. (3)

(ii) Mention the impacts of Buddhism on the socio-religious life of the people? (3)

(iii) Describe the role of Sangha in Buddhism. (4)

Ans. (i) For answer, refer to Q.4 of Long Answers Type Questions.

(ii) Buddhism played a significant role in transforming the social and religious fabric of society in the following ways

- It inspired a reform movement within Hinduism, challenging the expensive yajnas and sacrifices, as well as the rigid caste system.
- Buddhism promoted intellectual growth and highlighted the flaws within the existing societal structures.
- It also provided the marginalised and oppressed sections of society with an opportunity to voice their concerns, granting them a more active role in political and social matters.

(iii) In Buddhism, Sangha is an organisation that helps to spread the teachings of Buddha. It include monks (bhikshus) and nuns (bhikkunis) who live together in monasteries and follow strict rules. The Sangha provides a place for these followers to practice meditation, study, and live a simple, disciplined life. They follow the ten commandments, which include speaking the truth, avoiding violence, and not owning property.

The Sangha plays a vital role in teaching people about Buddhism and guiding them on the path to enlightenment. It helps keep the teachings alive and accessible to others.

Q.4 With reference to the sources of information about Jainism and Buddhism, state the significance of the following.

(i) What are the Angas and what role do they play in Jainism? (3)

(ii) How Tripitakas are significant in Buddhism? (3)

(iii) Explain, how Jataka contribute to understanding the teachings of Buddhism. (4)

Ans. (i) The Angas are the central texts of Jainism, containing the main teachings of Lord Mahavira after he attained complete knowledge. These teachings were written down in twelve parts, called the Dwadashangi.

Two important texts within the Angas are the Aacharang Sutra, which gives rules for Jain monks, and the Vyakhya Pragnapti (or Bhagavati Sutra), which explains Jain philosophy.

The Angas cover a variety of topics like ethics, religious rituals, vows, and the philosophy of Jainism.

The Upangas are additional texts that further expand on these teachings, providing a deeper understanding of Jain principles and practices.

(ii) The Tripitakas are the main texts in Buddhism, and they play a vital role in preserving the teachings of Buddha. They are divided into three parts

(a) **Vinaya Pitaka** This explains the rules for monks and nuns, as well as giving insights into Buddha's life and times.

(b) **Sutta Pitaka** This contains Buddha's discourses and teachings, which forms the core of Buddhist philosophy, including the famous Dhammapada.

(c) **Abhidhamma Pitaka** This focuses on Buddhist philosophy and explains how the mind and matter work.

Together, the Tripitakas guide Buddhists in their practice and offer a deeper understanding of their faith and history.

(iii) The Jatakas are stories about the Buddha's past lives, where he takes different forms like a king, animal, or deity. These stories highlight the Buddha's virtues, such as kindness, patience, and wisdom, showing how he practiced these qualities in various lifetimes.

While the Jatakas don't give many details about Buddha's life, they offer insights into the social, economic, and political conditions of ancient times. They also teach important Buddhist values like compassion, selflessness, and moral behaviour, making them a valuable tool for understanding the core principles and ethics of Buddhism.

Q.5 With reference to Jainism and Buddhism, answer the following questions.

(i) Mention any three causes for the rise of Jainism and Buddhism. (3)

(ii) How did Jainism influence art and architecture? (3)

(iii) What was the impact of Buddhism on social and religious life in India? (4)

Ans. (i) The rise of Jainism and Buddhism can be attributed to three primary factors

(a) **Reaction Against Ritualism** Religious ceremonies had become increasingly costly, placing them beyond the reach of ordinary people. This led to the emergence of faiths that were simple, accessible, and less dependent on elaborate rituals.

(b) **Corruption in Religion** Priests often exploited the faithful, demanding money for yajnas and other rituals. This widespread corruption prompted protests, especially from Kshatriya rulers. Both Jainism and Buddhism were founded by Kshatriya princes who sought to challenge such practices.

(c) **Rigid Caste System** The caste system had become highly inflexible, restricting social mobility and preventing individuals from changing their caste. Jainism and Buddhism offered a more egalitarian and liberal approach, providing an alternative to the rigid social structure of the time.

(ii) Jainism influenced art and architecture through its focus on non-violence and simplicity and creating serene spaces for meditation and worship.

Jain rulers and patrons supported the construction of impressive temples and sculptures, such as the famous statue of Bahubali at Shravanabelgola. Jain temples, like those at Dilwara in Mount Abu, showcase intricate carvings and detailed architectural designs.

Jainism's emphasis on austerity and spirituality also inspired cave art, such as at Udayagiri and Ellora, reflecting the religion's cultural impact on Indian art and architecture.

(iii) The significant impact of Buddhism on social and religious life in India were

(a) It promoted the idea of ahimsa (non-violence), encouraging people to be kind to all living beings, which led to animal protection becoming more important.

(b) It also rejected caste distinctions, allowing people from all social backgrounds to participate in religious and political matters.

(c) Buddhism challenged traditional Hindu practices, like sacrifices, by focusing on personal effort and meditation.

(d) The religion offered a new way of thinking, promoting peace, equality, and intellectual growth. This helped reduce social divisions and gave more opportunities to weaker sections of society.

Q.6 With reference to the given pictures, answer the following questions.

A

B

(i) Identify the two preachers, whose images are given. Name the religions founded by them. (3)

(ii) Mention three main teachings of each of the two religions founded by these preachers. (3)

(iii) There have been few similarities and differences in both of the religions, Buddhism and Jainism. Mention any two similarities and two dissimilarities between the two religions. (4)

Ans. (i) The given images and religion founded by them are

- **A - Gautama Buddha**. He founded the religion, Buddhism.
- **B- Mahavira** He founded the religion, Jainism.

(ii) Three main teachings of Buddhism are

(a) **Karma** Buddhism believed in the theory of Karma. It said that man is the maker of his own destiny and it believed in rebirth.

(b) **Nirvana** The ultimate goal of life is to attain Nirvana or salvation which is freedom from the cycle of birth and death.

(c) **Ahimsa** Buddhism insisted on the path of non-violence.

Three main teachings of Jainism are

(a) **Ahimsa** (Non-violence) It urges followers to avoid harming any living being, in thought, speech or action.

(b) **Satya** Jainism emphasises speaking and acting truthfully and avoid deception and falsehood.

(c) **Aparigraha** This principle encourages detachment from material possessions and worldly desires, which promotes a simple and minimalist lifestyle.

(iii) **Similarities between Jainism and Buddhism**

(a) **Rejection of the Caste System** Both Jainism and Buddhism rejected the caste system and promoted the idea of equality among all individuals, regardless of their social background. They emphasised spiritual liberation as attainable by anyone, not limited to a specific caste or class.

(b) **Emphasis on Non-Violence (Ahimsa)** Both religions place a strong emphasis on ahimsa (non-violence). Jainism advocates absolute non-violence in thought, speech, and action, while Buddhism also teaches compassion and non-harming as central principles to spiritual practice.

Dissimilarities between Jainism and Buddhism

(a) **Concept of God** Jainism does not believe in God but acknowledge the existence of deities including the tirthankaras. While Buddhism does not believe in God and focuses on the teaching of Buddha.

(b) **Beliefs** Jainism believed in hard penance, advocating for rigorous self-discipline and ascetic practices to attain spiritual liberation while Buddhism followed a middle path, emphasising a balanced approach to life, avoiding both extreme indulgence and severe austerity.

4

THE MAURYAN EMPIRE

The Mauryas

- The Mauryan Empire was the first major empire in the history of India, ruled by Mauryan dynasty from 321 BCE to 185 BCE.
- It was founded by Chandragupta Maurya. He overthrew the Nandas from Magadha and the Greek Satraps from the North-West Frontier and unified a large part of the Indian sub-continent under his centralised government.

Sources about Mauryan Empire

The sources to know about the Mauryan Empire can be divided into two parts i.e. literary sources and archaeological sources.

Literary Sources

(i) Arthashastra of Kautilya

- Arthashastra was written in Sanskrit by Chanakya (Kautilya), also known as the Indian Machiavelli.
- Chanakya was the Prime Minister and Advisor to Chandragupta Maurya and he was an expert in politics and governance.
- Arthashastra is divided into three parts
  (i) The first part deals with the ruler, council of ruler, and government departments.
  (ii) The second part deals with civil and criminal law.
  (iii) The third part deals with war and diplomacy.

(ii) Indika

- Indika was written in Greek by Megasthenes, who was the Greek Ambassador at the court of Chandragupta Maurya. Megasthenes spent five years in the court of Chandragupta Maurya.
- It describes the political, social, religious and economic conditions of Mauryan period. It also describes the capital city of Mauryas, the Pataliputra.

Archaeological Sources

(i) Edicts of Ashoka

- An edict is a decree issued by a King. The edicts of Ashoka form the most important source of Mauryan history.
- In 1837, James Princep deciphered Ashoka's edicts, written in Pali and Prakrit languages using Brahmi and Kharosthi scripts.
- The edicts of Ashoka deal with Ashoka's Dhamma and also about the instructions given to his officials. These edicts are inscribed on rocks and pillars.
- There are 14 major rock edicts, including Rock Edict XIII, which describes the Kalinga war.
- Minor edicts include the Queen's edict, Barabar cave edict, and Kandahar bilingual inscription.
- There are seven pillar edicts, The Pillar Edict VII describe about Ashoka's efforts to spread dhamma.

(ii) Sanchi Stupa

A stupa is a semi-spherical solid dome like structure made of unburnt bricks and stones.

- The Sanchi Stupa was built by Ashoka in the 3rd century BC. It is one of the best-preserved stupas in Central India.
- It is 36.5 m in diameter and 16.5 m high, surrounded by a railing with four carved gateways facing all directions.

- During the Shunga period, it was enlarged and decorated with railings, a staircase, and a harmika on top.
- There is a circumambulatory path around the main stupa, and the railings and gates are richly sculpted with various motifs and designs.
- Gautam Buddha is symbolically represented through trees, footprints, wheels, thrones, and other non-living forms.
- The gateways feature incidents from Buddha's life and his past incarnations as described in the Jataka tales.

Sanchi Stupa

Rulers of the Mauryan Empire

Chandragupta Maurya (321-297 BCE)

- Chandragupta Maurya founded the Mauryan Empire. He united most of the Indian subcontinent after taking over the states previously conquered by Alexander.
- In 305 BCE, he defeated Seleucus Nicator, leading to a treaty where Chandragupta gained Kandhar, Kabul, Herat, and Baluchistan.
- He married Helen, Seleucus's daughter, and appointed Pushyagupta as the Governor of the North-Western province.
- Chandragupta's empire stretched from Kabul and Kandhar in the North-West to Mysore in the South and from Saurashtra in the West to Bengal in the East.
- During his reign, ambassadors Deimachus from Greece and Dionysius from Egypt visited the Mauryan court.
- According to Jain tradition, after ruling for 24 years, Chandragupta renounced the world and handed over the Kingdom to his son, Bindusara.

Bindusara (297-273 BCE)

- He was known to the Greeks as Amitrochates (Slayer of Foes).
- Bindusara campaigned in the Deccan and extended Mauryan control in the Peninsula as far as South Mysore. He conquered the land between the two seas, the Arabian Sea and the Bay of Bengal.
- He maintained friendly relations with the rulers of Greece.
- During his reign, a revolt took place in Taxila which was ended by his son Ashoka, who was the Governor of Taxila.

Ashoka (268-232 BCE)

- Ashoka succeeded to the throne after his father Bindusara's death. He took the titles Devanamapriya (The Beloved of the Gods) and Priyadarshi (The Beautiful One).
- Under Ashoka, the Mauryan Empire extended from the Hindukush mountains in the North-West to River Pennar in the South. Key regions included Tamralipti (Tamluk), a Bengal port connecting to Burma and Sri Lanka, as well as Kabul, Herat, and Kandahar.
- He maintained good relations with Central Asia's Khotan Empire and Southern Indian kingdoms like the Cholas, Cheras, and Pandyas.
- After the Kalinga war, he converted to Buddhism.
- He promoted peace, tolerance and the welfare of his people.

Kalinga War and Ashoka's Dhamma

Kalinga War

- In 261 BCE, Ashoka fought Kalinga War which had far reaching consequences for him and his empire.
- The main possible reason that led Ashoka to conquer Kalinga was its strategic locations, as it controlled the land and sea routes to South India and South-East Asia.

Consequences of Kalinga War

(i) The Kalinga war filled Ashoka's heart with grief and regret. The mass violence that was committed in Kalinga, developed hatred in Ashoka's heart regarding violence.

(ii) Kalinga changed Ashoka's personal life. He stopped hunting and eating meat and abandoned the life of luxury.

(iii) The prisoners of war were used for agricultural work, which resulted in an increase in production and brought economic prosperty in his empire.

(iv) Ashoka declared Buddhism as the state religion.

(v) Ashoka abandoned the policy of 'conquest by force' (Bherigosha) and 'ambition of victory in all directions' (Digvijay) and embraced 'the policy of religion' (Dhammagosha).

Ashoka's Dhamma

- The term Dhamma comes from the Sanskrit word Dharma, meaning custom or law.
- In his Edicts, Dhamma is described not as a religion or religious system but as a 'Moral Law', 'Code of Conduct' or an 'Ethical Order' which is common for all religions.

Principles of Ashoka's Dhamma

Ashoka's Dhamma has the following salient points

(i) Service to father and mother, practice of ahimsa, tolerance and respect for all people and their belief.

(ii) Prohibition of animal sacrifices and festive gatherings. Avoiding expensive and meaningless ceremonies or rituals.

(iii) Efficient organisation of administration in the direction of social welfare and maintenance of constant contact with people through the system of Dhammayatras.

(iv) Human treatment of servants by masters and prisoners by government officials.

(v) Consideration and non-violence to animals and courtesy to relations and liberality to Brahmins.

(vi) Tolerance among all the religious sects and appropriate treatment of ascetics.

Spread of Dhamma

(i) To record the doctrines of the Dhamma permanently, Ashoka inscribed them on rocks and pillars. The language of common man, Pali was used to spread the message to all corners of this empire.

(ii) Ashoka also appointed a special class of officers called Dhamma Mahamattas for propagating Dhamma and for promoting its practice throughout the Kingdom.

(iii) He conducted the 3rd Buddhist Council in 250 BCE in Pataliputra.

(iv) He sent his own son, Mahendra and daughter, Sanghamitra to Sri Lanka to propagate Buddhism.

Impact of Dhamma

(i) **Moral Value** People started to lead a moral life.

(ii) **Religious Unity** People gave support to the policy of religious tolerances propagated by their Emperor.

(iii) **Public Welfare** After the wars ended, officials focused on welfare schemes for the common people, leading to the nation's prosperity.

(iv) **End of Crimes** The policy of ahimsa impacted the people morally, thereby decreasing crimes like theft and various illegal activities.

Other Mauryan Kings

- **Dasharatha (232- 224 BCE)** He was a grandson of Ashoka and is commonly held to have succeeded him as the Emperor of Magadha.
- **Samprati (224- 215 BCE)** He was the grandson of Ashoka and is remembered for his efforts in spreading Buddhism across India and supporting religious tolerance during his reign.
- **Shalishuka (215- 202 BCE)** His reign is not well-documented. He is often considered to have ruled in the later phase of the Mauryan Empire's decline.
- **Devavarman (202- 195 BCE)** He ruled in a transitional period after the Maurya Empire began weakening.
- **Shatadhanvan (195- 187 BCE)** He was another of the lesser-known Mauryan emperors. His reign didn't significantly impact the empire's history.

- **Brihadratha (187- 184 BCE)** He was the last Mauryan ruler and his reign ended with his assassination by his general, Pushyamitra Shunga, which marked the fall of the Maurya Empire.

Administration of the Mauryan Empire

Mauryan administration had two main divisions - Civil Administration (Central Government and Provincial Government) and Military Administration.

(i) Central Government

- The King was the central figure in administration, holding supreme executive, legislative, and judicial powers. He appointed ministers and higher officials to manage law making, revenue and supervised the government workers.
- The King was assisted by Mantriparishad (Council of Ministers). The mantriparishad include Yuvaraj (the Crown Prince), Purohita (the Chief Priest of the State), Senapati (the Commander in Chief), Amatya (the Civil Servants), Samaharta (the Taxation Expert) and Sannidhata (the Supreme Treasurer).
- The Prime Minister was the head of the Mantriparishad and for each department, separate Minister was appointed. Adhyaksha (Superintendent) headed each of these departments.
- The other key officers included those responsible for agriculture, managing mines, overseeing ports, checking weights and measures, handling accounts and controlling trade.
- Ashoka brought some changes in the administrative system of Chandragupta Maurya. He appointed Mahamatras (Governors) to look after the welfare of his subjects.

(ii) Provincial Government

- Each province (headed by Kumara or Aryaputra) was sub-divided into number of districts called *Janapadas*, headed by Sthanika. Each district was again sub-divided into number of units.
- The village was at the lowest unit headed by Gramika.
- The Mauryan emperor directly governed the central and eastern parts of the empire, while provincial governors (Mahamatras) managed other regions.
- There were also officers like Pradeshikas (Tax collector), Rajuka (modern day Tehsildar or Revenue Officer) and Yukta (the Treasurer).

(iii) Military Administration

- The King was the Supreme Commander of the army and head of the military administration of Mauryan Empire.
- The war office of Mauryas were managed by a board of 30 members. They were also divided into six committees. Each of the committee had five members to look after navy, transport, supply, infantry, cavalry, the war chariots and war-elephants.
- The Mauryan Kings had constructed forts at strategic places for security and safety of the empire.

Revenue System of the Mauryan Empire

- **Land revenue** was the chief source of income of Mauryan Empire. Two types of taxes namely Bali and Bhaga were there. Toll tax, tax on liquor, gambling houses, etc., were some other taxes.
- **Samaharta**, the Chief of the Revenue Department, was in-charge of the collection of all revenues of the empire.
- The revenues came from land, irrigation, customs, shop tax, ferry tax, forests, mines and pastures. License fee from craftsmen and fines were also collected in the law-courts.
- Land revenue was set at 1/6th of the produce. State expenses included the King's household, army, government servants, public works, poor relief, and religion.

Spy System of the Mauryan Empire

- The detectives were known as Gudhapurushas. According to the Arthashastra, there were two kinds of spies, Sansthana (stationary) and Sanchari (wandering).
- Spies kept the king informed about the bureaucracy. The agents included householders, merchants, disciples, ascetics, poisonous girls which were called 'Vishkanyas'.
- The ambassadors who were appointed in the foreign countries also acted as spies.

EXAM ORIENTED QUESTIONS

TYPE - 1 1 Mark

Multiple Choice Questions

Q.1 Identify the odd one out in the following

(a) Chandragupta Maurya (b) The Great Ashoka
(c) Bindusara (d) Harsha

Ans. (d) Harsha

Exp. Chandragupta Maurya, Ashoka, and Bindusara were part of the Mauryan Empire, but Harsha was a ruler from the Vardhana dynasty.

Q.2 Emperor Ashoka, after witnessing the horrors of the Kalinga War, embraced Buddhism and dedicated his rule to promoting peace, tolerance, and compassion through moral edicts. *- The times of India 2nd Nov., 2024*

Which of the following languages were used in Ashoka's edicts?

(a) Sanskrit and Latin (b) Greek and Prakrit
(c) Greek and Persian (d) Tamil and Kannada

Ans. (b) Greek and Prakrit

Q.3 Consider the following statements regarding the rise of Chandragupta Maurya and choose the correct option

P : Chandragupta Maurya was influenced by Chanakya, who played a key role in his rise to power.

Q : Chandragupta Maurya expanded his empire by defeating the forces of Alexander's successor, Seleucus Nicator.

R : Chandragupta Maurya's empire began in the Southern parts of India and expanded Northward.

S : Chandragupta Maurya's empire was characterised by a decentralised administration with strong local assemblies.

(a) P and Q (b) P and R
(c) Q and S (d) P and S

Ans. (a) P and Q

Q.4 Chandragupta Maurya established a vast empire overthrowing

(a) Guptas and Chalukyas
(b) Nandas and Greek Satraps
(c) Rashtrakutas and Nandas
(d) Greek Satraps and Guptas

Ans. (b) Nandas and Greek Satraps

Q.5 Which of the following is most likely to be a feature of Ashoka's rule?

(a) Conquering more kingdoms.
(b) Spread of Buddhism through missions.
(c) Rejection of social welfare policies.
(d) Increase in the use of Sanskrit for administrative purposes.

Ans. (b) Spread of Buddhism through missions.

Exp. Ashoka sent people to other countries to teach Buddhism. He wanted peace instead of wars. He cared for people and worked for their happiness and well-being.

Q.6 Look at the picture below and answer the question

Who was the first person to decipher, the Ashokan Inscription?

(a) James Prinsep (b) Alexander Cunningham
(c) Colin Mackenzie (d) R.E.M. Wheeler

Ans. (a) James Prinsep

Exp. James Prinsep was the first person to read and understand the Ashokan inscriptions. He discovered their meaning in 1837, which helped people learn about Ashoka's reign and his messages.

Q.7 Read the description and answer the following question

The ruler of this empire was known for his conversion to Buddhism after the Kalinga War. He implemented policies of non-violence and religious tolerance, and his administration was based on moral and ethical governance. He also sent missionaries to foreign lands to spread Buddhism.

Who is being described in the above passage?

(a) Chandragupta Maurya (b) Bindusara
(c) Ashoka (d) Alexander

Ans. (c) Ashoka

Exp. Ashoka became a Buddhist after the Kalinga War, followed non-violence, treated everyone fairly, and spread Buddhism to other countries through missionaries.

Q.8 Which of the following was not a consequence of the Kalinga War?
(a) It changed Ashoka's personal life.
(b) It increased agricultural output.
(c) It increased military preparedness.
(d) It increased Buddhist missionary activity.

Ans. (c) Increased military preparedness.

Q.9 Complete the given analogy.
Amatya: Civil Servants:: Samaharta: ?
(a) Council of Minister (b) Taxation expert
(c) Crown prince (d) Commander in chief

Ans. (b) Taxation expert

Q.10 Which of the following is not likely to be true about the Mauryan Administration?
(a) The empire had a centralised bureaucracy.
(b) Provinces were governed by appointed officials.
(c) Local rulers had complete autonomy to rule.
(d) The state controlled both military and judicial functions.

Ans. (c) Local rulers had complete autonomy to rule.

Q.11 Which of the following were officers in the Provincial Government of the Mauryan Empire?
(a) Purohit, Senapati, Sannidhata, Samaharta
(b) Mahamatra, Prashika, Rajuka, Yukta
(c) Pradeshika, Rajuka, Yukta
(d) Bali, Bhaga

Ans. (c) Pradeshika, Rajuka, Yukta

TYPE - 2 1 Mark

Assertion-Reason Questions

Q.1 Read the two statements given below about the Mauryan Empire and select the option that shows the correct relationship between (A) and (R).

Assertion (A) Chandragupta Maurya founded the Mauryan Empire in 321 BCE and unified most of the Indian subcontinent.

Reason (R) Chandragupta Maurya's military conquests, along with the strategic support of his advisor Chanakya, enabled him to defeat the Nanda dynasty and establish the Mauryan Empire.
(a) R contradicts A
(b) R is the reason for A
(c) A is true but R is false
(d) A and R are independent of each other

Ans. (b) R is the reason for A

Q.2 Read the two statements given below about Ashokan Edicts and select the option that shows the correct relationship between (A) and (R).

Assertion (A) Most of the Ashokan Edicts are engraved in the Brahmi script, written from left to right.

Reason (R) The Ashokan edicts provide a useful insight into the life and ideals of Ashoka.
(a) R contradicts A
(b) R is the reason for A
(c) A is true but R is false
(d) A and R are independent of each other

Ans. (d) A and B are independent of each other

Q.3 Read the two statements given below about the Mauryan Empire and select the option that shows the correct relationship between (A) and (R).

Assertion (A) Ashoka is known for his promotion of Buddhism after the Kalinga War.

Reason (R) Ashoka embraced Buddhism because of the immense destruction caused by the Kalinga War, leading him to adopt a policy of non-violence and moral governance.
(a) R contradicts A
(b) R is the reason for A
(c) A is true but R is false
(d) A and R are independent of each other

Ans. (b) R is the reason for A

Q.4 Read the two statements given below about the Mauryan Empire and select the option that shows the correct relationship between (A) and (R).

Assertion (A) The Mauryan Empire was one of the most powerful and vast empires in ancient India.

Reason (R) The Mauryan Empire had a strong and efficient administration, a large standing army, and a well-developed system of roads, which contributed to its vastness and power.
(a) R contradicts A
(b) R is the reason for A
(c) A is true but R is false
(d) A and R are independent of each other

Ans. (b) R is the reason for A

TYPE - 3

2 Marks

Very Short Answer Type Questions

Q.1 Mention any two sources of information about the Mauryan Empire.

Ans. Two key sources of information about the Mauryan Empire are

(i) **Arthashastra** Written by Kautilya (also known as Chanakya), the Prime Minister of Chandragupta Maurya, this text serves as an extensive guide on political theory, diplomacy, administration, and governance.

(ii) **Indika** Composed by Megasthenes, a Greek ambassador at Chandragupta Maurya's court, the work offers a detailed account of the culture, society, and politics of the Mauryan Empire. It also provides a unique foreign perspective on the Indian subcontinent during that era.

Q.2 Who is the author of Indika, and what does it contain?

Ans. The author of Indika is Megasthenes, a Greek ambassador at Chandragupta Maurya's court. It describes the political, social, religious, and economic conditions of the Mauryan Empire, including details about its capital, Pataliputra.

Q.3 What is a Stupa? Mention any one stupa built by Ashoka.

Ans. A stupa is a semi-spherical solid dome like structure made of unburnt bricks and stones. It represents the spiritual body of Buddha containing his relics such as hair, teeth or bones. Ashoka built the Sanchi Stupa in Madhya Pradesh.

Q.4 Write any two points on significance of Ashoka's edicts.

Ans. The two significance of Ashoka's edicts are

(i) **Promotion of Dhamma** They spread Ashoka's teachings of moral values, non-violence, and tolerance.

(ii) **Record of Governance** The edicts provide insight into his policies, administration, and welfare initiatives.

Q.5 In context to the edicts of Ashoka, explain briefly the following terms

(i) Bhaga (ii) Bali

Ans. (i) **Bhaga** It was a form of tax, paid by the people on agriculture produce and the cattle to the state. It was 1/6th of the produce.

(ii) **Bali** It was a form of tax, paid by the people on religious offerings and sacrifices.

Q.6 Read the extract given below and answer the question which follows

"Ashoka's edicts, inscribed on pillars and rocks across his empire, were a key source of information about his reign. They communicated his policies on moral conduct, religious tolerance, and the welfare of his people. These inscriptions, which also included messages of non-violence and the importance of respecting all living beings, were meant to guide the citizens of his empire".

What message did Ashoka convey through his edicts?

Ans. Through his edicts, Ashoka conveyed messages of moral conduct, non-violence, religious tolerance, and respect for all living beings.

These inscriptions aimed to guide his subjects towards ethical living and promote the welfare of the people.

Q.7 Mention any two contributions of Chandragupta Maurya in establishing the Mauryan Dynasty.

Ans. The contributions of Chandragupta Maurya in establishing the Mauryan Dynasty are

(i) **Unification of the Indian Subcontinent** Chandragupta Maurya united a large part of the Indian subcontinent by taking control of the states previously conquered by Alexander, extending his empire from the North-Western regions to the South.

(ii) **Establishing a Centralised Administration** Chandragupta Maurya created a highly efficient and centralised administration, supported by a strong military, regional governors and a well-structured civil service. This system ensured effective governance, maintained law and order and facilitated the management to expand the territories.

Q.8 Give a brief description about the impact of the Kalinga war in the Ashoka's personal life?

Ans. The Kalinga War had a profound impact on Ashoka's personal life in the following ways

- He gave up hunting, stopped eating meat, and gave up leading a luxurious life.
- He became a follower of Buddhism, adopting its teachings like non-violence and rejecting unnecessary rituals.

Q.9 Imagine that you met a person, whose family suffered the consequences of the Kalinga War waged by Ashoka. Describe the horrors of the war as told by him.

Ans. When I met that person, he described me about the Kalinga War as a brutal and devastating conflict, where countless lives were lost, and entire families were broken. The fields were covered in blood, and the peaceful land was destroyed. The survivors were left with memories of the terrible things they had seen.

Q.10 What was the meaning of Ashoka's Dhamma?

Ans. Ashoka's Dhamma was a set of moral principles focused on kindness, non-violence, respect for all living beings, and tolerance. It encouraged ethical living, truthfulness, and compassion, aiming to create a peaceful and just society under Ashoka's rule.

TYPE - 4 — 3 Marks

Short Answer Type Questions

Q.1 Mention any three basic principles of Ashoka's Dhamma.

Ans. The basic principles of Ashoka's Dhamma are

Respect and Kindness Ashoka emphasised respect for elders, love for children and humane treatment of servants and prisoners. He promoted kindness and non-violence towards all living beings.

Religious Tolerance He encouraged harmony among different religious sects and discouraged meaningless rituals and animal sacrifices, fostering unity and understanding.

Social Welfare Ashoka focused on public welfare by organising Dhammayatras, planting medicinal herbs, digging wells and building hospitals and ensured the well-being of the people.

Q.2 Ashoka's reign is considered one of the brightest periods in Indian history. Justify the statement by mentioning any three points.

Ans. Ashoka's reign is considered one of the brightest periods in Indian history because

(i) **Spread of Dhamma** Ashoka promoted peace, non-violence, and respect for all religions through his Dhamma, which helped to unite people.

(ii) **Social Welfare** Ashoka built hospitals, roads, and rest houses, improving the well-being of his people.

(iii) **Cultural Growth** Ashoka supported art, architecture, and Buddhism, leading to the creation of great monuments like the Sanchi Stupa and spreading Buddhist teachings across India and beyond.

Q.3. "The Mauryan Empire was a model of centralised administration and effective governance". Justify the statement.

Ans. The above statement can be justified based on several key aspects

- **Centralised Administration** The Mauryan Empire had a centralised system, with the emperor holding supreme authority, ensuring uniform policies and efficient governance across the empire.
- **Well-Organised Bureaucracy** The empire was divided into provinces and districts, each managed by appointed officers to oversee tax collection, law enforcement, and other administrative tasks.
- **Legal and Economic Systems** The Mauryas implemented standardised laws and a uniform taxation system, as detailed in the Arthashastra, focusing on governance, economic management, and welfare measures like trade regulations.

Q.4 Discuss the role of the Samaharta and the use of land revenue in maintaining the empire.

Ans. In the Mauryan Empire, the Samaharta was the chief revenue officer, responsible for overseeing the collection of all state revenues. He supervised various departments, including those handling land, irrigation, customs, and other taxes.

Land revenue was set at one-sixth of the produce. It was the primary source of income, funding the king's household, the army, public works, and welfare programs.

Q.5 Explain the spy system of the Mauryan Empire as outlined in the Arthashastra.

Ans. The Mauryan Empire's spy system, as detailed in the Arthashastra, was highly organised and vital for governance. Spies were categorised into two main types: stationary (Sansthana) and wandering (Sanchari).

- Stationary spies operated undercover in various professions, such as students, ascetics, householders and merchants, to gather information secretly.
- Wandering spies were more active, engaging in covert operations, including the use of poisons and impersonation.

This extensive network ensured the king received accurate intelligence on both internal and external matters, maintaining the empire's stability and security.

TYPE - 5

4 Marks

Long Answer Type Questions

Q.1 Explain the significance of the Arthashastra written by Kautilya in understanding the political and administrative structure of the Mauryan Empire.

Ans. The Arthashastra, written by Kautilya (Chanakya), is a crucial text for understanding the political and administrative structure of the Mauryan Empire in the following ways

- **Political Framework** The Arthashastra provides a detailed guide on governance and statecraft. It highlights the duties of the king, the council of ministers and various government officials.
- **Efficient Administration** The Arthashastra outlined the structure and functioning of various departments like taxation, trade and agriculture. He proposed methods for revenue collection and economic policies.
- **Military Strategy** The Arthashastra covers strategies for maintaining a strong military. It discusses defense tactics, war planning and the use of spies, which were crucial for safeguarding the empire's borders and ensuring internal security.
- **Foreign Relations** The Arthashastra emphasised diplomacy and alliances to manage relations with neighbouring states. These principles guided the Mauryan Empire in expanding its territories and maintaining peace with other regions.

Q.2 What were the major achievements of Bindusara during his reign?

Ans. Bindusara was the second Mauryan emperor. He ruled from around 297 BCE to 273 BCE. Some of his major achievements include

- **Expansion of the Maurya Empire** Bindusara continued the work of his father Chandragupta Maurya in expanding the empire. He successfully conquered the land between the Arabian sea and the Bay of Bengal. He extended the Mauryan control to Mysore in South India.
- **Consolidation of Power** He maintained the administrative and political structures established by his father, Chandragupta Maurya, ensuring the empire's stability.
- **Relations with Foreign Countries** He established diplomatic relations with the Hellenistic kingdoms in the West, including the Seleucid Empire, after negotiating peace and alliances.
- **Promotion of Buddhism** Though he was not a follower of Buddhism, he is believed to have been tolerant of it. He provided patronage to Buddhism and paved the way for his son, Ashoka, to promote Buddhism more actively.

Q.3 What were the impacts of Dhamma on Ashoka's policies?

Ans. The impact of Dhamma on Ashoka's policies are

- **Focus on Welfare** Ashoka directed his administration towards improving the well-being of people and animals. He initiated welfare measures such as planting trees, digging wells and establishing hospitals. His policies reflected care for every section of society and enhanced social prosperity.
- **Promotion of Moral Values** Ashoka advocated for moral living. His policies emphasised non-violence (Ahimsa), respect for elders, kindness to servants and animals and tolerance among religions.
- **Religious Tolerance** Ashok's policy promoted respect for all religions and discouraged religious persecution, which aims for social harmony and unity within his diverse empire.
- **End of Wars** After the Kalinga War, Ashoka renounced violent conquests and embraced 'Dhammagosha' (policy of religion). This shift resulted in a peaceful rule, allowing focus on economic and social development.

Q.4. The Mauryan administration had a unique structure. Discuss the role and responsibilities of the key officials in the Central Government.

Ans. The Mauryan administration had a well-organised structure with key officials in the Central Government. Their roles and responsibilities were

(i) **King** The king was the supreme authority, overseeing the entire empire. He made important decisions and ensured peace and prosperity.

(ii) **Mantri Parishad (Council of Ministers)** The council helped the king in decision-making and managing state affairs. They advised on matters like military, taxation, and justice.

(iii) **Samaharta (Tax Collector)** This official was in charge of collecting taxes from the people, which funded the administration and the army.

(iv) **Senapati (Commander-in-Chief)** The Senapati oversaw the army and defence of the empire, ensuring security.

(v) **Pradeshika (Provincial Governors)** They were appointed to manage different regions, ensuring the smooth running of local affairs.

TYPE - 6 10 Marks

Structured Questions

Q.1 With reference to Ashokan edicts and answer the following questions

(i) What is an edict? Where are these edicts inscribed? **(3)**

(ii) Edicts provide insights into the ruler's policies and ideals. What is the significance of edicts as a source of information? **(3)**

(iii) How many major rock edicts did Ashoka issued? Explain any two. **(4)**

Ans. (i) An edict refers to a decree issued by a ruler or sovereign. In India, they are among the oldest, most well-preserved, and accurately dated historical records.

These edicts are engraved on rocks and pillars across the country and include 14 major rock edicts, 7 pillar edicts, along with several minor rock edicts.

(ii) Edicts hold great significance as a source of historical information because they offer valuable insights into the life and principles of Ashoka, as well as the broader history of the Mauryan Empire.

The edicts reveal Ashoka's commitment to justice, moral governance, and religious tolerance, offering a glimpse into his transformation after the Kalinga War. They also explain about the administrative structure and the emperor's efforts to communicate with his peoples.

(iii) Ashoka issued 14 major rock edicts, each addressing different aspects of his governance and moral principles. For example,

(a) Rock Edict I emphasises the importance of non-violence and compassion towards all living beings.

(b) Rock Edict XIII describes the Kalinga War, highlighting the immense suffering caused and Ashoka's subsequent commitment to peace and dhamma.

Q.2 Study the picture given below and answer the following questions.

(i) Name the structure given in the picture. Name the dynasty and the king who built it. **(3)**

(ii) Where is it located? Mention any two architectural features of this structure. **(3)**

(iii) This structure is considered a sacred structure, representing the Buddha's burial mound. What is the significance of this structure? **(4)**

Ans. (i) The structure given in the picture is Sanchi Stupa. It was built by King Ashoka of the Mauryan dynasty.

(ii) It is located at Sanchi, 45 km from Bhopal in Madhya Pradesh. Two architectural features of this structure are

(a) The stupa, with its hemispherical dome-like shape, is constructed from unburnt bricks and stones. It consists of a circular cylindrical drum with a Harmika and Chhatri on the top.

(b) It has four gateways, each facing a different direction, adorned with intricately carved panels that depict scenes from Buddha's life and various Jataka tales. Each gateway has two square pillars with a grid of three architraves.

(iii) The significance of Sanchi Stupa are

- A Buddhist Stupa holds great spiritual significance as it symbolises the physical form of Buddha, housing his sacred relics, such as hair, teeth, or bones. These relics are kept in a casket, which is placed at the base of the stupa's dome.
- The stupa serves as a focal point for meditation and pilgrimage, representing the path to enlightenment.

- It also symbolises the Buddha's presence and the teachings of Buddhism, offering a place for followers to reflect on his life and attain spiritual growth.
- It feature intricate carvings and inscriptions that showcases the architectural skills of that time.

Q.3 With reference to the Ashoka's reign answer the following questions.

(i) Explain the significance of the Kalinga War in shaping Ashoka's reign. How did it influence his policies and actions? (3)

(ii) Mention any three principals of Ashoka's Dhamma. (3)

(iii) How do literary sources like the Arthashastra help us understand the political and administrative structure of the Mauryan Empire? (4)

Ans. (i) The Kalinga War, fought by Ashoka, was a turning point in his reign. After a brutal victory, Ashoka was deeply moved by the suffering and loss of life he saw. This changed his outlook on war and violence. He adopted Buddhism and promoted peace, non-violence, and religious tolerance across his empire.

- Ashoka's policies focused on the welfare of his people, building hospitals, roads, and promoting ethical behaviour. The war's impact led him to shift from military conquest to spreading Dharma (moral teachings) and seeking to rule through compassion rather than force.

(ii) For answer, refer Q.1 of Short Answer Type Questions.

(iii) For answer, refer Q.1 of Long Answer Type Questions.

Q.4. With reference to the Mauryan Empire answer the following questions.

(i) Explain the role of the provincial government in the Mauryan Empire. How did it contribute to the empire's stability? (3)

(ii) Discuss the impact of Ashoka's Dhamma on the social and cultural life of the Mauryan Empire. What changes did it bring to people's daily lives? (3)

(iii) Historians have used a variety of sources to reconstruct the history of the Mauryan Empire. Justify the statement. (4)

Ans. (i) The provincial government in the Mauryan Empire played a key role in maintaining stability. The empire was divided into several regions, each ruled by a Governor who reported to the central authority.

These Governors were responsible for local administration, collecting taxes, maintaining law and order, and ensuring the welfare of the people. They also oversaw the military, which helped keep control over vast territories.

By managing resources, resolving local issues, and enforcing the king's policies, the provincial government helped keep the empire strong and unified. This system of governance ensured effective administration and stability across the empire.

(ii) Ashoka's Dhamma had a significant impact on the social and cultural life of the Mauryan Empire as

- It promoted values like non-violence, respect for all religions, and care for living beings. People were encouraged to live with kindness, truthfulness, and tolerance.
- Ashoka's Dhamma led to the construction of hospitals, rest houses, and wells, improving public welfare. It also encouraged social harmony and the importance of family values.
- The teachings of Dhamma helped people live in peace and work together. It made the empire kinder and more united. It helped people live morally and focus on spiritual growth.

(iii) The historians have used a variety of sources to reconstruct the history of Mauryan Empire. Some of the important sources include

Literary Sources

- **Arthashastra** This text was written by Kautilya and it provides insights into the Mauryan polity, governance, administration and economy.
- **Indika** Megasthenes, a Greek ambassador to Chandragupta Maurya's court, wrote Indika. It offers information about the Mauryan administration and social structure.

Archaeological Sources

- **Ashokan Inscriptions** The inscriptions of Ashoka, found on rocks and pillars, are a crucial source for understanding the Mauryan empire's administrative structure, policies and the concept of 'Dhamma' (righteous conduct).
- **Material Remains** Archaeological excavations have unearthed coins, pottery and architectural remains that provide insights into the Mauryan economy, culture and technological advancements.

Q.5 With reference to Mauryan administration, answer the following questions

(i) Chandragupta Maurya is regarded as the chief architect of the system of administration. Justify this statement. **(3)**

(ii) "Under the leadership of Chandragupta Maurya and his successors, the Mauryan Empire unified diverse regions, cultures, and peoples into a single political entity". Explain briefly the Pan-Indian character of the Mauryan administration. **(3)**

(iii) Under the Mauryan rule, the civil and military administration was highly organised, efficient, and designed to manage the vast and diverse empire effectively. Briefly describe the main features of civil and military administration under Mauryan rule. **(4)**

Ans. (i) The Chandragupta Maurya is regarded as the chief architect of the administrative system and this can be justify by the following

- **Foundation of a Centralised Empire** Chandragupta Maurya, with the help of his advisor Kautilya, founded the Mauryan Empire, which unified a vast territory under one administration and marked a significant shift from the decentralised political landscape of the time.
- **Influence of Arthashastra** Chandragupta implemented the principles of Arthashastra, covering areas like taxation, justice and military strategies and laid down the foundation of an efficient administration.
- **Military and Espionage System** Chandragupta organised a strong military and espionage system, which ensured the safety and stability of the empire while maintaining law and order throughout his reign.

(ii) The Mauryan Empire extended from Hindukush in North-West to River Pennar in South. The Pan-Indian character of Mauryan empire are

- It marked the end of small states.
- It helped in establishing trade links with foreign countries.
- It made Mauryan empire strong and helped the Mauryan kings face foreign aggressions successfully.
- This helped the Mauryan kings to pay more attention to the social and economic life of the people. Hence, there was an all-round economic prosperity.

(iii) The main features of civil and military administration under Mauryan rule are described below

Civil Administration

- The civil administration had two main divisions - the Central Government and the Provincial Government. The Mauryan Government was centralised and was managed by several officials at different ranks.
- The king was supreme authority and supreme judge. His throne was hereditary. The king was assisted by the council of ministers headed by the Prime Minister.
- The provincial government was headed by Kumar or Aryaputra and the district administration was looked after by Pradeshika, Rajuka and Yukta. There were Mahamatras to assist Kumars.
- Pradeshika was the tax collector. There was an efficient Spy system to keep the king informed. Two kinds of taxes, namely Bali and Bhaga were levied.

Military Administration

- There was a huge army consisting of infantry, cavalry, elephants and chariots.
- The army had 6,00,000 infantry, 30,000 cavalry, 9000 war elephants and 8000 chariots The chief weapons used were bows, arrows, shields, swords etc.
- The king was the commander in chief of the army. The whole army was under a military commission of 30 members and they had a well laid recruitment policy. The soldiers were paid in cash.
- The Mauryan king had built forts at strategic places for the safety and security of the empire.

THE SANGAM AGE

- The Sangam Age refers to the period when bulk of Tamil literature was composed by Tamil scholars and poets in three successive literary gatherings called Sangam.
- The word 'Sangam' is the Tamil form of the Sanskrit Sangha which means an assembly or an association.
- The Sangam Age had three Sangams
  - (i) **First Sangam** (Irai Sangam) Held in Madurai and attended by Gods and Legendary sages. All its works have perished.
  - (ii) **Second Sangam** (Idai Sangam) Held in Kapatpuram and attended by several poets. Only Tolkappiyam (early Tamil grammar) remains.
  - (iii) **Third Sangam** (Kadai Sangam) Held in Madurai and created vast literature, but only some of them has survived.

Sources of the Sangam Age

The primary sources of information about the Sangam Age include the following -

1. Tirukkural

- It was written by **Tiruvalluvar.** It is a classic of couplets or Kurals. It is a part of the eighteen minor works (Patinenkilkanakku) of the Sangam literature. The Tirukkural (or Kural) explains various aspects of life and is one of the most important works in the Tamil language.
- **Tirukkural** is a Tamil work with 1330 couplets in 133 chapters. It has three sections: i.e. **Aram** (righteousness), **Porul** (wealth) and **Inbam** or **Kamam** (pleasure). Each chapter has a specific subject ranging from 'ploughing a piece of land' to 'ruling a country'. It preaches simplicity and truth throughout its verses.
- While **Aram** and **Inbam** discuss about ethical living in private life, **Porul** deals with public affairs.
- Besides these, Tamil literature comprises five epics, namely - *Jivakachintamani, Manimekalai, Silappadikaram, Valayapathi* and *Kuntalakeshi.*

2. Megaliths

- Megaliths are large stones or structures made of stones that were used to create monuments by ancient people. During the Sangam Age, megaliths were used to mark burial sites or commemorative memorials.
- Some megaliths are visible on the surface, while others are underground.
- Multiple skeletons in some megaliths has been found. This indicates that people belonging to the same family were buried in the same place but at different time periods.
- Things like pitchers, baskets, ornaments, tools, weapons of iron and stone, etc., are found in burials which indicated life of the people during the Sangam Age. It indicates their belief of life after death.
- Megaliths have been found in Tamil Nadu districts like Kanchipuram, Vellore, Thiruvannamalai, and others.

Megaliths

Megalith Burial

Tamil Kingdoms

- The Sangam poems mention the term 'muvendar', which is a Tamil word meaning three chiefs. It was used for the heads of three ruling families, namely - Chera, Chola and Pandya in the Tamil country during the Sangam Age.
- In addition to these kingdoms, there was local chieftains.

Chera Kingdom

- The Chera kingdom included major parts of modern Kerala/Malabar areas.
- Their capital was Vanji or Karur. Their symbol on the flag was bow and arrow.
- **Cheran Senguttuvan** (2nd century AD) was a prominent Chera ruler.
- His military achievements have been chronicled in Silappadikaram (epic) which was composed by his brother Ilango Adigal.
- He crossed the river Ganges and defeated the North Indian rulers and led a Himalayan expedition.
- He also introduced the Pattini cult (worship of Kannagi as the ideal wife).
- He was the first South Indian ruler to send an embassy to China.

Chola Kingdom

Kallanai dam

- The Sangam Chola kingdom included Thanjavur, Tiruchirappalli, Northern Tamil Nadu and Southern Andhra Pradesh, with Uraiyur as its first capital.
- The Chola symbol was a tiger.
- King Karikala, a famous Chola ruler, is known for his military conquests and development works.
- The Pattinappalai describes his life and victories, including the Battle of Venni, where he defeated the Cheras, Pandyas, and eleven minor chieftains.
- He built the Kallanai dam on the Kaveri river for irrigation and reclaimed forest land for farming.
- Karikalan had fortified the port city Kaveripoompattinam or Puhar and made it his second capital. He promoted trade and literature.

Pandyan Kingdom

- The Pandyan kingdom during the Sangam Age included Madurai, Tirunelveli and Ramanathapuram.
- Pandyan kings were called Maran, Valudhi and Chezhiyan.
- Their symbol was the carp (fish).
- Their capital was Madurai, and their main port was Korkai, described in Maduraikkanji by Mangudi Maruthanar.
- The Pandyas were known for supporting Tamil Sangam literature, with Madurai as a cultural hub.
- Pandyan ruler Thalaiyalanganathu Nedunchezhiyan defeated the combined forces of Chera, Chola and other Chieftains at Tholaiyalanganam.

Local Chieftains

- A number of local chieftains ruled in different parts of Tamil Nadu apart from the three Tamil kingdoms i.e. Chera, Chola and Pandya. They were known as Velirs.
- The most famous among the Velirs were called Seven Patrons or Kadaiyelu Vallalgal. They were - Pari, Ori, Malayan, Elini, Pegan, Aay and Nalli.
- Tamil poets like Kabilar, Avvaiyar, Nallathanar and Perunchithiranar received patronage from the local chieftains. In return, these poets hailed them for their generosity. They also helped to resolve any disputes between the rulers.

- The local chieftains made generous donations to the poets, bards and their consorts. They had also played a significant role in the political, social and cultural domains during the Sangam Age.

Society of the Sangam Age

In the Sangam Age, the Tamil people had a common language and culture, but they lived in five different natural landscapes.

Social Class

- Tolkappiyam text refers to the five Tinais or divisions of lands and the people living in these five divisions had their respective chief occupations as well as Gods for worship. These divisions were
  - **Kurinji (Hilly tract)** Deity - Murugan, occupation - hunting and honey collection.
  - **Mullai (Pastoral tract)** Deity - Mayon (Vishnu), occupation - shifting agriculture and animal husbandary.
  - **Marutam (Wet land)** Deity - Indra, occupation - agriculture.
  - **Neital (Littoral land)** Deity - Varunan, occupation - fishing and salt extraction.
  - **Palai (Parched zones)** Deity - Korravai, occupation - robbery, cattle lifting.

Caste System

- The Tamil Sangam society was divided on the basis of high born or low born that differentiated Brahmins and their patrons from the common men.
- The Tolkappiyam text refers to the existence of four-fold caste system and social inequalities in the Sangam society. The four castes were Arasar (ruling class), Anthanars, Vellalar and Vaishyas.
- The Brahmins of Sangam society were ideal priests. They acted as the chief advisor to the kings as scholars and philosophers. Though, the Brahmins played a constructive role in society and administration, the Sangam society was not priest-dominated.
- Vellalars held key positions and engaged in trade, with close ties to the Cheras, Cholas and Pandyas.
- Vaishyas were involved in agriculture, trade, commerce and sacrifices.
- Ordinary ploughmen were called uzhavar, while landless labourers were known as adimai or kadasiyar.

Position of Women

- The women enjoyed a respectable position, but their status was not equal to men in the society.
- Education was provided to women as there were women poets like Avvaiyar, Nachchellaiyar and Kakkaipadiniyar who flourished and contributed to Tamil literature.
- Love marriage was a common practice and women were allowed to choose their life partners. But, life of widows was miserable.
- The practice of Sati was prevalent in the higher level of society.
- The worship of Kannagi or Pattini (the Chaste Lady) was an extension of the worship of the Goddess of chastity.

Marriage

- According to texts like the Tolkappiyam and the Kalaviyal, the Aryans introduced the rituals and ceremonies of marriage (karanam).
- They refer to eight forms of marriage mentioned in the Sanskrit Dharmashastras and included them in the framework of Tamil scheme.

Food

- Rice was the staple food during the Sangam period. Apart from it, meat, fish, vegetables, milk and milk products were the chief articles of food.
- The food-habits among the people varied according to their economic status. The rich had their feasts every day, while the poor took simple food.
- Chewing betel leaves was most common among the people. Offering betel leaves to guests had become a social formality.

REVISION NOTES

Dress and Ornaments

- People of Sangam Age dressed according to their staus. The rich wore silk and fine cotton garments, while the middle class generally wore two pieces of cotton clothing.
- Women paid much attention to their hairstyle. They used flowers like Jasmine to decorate their plaits and tufts. Both men and women used perfumes made of sandal and flowers.
- Sangam literature mentions a variety of ornaments worn by both men and women, made of gold, silver, pearls, and precious stones. Poor people wore ornaments made of shells and beads.

Entertainment

- Music and dance were a good part of the spare time of men and women.
- Cock fighting, goat fighting and gambling were popular in the villages.
- Wrestling was another form of entertainment enjoyed by the youth, though at times it led to death of one of the contestants.
- The children played various games for entertainment.

Economy of the Sangam Age

Agriculture

- Agriculture was the chief occupation. The main crops were rice, cotton, sugarcane, ragi, different varieties of fruits, etc.
- The Sangam literature mentions rural activities like cultivation of ragi and sugarcane, harvesting and drying of grain and the making of sugar from the sugarcane.

Handicrafts

- The handicrafts included weaving, metal works and carpentry, ship building and making of ornaments using beads, stones and ivory.
- People during this time became highly skilled in spinning and weaving cotton and silk clothes. These fabrics, especially the cotton clothes made in Uraiyur, were in high demand in the Western world.
- Besides cotton and silk, cloth made of wood fibre was also used by the priestly class. Dyeing was a common industry that supported the process of weaving.

Trade

- Both internal and foreign trade was well organised and briskly carried throughout the period. Most of the trade was carried on by barter system.
- The port city of Puhar became an important place of foreign trade, as big ships entered this port containing precious goods. Other significant ports of commercial activity were Tondi, Musiri, Korkai, Arikkamedu and Marakkanam.
- The Periplus (sailing around or voyage) of Red sea described the navigation and trade of Roman Empire with India. It mentioned the ports of Naura (Cannanore), Tyndis (Ponnani) and Muziris (Cranganore) were important ports on the West coast. The pearls from the coast were sent to Uraiyur and exported.
- There were established markets called Angadi in the bigger towns, while at other places, goods were carried by hawkers to the houses of the people.
- Many gold and silver coins that were issued by the Roman Emperors like Augustus, Tiberius and Nero have been found in all parts of Tamil Nadu indicating flourishing trade.
- Major exports of the Sangam Age were cotton fabrics and spices like pepper, ginger, cardamom, cinnamon and turmeric along with ivory products, pearls and precious stones.
- Major imports for the traders were horses, gold and sweet wine.

EXAM ORIENTED QUESTIONS

TYPE - 1   1 Mark

Multiple Choice Questions

Q.1 Read the description and answer the following question.

This literary work is one of the two major divisions of Sangam literature, which deals primarily with the themes of love, relationships and inner feelings. It consists of poems that describe personal emotions and the lives of lovers.

Which of the following categories of Sangam literature is described in the passage?

(a) Puram   (b) Akam
(c) Itihasa   (d) Vedic Literature

Ans. (b) Akam

Q.2. Identify the odd one out regarding the literary works of the Sangam Age.

(a) Tirukkural   (b) Ettuthokai
(c) Manimekalai   (d) Indika

Ans. (d) Indika

Exp. Indika is a historical account written by the Greek traveller Megasthenes, while Tirukkural, Ettuthokai, and Manimekalai are all Tamil literary works from the Sangam Age.

Q.3 Which of the following best describes the significance of Tirukkural in Tamil literature?

(a) It is an epic describing the victories of Chera rulers.
(b) It is a work of 1330 couplets that explains aspects of life.
(c) It is a religious text focused on worship and rituals.
(d) It is a historical document narrating the Sangam Age wars.

Ans. (b) It is a work of 1330 couplets that explains aspects of life.

Q.4. What are the box-like structures erected with the stone slabs, resting on each other without any mortar called?

(a) Megaliths   (b) Tirukkural
(c) Couplets   (d) Malaiyar

Ans. (a) Megaliths

Exp. Megaliths are large stone structures built by ancient people. These stone slabs were placed on top of each other to create box-like shapes, often used for burial or as memorials.

Q.5 Read the description given below and identify the ruler. He built the Kallanai dam on the Kaveri River for irrigation.

(a) Karikalan Chola
(b) Rajendra Chola
(c) Cheran Senguttuvan
(d) Vijayalaya Chola

Ans. (a) Karikalan Chola

Exp. Karikalan Chola, a famous king from the Chola dynasty, built the Kallanai dam on the Kaveri River to improve irrigation and support agriculture in the region. This dam is one of the oldest in the world.

Q.6. Look at the picture below and answer the following question.

A   B   C

The emblem which resembles to the Pandyas of the Sangam Age is

(a) B   (b) C
(c) A   (d) None of these

Ans. (c) A

Q.7 Complete the given analogy.

Chola : Uraiyur : : Pandya : ?

(a) Vanji   (b) Madurai
(c) Kanyakumari   (d) Vellore

Ans. (b) Madurai

Q.8 Which of the following is most likely to have been a characteristic of the Sangam Age?

(a) The use of Sanskrit as the primary language for literature.
(b) A thriving trade network with the Roman Empire.
(c) The spread of Buddhism throughout Tamil Nadu.
(d) The dominance of the Gupta Empire in South India.

Ans. (b) A thriving trade network with the Roman Empire.

Q.9 Identify the statements about the Sangam Age and choose the correct option.

P : The Sangam Age is known for the creation of Tamil literature, which includes works composed by Tamil poets.

Q : The Chola dynasty was the only dynasty that ruled during the Sangam Age.

R : The Sangam Age saw the establishment of trade relations between Tamil kingdoms and the Roman Empire.

S : The Sangam literature does not include Akam and Puram.

(a) P and Q (b) P and R

(c) R and S (d) Q and S

Ans. (b) P and R

Q.10 Which of the following was not a feature of the class system of the Sangam Age?

(a) The Vellalars were the ruling class

(b) The social structure was largely influenced by birth

(c) Merchants and traders were an important part of society

(d) The role of women was equal to men in all social aspects

Ans. (d) The role of women was equal to men in all social aspects.

Exp. In the Sangam Age, while women had respect and could be educated, their status was not equal to men. Men held more power in society and family.

Q.11 Which of the following was a major export item from the Tamil kingdoms during the Sangam Age?

(a) Wheat (b) Spices

(c) Silver (d) Iron

Ans. (b) Spices

TYPE - 2

1 Mark

Assertion-Reason Questions

Q.1. Read the two statements given below about the Cheras of Sangam Age and select the option that shows the correct relationship between (A) and (R).

Assertion (A) The capital of the Cheras was Vanji and their chief port was Thondi.

Reason (R) Their symbol on the flag was tiger.

(a) R contradicts A

(b) R is the reason for A

(c) A is true but R is false

(d) A and R are independent of each other

Ans. (c) A is true but R is false

Q.2. Read the two statements given below about the Chola kingdom of Sangam Age and select the option that shows the correct relationship between (A) and (R).

Assertion (A) The Chola kingdom was rich in water resources.

Reason (R) The river Kaveri flowed through the Chola kingdom.

(a) R contradicts A

(b) R is the reason for A

(c) A is true but R is false

(d) A and R are independent of each other

Ans. (b) R is the reason for A

Q.3. Read the two statements given below about the local chieftains of Sangam Age and select the option that shows the correct relationship between (A) and (R).

Assertion (A) The local chieftains who ruled in different parts of Tamil Nadu were called Velirs.

Reason (R) They helped to resolve the disputes among the rulers.

(a) R contradicts A

(b) R is the reason for A

(c) A is true but R is false

(d) A and R are independent of each other

Ans. (d) A and R are independent of each other

Q.4. Read the two statements given below about the food habits of Sangam Age and select the option that shows the correct relationship between (A) and (R).

Assertion (A) The people of the Sangam Age consumed a variety of food, including rice, fruits and meat.

Reason (R) The people of the Sangam Age followed an agrarian economy, and their diet was largely based on the crops they grew, along with the availability of meat and fruits from the forests.

(a) R contradicts A

(b) R is the reason for A

(c) A is true but R is false

(d) A and R are independent of each other

Ans. (b) R is the reason for A

TYPE - 3 2 Marks

Very Short Answer Type Questions

Q.1 Who wrote the Tirukkural? Also, name the three sections into which its chapters are categorised.

Ans. Tirukkural was written by Tiruvalluvar, a Tamil poet and philosopher.

The three sections into which the chapters of Tirukkural are categorised are - Aram (righteousness), Porul (wealth), Inbam or Kamam (pleasure).

Q.2 Give a brief account on Megaliths?

Ans. The Megaliths are box-like structures erected with the stone slabs, resting on each other without any mortar. Sometimes there was an opening cut into one of the sides.

Some megaliths are seen on surface while some are underground with stone circles or boulders placed on surface to serve as signpost to find the burial site.

Q.3 Mention any two sources of information about the Sangam Age.

Ans. Two sources of information about the Sangam Age are

(i) **Sangam Literature** Ancient Tamil texts like *Tolkappiyam* and *Ettuthokai* provide detailed insights into the social, cultural, and political life of the Sangam period.

(ii) **Archaeological Evidence** Excavations at sites like Arikamedu and Keeladi reveal information about trade, urban settlements, and daily life during the Sangam Age.

Q.4 Mention any two famous poets from the Sangam Age.

Ans. The two famous poets from the Sangam Age are

(i) Avvaiyar (ii) Nallathanar

Q.5 Who were the Vellalars during the Sangam Age? Examine the relationship with the rulers of the Sangam Age.

Ans. During the Sangam Age, the Vellalars were wealthy landowners who cultivated the fertile wetlands. In addition to farming, the Vellalars were also involved in trade.

They had strong connections with the three major dynasties-the Cheras, Cholas and Pandyas and held important positions in their courts.

Q.6 Mention the two major crops grown during the Sangam period.

Ans. Two major crops grown during the Sangam period were rice and sugarcane.

Rice was the primary staple crop, cultivated extensively in the fertile plains, while sugarcane was important for producing jaggery, a sweetener used in various foods and offerings.

Q.7 Mention one major cotton trade during the Sangam Age, and what products were exported to foreign countries.

Ans. Uraiyur was one major center of cotton trade.

The products exported to foreign countries during the Sangam Age were pepper, ginger, cardamom, cinnamon, turmeric, ivory products, pearls and precious stones.

Q8 Name two ports that were important for trade during the Sangam Age.

Ans. Two important ports for trade during the Sangam Age were

(i) Puhar (Kaveripattinam) (ii) Muziris (Muchiri)

Q.9 Imagine you are a merchant during the Sangam Age. How would you describe the role of trade and commerce in context to the economy during that time?

Ans. If I were a merchant during the Sangam Age, then I would describe the economy as being heavily dependent on trade. Coastal towns like Puhar were bustling with activity as they facilitated both local and international trade. We traded goods like spices, textiles, and pearls with other regions, including the Roman Empire.

Q.10 Give two reasons why the Sangam Age is considered a significant period in the history of Tamil Nadu.

Ans. The two reasons why the Sangam Age is considered a significant period in the history of Tamil Nadu include

(i) The Sangam Age is known for its rich and diverse Sangam literature, which provides valuable insights into the social, political and cultural life of the time.

(ii) It was a period of flourishing trade and economic prosperity, with significant external trade connections, including with the Roman Empire and other parts of Asia.

TYPE - 4 3 Marks

Short Answer Type Questions

Q.1 Who were the major rulers of the Sangam Age? Describe their contributions.

Ans. The major rulers of the Sangam Age were

(i) **Karikalan Chola** He was known for his military power and administrative skills.

He expanded the Chola Empire and is credited with building extensive irrigation works, including the Kallanai dam.

(ii) **Cheran Senguttuvan** He was a famous Chera ruler, known for his valor and his contributions to the development of Tamil culture. He also played a significant role in the trade with foreign nations.

Q.2. Mention any three important sources of income in Sangam Age.

Ans. The three important source of income in Sangam Age were

(i) **Agriculture** It was the backbone of the Sangam Age economy, with rice as the staple crop and others crops like millets, sugarcane, and cotton. Fertile lands near rivers like Kaveri ensured surplus production, supporting trade.

(ii) **Trade** Coastal cities like Muziris and Kaveripattinam were major trade hubs, exporting spices, pearls, silk, and cotton while importing Roman wine, glassware, jewels and luxury items.

(iii) **Craftsmanship** Skilled artisans produced jewellery, metalwork, pottery, textiles, and tools. Pearl-making, carpentry, and blacksmithing were highly valued, contributing to trade and economic prosperity.

Q.3 Describe the role of local chieftains during the Sangam Age.

Ans. During the Sangam Age, local chieftains played an important role in society in the following ways

- They ruled smaller regions under the bigger kingdoms of the Cheras, Cholas, and Pandyas. These chieftains were responsible for maintaining law and order, protecting their people, and collecting taxes.
- They also supported poets and artists by offering them gifts and rewards.
- Many chieftains were brave warriors who participated in battles and expanded their territories. They were respected by their people and were important in keeping the local administration running smoothly.

Q.4 Describe the social structure during the Sangam Age.

Ans. The social structure of the Sangam Age was based on a hierarchical system. At the top were the Brahmins, who were priests and scholars. The Vellalars, who were landowners and agriculturists, formed the majority of the population and played a significant role in society.

The Kshatriyas were the warriors and rulers, responsible for maintaining law and order.

Artisans, traders, and farmers formed the lower strata. There was also a significant distinction between the urban and rural population. Women had a relatively higher status compared to other contemporary cultures, though their roles were still often limited to domestic spheres.

Q.5 Mention any four types of handicrafts that flourished during the Sangam Age and explain their significance.

Ans. The Sangam Age was known for its remarkable handicrafts. Four types of handicrafts that flourished during the Sangam age were weaving, metalwork, carpentry, and ornament making.

(i) Weaving was highly advanced, with cotton and silk clothes, especially from Uraiyur, being in great demand worldwide.

(ii) Metalwork and carpentry supported industries like shipbuilding.

(iii) Ornament making used beads, stones, and ivory to create beautiful designs.

(iv) Additionally, cloth made from wood fiber was used by priests, and dyeing was a widespread craft that enhanced the weaving industry.

TYPE - 5 — 4 Marks

Long Answer Type Questions

Q.1 List the three Sangams held during the Sangam Age and briefly mention their significance.

Ans. The Sangam Age had three Sangams (gatherings of poets and scholars) in ancient Tamil Nadu.

(i) **First Sangam** Held in Madurai, this Sangam included legendary poets, but no works from this period has survived.

(ii) **Second Sangam** Held in Kapatapuram, a few works from this period remain, showing early Tamil literary growth.

(iii) **Third Sangam** Held in Madurai, it produced famous works like *Tirukkural* and *Silappadikaram*, reflecting Tamil culture, society, and values.

These Sangams were significant because they preserved Tamil language and literature, offering insights into the life and achievements of ancient Tamil society.

Q.2 **Megaliths are found in various districts of Tamil Nadu, such as Kanchipuram and Vellore. How do these megalithic structures help us understand the cultural and religious practices of the people during the Sangam Age?**

Ans. Megaliths found in districts like Kanchipuram and Vellore offer valuable insights into the cultural and religious practices of the Sangam Age. These large stone structures were primarily used to mark burial sites, suggesting a strong belief in the afterlife.

The presence of multiple skeletons in some megaliths indicates that family members were buried together over different periods, reflecting the importance of kinship and family ties.

Artifacts such as pitchers, baskets, tools, and weapons found in these burial sites show the daily life, skills, and material culture of the people. Additionally, these megaliths symbolise the respect for ancestors and the belief in an ongoing spiritual existence, linking them to broader religious and social customs of the time.

Q.3 **How was the society in the Sangam Age different from that in the Vedic Age?**

Ans. The society in the Sangam Age was different from that in the Vedic Age in following ways

- The society in the Sangam Age was organised by occupational groups while the society in Vedic Age was organised on the basis of castes.
- Women in Sangam Age were respected and were allowed intellectual pursuits. There were women poets like Avvaiyar and Nachchellair. Women in Vedic Age were also in respectable position but their education was not given importance. Also their position in society declined towards later Vedic age.
- Sati-pratha was prevalent in Sangam Age, while in Vedic age, women were allowed to remarry after husband's death.
- Primary deity of Sangam Age was Murugan and that of Vedic Age were - Indra, Agni and Varuna.
- Economy of Sangam Age was based on agriculture while Vedic economy was pastoral.

TYPE - 6   10 Marks

Structured Questions

Q.1 **With reference to the society of the Sangam Age answer the following**

(i) Discuss the position of the women in Sangam society. **(3)**

(ii) What is the Tolkappiyam, and what does it describe? (3)

(iii) Discuss the dress and ornaments of the Sangam Age people. How did clothing and accessories vary among different classes? (4)

Ans. (i) In Sangam society, women held a respectable position but were not equal to men. Education was provided to some women, and talented poets like Avvaiyar contributed to Tamil literature. Love marriages were common, and women could choose their life partners. However, widows faced hardships, and the practice of Sati was prevalent among the higher classes. Women worshipped Kannagi, the symbol of chastity. They took great care of their appearance, using ornaments, perfumes, and hairstyles decorated with flowers. Despite some freedoms, their status reflected both respect and limitations.

(ii) The Tolkappiyam is an ancient Tamil text and one of the oldest works in Tamil literature. It is a grammar book that explains the rules of Tamil language and literature. Besides grammar, it also gives insights into the culture, society, and traditions of the Sangam Age. It describes the division of people based on natural landscapes (Kurinji, Mullai, Marutam, Neital, Palai), their occupations, deities, and social structure. It also mentions the caste system, marriage customs, and daily life, making it a valuable source to understand early Tamil society.

(iii) During the Sangam Age, clothing and ornaments reflected social status and vary among different classes in the following ways

- The rich wore silk and fine cotton garments, while the middle class wore simple cotton clothing.
- Women styled their hair with flowers like jasmine and used perfumes made of sandalwood and flowers.
- Both men and women adorned themselves with ornaments made of gold, silver, pearls, and precious stones. The poor people used shells and beads.
- Jewellery included necklaces, bangles, earrings, and anklets. Clothing and accessories varied greatly based on economic status, with the wealthy showcasing their prosperity through luxurious attire.

Q.2 **With reference to the society and culture during the Sangam Age, answer the following questions**

(i) The Sangam Age society was divided into five different land divisions, each associated with specific occupations and deities. Discuss the social significance of these divisions. (4)

(ii) Discuss the caste system and the position of women in the Sangam society. **(3)**

(iii) How did Sangam literature reflect the values and beliefs of the people during that period? **(3)**

Ans (i) The society during the Sangam Age was divided into five land divisions, each with its own occupations and deities. These divisions were

(a) **Kurinji** (Hilly tract) People were hunters and gathered honey, worshipping the deity, Murugan.

(b) **Mullai** (Pastoral tract) People raised cattle and worshipped Mayon (Vishnu).

(c) **Marutam** (Wet land) People were farmers, grew crops, and worshipped Indira.

(d) **Neithal** (Littoral land) People were involved in fishing and salt production, worshipping Varunan.

(e) **Palai** (Desert) People led a harsh life and were known for robbery. They worshipped Korravai.

These divisions helped in organising the community based on natural resources and occupations, influencing the social roles of individuals.

(ii) In the Sangam society, the caste system was based on social hierarchy. The four main castes were Arasar (ruling class), Anthanars, Vellalar, and Vaishyas. Brahmins held important roles as priests and advisors to kings. Vellalars were involved in administration and trade, while Vaishyas focused on agriculture and commerce.

Women had a respectable position but were not equal to men. Some women, like Avvaiyar, became famous poets. Love marriages were common, and women could choose their partners, but widows faced difficult lives. The practice of Sati and worship of Kannagi (the chaste lady) were also present.

(iii) Sangam literature reflects the values and beliefs of the people during the Sangam Age by portraying their daily lives, ethical ideals, and social practices.

Works like *Tirukkural* and *Silappadikaram* emphasised the importance of righteousness (Aram), wealth (Porul), and pleasure (Inbam), guiding people in their personal and public lives.

It also highlighted the roles of love, duty, and justice, as well as the respect for elders and hospitality. The literature also portrayed the belief in life after death, shown by the megalithic burial practices, and the significance of family, especially in the form of marriage and relationships.

Q.3 With reference to the economy during the Sangam Age, answer the following questions.

(i) Discuss the occupations of the people and the activities associated with it. **(3)**

(ii) "Internal trade during the Sangam Age flourished through an organised way". Explain the organisation of internal trade during Sangam Age **(3)**

(iii) Discuss the extent and significance of external trade during the Sangam Age. **(4)**

Ans. (i) Agriculture was the main occupation of the people during the Sangam period. Rice was the primary crop, while other crops included cotton, ragi, sugarcane, pepper, ginger, cardamom, turmeric, cinnamon, and various fruits.

The State took responsibility for building embankments and canals to help with irrigation. The Sangam poems provide detailed descriptions of rural activities such as growing ragi and sugarcane, making sugar from the cane, and harvesting and drying grains.

(ii) During the Sangam Age, internal trade flourished in a well-organised manner. Established markets, known as Angadi, were present in towns for trading goods, while hawkers carried goods to people's homes in smaller areas. The barter system was predominantly used for transactions.

Key trade hubs, such as the city of Puhar and ports like Tondi and Korkai, facilitated commerce and connected urban and rural areas. Efficient trade routes further strengthened the system, ensuring smooth and structured trade across the region.

(iii) During the Sangam Age, there was a large amount of trade with foreign countries. According to Sangam literature, Tamil land had valuable goods that were highly sought after in foreign markets, such as pepper, ginger, cardamom, cinnamon, turmeric, ivory products, pearls, and precious stones. The main imports included horses, gold, and glass.

The port cities played a key role in foreign trade, with Saliyur in the Pandya kingdom and Bandar in the Chera kingdom being the most important. The discovery of Roman gold and silver coins in Tamil Nadu shows how extensive this trade was.

The Periplus of the erythraean sea, a Roman text, provides details about trade between India and the Roman Empire and mentions Uraiyur as the place where pearls from the coast were sent for export. Other important ports on the West coast included Naura, Tyndis, and Muziris.

THE AGE OF THE GUPTAS

- The Gupta Empire rose in Magadha around fourth-century AD. The Gupta dynasty ruled for more than 200 years from 320 to 540 AD. This period is also known as Imperial Age of the Guptas.
- The Gupta period is popularly known as the Classical Age or Golden Age of India.
- The rulers of this dynasty established a vast empire comprising almost the entire Northern India.

Sources of the Gupta Age

1. Accounts of Fa-hien

- Fa-hien was the first Chinese pilgrim, who visited India on a religious mission during the reign of Chandragupta II.
- The various aspects of Chandragupta's empire, i.e. political, religious, social and economic, were clearly reflected in his writings.
- Fa-hien observed that India was a peaceful place where different religions like Vaishnavism, Shaivism, Buddhism, and Jainism lived together in harmony.
- In North India, the death penalty was not imposed. Instead, most crimes were punished with fines, and only serious rebellions were punished by cutting off one hand.
- Besides agriculture, there were other professions like carpentry, spinning, weaving, goldsmith etc.
- The Shudras lived outside the town and could only enter by making noise with a stick. They worked as butchers, hunters, and fishermen.
- The income of the government was mainly based on the revenue taxes, which were one-sixth of the total production. The roads were kept safe for travellers.
- The coin sculptures and paintings depicted the Hindu Gods and Goddesses.
- His account gave an information of Pataliputra city that had many charitable institutions including a hospital funded by wealthy citizens and the huge palace of the Great Ashoka.
- He also provided a detailed account of Magadha which was a prosperous empire having large towns and wealthy population.

2. The Allahabad Pillar Inscription (Prayaga Prashasti)

- Harisena, the Mahadandnayaka (Commander-in- Chief)/Chief Judicial Officer) and the court poet of Samudragupta, composed the contents that are inscribed on Allahabad pillar.
- It records the name and achievements of Samudragupta, the ruler of the Gupta Empire.
- It also provides the list of kings and tribal republics that were conquered by Samudragupta.

Allahabad Pillar

- The first part of the pillar inscription describes Samudragupta as the one who resolved the eternal conflict between poetry and propriety.
- The next part gives a list of the conquests of Samudragupta during his Deccan expedition.

Ashwamedh-Type Coins

Rulers of Gupta Dynasty

The Gupta dynasty was founded by Sri Gupta but his reign and details are not well-documented. He was succeeded by his son Ghatotkacha but his reign is obscure. Thereafter, following were significant rulers of Gupta dynasty.

Chandragupta I (320-330 AD)

- He was the son and successor of Ghatotkacha.
- He was a powerful Gupta ruler, who had waged many battles to attain his title of Maharajadhiraja (King of kings).
- He extended his Empire through matrimonial alliance by marrying a Lichchavi princess Kumaradevi.
- He is considered as the real founder of the Gupta Empire.

Samudragupta (330-380 AD)

- He was the son and successor of Chandragupta I. He was also known as the 'Napolean of India' because of his braving and generalship.
- His greatest achievement was 'political unification of India'.
- He issued gold coins to remember the Ashwamedha sacrifices he performed after his military victories. These coins are known as Ashwamedh-Type coins.
- The Allahabad pillar inscription gave following information about Samudragupta
  - Samudragupta defeated 'nine rulers of Aryavarta' and made their Kingdoms as a part of his Empire.
  - Samudragupta conquered neighbouring states of Assam, Coastal Bengal, Nepal and a number of Gana Sanghas (organisation of the Kings) in the North-West. They paid tribute to him and followed his orders.
  - It mentions about Samudragupta's expedition of South India (Dakshnipatha), whose twelve rulers surrendered to him after being defeated, were liberated and allowed to rule again over their kingdoms.
  - Samudragupta had close contacts with the kingdom of Ceylon and South-East Asian colonies.
  - The Shakas and Kushanas, who ruled in the West, gave up their control and paid tribute to Samudragupta.
  - He was called by different names, one of them was Kaviraja because of his ability to compose verses.
  - Certain coins show him playing the Veena. He was a follower of Brahmanism and worshipped Lord Vishnu.
  - He also patronised the Great Buddhist scholar, Vasubandhu.
  - He also had faith in vedic sacrifices and was tolerant towards other religions.

Chandragupta II (380-415 AD)

- He was the son and successsor of Samudragupta. He expanded his empire by winning battles and through marriage alliances. His capital city was Pataliputra.
- Chandragupta II conquered the territories of Western Malwa and Gujarat by defeating the Shaka rulers, who had ruled for about four centuries in the region. This earned him the title of Sakari (conqueror of Sakas) and Vikramaditya.
- After this victory, Chandragupta II gained control over the Arabian sea and access to the sea ports under his reign. This enabled the Gupta Empire to control trade with the Western countries.
- Chandragupta II was the first Gupta ruler to issue silver coins.
- He is renowned for his patronage to art, literature, architecture and administration.

- His court is believed to have been adorned with Navratna (the Nine Gems) including Kalidasa, Amarasimha and Varahamihira.

Kumaragupta I (415 - 455 AD)

- He assumed the titles of 'Shakraditya' and 'Mahendraditya' as part of his royal designations.
- He established Nalanda University, which gained global recognition as a prestigious educational institution.
- In the last years of his reign, the peace and prosperity of the empire were disturbed due to the invasion of the Turko-Mongol tribe, the Huns. During the war with the Huns, Kumaragupta died.
- The inscriptions of Kumaragupta I's reign are - Karandanda, Mandsor, Bilsad inscription (oldest record of his reign) and Damodar Copper plate Inscription.

Skandagupta (c. 455 - 467 AD)

- He assumed the title of 'Vikramaditya' as part of his royal designation.
- An inscription found in Junagarh/Girnar during his reign mentions that his governor Parnadatta, undertook the repair of the Sudarshan Lake.
- During the reign of Skandagupta, the successor of Kumaragupta and the last illustrious ruler of the Gupta Empire, the Huns attacked but were successfully repelled.
- After Skandagupta's death, his successors-Purugupta (467-473 AD), Kumaragupta II (473-479 AD), Budhagupta (476-495 AD), Narasimhagupta, Kumaragupta III, and Vishnugupta (540-550 AD) failed to prevent further Huns invasions. This led to the gradual disintegration of the Gupta empire.

Gupta Administration

The Gupta Empire had a strong and well-organised administration. The main features of Gupta Administration were

1. Central Administration

- Gupta Empire was a monarchical government which means all powers vested to the Kings. The Kings were seen as divine and were regarded as gods or their representatives.
- The imperial Gupta Kings adopted pompous titles such as Maharajadhiraja, Paramabhattaraka, Chakravarti, Paramesvara, etc.
- The King was assisted by a Council of Ministers. The Minister's office was almost hereditary.
- The supreme judicial power was invested in the King, but the Mahadandnayaka carried out the judicial functions.
- The central secretariat also worked under the supervision of the King and the King was the source of all honors and titles.
- All land in the country was the property of the King. He had the sole right to build infrastructure, collect taxes, and provide justice.
- The Gupta Kings created two new classes - Sandhivigrahika (Minister of War and Peace) and Kumaramatyas (Offices of the Crown Prince).
- Civil and criminal crimes were clearly defined and separated in the Gupta Empire.

2. Provincial and the Local Administration

- The Gupta rulers evolved the first systematic provincial and local administration, which was primarily concerned witht the collection of revenues and the maintenance of law and order.
- The Empire was divided into a number of provinces, called Bhuktis.
- The bhuktis were further divided into Vishayas. A Bhukti was placed under Uparika (the Governor) and Vishaya under Vishayapati.

- The village level disputes were solved by the village headman called Gramapati or Gramadhyaksha and this was the smallest administration unit.
- There were various towns (janapadas) which were administered by a committee of five members. They were headed by an officer called Purapala.
- Chiefs of the guilds were called Nagarseths, who represented the guild in the urban trading circles.
- The Sarthavaha represented the trading communities. The terms Nivartana, Kulyavapa and Dronavapa were used for land measurements.
- The Araghatta (Persian wheel) or Ghati Yantras were the tools of irrigation, which became more popular during the Gupta era.

Contribution of Gupta Empire

During the Gupta period, India reached a high level of civilisation and culture due to its contribution in the fields of education, science, literature, art and architecture. Therefore, Gupta period is known as the period of Golden Age of Indian Culture.

Nalanda University

Education

- Primary education could be obtained by the people. Formal and higher education was obtained by staying in Agraharas or Monasteries. Women could obtain education, unlike in other parts of the world.
- Cities like Pataliputra, Ayodhya, Valabhi, Ujjain and Nasik were significant educational centers of those times.
- Nalanda University situated near Rajagriha in Bihar, was probably the highest seat of Buddhist learning during the Gupta period.

Nalanda University

- The site of Nalanda is located at South-East of Patna in Bihar. It has been called one of the first great universities recorded in history.
- Initially, this was a Buddhist monastery, but later became a University. The University was founded in the 5th century BC. In the 7th century AD, the Chinese scholar Xuanzang visited the Nalanda University.
- Historical studies indicate that the University of Nalanda was established during the reign of the Gupta Emperor, Kumaragupta.
- The complex was built with red bricks and its ruins occupy an area of 14 hectares. The University attracted scholars and students from other countries also such as China, Greece and Persia.
- Panini, Jivaka, Prasenjit and Chanakya were the students of Nalanda University.
- The library of Nalanda, called Dharma Gunj (Mountain of Truth) or Dharmaganja (Treasury of Truth), was the most famous center of Buddhist knowledge in the world at that time. The library had three main buildings - Ratnasagara (Sea of Jewels), Ratnodadhi (Ocean of Jewel) and Ratnaranjaka (Delighter of Jewels).
- In this University, courses were drawn from every field of learning such as, Buddhist and Hindu, sacred and secular, foreign and native.
- The subjects were Science, Astronomy, Medicine, Logic, Samkhya, Yoga-shastra, the Veda and the scriptures of Buddhism.
- Nalanda was ruined by Turkish Muslim invaders under Mohammad-bin Bakhtiyar Khilji in 1193, who was a General of Mohammad Ghori.

Science

- The Gupta period saw the rise in Mathematics, Astronomy, Astrology and Medicine.
- Metallurgy or science of metals had also made a wonderful progress during the Gupta period.
- Aryabhatta was a great mathematician and astronomer. He wrote the book Aryabhattiyam in 499 AD that deals with mathematics and astronomy. He also wrote Surya Siddhanta in which he explained the exact causes of solar and lunar eclipses.
- He was the first to declare that the Earth was spherical in shape and that it rotates on its own axis. However, these views were rejected by later astronomers like Varahamihira and Brahmagupta.
- Aryabhatta was acquainted with the decimal system and the use of zero. He also calculated the exact value of *Pi* (π) which was equal to 3.1459.
- Varahamihira was a great astronomer who composed Pancha Siddhantika, the five astronomical systems. His work 'Brihadsamhita' is a great work in Sanskrit literature.
- Brahmagupta was an Astronomer and Mathematician. He described the Law of Gravitation centuries before Newton.

3. Medicine

- In the field of medicine, the Great Physicians during Gupta period were Charaka, Sushruta and Dhanwantri. They wrote treatises on Ayurvedic science of medicine, prevention, treatment and cure.

4. Culture

- The Gupta empire had strong and capable rulers who brought stability and growth.
- There was political stability, so trade and commerce flourished during the Gupta period which led to economic prosperity.
- Economic prosperity allowed people to pursue various arts and crafts and literary activities.

Works of Kalidasa

- Mahakavi Kalidasa was a great Indian poet and playwright in the 4th century CE. Kalidasa's works provide reliable information about the government, society and religion of the Gupta period and also contain the traces of political history.
- His dramatic works include Abhijnanashakuntalam (love story of King Dushyanta and Shakuntala), Vikramorvasiyam (Urvashi won by Valour) and Malavikagnimitram (love story of Malavika and Agnimitra)
- His poetic works include Raghuvamsa (Dynasty of Raghu), Kumarasambhava (Birth of the War God) and the Meghaduta (the Cloud Messenger).

The Vishnu Temple at Deogarh

- It was built in the beginning of the 6th century AD, located near Jhansi in Uttar Pradesh. This temple was made of stone and bricks.
- This temple was first described in detail by Alexander Cunningham in his tour of 1874-77. It is also known as Dashavatara Temple due to presence of ten incarnations of Vishnu depicted on the temple and locally known as 'sagar marh' due to the presence of rock-cut well nearby.
- It was built on a platform with a height of 1.5 m. It is the first North Indian temple with Shikhara (tower).
- The walls of the temple were decorated with the scenes depicting Ramayana and Lord Krishna's life.
- The interior of temple has four Verandahs. An important feature of this temple is the sculpture of Lord Vishnu in which he is shown asleep on the coil of the giant Serpent, Sheshnaga.

Vishnu Temple at Deogarh

EXAM ORIENTED QUESTIONS

TYPE - 1 — 1 Mark

Multiple Choice Questions

Q.1 Which of the following is described by the Chinese traveller, Fa-hien?

(a) Though people were prosperous, they led simple lives
(b) Though people were poor, they led extravagant lives
(c) People were rich and extravagant
(d) Though the cities were flourishing, people were poor

Ans. (a) Though people were prosperous, they led simple lives.

Exp. According to Fa-hien, India during the Gupta period was peaceful, and the people, although wealthy, led modest and simple lives, focusing on basic professions and living harmoniously.

Q.2 Look at the picture below and answer the following question.

What is the primary purpose of this inscription?

(a) To commemorate the Gupta Empire's cultural achievements.
(b) To describe the religious practices of the Gupta Empire.
(c) To record the military conquests of Samudragupta.
(d) To praise the architectural achievements of the Gupta Empire.

Ans. (c) To record the military conquests of Samudragupta.

Exp. The primary purpose of the Allahabad Pillar inscription is to record the military conquests of Samudragupta. It lists the rulers and tribes he defeated and brought under his control, showcasing his power and success in expanding the Gupta empire.

Q.3 Read the description and identify the person.
He was the first independent king with the title of 'Maharajadhiraja' or 'the King of Kings'.

(a) Chandragupta I (b) Chandragupta II
(c) Samudragupta (d) Srigupta

Ans. (a) Chandragupta I

Q.4 How did Samudragupta rule the Southern kingdoms?

(a) He kept the kingdoms under his direct control.
(b) He allowed the defeated rulers to rule their kingdoms.
(c) The defeated rulers paid tribute and attended Samudragupta's court.
(d) All of the above

Ans. (b) He allowed the defeated rulers to rule their kingdoms.

Q.5 This ruler's reign marked the peak of the Gupta Empire's cultural achievements. He is known for his patronage of the arts, and he promoted Sanskrit literature. He was also a lover of poetry and drama, and Kalidasa's works flourished during his rule. *World History Encyclopedia*

Who is being described in the above description?

(a) Chandragupta I (b) Samudragupta
(c) Chandragupta II (d) Harsha

Ans. (c) Chandragupta II

Q.6 Which of the following is not associated with the reign of Chandragupta II (Vikramaditya)?

(a) Expansion of the Gupta Empire to its greatest territorial extent.
(b) Patronage of arts, literature and science.
(c) The support for Buddhism as the state religion.
(d) Military victories over the Shakas.

Ans. (c) The support for Buddhism as the state religion.

Exp. Chandragupta II supported various religions, but his reign is more closely associated with the growth of Hinduism and the promotion of arts, literature, and military victories.

Q.7 Who is represented as slaying a lion on some coins with the legend Simha-Vikrama?

(a) Chandragupta I (b) Chandragupta II
(c) Samudragupta (d) Rudrasena II

Ans. (b) Chandragupta II

Q.8 Which of the following is not correct about Chandragupta II ?

(a) He was called as Napoleon of India.

(b) He conquered the Western Malwa and Gujarat by defeating the Saka rulers.

(c) His court said to have been adorned with Navratna.

(d) Kalidasa was contemporary of Chandragupta II.

Ans. (a) He was called as Napoleon of India.

Exp. 'Napoleon of India' title was given to Chandragupta II's predecessor, Samudragupta. Chandragupta II was known for his conquests, cultural contributions, and the support of famous scholars like Kalidasa.

Q.9 Look at the picture below and answer the following question.

The image shows the ruins of an ancient university that was once a great center of learning. Which famous traveller visited this university and wrote about its teachings and scholars?

(a) Ibn Battuta (b) Hiuen Tsang

(c) Marco Polo (d) Al-Masudi

Ans. (b) Hiuen Tsang

Exp. Hiuen Tsang was a Chinese scholar who came to India during the Gupta period and studied at Nalanda University.

Q.10 Complete the given analogy.

Dharma Gunj: Mountain of Truth:: Dharmaganja: ?

(a) Treasury of Truth (b) Sea of Jewels

(c) Ocean of Knowledge (d) Ocean of Jewel

Ans. (a) Treasury of Truth

Q.11 Identify the statements regarding the Gupta Age.

P : The Gupta rulers practiced a centralised form of governance with autonomous local rulers.

Q : The reign of the Gupta Empire is regarded as the Golden Age.

R : Gupta society was known for its flexible caste system.

S : Gupta rulers promoted scientific advancements, including in the field of astronomy.

(a) P and Q (b) Q and S (c) P and R (d) R and S

Ans. (b) Q and S

Q.12 Which of the following is most likely to have been a major achievement during the Gupta Empire?

(a) The construction of the Great Wall of India

(b) Advances in Mathematics and Astronomy

(c) The creation of the first Indian Empire

(d) The spread of Zoroastrianism

Ans. (b) Advances in Mathematics and Astronomy

Exp. During the Gupta empire, Aryabhatta and Brahmagupta made significant contributions in mathematics and astronomy. Aryabhatta introduced the concept of zero, the decimal system and explained solar and lunar eclipses.

Q.13 Complete the given analogy.

Aryabhata: Astronomer : : Sushruta: ?

(a) Physician (b) Astrologer

(c) Mathematician (d) Poet

Ans. (a) Physician

Q.14 Which of the following rulers was the last ruler of the Gupta Empire?

(a) Kumaragupta I (b) Samudragupta

(c) Chandragupta II (d) Vishnugupta

Ans. (d) Vishnugupta

Q.15 What is mentioned in the Junagarh/Girnar inscription during Skandagupta's reign?

(a) Construction of the Iron Pillar of Delhi

(b) Establishment of Nalanda University

(c) Repair of the Sudarshan Lake

(d) Defeat of the Shakas

Ans. (c) Repair of the Sudarshan Lake

TYPE - 2 1 Mark

Assertion-Reason Questions

Q.1 Read the two statements given below about Fa-hien and select the option that shows the correct relationship between (A) and (R).

Assertion (A) Fa-hien made careful unbiased observations about conditions during the Gupta period.

Reason (R) According to him, the Gupta Empire was prosperous and governed by enlightened principles.

(a) R contradicts A

(b) R is the reason for A

(c) A is true but R is false

(d) A and R are independent of each other

Ans. (b) R is the reason for A

Q.2 Read the two statements given below about the Gupta administration, and select the option that shows the correct relationship between (A) and (R).

Assertion (A) According to Fahien's accounts, during the Gupta period, professions such as agriculture, carpentry, spinning, weaving and goldsmithing were practiced.

Reason (R) Local kings and smaller chiefs ruled a large part of the Gupta empire.

(a) R contradicts A (b) R is the reason for A
(c) A is true but R is false
(d) A and R are independent of each other

Ans. (d) A and R are independent of each other

Q.3 Read the two statements given below about Fahien and select the option that shows the correct relationship between (A) and (R).

Assertion (A) Fa-hien mentioned that the Shudras were kept outside the town and had to make noise with a stick before entering to the town.

Reason (R) Fa-hien described that agriculture, carpentry, and goldsmithing were among the major professions in the Gupta empire.

(a) R contradicts A (b) R is the reason for A
(c) A is true but R is false
(d) A and R are independent of each other

Ans. (d) A and R are independent of each other

Q.4 Read the two statements given below about the Samudragupta, and select the option that shows the correct relationship between (A) and (R).

Assertion (A) Samudragupta performed Ashwamedha sacrifices after his military victories.

Reason (R) The Ashwamedha sacrifice was a religious ritual that symbolised the king's dominance over his territory.

(a) R is the reason for A (b) R contradicts A
(c) A is true but R is false
(d) A and R are independent of each other

Ans. (a) R is the reason for A

Q.5 Read the two statements given below about the culture during the Gupta Age, and select the option that shows the correct relationship between (A) and (R).

Assertion (A) Unlike the earlier phase in history, the Gupta temples were not made of perishable material.

Reason (R) The Gupta period marked the beginning of writing of important works like the Puranas.

(a) R contradicts A (b) R is the reason for A
(c) A is true but R is false
(d) A and R are independent of each other

Ans. (d) A and R are independent of each other

TYPE - 3 2 Marks

Very Short Answer Type Questions

Q.1 Who was the founder of Gupta Empire? What were the achievements of Samudragupta during his reign?

Ans. Sri gupta was the founder of the Gupta empire but Chandragupta I is considered the real founder of the Gupta empire.

Samudragupta also known as the 'Napoleon of India', he was a bold and great conqueror who expanded his empire from the Brahmaputra in the East to the Narmada in the South.

Q.2 Mention any two titles adopted by the Gupta rulers.

Ans. Two titles adopted by the Gupta rulers were

(i) **Maharajadhiraja** This title was adopted by Chandragupta I translates to 'King of Kings'. It was to indicate their supremacy over other regional kings and rulers in the empire.

(ii) **Shakraditya** This title was adopted by Kumaragupta I and it means son of Shakra. It refers to the Indian deity Indra (Shakra).

Q.3 Mention the administrative divisions of the Gupta empire and their respective officials.

Ans. The Gupta empire was divided into provinces, each ruled by a Governor. The provinces were further divided into smaller districts, managed by officers called Amatyas.

Villages were administered by local heads, called Gramins. The Central Government had officials like *Dandapashikas* for law and order, ensuring smooth governance.

Q.4 Explain the role of the Mahadandnayaka in Gupta administration?

Ans. The Mahadandnayaka in the Gupta administration was responsible for judicial functions. Though the supreme judicial power lay with the king, the Mahadandnayaka played a significant role in overseeing and executing the legal matters and administration of justice.

Q.5 What were the two new classes created by the Gupta Kings, and what were their roles?

Ans. The two new classes created by the Gupta Kings were

(i) **Sandhivigrahika** (Minister of War and Peace) responsible for handling matters related to diplomacy and military affairs.

(ii) **Kumaramatyas** (Officers of the Crown Prince) who assisted in governance and administration.

Q.6 Give two reasons why the Gupta period is considered as the golden age of Indian culture?

Ans. The two reasons why the Gupta period is considered the golden age of Indian culture are

(i) The Gupta period witnessed remarkable achievements in science, mathematics, literature, and art, including the works of Aryabhata in mathematics and astronomy.

(ii) It was a time of flourishing Sanskrit literature, with famous works like Kalidasa's 'Shakuntala', and the development of beautiful art and architecture.

Q.7 Imagine you are an archaeologist exploring the ruins of Nalanda University. What significant artifacts or structures would you expect to find that demonstrate its historical importance as a center of learning?

Ans. As an archaeologist exploring the ruins of Nalanda University, I would expect to find large, ancient buildings made of bricks and stones. There would be detailed carvings and sculptures, showing scenes from Buddhist teachings.

I might also find old manuscripts or inscriptions, describing the subjects taught, like science, medicine, and mathematics. The remains of the library, known as Dharma Gunj, would show it was a famous center for learning and knowledge.

Q.8 Name two main buildings of the Nalanda University library.

Ans. The two main buildings of the Nalanda University library were Ratnasagara (Sea of Jewels) and Ratnodadhi (Ocean of Jewel).

Q.9 State any two famous literary figures of the Gupta Age.

Ans. Two literary figures of the Gupta Age were

(i) **Kalidasa** He was one of the greatest Sanskrit playwrights and poets, known for his famous works like 'Shakuntala' and 'Meghaduta', which are considered masterpieces of Indian literature.

(ii) **Harisena** He was a court poet of Samudragupta and is known for his works, including the 'Prayag Prashasti', a famous inscription praising the achievements of Samudragupta.

Q.10 With reference to the dramas written by the poet, Kalidasa answer the following.

(i) Abhijnanashakuntalam (ii) Malavikagnimitram

Ans. (i) **Abhijnanashakuntalam** It was a love story between Shakuntala and the King Dushyanta.

(ii) **Malavikagnimitram** It tells the love story of Agnimitra and malvika.

TYPE - 4 3 Marks

Short Answer Type Questions

Q.1 Who was Fa-hien? What did he observed about India?

Ans. Fa-hien was a Chinese buddhist monk who visited India during the reign of Chandragupta II on a religious journey. He made careful and unbiased observations about the society and conditions at that time. According to Fa-hien

- Magadha was a prosperous region with large towns and a wealthy population.
- Pataliputra was a thriving city with many charitable institutions, including hospitals.
- Despite their wealth, people led simple lives and followed Buddhist principles.
- Vaishnavism, Shaivism, Buddhism, and Jainism were the major religions, and people coexisted peacefully.
- Hindu Gods and Goddesses were depicted on coins, sculptures, and paintings.
- The penal code was lenient, with most crimes were punished by fines and most rebellions were punished by cutting off one hand.

Q.2 Mention any three points that the inscriptions on the Allahabad Pillar tell us about Samudragupta's reign.

Ans. The inscriptions on the Allahabad Pillar provide following details of Samudragupta's reign.

(i) They highlight his military conquests, such as defeating nine rulers of Aryavarta, conquering regions like Assam, Bengal, Nepal, and parts of South India.

(ii) They also mention his diplomatic relations with foreign states, including the Shakas and Kushanas.

(iii) The inscriptions praise Samudragupta's patronage of arts and his reputation as a skilled poet and Vaishnavism follower.

Q.3 Explain the contributions of Varahamihira and Brahmagupta in the fields of mathematics and astronomy during the Gupta period.

Ans. The contribution of Varahamihira and Brahmagupta in the fields of mathematics and astronomy during the Gupta period were

- **Varahamihira** was an expert in astrology and astronomy, known for his work Pancha Siddhantika and Brihatsamhita. He contributed to weather predictions and planetary movements.

- **Brahmagupta**, another brilliant mathematician, described the 'Law of Gravitation' centuries before Newton and made advancements in algebra. Varahamihira and Brahmagupta shaped India's scientific achievements during the Gupta period.

Q.4 Discuss the economic policies of the Gupta Empire, especially with respect to trade, taxation and the management of land.

Ans. The Gupta Empire had a strong economy supported by trade, taxation and efficient land management as follows

- **Trade** They traded goods like silk, spices, and precious metals with South-East Asia, the Roman Empire, and China, using ports on the Arabian Sea.
- **Taxation** Taxes were collected on land, goods and trade, ensuring steady revenue.
- **Land Management** Land was classified and taxed based on fertility, and irrigation systems like Araghatta improved agriculture. The state also gave tax-free land to Brahmins and religious institutions, promoting learning and culture.

Q.5 The Gupta empire was known for its advancements in art, literature, and science. Justify the statement by mentioning any three points.

Ans. The Gupta empire is often called the 'Golden Age' due to its advancements in various fields, such as art, literature and science. This can be justified as

- Gupta artists created beautiful sculptures and carvings, especially in temples.
- Literature flourished, with famous works like Kalidasa's plays and the writing of the Puranas.
- The Guptas made significant progress, including the invention of the number zero and advances in astronomy, medicine, and mathematics.

Q.6 List the inscriptions associated with Kumaragupta I and what does the oldest record of his reign reveal?

Ans. The inscriptions associated with Kumaragupta I include the Karandanda inscription, Mandsor inscription, Bilsad inscription and Damodar Copper Plate inscription.

Among these, the Bilsad inscription is the oldest record of his reign. These inscriptions provide valuable insights into his rule, achievements and administration. They serve as historical evidence of his governance and contributions, such as the establishment of Nalanda University. Additionally, these records highlight the challenges he faced, including the Huns invasions that marked the later years of his reign and contributed to the empire's instability.

TYPE - 5   4 Marks

Long Answer Type Questions

Q.1 The reign of Chandragupta II saw significant territorial expansion and political alliances. How did Chandragupta II's matrimonial alliances and military conquests shaped the Gupta empire?

Ans. Chandragupta II expanded the Gupta empire through strategic matrimonial alliances and military conquests. His marriage to the daughter of the powerful Shaka ruler helped him gain control over Western India, securing key trade routes.

Chandragupta II's military conquests significantly shaped the Gupta empire by expanding its territories and ensuring security. His victory over the Shakas, who controlled Western India, brought crucial trade routes under Gupta control, boosting the empire's economy. The success of these conquests not only increased the empire's size but also established its dominance over rival states.

Q.2 Discuss the role and significance of Nalanda University during the Gupta period as a center of learning.

Ans. Nalanda University, established during the Gupta period, was one of the most important centers of learning in ancient India. It attracted scholars from different parts of the world, including China, Greece, and Persia. The university offered a wide range of subjects such as, science, medicine, astronomy, and logic. Its library, known as Dharma Gunj, was a renowned storehouse of knowledge.

Scholars like Xuanzang from China visited Nalanda to study. The teachings at Nalanda helped spread Indian knowledge across Asia. Buddhism influenced the development of education in many countries. The university played a significant role in preserving ancient texts and promoting intellectual exchange.

Q.3 How was land ownership structured under the Gupta empire, and what rights did the king hold over it?

Ans. Under the Gupta Empire, all land in the kingdom was considered the property of the king.

The king had the supreme authority over the land and could use it as he wished in the following ways

- He had the sole right to grant land to individuals or institutions, often as rewards or donations.
- The king could also impose, recover, or exempt taxes on the land.
- Additionally, the construction of infrastructure, such as roads and canals, was managed under the king's authority.

- This system reflected the centralised power of the king, where his control over land ensured political stability and economic strength for the empire.

Q.4 Mention any four contributions of Aryabhatta's in the field of science.

Ans. The four contributions of Aryabhatta's in the field of science were

(i) He proposed that the Earth revolves around the Sun.

(ii) He discovered the formula for calculating the area of a triangle.

(iii) He accurately calculated the value of pi (π) as 3.14159 and is credited with the development of trigonometry.

(iv) In his work 'Surya Siddhanta', he explained the causes of solar and lunar eclipses.

(v) He was familiar with the decimal system and the concept of zero.

Q.5 Explain, how did literature flourished during the Gupta period?

Ans. The Gupta period is called the "Golden Age of Literature" due to the growth of Sanskrit literature. Writers like Kalidasa created timeless works, including plays like Abhijnanashakuntalam and poems like Meghaduta, which beautifully describe nature, emotions, and culture.

Other scholars like Amarasimha wrote important texts like Amarakosha, a famous Sanskrit dictionary. Literature covered diverse topics like religion, science, and philosophy, reflecting the knowledge and creativity of the time.

Buddhist and Jain texts were also written, promoting different ideas. The Gupta rulers supported scholars and encouraged writing, with many works written in Sanskrit, the official language of the empire. This patronage helped literature flourish and made the Gupta period a landmark in India's cultural history.

TYPE - 6 — 10 Marks

Structured Questions

Q.1 With reference to the Gupta empire, answer the following questions.

(i) The Gupta period is marked by the establishment of great learning centers like Nalanda University. What role did Nalanda University play in promoting education and intellectual growth during the Gupta period? (3)

(ii) What insights do Fa-hien's accounts provide about the Gupta period's socio-political and religious conditions? (3)

(iii) Discuss the role and responsibilities of the different officials in the Gupta administration, such as the minister, governors, and local officers. How did their roles contribute to the functioning of the empire? (4)

Ans. (i) For answer, refere Q.2 of Long Answer Type Questions.

(ii) Fa-hien, a Chinese traveller, provides valuable insights into the Gupta period through his accounts. He describes a peaceful and prosperous society under Gupta rule, where people lived with security and enjoyed economic stability.

He also highlights the role of religion, particularly Buddhism, which flourished during this time. Fa-hien mentions the support given to Buddhist monasteries and the peaceful coexistence of various religious communities.

His accounts reflect the high moral standards of the time, with a strong focus on ethics, education, and culture, giving us a glimpse of the socio-political and religious harmony in the Gupta empire.

(iii) In the Gupta empire, the administration was divided into different levels, each with specific responsibilities as follows

- King was the supreme ruler, overseeing the entire empire.
- Minister assisted the king in making decisions and advising on important matters.
- Governors were in charge of provinces or regions, ensuring law and order, collecting taxes, and managing resources.
- Local officers looked after smaller areas, dealing with daily administration and helping with public works and local issues.

These officials helped maintain stability by ensuring proper governance, promoting trade, and protecting the empire from external threats. Their cooperation and clear roles contributed to the smooth functioning and growth of the Gupta empire, making it one of the most prosperous in Indian history.

Q.2 With reference to the administrative system of the Guptas, answer the following questions.

(i) The King during the Gupta Age enjoyed many powers, often compared to gods for his role as protector of the people. Explain the position and powers of the King during the Gupta Age. (4)

(ii) "Village administration was essential for the functioning of daily affairs". Describe briefly the administration of villages during the Gupta period. **(3)**

(iii) According to the Allahabad Pillar inscription, which regions and kingdoms did Samudragupta conquer or bring under his control? **(3)**

Ans. (i) The position and powers of the King during the Gupta Age were

- During the Gupta Age, the king was considered almost divine, often compared to gods like Vishnu, Indra, and Yama for his role as the protector and guardian of the people.
- The king was the head of the government and had authority over political, administrative, military, and judicial matters.
- He acted as the commander-in-chief of the army and controlled all military affairs.
- The king appointed governors and important civil and military officers, all of whom worked under his guidance.
- As the ultimate authority, the king could levy taxes, construct infrastructure like dams, provide justice, and manage unclaimed property.
- All land in the empire was considered the king's property, showing his absolute control over the empire's resources.

(ii) In the Gupta period, the administration of villages was overseen by the village headman. Small towns or villages, known as vithis, were governed with the involvement of local leaders and influential figures. These individuals played a crucial role in decision-making, as no land transactions or significant matters could take place without their approval. This system ensured that village administration was effectively managed at the local level during the Gupta age.

(iii) According to the Allahabad Pillar inscription, Samudragupta conquered several regions and kingdoms during his reign, as follows

- He defeated the 'Nine rulers of Aryavarta' and added their kingdoms to his empire.
- He also conquered neighbouring states like Assam, Coastal Bengal, Nepal, and several Gana Sanghas (groups of kings) in the North-West.
- These kingdoms paid tribute and obeyed his commands. Additionally, Samudragupta's expedition to South India was successful, as twelve rulers from the South surrendered to him after defeat.
- The inscription also mentions his relations with Ceylon and South-East Asian colonies.

Q.3 With reference to the picture given below, answer the following.

(i) Identify the temple given in the picture. Where is it located, and which deity does it honor? **(3)**

(ii) Mention the architectural features of this temple. **(3)**

(iii) Explain the historical and cultural importance of the Dashavatara Temple, built in the early 6th century, and how its features, such as the depictions of the ten incarnations of Vishnu and scenes from the Ramayana, reflect the religious beliefs of the time. **(4)**

Ans. (i) The given temple is Dashavatara Temple (also called Vishnu temple). It is located in Deogarh. This temple is dedicated to Lord Vishnu, the God of preservation.

(ii) The Dashavatara Temple is known for its distinctive architectural features

- It was constructed using stone and bricks, standing on a platform that is 1.5 meters high.
- The interior of temple has four Verandahs.
- An important feature of this temple is the sculpture of Lord Vishnu in which he is shown asleep on the coil of the giant Serpent, Sheshnaga.

(iii) The Dashavatara Temple, built in the early 6th century, holds great historical and cultural importance as it reflects the religious beliefs of that time.

The temple is dedicated to Lord Vishnu, and its walls display the ten incarnations (Dashavatara) of Vishnu, showing his various forms, such as a fish, tortoise, and boar. This highlights the belief in Vishnu's role as the protector and preserver of the universe.

The temple also depicts scenes from the Ramayana and Lord Krishna's life, emphasising the importance of these Hindu epics. The temple's architecture, with its Shikhara (tower) and intricate sculptures, represents the growing influence of Hinduism and its symbolism in the 6th century in India.

7

THE CHOLAS

- The Cholas became powerful in the 9th-century and established an empire covering most of South India.
- They successfully united South India under their rule and through their naval strength, they extended their influence in the South-East Asian countries.
- They dominated the political affairs of Sri Lanka for over two centuries through repeated invasions. The Cholas maintained trade relations with the Arabs in the West and the Chinese Empire in the East.
- By the end of the 9th-century, the Cholas defeated the Pallavas of Kanchi and weakened the Pandyans, gaining control over the Tamil region (Tondamandalam).

Sources of Chola Dynasty

1. Inscriptions

- The inscriptions of the Cholas are in the form of Copper-plate grants, stone inscriptions inscribed on the walls and pillars of the temples.
- Thiruvananthapuram inscriptions give information about the reign of Rajendra III.
- The Uttaramerur inscriptions give information about the village administration, taxation and land revenue.
- The copper-plate grants known as Anbil plates, the Kanyakumari stone inscription, Karandi plates and Thiruvalangadu copper plates gives useful information about the Chola dynasty. These plates are written in Sanskrit and Tamil.

Copper Plate Inscription

- The Tanjore Peruvudaiyar temple inscriptions give information about the existence of Shaivism.
- The inscriptions of contemporary rulers like Cheras, Pandyas, Rashtrakutas and Gangas give information about the Cholas' records of land grants villages, plots of farmland or other privileges given by the kings to private individual or institutions.
- Chola inscriptions displayed a variation in language and script depending on the time period and location where the records were made. Sanskrit inscriptions used the Grantha script, which was closely related to Tamil in its development.

2. The Brihadeshwara Temple

- The Brihadeshwara temple is a famous example of Chola architecture, built at Thanjavur (Tanjore). It is also called the Rajarajeshwara temple after the name of king Rajaraja I who built it in honour of Lord Shiva.
- This temple is a prime example of Dravidian style of architecture and has been declared as World Heritage Site by UNESCO.

The Brihadeshwara Temple

- The gateway of the temple is called 'gopuram'.
- The main shrine is known as 'garbhagriha' where the images of gods and goddesses were kept. Those images were made either of stone or bronze.
- The main structure of the temple is vimana (or tower) which rises to a height of 66 metres.
- The temple has a massive dome made from a single stone block, which is 7.6 meters high and weighs about 80 tons.
- The inner walls of the temple have extensive paintings and sculpture.
- The temple has a portrait of Rajaraja Chola bowing down to Lord Nataraja.
- Inscriptions in the temple point towards Rajaraja as the chief architect of the temple.
- The temple features carvings of dancers displaying 81 out of the 108 karanas (synchronised hand and foot movements) of Bharatanatyam.
- It is one of the few temples that have Ashta-dikpaalakas (Guardians of the eight directions) idols.

Rulers of the Chola Dynasty

- The early Cholas ruled during the Sangam period. Karikala was the greatest king among the early Chola kings.

Vijayalaya Chola (848–891 AD)

- He was the founder of the later Chola Empire. He took the title Parakesarivarman, and built the Solesvara Temple at Narttamalai.

Aditya I (870–907 AD)

- He was the son of Vijayalaya. He defeated the Pallavas and Western Gangas, built 108 Shiva temples and was known as Kodandarama.

Parantaka Chola I (907–950 AD)

- He expanded the Chola empire. He conquered Madurai and Sri Lanka and took the title Maduraiyum Elamum Konda Parakesarivarman.

Rajaraja Chola I (985–1014 AD)

- He was the son of Parantaka II and Vanavan Mahadevi. He was the greatest Chola ruler.
- He defeated the Chera Army at Thiruvananthapuram. He also defeated Bhaskar Ravi, the Raja of Kollam.
- He defeated Mahinda V, the King of Ceylon and occupied Anuradhapuram and the Northern part of Ceylon.
- He got the title Mummudi Cholan after the conquest of three Southern kingdoms, Cheras, Pandyas and Ceylon.
- He introduced land survey system and encouraged local self-government throughout his empire.

Rajendra Chola I (1012–1044 AD)

- He was a great administrator and warrior. He succeeded by his father Rajendra I.
- He shifted his capital from Tanjore to Gangaikonda-Cholapuram in the present state of Tamil Nadu.
- He captured the whole of Ceylon and consolidated the Chola domination over Ceylon.
- He sent a fleet (ship) across Bay of Bengal and conquered Pegu (in Burma) as well as Andaman and Nicobar Islands.
- Rajendra I defeated the Bengal king Mahipala I and brought water from Ganges to Tanjore.
- During his rule, Rajendra I constructed many Shiva and Vishnu temples, magnificent palaces at his new capital Gangaikonda-Cholapuram.
- His son Rajadhiraja Chola (1044–1054 AD) performed the Ashvamedha sacrifice. He conquered Lanka, Vengi, and Kalinga.

Rajendra Chola II (1054–1063 AD)

- He played a key role in the Battle of Koppam against the Chalukyas.

Kulothunga Chola I (1070–1122 AD)

- He got the title Kulottunga, literally meaning the exalter of his race.
- He established Chola overlordship over the Sri Vijaya province Kedah in Malaysia.
- After Kulothunga Chola I, the Chola rulers weakened. Vikrama Chola (1118–1135 AD) and Kulothunga Chola II (1133–1150 AD) saw brief stability, but Rajaraja Chola II (1146–1173 AD), Rajadhiraja Chola II (1166–1178 AD) and Kulothunga Chola III (1178–1218 AD) faced decline.

Rajendra Chola III (1246–1279 AD)

- He was the last ruler of this dynasty.
- He was defeated by Pandya King Jatavarman Sundarapandya II.

The Chola Administration

General Administration

- The King was the head of the administration. The kings and queens were seen as representatives of God, and their idols were placed in temples.
- The Chola kingship was hereditary, following the principle of primogeniture, where the eldest son became the successor. The apparent heir to the throne was called the Yuvaraja.
- The Cholas had three major administrative divisions called – 'Central government', 'Provincial government' and 'Local government'.

1. Central Government

- The king was the most important person in the Chola administration.
- Council of Ministers and officials took active part in running the administration of Central government.
- The higher officials were called Peruntaram and the lower officials were called Siruntaram.
- The Central government looked after the matters like external defence, internal peace and order cultural progress and promotion of general prosperity of the empire.

2. Provincial Government

- The Chola empire was divided into provinces or mandalams. The head of the province was called Viceroy.
- Each mandalam was divided into number of Kottams or Valanadus. Each Kottam was sub-divided into Nadu.
- Each Nadu was further divided into Urs (villages) which form part of the last unit of the administration.
- Princes of the royal family were appointed Governors of provinces.

3. Local Government

- There were general assemblies in the Chola Empire which included most of the local residents. They were of three categories
  - (i) **Ur** It was the assembly of local members. It consisted of the tax paying residents of an ordinary village.
  - (ii) **Sabha** It was restricted to the Brahmin assembly of the villages where all the land belonged to the Brahmins.
  - (iii) **Nagaram** It was an assembly of merchants. It was found more commonly where traders and merchants were in a dominant position.
- The lands donated to temples were known as the devadaya or devadana.
- The temple was also a centre for education. The priests of the temple were the local teachers as there were no separate schools.

- The schools were housed in the temple courtyard. The students learnt their lessons in two languages Sanskrit and Tamil.

Military Administration

- The Chola army consisted of elephant, cavalry and infantry.
- The army of Cholas had three organs – *Nayak, Senapati* and *Mahadandnayak.*
- Personal bodyguards called *Vilaikkaras* were kept by most of the Kings.
- Cantonments called *Kadagam* were established for the soldiers.
- The cholas had a strong navy through which they controlled the Malabar and Coromandel Coast and the entire Bay of Bengal.

The Revenue

- The taxes on land, the produce of the land, and tax on trade were the main sources of revenue for the Chola kingdom.
- Generally, 1/6th of the land yield was collected as tax.
- Professional tax and house tax were also collected.
- Taxes on mines, ports, forests and salt pans were collected.
- The officials collected taxes on land from village councils.
- A portion of the revenue was reserved for the king. The rest of the revenue was used on public works like building roads, tanks, paying the salary of navy and army, etc.

The Chola Art

- The art of making stone and metal images had made rapid progress under the Chola rulers.
- The bronze image of Lord Shiva as 'Nataraja' – Lord of Dance, is an excellent work of art.
- The image of Nataraja has been described as the 'cultural epitome' of the Chola period.

The Nataraja

EXAM ORIENTED QUESTIONS

TYPE - 1 — 1 Mark

Multiple Choice Questions

Q.1 Which of the following is most likely to be found in the inscriptions of the Chola period?

(a) Descriptions of the Chola kings' religious activities.
(b) Descriptions of the Chola military victories in South-East Asia.
(c) Paintings of medieval warfare tactics.
(d) Records of foreign kings visiting the Chola empire.

Ans. (b) Descriptions of the Chola military victories in South-East Asia.

Exp. Chola inscriptions mainly describe military victories, especially in South-East Asia, rather than paintings or records of foreign kings. They highlight the Chola empire's expansion and influence.

Q.2 The Uttaramerur inscriptions provide valuable insights into the Kudavolai system, which was a unique method of electing village representatives during the Chola period. These inscriptions also give detail information on taxation and land revenue policies.

What aspect of Chola administration is highlighted in the Uttaramerur inscriptions?

(a) Military conquests
(b) Village administration
(c) Maritime trade
(d) Temple architecture

Ans. (b) Village administration

Q.3 Identify the odd one out in context to the Brihadeshwara temple.

(a) It is also called the Rajarajeshwara temple
(b) The gateway of the temple was called 'gopuram'.
(c) The main structure of the temple is vimana.
(d) The temple is 10.1 meters high

Ans. (d) The temple is 10.1 meters high

Exp. The Brihadeshwara temple is much taller, with its vimana (main tower) reaching about 66 meters.

Q.4 Identify the statements regarding the Cholas and choose the correct option.

P : Rajaraja Chola I built the Brihadeshwara temple at Thanjavur.
Q : The Chola dynasty expanded into South-East Asia, including Indonesia and Malaysia.
R : The Cholas were known for promoting Buddhism and its spread across the Indian subcontinent.
S : The Cholas built many Buddhist stupas during their rule.

(a) P and Q
(b) Q and S
(c) P and R
(d) R and S

Ans. (a) P and Q

Q.5 Identify the odd one out in context to the Chola rulers.

(a) Rajendra I
(b) Rajaraja I
(c) Vijayalaya Chola
(d) Ranjit Singh

Ans. (d) Ranjit Singh

Q.6 Look at the picture given below of Nataraja (Lord Shiva), and answer the following question.

What does this image represent in terms of artistic achievement during the Chola period?

(a) Stone carving
(b) Bronze casting and sculpture
(c) Iron work
(d) Calligraphy

Ans. (b) Bronze casting and sculpture

Exp. The image represents bronze casting and sculpture, a great artistic achievement of the Chola period. Chola artisans created beautiful bronze statues of gods and kings using the lost-wax technique, showing fine details and elegance.

Q.7 Read the description and identify the ruler.

"This ruler founded the Chola dynasty after defeating the Pandya rulers. He established the Chola capital at Thanjavur and began the dynasty's reign of power in Southern India".

(a) Vijayalaya Chola
(b) Rajaraja Chola I
(c) Rajendra Chola I
(d) Kulothunga Chola I

Ans. (a) Vijayalaya Chola

Q.8 Rajaraja Chola I, one of the greatest rulers of the Chola dynasty, undertook the construction of the Brihadeshwara temple at Thanjavur, which became a major religious and cultural center.

Which of the following is not likely to have been a contribution of Rajaraja Chola I during his reign?

(a) He defeated the Chera Army at Thiruvananthapuram.
(b) He expanded the Chola Empire's territory to include parts of the Malayan Peninsula.
(c) He led military campaigns in the Northern regions of India.
(d) He promoted Tamil literature and culture.

Ans. (c) He led military campaigns in the Northern regions of India.

Q.9 Which of the following statements is not true about Rajaraja I?

(a) He conquered Sri Lanka and made Polonnaruva his capital.
(b) He introduced land surveys and encouraged local self-government.
(c) He was a great patron of Buddhism.
(d) He expanded the Chola empire through successful military campaigns.

Ans. (c) He was a great patron of Buddhism.

Exp. Rajaraja I was a strong supporter of Hinduism, especially Shaivism. He built the famous Brihadeshwara temple. While he respected other religions, he mainly promoted Hindu temples and traditions.

Q.10 Read the description and identify the person

He defeated the Bengal king Mahipala I and brought water from Ganges to Tanjore.

(a) Rajaraja I (b) Rajendra I
(c) Parantaka I (d) Parantaka II

Ans. (b) Rajendra I

Q.11 During the reign of Rajendra Chola I, the Chola empire expanded its control over Ceylon, Bengal, and parts of South-East Asia. His administration ensured efficient governance and he even brought water from the Ganges to Tanjore to mark his victory over Bengal. He shifted the capital to Gangaikonda-Cholapuram, emphasising his authority.

Which feature of Rajendra Chola I's rule is highlighted in the above case?

(a) Military expansion (b) Religious tolerance
(c) Maritime trade (d) Local self-governance

Ans. (a) Military expansion

Q.12 Rajendra Chola adopted the title Gangaikonda to commemorate which victory?

(a) Odisha (b) Bengal
(c) Sri Lanka (d) Mysore

Ans. (b) Bengal

Q.13 Which Chola king played a key role in the Battle of Koppam against the Chalukyas?

(a) Rajaraja Chola I (b) Rajendra Chola I
(c) Rajendra Chola II (d) Kulothunga Chola I

Ans. (c) Rajendra Chola II

Q.14 Complete the given analogy:

Higher officials: Peruntaram:: Lower officials :?

(a) Senapati (b) Nayak
(c) Viceroy (d) Siruntaram

Ans. (d) Siruntaram

Q.15 Under the Cholas' rule, land-revenue was collected through the

(a) Senapati
(b) Village Council (Assembly)
(c) Government official
(d) All of the above

Ans. (b) Village Council (Assembly)

Exp. Under the Cholas, the Village Council (Assembly) managed land revenue collection. They kept records, decided taxes, and ensured fair collection, making local governance strong and efficient.

Q.16 Which of the following did not contribute to the revenue of the Chola Empire?

(a) Overseas trade (b) Taxes on land
(c) Trade-tax (d) Taxes on produce

Ans. (a) Overseas trade

Q.17 Which of the following is not correct about Chola temples?

(a) They were centers for religious worship and spiritual activities
(b) They served as centers for cultural activities like dance and music
(c) They were also used as military fortresses.
(d) They played a role in administration and local governance.

Ans. (c) They were also used as military fortresses.

Exp. Chola temples were not used as military fortresses. Instead, they were important centers for religion, culture, and administration, where people worshipped, learned music and dance, and managed local governance.

TYPE - 2 1 Mark

Assertion-Reason Questions

Q.1 Read the two statements given below about Brihadeshwara temple and select the option that shows the correct relationship between (A) and (R).

Assertion (A) The Brihadeshwara temple is the first example of having a portrait of a ruler, i.e., Rajaraja Chola.

Reason (R) It has been declared as a World Heritage site by UNESCO.

(a) R contradicts A
(b) R is the reason for A
(c) A is true but R is false
(d) A and R are independent of each other

Ans. (d) A and R are independent of each other

Q.2 Read the two statements given below about Rajaraja I and select the option that shows the correct relationship between (A) and (R).

Assertion (A) Chola ruler, Rajaraja I took out a naval expedition and attacked both Sri Lanka and Maldives.

Reason (R) Rajaraja I established Chola rule during the middle of 7th century.

(a) R contradicts A
(b) R is the reason for A
(c) A is true but R is false
(d) A and R are independent of each other

Ans. (c) A is true but R is false

Q.3 Read the two statements given below about Chola rulers and select the option that shows the correct relationship between (A) and (R).

Assertion (A) The Chola rulers promoted local self-government in villages.

Reason (R) The Cholas believed in a centralised form of administration with no role for local governance.

(a) R contradicts A
(b) R is the reason for A
(c) A is true but R is false
(d) A and R are independent of each other

Ans. (c) A is true but R is false

Q.4 Read the two statements given below about Rajendra Chola and select the option that shows the correct relationship between (A) and (R).

Assertion (A) On the complaint of Indian merchants, Rajendra Chola sent out a huge army and defeated Shrivijaya, the ruler of present day Indonesia.

Reason (R) There were problems for Indian merchants who had been trading with various parts of South-East Asia and Southern China.

(a) R contradicts A
(b) R is the reason for A
(c) A is true but R is false
(d) A and R are independent of each other

Ans. (b) R is the reason for A

Q.5 Read the two statements given below about temples in the Chola Dynasty, and select the option that shows the correct relationship between (A) and (R).

Assertion (A) The temples were centers of education in the Chola kingdom.

Reason (R) The students learnt their lessons in two languages, i.e., Hindi and Sanskrit.

(a) R contradicts A
(b) R is the reason for A
(c) A is true but R is false
(d) A and R are independent of each other

Ans. (c) A is true but R is false

TYPE - 3 2 Marks

Very Short Answer Type Questions

Q.1 Name any two important sources of information about the Cholas.

Ans. Two important sources of information about the Cholas are

(i) Thiruvananthapuram inscriptions
(ii) Uttaramerur inscriptions

Q.2 State two types of sculptures found in the Brihadeshwara temple.

Ans. Two types of sculptures found in the Brihadeshwara temple are

(i) **Bronze Sculptures** Including depictions of Lord Shiva and other deities.

(ii) **Stone Sculptures** Representing various gods, goddesses, and dancers.

Q.3 (i) Who was the founder of the Chola dynasty?

(ii) In which region the Chola dynasty was established?

Ans. (i) Vijayala was the founder of Chola dynasty.

(ii) The Chola dynasty was established in the Tamil region.

Q.4 Name any two great rulers of the Chola dynasty.

Ans. Two great rulers of the Chola dynasty were

(i) Rajaraja I (ii) Rajendra Chola I

Q.5 **Who was the son of Parantaka II and which title did he earn after conquering the three Southern kingdoms?**

Ans. The son of Parantaka II was Rajaraja Chola I and he earned the title Mummudi Cholan after conquering the three Southern kingdoms—Chera, Pandya and Ceylon.

Q.6 **Mention any two achievements of Rajendra Chola I.**

Ans. Two achievements of Rajendra Chola were

(i) He conquered the entire Island of Sri Lanka and Sri Lanka remained under Chola control for the next 50 years.

(ii) His army defeated Mahipala I, the king of Bengal, and he built a new capital called Gangaikonda- cholapuram.

Q.7 **The later Chola rulers struggled to maintain control over their empire. Give two reasons for their weakening power.**

Ans. The later Chola rulers struggled to maintain control over their empire due to

(i) **External Invasions** Continuous attacks from the Pandyas and Hoysalas weakened Chola dominance, leading to territorial losses.

(ii) **Internal Conflicts and Weak Administration** Ineffective leadership, succession disputes and administrative decline further destabilised the empire, accelerating its downfall.

Q.8 **Explain the role of local assemblies in the Chola administration.**

Ans. Local assemblies like the Ur, Sabha, and Nagaram were responsible for managing village affairs, regulating taxes, water supply, and running educational institutions, ensuring efficient local governance.

Q.9 **Imagine you are a foreign merchant visiting the Chola Empire to trade goods during the reign of Rajendra Chola I. What two features of the Chola Empire's economy would attract you as a merchant?**

Ans. I would be attracted firstly by the thriving agricultural economy, which ensured a steady supply of goods, and secondly the strategic position of the Cholas' ports for maritime trade, which provided easy access to trade routes across South-East Asia, facilitating profitable exchanges of goods.

Q.10 **What was the role of the 'Sabha' in the Chola administration, and how did the village assemblies contribute to local governance?**

Ans. The 'Sabha' was a special assembly of Brahmins in Chola villages, responsible for managing land and local affairs. Village assemblies, like the 'Ur' and 'Nagaram', helped in collecting taxes, managing water supply, and running schools and temples, ensuring smooth local governance and community welfare.

Q.11 **Describe two main features of the Chola military administration.**

Ans. Two main features of the Chola military administration were

(i) **Organised Army** The Chola army was divided into three parts-cavalry, infantry, and elephants, which helped them in land and sea battles.

(ii) **Powerful Navy** The Chola navy controlled coastal regions and trade routes, extending their power in Southeast Asia.

TYPE - 4 — 3 Marks

Short Answer Type Questions

Q.1 **Give any three reasons why Rajaraja I undertook a naval expedition against Ceylon and Maldives?**

Ans. The three reasons why Rajaraja I undertook a naval expedition against Ceylon and Maldives include

(i) Rajaraja aimed to extend the Chola empire's power and influence over neighbouring regions, especially Sri Lanka and the Maldives, which were strategically important for controlling maritime trade routes in the Indian Ocean.

(ii) He sought to control the trade routes in the Indian Ocean.

(iii) He wanted to defeat the local rulers of Ceylon and the Maldives who were resisting the Chola authority, asserting the Cholas' supremacy in the region.

Q.2 **"Rajaraja I and Rajendra I strengthened the Chola naval power." Justify this by mentioning any three points.**

Ans. Rajaraja I and Rajendra I strengthened the Chola naval power in the following ways

(i) **Building a strong navy** They expanded the Chola fleet, enabling control over the Bay of Bengal.

(ii) **Conquering overseas territories** They controlled regions like Sri Lanka and South-East Asia, securing trade routes.

(iii) **Protecting trade** Their navy helped protect important sea trade and merchant routes.

Q.3 Mention any three reasons that made the Chola administration strong and effective.

Ans. The three reasons that made the Chola administration strong and effective were

(i) The King was holding all the power and authority at the center of the administration.

(ii) The King regularly toured the empire to ensure the administration was running smoothly.

(iii) The Cholas were skilled administrators. Villages were self-governed, with no direct government officials. Instead, they had three types of local assemblies – Ur, the Sabha, and the Nagaram.

TYPE - 5 4 Marks

Long Answer Type Questions

Q.1 Mention four significant features of inscriptions providing information about the Cholas.

Ans. Four significant features of inscriptions providing information about the Cholas includes

(i) These inscriptions tell us about the Chola administration. For example, the Uttaramerur inscription gives information on the village administration, taxation and land revenue.

(ii) Some inscriptions contain royal orders regarding taxation and land revenue, decisions made by village assemblies, and judgements passed on individuals guilty of crimes such as theft and murder.

(iii) The inscriptions of contemporary rulers like Cheras, Pandyas, Rashtrakutas and Gangas give information about the Cholas' records of land grants villages, plots of farmland or other privileges given by the kings to private individual or institutions.

(iv) The Tanjore Peruvudaiyar temple inscriptions give information about the existence of Shaivism.

Q.2 Explain the Chola administrative system at the central, provincial, and local levels, and describe how it contributed to the efficient governance of the empire.

Ans. The Chola Empire had a highly structured administrative system with three main levels: central, provincial and local.

- At the central level, the king was the head of the government, supported by a council of ministers.
- Provinces, called mandalams, were governed by viceroys, and were further divided into Kottams, Nadus, and villages.
- Local governance was organised through assemblies like the Ur (ordinary villages), Sabha (Brahmin villages), and Nagaram (trade centers), where local residents or merchants managed taxes, water supplies, and charity institutions.

This system ensured effective management, encouraged local participation, and helped maintain peace and stability throughout the empire by distributing power and responsibilities.

Q.3 Describe the military achievements of Rajendra I and how his conquests impacted the Chola Empire's influence in South-East Asia.

Ans. Rajendra I continued the expansionist policies of his father, Rajaraja I, and became renowned for his military powers. He conquered the entire island of Ceylon, consolidating Chola control over the region.

Rajendra I also expanded Chola influence beyond India by sending a powerful navy across the Bay of Bengal to conquer territories in South-East Asia. His conquest of Pegu (Burma), the Andaman and Nicobar Islands, and the Malaya region marked the Cholas as a dominant naval power. His victory over the Srivijaya king in South-East Asia secured Indian trade routes and established the Chola Empire as a major maritime and cultural power in the region.

Q.4 The Chola Empire reached its peak under rulers like Rajaraja Chola I and Rajendra Chola I but declined after the reign of Kulothunga Chola I. Analyse this statement by stating any four factors that contributed to the decline of the Chola dynasty.

Ans. The Chola Empire flourished under Rajaraja Chola I and Rajendra Chola I due to their military conquests, administrative efficiency, and economic prosperity. However, after the reign of Kulothunga Chola I, the empire gradually declined due to several factors

1. **Weak Successors** Later Chola rulers lacked the military and administrative capabilities of their predecessors, leading to internal instability.

2. **Pandya and Hoysala Threats** The rising power of the Pandyas and Hoysalas weakened Chola dominance, leading to territorial losses.

3. **Declining Naval Power** The once-powerful Chola navy lost its influence, affecting overseas trade and control over South-East Asian regions.

4. **Internal Revolts** Frequent rebellions by feudatories and local chieftains eroded Chola authority, making governance difficult.

TYPE - 6 (10 Marks)

Structured Questions

Q.1 The inscriptions of the Cholas are in the form of copper plate grants, stone inscriptions and inscriptions inscribed on the walls of the temples.

With reference to the Chola inscription, answer the following questions.

(i) What information about the Chola dynasty can we get from these inscriptions? **(3)**

(ii) Discuss the role of inscriptions in understanding the political, social, and cultural aspects of the Chola dynasty. **(3)**

(iii) Mention the inscription that gives us information about the village administration. Explain briefly the various forms of Chola inscriptions. **(4)**

Ans. (i) For answer, refer Q.1 of Long Answer Type Questions.

(ii) Inscriptions were a key source of information about the Chola dynasty, serving as records of royal orders, land grants, and cultural activities. Rajaraja I's use of inscriptions to document his reign was a significant development. They provide insights into the political and administrative structure, such as the Kudavolai system (village administration) and taxation methods.

The inscriptions in temples like the Brihadeshwara temple and the Tanjore Peruvudaiyar temple highlight the prominence of Shaivism and local self-government. Furthermore, they highlight the culture, art, and crafts of that time, including the use of Sanskrit and Tamil in records and the evolving script used in the inscriptions.

(iii) The Uttaramerur inscriptions give information about the Kudavolai system (village administration), taxation and land revenue.

The various forms of Chola inscriptions are as follows

- **Copper-plate grants** These were metal plates, usually copper, used to record royal decrees, land grants, and other important matters.
- **Stone inscriptions** Carved into stone, these inscriptions were used for public records, proclamations, and religious texts.
- **Inscriptions inscribed on the walls** These inscriptions were often found on the walls of temples or other significant structures, detailing royal orders and religious offerings.
- **Inscriptions on pillars of the temple** These were engraved on temple pillars, often commemorating victories, donations, and religious events.

Q.2 With reference to the given picture, answer the following questions.

(i) Identify the temple given in the picture. Who built this temple? Where is it located? **(3)**

(ii) To which deity is the temple dedicated? Mention two special features of this temple? **(3)**

(iii) This temple has several architectural features like gopuram, garbhagriha, mandapa and vimana. Explain these features. **(4)**

Ans. (i) The given temple is Brihadeshwara temple, also known as Rajarajeshwara temple.

The Chola King, Rajaraja I built this temple.

It is located at Thanjavur in Tamil Nadu.

(ii) The temple is dedicated to 'Lord Shiva'.

Two special features of this temple are

(a) The main structure of the temple is Vimana (or tower) which rises to a height of 66 metres.

(b) It has a huge 'Shiva Lingam', cut in monolithic rock about 8.87 metres high.

(iii) The given architectural features of Brihadeshwara temple are discussed below

- **Gopuram** (Gateway) It is a towering, sophistically carved structure that marks the entrance to the temple.
- **Garbhagriha** (Shrine) It is the innermost and most sacred part of the temple, housing the main idol or deity. It is usually a small, dark and enclosed space where only priests or selected individuals can enter.
- **Mandapa** (Audience Hall) It is a pillared hall or pavilion located in front of or near the Garbhagriha. It serves as a space for people to gather, participate in rituals, listen to hymns, or watch religious performances.

- **Vimana** (Towers) It is the tower above the Garbhagriha, typically in a pyramid-like shape. The Vimana's height and design vary depending on the region and style of the temple.

Q.3 With reference to the Cholas period explain the following.

(i) **"Taxes levied by the Cholas were big sources of revenue collection to support administration and temple activities". Briefly explain about those taxes imposed by the Cholas.** **(3)**

(ii) **What were the three types of village assemblies in the Chola administration?** **(3)**

(iii) **How was the administration of the Chola Kingdom organised?** **(4)**

Ans. (i) Taxes imposed by Cholas were taxes on land, taxes on the produce of the land and taxes on trade. The taxes on land were collected by the officials from the village councils. Part of revenue was kept for the king. The rest was used on the public works, on salaries of officials, on paying for the upkeep of the army and on the building of temples.

(ii) The three types of village assemblies in the Chola administration were as follows

(a) The Ur was common type of assembly of the villages where the land was held by all classes of people who were, therefore, members of the local assembly.

(b) The Sabha was exclusively Brahmin assembly of the villages, where all the land belonged to the Brahmins.

(c) The Nagaram was the assembly of merchants and traders. It was prevalent at the places where they were dominant.

(iii) The Cholas had a very efficient and organised administration. All authority was vested in the King. There was a Council of Ministers to advise the King. The administration was made even more simpler and efficient by distribution of power at different stages of administration.

The empire was divided into province (mandalams), which were further divided into Valanadu and Nadu. Princes of the royal family were appointed governors of provinces. There was self-governance in the villages and they were not ruled by any government officials. The Central government looked after external defence, internal peace and order, promotion of general prosperity and cultural progress of the empire.

8

THE DELHI SULTANATE

- The period between 1206 AD and 1526 AD in the Indian history is known as the period of Delhi Sultanate.
- During this time, the five dynasties that ruled over Delhi were the Mamluks (Slave), Khiljis, Tughlaqs, Sayyids, and Lodhis.
- The rulers of the various dynasties ruled from their capital at Delhi were called the Sultans.
- The Slave dynasty was the first ruling dynasty of the Delhi Sultanate, and the Lodhi dynasty was the last ruling dynasty of the Delhi Sultanate.

Sources of Delhi Sultanate

The important sources of information about the Delhi Sultanate are

1. Inscriptions

- The inscriptions are found on coins, monuments, milestones and tombstones.
- Inscriptions found in Delhi and Uttar Pradesh provide information about land grants, rulers' battles, etc.
- Many inscriptions record land-grants made by various rulers and chiefs; others are descriptions of battles or speeches and writings to rulers.
- Early records of the Delhi Sultanate are written in Arabic and most records are in Persian as it was the official language. Some inscriptions are also written in Sanskrit.
- The first coin issued by Muhammad Bakhtiyar Khalji bears both Arabic and Sanskrit inscriptions.

2. Monuments

The most significant monuments of Delhi Sultanate is Qutub Minar in Delhi. The construction of Qutub Minar was started by Qutub-ud-din Aibak and was dedicated to the Sufi saint, Qutb-ud-din Bakhtiyar Kaki, who was greatly respected by the people of Delhi. The structure was completed by Iltutmish.

The special features of Qutub Minar are

(a) Originally, Qutub Minar had only four storeys with the height of 71.4 metres.

(b) The tower was damaged by lightning in 1369. In the course of repairs and renovations, Feroz Shah Tughluq further raised its height.

(c) The fifth storey and some changes were added in 14th century by Firoz Shah Tughlaq.

(d) The tower is made of red sandstone, grey quartzite and marble. The entrance of tower is through the doorway on the northern side. Each storey has a projecting balcony.

(e) The walls of the minaret are covered with Indian floral motifs and verses from the Quran.

(f) The Minar is a circular tower of about 13.8 metres in diameter at the base and tapers to the width of about 3 metres at the summit. It has a circular stairway of 379 steps leading to the top.

Qutub Minar

Ruling Dynasties of Delhi Sultanate

The real founder of Muslim Empire in India was Shihab al-Din Muhammad Ghori or Muhammad of Ghor.

- In 1193 AD, Muhammad Ghori defeated the ruler of Kannauj in the Battle of Chandawar. This battle laid the foundation of Turkish rule in Northern India.
- From Delhi, the Turkish rule was extended into the Gangetic plains and to Bihar and Bengal.

The Slave Dynasty (1206 - 1290 AD)

- Mohammad Ghori left his slave General Qutub-ud-din Aibak as Viceroy of the conquered lands.
- After Mohammad Ghori's death in 1206 AD, all the Muslim rulers of Delhi till 1290 AD were either slaves or descendants of slaves. These rulers are known as the 'Slave Rulers' or Mamluk Sultans, and the dynasty is called the Slave dynasty.
- Qutb-ud-din Aibak was an important ruler of this dynasy.
- Qutb-ud-din Aibak (1206 - 1210 AD) is regarded as the founder of the Slave dynasty.
- He earned the title of Lakhbaksh (Giver of Lakhs) because of liberal distribution of money and his generosity.
- He was a brave and capable military general and a man of letters.
- Scholars like Hasan Nizami and Fakhre Mudir adorned his court.
- He began a series of conquest and captured the fort of Kalinjar in Bundelkhand and Anhilwara (capital of Solankis) in Gujarat.
- He was intolerant in the matters of religion. He had destroyed some Hindu temples and had constructed mosques.
- His main concerns were the affairs in the North-West and Bengal in the East.
- In 1210 AD, Aibak died of a sudden fall from a horse at Lahore while playing chaugan (polo).
- Iltutmish (1210 – 1236 CE) strengthened the Delhi Sultanate by introducing the Iqta system. He gained recognition from the Abbasid Caliph.
- Razia Sultan (1236 – 1239 CE) was the daughter of Iltutmish who ruled from 1236 to 1240 as the first and only female ruler of the Delhi Sultanate. She faced opposition from nobles and was eventually defeated and killed.
- The last ruler of the Slave Dynasty was Muiz-ud-din Muhammad Qaiqabad who was overthrown by Jalal ud-din Firuz Khalji in 1290.

The Khilji Dynasty

- After the Slave dynasty, Khilji dynasty ruled over Delhi.
- Jalal-ud-din Khilji founded the Khilji dynasty in 1290 AD.
- Alauddin Khilji was an imporant ruler of Khilji dynasty.
- The Khiljis were actually Turks who had settled in the Khilji region of Afghanistan for a long time.
- Alauddin Khilji (1296 - 1316 AD) was the nephew of Jalal-ud-din Khilji and was considered to be the most powerful ruler of the dynasty.
- He killed Jalal-ud-din and succeeded the throne in 1296 AD.
- He was the first Turkish Sultan of Delhi who separated religion from politics.
- He proclaimed Kingship knows no Kinship. The phrase is a principle of kingship which states that kinship is not a factor in determining who becomes a king.
- Alauddin Khilji annexed - Gujarat, Ranthambhore, Mewar, Malwa and Jalor.
- In Deccan, Alauddin's army led by Malik Kafur defeated - Ram Chandra of Devagiri, Pratap Rudradeva of Warangal, Vir Ballal III of Dwarasamudra and Vir Pandya of Madurai.

Reforms of Alauddin Khilji

(i) Revenue Reforms

- He introduced the practice of measuring the land and fixed the share of state accordingly.
- He created new department i.e., 'Diwan-i-Mustakhraj' to enquire into the revenue arrears and to collect them.
- He established the separate markets for food-grains, cloth, horses and fruits etc.
- He increased the land revenue from one-third to one-half and demanded it to be paid in cash and not in kind.

(ii) Measures against Nobility

- He re-organised the spy system to keep a check on the activities of the nobles.
- The use of wine and intoxicants was banned.
- Nobles should not intermarry without the permission of the sultan.
- He seised the properties of noble classes.
- He restricted gambling and those who gambled were severely punished.

(iii) Military Reforms

- He introduced the first permanent standing army of Delhi.
- He abolished the Iqtas on royal troopers and the payment of their salaries in cash.
- He introduced Dagh (branding of horses) and Chehra (branding or identity of soldiers).

(iv) Market Regulations

- He fixed the commodities of food grains, sugar and cooking oil.
- Each market was under the charge of a controller of market (shahna).
- The strict punishments were prescribed for cheating and underweighing goods.

(v) Deccan Expeditions

- Alauddin was more interested in acquiring the wealth for the maintenance of his huge army.

Decline of the Khilji Dynasty

- The rulers of Deccan were forced to accept the overlordship to pay annual tribute to him.
- After Alauddin Khilji's death, his son Qutbuddin Mubarak Shah became the ruler. He removed all the strict regulations imposed by his father.
- Qutb al-Din Mubarak Shah was the last ruler of the Khilji dynasty. He was killed in 1320 by Khusro Khan, his military commander.
- Khusro Khan was then killed by Ghazi Malik, who became the first ruler of the Tughlaq dynasty.

The Tughlaq Dynasty (1320-1414 AD)

- Tughlaq dynasty was founded by Ghiyas-ud-din Tughlaq or Ghazi Malik in 1320 AD.
- Muhammad bin Tughlaq was an important ruler of this dynasty.

Muhammad bin Tughlaq (1325-1351 AD)

- He was the son of Ghiyas-ud-din Tughlaq Shah who ascended the throne in 1325 AD. He was an excellent warrior.
- He had complete command over - astronomy, mathematics, medicine and had great interest in religion and philosophy.

Experiments Carried out by Muhammad bin Tughlaq

1. Transfer of Capital

- He shifted his capital to Devagiri near Aurangabad and renamed it Daultabad due to following reasons
  - Delhi was in the grip of severe famine.
  - Delhi was constantly threatened by the Mongal invasions.
  - Daultabad was centrally located from where he could control the Deccan territories.

2. Token Currency

- He introduced token currency in 1330, using copper and brass coins also called 'Jital' in place of silver tankas.
- But the scheme failed due to the circulation of counterfeit or fake coins.
- This resulted in chaos in trade and commerce.

3. Taxation in Doab

- To get more revenue, he increased the new land tax called 'Kharaj-i-ala', in the Ganga-Yamuna Doab.
- Due to drought and famine, the people refused to pay extra taxes and rose in rebellion.
- The tax collectors showed no mercy and took stern measures to collect the taxes.
- The peasants abandoned their land and flee to jungles as they were unable to pay the tax.

4. Plan of Conquests

- Muhammad bin Tughlaq dreamt of conquering the world.
- He organised an army and paid full year's salary in advance to his soldiers.
- But due to failure of token currency he abandoned the project and disbanded the army.

Firoz Tughlaq (1351 – 1388 CE)

- After Muhammad bin Tughlaq he was chosen as the Sultan by the nobles.
- He repaid all of Muhammad-bin-Tughlaq's Taquavi (agricultural) debts, increased the salaries of revenue officials and abolished unfair taxes.
- He also founded cities like Firozabad, Hissar, Jaunpur and Fatehabad.
- The last ruler of the Tughlaq dynasty was Nasir-ud-Din Mahmud Shah Tughluq, who was also known as Nasiruddin Mohammad Shah.

Sayyid Dynasty

- **Khizr Khan (1414 – 1421 CE)** He took control of Delhi and started the Sayyid dynasty. He did not adopt the title of Sultan and was chose to be known as Rayat-i-Ala. He tried to make the Delhi Sultanate strong but could not succeed and died in 1421 CE.
- **Mubarak Shah (1421 – 1433 CE)** After Khizr Khan, his son Mubarak Shah became the next ruler, but he faced many problems and lost control over his nobles.
- **Alam Shah (c. 1445 – 1451 CE)** He was the last ruler of the Sayyid dynasty. His wazir, Hamid Khan, asked Bahlul Lodhi to take charge of the army. Alam Shah realised that it would be difficult to continue as a ruler, so he retired to Badaun.

Lodhi Dynasty

- The Lodhis/Lodis were the last ruling dynasty of the Sultanate period.
- **Bahlol Lodhi (1451 – 1489 CE)** He founded the Lodhi dynasty. He expanded his rule by defeating Jaunpur and bringing Kalpi and Dholpur under his control. He annexed the Sharqui dynasty and introduced Bahlol copper coins. He died in 1489 CE and was succeeded by his son, Sikander Lodhi.
- **Sikander Lodhi (1489–1517 CE)** He was the strongest Lodhi ruler. He expanded his kingdom, improved administration, built roads, and introduced the Gazz-i-Sikandari measurement system.
- **Ibrahim Lodhi (1517–1526 CE)** Sikander Lodhi was succeeded by his eldest son, Ibrahim Lodhi. He was a harsh ruler who insulted his nobles.
- Daulat Khan Lodhi, the governor of Punjab, invited Babur, who defeated and killed Ibrahim in the First Battle of Panipat (1526 CE). This led to the end of Lodhi dynasty.

Administration of Delhi Sultanate

1. Central Administration

- In central administration of Delhi Sultanate, the Sultan was the supreme executive, legislative, judicial and military authority. A number of ministers assisted him in administration.
- The Wazir was an important key figure in the administration who acted as the Prime Minister. The work of the official was supervised by the Wazir. However, the final decisions were always taken by the Sultan.
- The nobles formed an extremely powerful group as they held positions of military commanders and provincial governors.

2. Provincial and Local Administration

- During Delhi Sultanate, the empire was divided into provinces called Iqtas.
- Each province was controlled by officials called muqtis.
- The provinces were further divided into shiqs and parganas or districts in order to facilitate local administration.
- The lowest administrative unit was the village which included officials like the muqaddam (the village headman), the patwari (the record keeper) and the mushrif (the village accountant).
- There was a panchayat in each village to settle local disputes.

3. Military Administration

- 'Ariz-i-mumalik' was the minister in charge of the army.
- The special responsibility of the ariz's department was to recruit, equip and pay the army.
- The Sultan himself was the commander-in-chief of the army.

4. Judicial Administration

- There were two departments in judicial administration of Delhi Sultanate which were - Diwan-i-Risalat and Diwan-i-Insha.
- The Diwan-i-Risalat was presided by the Chief Sadar (a leading qazi) and it dealt with religious matters.
- The qazi was the head of the department of justice and advised the Sultan on civil and religious matters.
- The Diwan-i-Insha was responsible for writing and managing official letters and communication of state (Royal correspondence).

5. Revenue Administration

- 'Iqta system' was followed in Delhi Sultanate which was the practice of giving grants of revenue from a territory. Those who were given iqtas were called 'Iqtadars'.
- Under the Iqta system, Iqtadars used the revenue collected from those lands to maintain themselves, their families, and soliders for the sultan's military needs.
- Many of these iqtadars functioned as independent rulers of the territories under their command when the central authority became weak.

EXAM ORIENTED QUESTIONS

TYPE - 1   1 Mark

Multiple Choice Questions

Q.1 Identify the odd one out from the following.
(a) Slave dynasty   (b) Khilji dynasty
(c) Tughlaq dynasty   (d) Mughal dynasty

Ans. (d) Mughal dynasty

Q.2 Which dynasty was the last ruling dynasty of the Delhi Sultanate before its fall?
(a) Khilji dynasty   (b) Tughlaq dynasty
(c) Lodhi dynasty   (d) Sayyid dynasty

Ans. (c) Lodhi dynasty

Q.3 Identify the key features of the Iqta system
P : It was a land revenue system where nobles were granted land in exchange for military service.
Q : The Iqtadars (holders of Iqta) could pass the land to their heirs.
R : The revenue collected from the Iqta was used for maintaining soldiers and administration.
S : It was first introduced by Balban.
(a) P and Q   (b) R and S
(c) P and R   (d) Q and S

Ans. (c) P and R

Q.4 Look at the image given below and answer the question.

Which of the following rulers is not linked to the construction of this monument?
(a) Qutb-ud-din Aibak   (b) Alauddin Khilji
(c) Iltutmish   (d) Feroz Shah Tughlaq

Ans. (b) Alauddin Khilji

Q.5 Read the description and answer the following question.
"He is best known for his market regulations".
(a) Razia Sultan   (b) Jalaluddin Khilji
(c) Alauddin Khilji   (d) Muhammad bin Tughlaq

Ans. (c) Alauddin Khilji

Q.6 Who is most likely to have expanded the Delhi Sultanate territory to its largest extent?
(a) Alauddin Khilji   (b) Balban
(c) Qutb-ud-din Aibak   (d) Iltutmish

Ans. (a) Alauddin Khilji

Exp. Alauddin Khilji expanded the Delhi Sultanate by conquering large parts of Southern India and the Deccan region, making it the largest in the Sultanate's history.

Q. 7 Which of the following scenarios best describes the rule of Alauddin Khilji?
(a) He focused on strengthening the military and implementing price control.
(b) He built the Qutub Minar and supported the architectural development.
(c) He was known for his religious tolerance and encouragement of cultural diversity.
(d) He did not expanded the Delhi Sultanate's territory.

Ans. (a) He focused on strengthening the military and implementing price control.

Exp. Alauddin Khalji is known for his military reforms, strengthening his army, and implementing market reforms like price control to ensure stability in the kingdom.

Q.8 Identify the correct statements regarding the reign of Muhammad bin Tughlaq and choose the correct option.
P : Muhammad bin Tughlaq introduced a token currency system in his empire.
Q : The token currency was made of copper and brass coins.
R : The introduction of token currency was successful.
S : The token currency was a conventional idea for its time.
(a) P and Q   (b) P and R   (c) Q and S   (d) P and S

Ans. (a) P and Q

Q.9 Which ruler transferred the capital from Delhi to Daulatabad?
(a) Muhammad bin Tughlaq
(b) Iltutmish
(c) Firoz Shah Tughlaq
(d) Ghiyas-ud-din Tughlaq

Ans. (a) Muhammad bin Tughlaq

Exp. Muhammad bin Tughlaq moved the capital to Daulatabad in 1327 to control the Deccan region better, but the decision caused many problems due to its distance.

Q.10 Which of the following is not likely to have been a policy of the Delhi Sultanate rulers?
(a) Centralised administration
(b) Implementation of market reforms
(c) Introduction of a uniform currency
(d) Religious tolerance and freedom

Ans. (d) Religious tolerance and freedom

Q.11 Complete the following analogy.

Diwan-i-Risalat : Religious matters :: Diwan-i-Insha :
(a) Army (b) Royal correspondence
(c) Land grants (d) Provincial administration

Ans. (b) Royal correspondence

Q.12 Identify the odd one out of the following sources of revenue during the Delhi Sultanate.
(a) Land tax (Kharaj) (b) Jizya tax on non-Muslims
(c) Customs duties on trade (d) Tax on religious offerings

Ans. (d) Tax on religious offerings

Exp. During the Delhi Sultanate, revenue sources like the land tax (Kharaj), Jizya tax on non-Muslims, and customs duties on trade were regular, state-imposed taxes, while a tax on religious offerings was not a typical or major source of revenue for the Sultanate.

Q.13 Which of the following statements is not true about the Delhi Sultanate?
(a) The Delhi Sultanate was established by Qutb-ud-din Aibak.
(b) The Delhi Sultanate lasted for more than 300 years.
(c) The Delhi Sultanate was known for its Hindu-majority rule.
(d) The Delhi Sultanate introduced administrative reforms and a centralised government.

Ans. (c) The Delhi Sultanate was known for its Hindu-majority rule.

Q.14 Identify the odd one out of the following reasons for the decline of Delhi Sultanate dynasties.
(a) Weak successors (b) Opposition from nobles
(c) Foreign invasions (d) Democratic elections

Ans. (d) Democratic elections

Q.15 In which battle was Ibrahim Lodhi defeated, marking the end of the Delhi Sultanate?
(a) First Battle of Tarain
(b) Second Battle of Panipat
(c) First Battle of Panipat
(d) Battle of Khanwa

Ans. (c) First Battle of Panipat

TYPE - 2 1 Mark

Assertion-Reason Questions

Q.1 Read the two statements given below about the Qutub Minar in India and select the option that shows the correct relationship between (A) and (R).

Assertion (A) Qutub Minar was dedicated to the Sufi saint, Qutb-ud-din Bakhtiyar Kaki.

Reason (R) The construction of Qutub Minar was started by Iltutmish.
(a) R contradicts A
(b) R is the reason for A
(c) A is true but R is false
(d) A and R are independent of each other

Ans. (c) A is true but R is false

Q.2. Read the two statements given below about the Qutub-ud-din Aibak and select the option that shows the correct relationship between (A) and (R).

Assertion (A) The Delhi Sultanate was established in 1206 by Qutub-ud-din Aibak.

Reason (R) Qutb-ud-din Aibak was a military general who rose to power after the death of Muhammad Ghori.
(a) R contradicts A
(b) R is the reason for A
(c) A is true but R is false
(d) A and R are independent of each other

Ans. (b) R is the reason for A

Q.3 Read the two statements given below about Alauddin Khalji and select the option that shows the correct relationship between (A) and (R).

Assertion (A) Alauddin Khilji was the first ruler who laid the foundation of a permanent standing army.

Reason (R) He was the first sultan of Delhi who ordered measurement of land.
(a) R contradicts A
(b) R is the reason for A
(c) A is true but R is false
(d) A and R are independent of each other

Ans. (d) A and R are independent of each other

Q.4. Read the two statements given below about the architecture of Delhi Sultanate and select the option that shows the correct relationship between (A) and (R).

Assertion (A) The Delhi Sultanate saw a rise in the development of architecture, particularly in the construction of mosques and tombs.

Reason (R) The rulers of the Delhi Sultanate encouraged the building of Islamic architectural monuments as a way to assert their power and culture.

(a) R contradicts A
(b) R is the reason for A
(c) A is true but R is false
(d) A and R are independent of each other

Ans. (b) R is the reason for A

Q.5 Read the two statements given below about the Delhi Sultanate and select the option that shows the correct relationship between (A) and (R).

Assertion (A) The establishment of the Delhi Sultanate led to the decline of the Rajput kingdoms.

Reason (R) The Delhi Sultans launched several military campaigns that weakened the Rajput rulers and integrated their territories into the Sultanate.

(a) R contradicts A
(b) R is the reason for A
(c) A is true but R is false
(d) A and R are independent of each other

Ans. (b) R is the reason for A

TYPE - 3 2 Marks

Very Short Answer Type Questions

Q.1 Describe any two key features of Qutub Minar.

Ans. The two key features of Qutub Minar are

- Qutub Minar is 72.5 meters tall, making it the tallest brick minaret in the world.
- The minaret is adorned with beautiful inscriptions and carvings, showcasing the art and architecture of that era.

Q.2 Who was the founder of the Slave dynasty and what were his major contributions?

Ans. The founder of the Slave dynasty was Qutb-ud-din Aibak. He was a former slave who became the sultan of Delhi after defeating the last ruler of the Ghaznavid dynasty.

His major contributions include starting the construction of Qutub Minar and establishing the first Muslim rule in Delhi.

Q.3 Mention any two reasons why Razia Sultan faced opposition during her rule.

Ans. Razia Sultan faced opposition during her rule because

1. **Gender Bias** The nobles and Turkish aristocracy were unwilling to accept a female ruler, as they believed that a woman should not rule the empire.

2. **Favoritism Towards Non-Turkish Nobles** Razia Sultan appointed an Abyssinian (African) slave, Yakut, to a high position, which angered the Turkish nobles and led to rebellion against her.

Q.4 **Alauddin Khalji was a powerful ruler from the Khalji dynasty who used to rule the sultanate of Delhi. He was the nephew and a son-in-law of his predecessor Jalaluddin. He killed his father-in-law and consolidated his power in Delhi.** *Times of India*

What reforms were associated with Alauddin Khalji's rule? Through which reform he controlled the prices of goods?

Ans. Alauddin Khalji was associated with - military reforms, market reforms, and land revenue reforms. He controlled the prices of goods through market reforms.

Q.5 Mention any two military reforms introduced by Alauddin Khalji.

Ans. Two military reforms introduced by Alauddin Khalji are

(i) He imported quality horses and started the system of branding horses (dagh) so that the soldiers could not replace them with inferior quality horses.

(ii) He introduced the system of chehra which meant giving a kind of identity card to every soldier.

Q.6 Give two reasons why Alauddin Khalji did not annex the Deccan kingdoms of Devagiri, Warangal, Dwarasamudra and Madurai?

Ans. Alauddin did not annex these kingdoms for two reasons

(i) He realised that practically it would be difficult to control these distant lands from Delhi.

(ii) He was more interested in acquiring the wealth of these Deccan kingdoms for the maintenance of his huge army.

Q.7 **Imagine you are a noble in the court of Alauddin Khilji. You are asked to advise the Sultan on how to implement his market reforms to control prices and maintain order in the empire. What steps would you suggest to ensure the success of these market reforms?**

Ans. If I were a noble in the court of Alauddin Khilji, I would suggest setting up strict price controls for essential goods. I would appoint market officials (Shahis) to oversee fair trade, and establish markets run by the government.

Q.8 What were the reasons for Muhammad bin Tughlaq's decision to shift the capital from Delhi to Daulatabad?

Ans. Muhammad bin Tughlaq shifted the capital from Delhi to Daulatabad to have a central location, which could control both the Northern and Southern parts of India better.

He also hoped it would improve administrative control and defence. However, the move caused hardship for people and failed due to poor planning.

Q.9 Mention the two controversial steps taken by Muhammad bin Tughlaq.

Ans. The two controversial steps taken by Muhammad bin Tughlaq include

(i) Shifting of Capital from Delhi to Devagiri (Daulatabad) and back to Delhi which caused lot of hardships to the people.

(ii) Introduction of token currency or bronze tanka to replace the silver tanka but the experiment failed due to the circulation of counterfeit or fake coins.

Q.10 Explain any two administrative reforms introduced by Firoz Tughlaq.

Ans. Two administrative reforms introduced by Firoz Tughlaq are

1. **Relief to Farmers** He repaid the agricultural (Taquavi) loans that were imposed during Muhammad bin Tughlaq's reign, providing financial relief to farmers and improving agricultural productivity.

2. **Tax Reforms** He abolished several unfair taxes and ensured a more systematic revenue collection, making taxation more just and efficient for the people.

Q.11 Mention any two achievements of Sikander Lodhi as a ruler.

Ans. Two achievements of Sikander Lodhi as a ruler are

1. **Territorial Expansion** He expanded his kingdom by conquering Bihar and parts of Bengal, strengthening the Lodhi dynasty's control over North India.

2. **Administrative Reforms** He improved governance by building roads, promoting trade and introducing the Gazz-i-Sikandari, a standardised measurement system for land assessment.

Q.12 Who was the commander-in-chief of the army during the Sultanate period? Name the department which dealt with state correspondence during the Sultanate period.

Ans. The Sultan himself was the commander-in-chief of the army during the Sultanate period.

The department which dealt with state correspondence during the Sultanate period was the Diwan-i-Insha.

TYPE - 4 — 3 Marks

Short Answer Type Questions

Q.1 Mention any three features of the inscriptions found during the reign of Delhi Sultanate.

Ans. The three features of the inscriptions found during the reign of Delhi Sultanate include

(i) The inscriptions are found on coins, monuments, milestones and tombstones.

(ii) Many inscriptions record land-grants made by various rulers and chiefs; others are descriptions of battles or speeches and writings to rulers.

(iii) Some of the inscriptions are in Sanskrit, some in Arabic and some in both the languages.

Q.2 "He was liberal in distributing money and was known as Lakhbaksh". Whom is this statement associated to? Mention any two of his qualities.

Ans. The given statement is associated with Slave ruler, Qutub-ud-din Aibak. Two of his qualities were

(i) He was a brave and capable military general.

(ii) He was a man of letters. Scholars like Hasan Nizami and Fakhre Mudir adorned his court.

Q.3 "Kingship knows no kinship". This is a statement that was proclaimed by Alauddin Khilji, a Sultan of the Delhi Sultanate. Justify this statement by mentioning any three points.

Ans. The statement 'Kingship knows no kinship' by Alauddin Khilji reflects his belief that leadership should be based on merit and loyalty, not family ties. Here are three key points justifying this

(i) Alauddin consolidated power in his own hands, disregarding family ties when necessary, even executing relatives if they threatened his rule.

(ii) He appointed officials based on capability rather than family connections, ensuring that competence was prioritised over kinship.

(iii) Alauddin prioritised the stability of his reign, eliminating potential rivals, including family members, to safeguard his throne.

Q.4 Explain, how did Alauddin Khilji expand his empire?

Ans. After conquering the bulk of Northern India, Alauddin Khilji sent an expedition to Deccan under Malik Kafur. The kingdoms of Devagiri, Warangal, Dwarasamudra and Madurai were conquered but not annexed.

Alauddin Khilji knew that it was difficult to control these distant lands from Delhi and also he was only interested in acquiring the wealth of these Deccan kingdoms for the maintenance of his huge army. That is why he forced the rulers of Deccan to accept his over-lordship and to pay annual tribute to him.

Q.5 Mention any three important reforms held under Muhammad bin Tughlaq.

Ans. The three important reforms held under Muhammad bin Tughlaq include

(i) Muhammad bin Tughlaq increased taxation in the Doab regions of Ganga and Yamuna as he wanted to raise a strong army for conquest. The taxation was raised by ten to twenty times more. The tax collectors continued to collect taxes by oppression which resulted in widespread revolts.

(ii) Muhammad bin Tughluq transfered the capital from Delhi to Devagiri, near modern Aurangabad and renamed it Daulatabad. One of the reason expected for shifting the capital was the consolidation of South India and to make Daulatabad the centre of Muslim culture.

(iii) The introduction of token currency was an innovational idea of its time. Muhammad bin Tughluq issued currency made of copper and bronze in place of silver. This was done because of the shortage of silver.

Q.6 How did the Sayyid dynasty come to an end? Mention any two key events.

Ans. The Sayyid dynasty ended due to weak rulers and the growing power of the Lodhis. Two key events led to its downfall are

1. **Weak Leadership of Alam Shah (1445–1451 CE)** The last ruler, Alam Shah, failed to control his nobles and administration, leading to instability in the empire.

2. **Transfer of Power to Bahlul Lodhi** Alam Shah's wazir, Hamid Khan, invited Bahlul Lodhi to take charge of the army. Realising his inability to rule, Alam Shah voluntarily stepped down and retired to Badaun in 1451 CE, marking the end of the Sayyid dynasty.

TYPE - 5

4 Marks

Long Answer Type Questions

Q.1 Describe the contribution of Qutub-ud-din Aibak to the Delhi Sultanate.

Ans. The contribution of Qutub-ud-din Aibak to the Delhi Sultanate include

(i) He became the first Sultan of Delhi and laid the foundation of the Delhi Sultanate, marking the beginning of Muslim rule in Northern India.

(ii) He is credited with initiating the construction of the Qutb Minar in Delhi, which is one of the most iconic monuments of Indo-Islamic architecture.

(iii) He encouraged the development of Islamic architecture in India. He built the Quwwat-ul-Islam Mosque in Delhi, which is one of the earliest examples of mosque architecture in India, utilising materials from Hindu temples.

(iv) He introduced a more organised administrative system in the Sultanate. He appointed officials based on merit, he set up a stable governance structure, and began the process of consolidating Muslim rule in India by bringing various regions under the Sultanate's control.

Q.2 Evaluate the impact of Muhammad bin Tughlaq's administrative reforms on the Delhi Sultanate. Were these reforms successful, and what were their long-term effects?

Ans. Muhammad bin Tughlaq's administrative reforms were ambitious but largely unsuccessful. One of his key reforms was the introduction of token currency, where he minted coins of copper and brass, hoping to make trade easier. However, people did not trust the new currency, and it led to widespread economic problems.

He also moved the capital from Delhi to Daulatabad, hoping to make it a more strategic location, but this caused hardship for people as they had to travel long distances. Although he attempted to improve administration, his policies created confusion and instability.

In the long term, his reforms weakened the Delhi Sultanate, and many of his changes were reversed by his successors.

Q.3 Describe the administrative reforms by Allaudin Khilji.

Ans. The administrative reforms by Allaudin Khilji include

- He established an efficient spy system to keep a check on the activities of the nobles.
- The use of wine and intoxicants was banned.
- People were not intermarry without permission of the Sultan.
- He seised the properties of noble classes.
- Gambling was forbidden and gamblers were severely punished.

Q.4 The Lodhi dynasty was the last ruling dynasty of the Delhi Sultanate before the Mughal invasion. Evaluate this statement by explaining any three factors that led to the downfall of the Lodhi dynasty.

Ans. The Lodhi dynasty was the last to rule Delhi before the Mughal invasion and its downfall was due to several factors

(i) **Weak Leadership** Ibrahim Lodhi, the last Lodhi ruler, was harsh and did not respect his nobles. His poor leadership created conflicts within his kingdom.

(ii) **Revolt by Nobles** Many nobles, including Daulat Khan Lodhi, were unhappy with Ibrahim's rule. Daulat Khan invited Babur from Kabul to invade India.

(iii) **Defeat in Battle** Babur defeated Ibrahim Lodhi in the First Battle of Panipat (1526 CE). His army was disorganised, while Babur used modern warfare techniques, including cannons.

Q.5 Explain the following terms.

(i) Diwan-i-Risalat

(ii) Diwan-i-Insha

Ans. (i) **Diwan-i-Risalat** The Diwan-i-Risalat was presided by the Chief Sadar (a leading qazi) and it dealt with the religious matters. The qazi was the head of the department of justice and gave advise to the Sultan on civil matters. It also oversaw the welfare of the religious community and managed religious affairs such as the appointment of religious leaders.

(ii) **Diwan-i-Insha** The Diwan-i-Insha dealt with the royal correspondence. It was responsible for managing official letters, royal decrees, and maintaining communication with other states, ensuring efficient administration. It also played a key role in drafting important documents and ensuring that the Sultan's policies were effectively communicated across the empire.

Q.6 The role of military officers in the administration of the Delhi Sultanate was crucial for maintaining law and order. Discuss how the Sultanate integrated military power into its administrative structure, especially at the provincial level.

Ans. During the Delhi Sultanate, military officers played a key role in both governance and maintaining law and order. The Sultan relied on his army to control vast regions and suppress rebellions.

At the provincial level, military commanders, known as 'iqtadars', were assigned territories and given land in return for military service. These commanders were responsible for collecting taxes and ensuring the security of their regions.

The military power was directly linked to administration, as the army helped enforce policies, defend borders, and maintain control over distant provinces. This military- backed system ensured the stability of the empire.

TYPE - 6 10 Marks

Structured Questions

Q.1 Look at the given picture below, and answer the following questions

(i) Who initiated the construction of this monument? Who completed it? Where is it located? **(3)**

(ii) Name the saint after whom the monument is named. What information do the monuments of the Sultanate period provide about the Sultanate era? **(3)**

(iii) Mention any four architectural features of the monument. **(4)**

Ans. (i) Qutub-ud-din Aibak initiated this monument. It was completed by Iltutmish. It is located in Delhi.

(ii) It is named after Sufi saint 'Qutub-ud-din Bakhtiyar Kaki'.

The monuments of the Sultanate period reveal the cultural trends, the living conditions, faiths and beliefs of the period. They offer valuable insights into the religious practices, beliefs, and the way of life during the period.

These structures also reveal the rulers' attitudes towards religion, art and culture, showcasing their devotion, power and desire to leave a lasting legacy. The architectural style, which combined Islamic and local influences, is a testament to the Sultanate's cultural synthesis.

(iii) Four architectural features of the Qutub Minar include

(a) Initially, the tower stood at a height of 71.4 meters with four storeys. After it was damaged by lightning in 1369, Feroz Shah Tughlaq repaired and extended the tower, further increasing its height (72.5 metres).

(b) The Qutub Minar features five storeys that taper as they rise, with each storey separated by projecting balconies, enhancing its visual outlook.

(c) The base of the Minar has a diameter of 13.8 meters, while the top narrows to just 3 meters in diameter. It is also equipped with a circular stairway comprising 379 steps leading to the top.

(d) The projecting balconies are designed in a way that allows the entire structure to evenly distribute the weight, ensuring stability and strength throughout the tower.

Q.2 With reference to the Khilji dynasty, answer the following questions.

(i) Mention the three important steps taken by Alauddin Khilji to regulate prices in his empire. (3)

(ii) Alauddin Khilji had to face a series of rebellions from the nobles. What were the methods adopted by him to diminish the power of the nobility? (3)

(iii) Alauddin Khilji implemented several measures to increase revenue to sustain his big army, and for the efficient governance. Mention any four measures which he took to increase the revenue? (4)

Ans. (i) The three important steps taken by Alauddin Khilji to regulate prices in his empire included

(a) Fixing the prices of essential commodities like foodgrains, sugar and cooking oil to maintain stability.

(b) Establishing three separate markets in Delhi - one for food grains, one for expensive cloth, and another for horses, slaves, and cattle. Each market was managed by a controller known as the 'Shahna'.

(c) Imposing strict penalties for dishonest practices, such as cheating and under-weighing goods, to ensure fair trade.

(ii) The methods adopted by Alauddin Khilji to diminish or crush the power of the nobility were

- Restricting nobles from holding parties, functions, or marriage alliances without the Sultan's approval.
- Banning the use of wine and intoxicants among the nobility.
- Forbidding gambling and imposing severe punishments on those who caught practicing gambling.
- Shifting the payment of soldiers from land grants to cash, reducing the nobility's control over military power.
- Establishing a robust spy network to monitor the activities and loyalty of the nobles.

(iii) The four measures Alauddin Khilji took to increase the revenue were

(a) He introduced the practice of measuring the land and fixed the state share accordingly, ensuring a more accurate and systematic assessment of land for tax purposes.

(b) He increased the state revenue from one-third to one-half, which significantly boosted the Sultanate's financial resources.

(c) He demanded the revenue in cash and not in kind, making the revenue collection more efficient and reducing the chances of corruption or exploitation.

(d) He appointed special officers for revenue collection, ensuring better oversight and preventing irregularities in the tax collection process.

Q.3 With the reference of the administration of Delhi Sultanate, answer the following questions.

(i) Administration in the provinces and villages played an important role during the Delhi Sultanate. Describe how provincial and local administration was organised during the rule of Delhi Sultanate. (3)

(ii) Mention any three functions of Judicial administration. (3)

(iii) Central administration had the jurisdiction over all local governments. Describe the organisation of central administration during the reign of the Delhi Sultanate. (4)

Ans. (i) During the rule of Delhi Sultanate, provincial and local administration was organised as follows

- During Delhi Sultanate, the empire was divided into provinces called 'Iqtas'.
- Each province was controlled by officials called 'muqtis'.

- The provinces were further divided into 'shiqs' and parganas or districts in order to facilitate local administration.
- The lowest administrative unit was the village which included officials like the muqaddam (the village headman), the patwari (the record keeper) and the mushrif (the village accountant).
- There was a panchayat in each village to settle local disputes.

(ii) The three key functions of the Judicial administration in the Delhi Sultanate include

(a) The judicial system ensured that justice was provided to the people, with courts set up to hear cases related to criminal, civil, and religious matters. Qazi's (judges) played a key role in delivering judgements based on Islamic law.

(b) The judicial system helped maintain law and order by punishing people who commited crimes, resolving disputes, and ensuring adherence to the rule of law across the Sultanate.

(c) Qazi's and other legal officers advised the Sultan on legal matters, including the interpretation of religious and civil laws, ensuring that the ruler's decisions were in accordance with both Islamic principles and the state's policies.

(iii) The organisation of central administration during the reign of the Delhi Sultanate include

(a) In central administration of Delhi Sultanate, the Sultan was the supreme executive, legislative, judicial and military authority.

(b) A number of ministers assisted him in the administration.

(c) Wazir was an important key figure in the administration who acted as the Prime Minister. The work of the official was supervised by the Wazir, however, the final decisions were always taken by the Sultan.

(d) The nobles formed an extremely powerful group as they held positions of military commanders and provincial governors.

9

THE MUGHAL EMPIRE

- The Mughal dynasty was one of the longest ruling dynasties in India.
- The Mughals were descendants of two great lineages of rulers.
- From their mother's side, they were descendants of Genghis (Chingiz) Khan, the Mongol ruler who ruled over parts of China and Central Asia.
- From their father's side, they were the successors of Timur (Tamerlane), the ruler of Iran, Iraq and Turkey.

Sources

The main sources of information about the mughals are

1. Ain-i-Akbari

- The Ain-i-Akbari is a 16th century, detailed document which records the administration of emperor Akbar's Empire.
- It was written by Wazir Abul Fazl, who was the minister and one of the nine jewels at Akbar's court.
- The Ain-i-Akbari is written in Persian language.
- It is divided into five books, which are
  - (i) The First book deals with the imperial household.
  - (ii) The Second book deals with the servants of the emperor, the military and civil services.
  - (iii) The Third book deals with the imperial administration. It consists of the regulations for the judicial and executive departments, and the divisions of the empire.
  - (iv) The Fourth book provides information about hindu philosophy, science, social customs and literature.
  - (v) The Fifth book contains quotes (wise sayings) of Akbar, as well as history of the author's family and biography of the author.

2. The Taj Mahal

- Taj Mahal is situated on the banks of Yamuna river in Agra. It was built by Shah Jahan in memory of his beloved wife Mumtaz Mahal.
- The work started in 1632 and finished in 1653. Ustad Ahmad Lahori was the master architect of this monument. Taj Mahal is made of pure white marble. The central dome rises to a height of 56.1 metres and has the appearance of an inverted Lotus.
- There are four smaller domes at the four corners of the building.
- The monument is built on a platform that is 6.6 metres high.
- The lower portion is square in design and rises to a height of 32 metres.

Taj Mahal

REVISION NOTES

- The interior and the exterior of the main building are decorated with screens, calligraphy and inlay work. The method of decoration used in Taj Mahal is called Pietra dura.
- Taj Mahal was designated as World Heritage Site by UNESCO in 1983 and was declared as one of the Seven Wonders of the World in 2007.

3. The Jama Masjid

- The Jama Masjid in Delhi was built by Mughal emperor Shah Jahan. The main architect of this monument was Ustad Khalil. He designed the mosque by blending Islamic and Mughal architectural styles.
- It is the largest mosque in India.
- There are three gateways to the Jama Masjid mosque i.e. on the South, East and North sides.
- The central dome is the largest and highest, made of white marble, decorated with stripes of black colour.
- The front of the large prayer hall has eleven arches, with the middle one rising higher than the roof level.

Jama Masjid

4. The Red Fort

- The Red Fort or Lal Qila was built by Shah Jahan. He began its construction in 1638 and completed it in 1648. Originally, it was known as Qila-e-Mubarak.
- It was built of red sandstone and marble on the banks of the Yamuna.
- The fort is in the form of a parallelogram measuring 930 metres by 495 metres.
- It is surrounded by a strong fortified wall.
- Some of the prominent buildings in this fort are *Diwan-i-Aam*, the *Diwan-i-Khas* and the *Rang Mahal.*
- These buildings are decorated with pure white marble, inlaid with precious stones.

The Red Fort, Delhi

- Later on, Aurangzeb built the Moti Masjid in the Red Fort.
- The Prime Minister of India every year hoists the national flag from its ramparts on Independence Day (15th August).

Rulers of the Mughal Empire

Babur (1526-1530)

- Babur was the founder of the Mughal Empire in India. His original name was Zahir-ud-din Muhammad.
- Babur succeeded to the throne of Farghana at a very early age of 11 years.
- He wrote his memoirs in Tuzuk-i-Baburi in Turkish language, describing the flora and fauna of India and detailed record of his entire career.
- Babur was succeeded by his son Humayun.
- Babur consolidated his empire through three major battles
  1. **First Battle of Panipat** (1526) Babur defeated Ibrahim Lodi, marking the start of Mughal rule in India. His use of artillery and superior tactics secured Delhi and Agra.

2. **Battle of Khanwa** (1527) Babur defeated the Rajput confederacy led by Rana Sanga, strengthening Mughal dominance in Northern India.

3. **Battle of Ghagra** (1529) Babur overcame the Afghans and the Sultan of Bengal, eliminating major resistance and solidifying his rule.

Humayun (1530-1540, 1555-1556)

- Humayun was the son of Babur.
- He introduced more systematic tax collection methods to improve revenue and reduce corruption.
- He lost the throne to Sher Shah Suri, but regained it later.

Akbar (1556-1605)

- He was the greatest ruler of Mughal Empire.
- He was crowned at Kalanaur at the age of 13 years and was guided by his tutor, Bairam Khan.
- Bairam Khan became the Wakil of the kingdom with the title of Khan-i-Khana.

Wars Fought and Campaigns led by Akbar

- Akbar's first conflict was with Hemu, a general of Adil Shah when he captured Agra and Delhi. Akbar's army under Bairam Khan defeated Hemu in the Second Battle of Panipat in 1556 and Akbar re-occupied Agra and Delhi.
- Akbar's other campaigns were against Durgavati of Garh-Katanga (Gond and Rajput principalities) followed by Chittor.
- In 1562, Akbar made his first visit to the tomb of the Sufi Saint, Sheikh Moinuddin Chishti, in Ajmer.
- In 1572, Akbar faced a rebellion in Gujarat, which was crushed by him and to mark this victory, he built the Buland Darwaza at Fatehpur Sikri.
- In 1576, the famous Battle of Haldighati was fought between Maharana Pratap (ruler of Mewar) and the Mughal army led by Raja Man Singh.

Steps towards Integration by Akbar

- To strengthen the liberal principles, Akbar enrolled a number of Hindus into the nobility.
- Akbar abolished the poll tax or Jazya tax, which the non-muslims were required to pay. He also abolished the pilgrim tax on bathing holy places such as Prayag and Benaras.
- In 1580, Akbar promulgated a new faith called Din-i-Ilahi. It was based on the principle of oneness of God.
- By 1595, Akbar's armies had conquered Kashmir, Sindh, Odisha, Central India and Qandhar.
- Akbar's last campaign was against Asirgarh, resulting in the annexation of Khandesh (1601).

Rajput Policy of Akbar

Akbar's Rajput policy focused on alliances through marriages, high-ranking appointments and respecting Rajput autonomy and religious freedom, ensuring their loyalty and integration into the Mughal Empire.

Key Features

- Akbar recognised the importance of Rajput support for consolidating his empire and adopted a policy of alliance and integration.
- He married Rajput princesses to strengthen his ties with Rajput rulers and establish a sense of kinship.
- Akbar appointed Rajputs to high positions in his court, recognising their martial skills and loyalty.
- He granted religious freedom to Rajputs, allowing them to practice their faith without interference.
- Akbar respected the internal autonomy of Rajput kingdoms, allowing them to maintain their traditions and customs.
- Unlike his treatment of other rulers, Akbar did not annex Rajput territories, but instead sought their allegiance and tribute.

Social and Educational Reforms by Akbar

Akbar implemented significant social and educational reforms, including abolishing forced sati, legalising widow remarriage, raising the minimum marriage age and promoting education for both Muslims and Hindus, emphasising moral and secular subjects.

Social Reforms

- Akbar issued orders to prevent the forced burning of widows on their husband's funeral pyre (sati), though he allowed it if done voluntarily.
- He legalised widow remarriage, a step that was crucial for women's rights and social mobility.
- Akbar raised the minimum age of marriage for girls to fourteen and for boys to sixteen, aiming to discourage child marriage.
- Akbar abolished laws that discriminated against non-Muslims and created a single legal system that incorporated laws from both Islam and Hinduism.

Educational Reforms

- Akbar recognised the importance of education and encouraged the establishment of schools and colleges for both Muslims and Hindus throughout his empire.
- He introduced changes to the curriculum, emphasising moral education, mathematics and secular subjects like agriculture, geometry, astronomy, logic and history.
- He established a library at Fatehpur Sikri exclusively for women and encouraged the development of bookbinding as a high art.
- Under his instruction, numerous maktabs (primary schools) and madrasahs (higher education institutions) were founded and richly endowed, for both resident and day-scholars.

Mansabdari System

- The mansabdari system was introduced by Akbar. The Mughal officers were known as mansabdars.
- These officers were given specific rank or mansab either in bureaucracy, military hierarchy or the nobility.
- The lowest rank was 10 and the highest was 5000 for nobles. These ranks had two divisions-zat and sawar.
  - (i) **Zat** It indicated the personal status or rank of a person and the salary due to him.
  - (ii) **Sawar** It was the designated number of horses with horseman, he had to maintain. For example, for every 10 cavalrymen, 20 horses were to be maintained.
- The mansabdars received their salaries as revenue assignments called jagirs.
- Another important feature of the mansabdari system was the law of zabti. According to it, when a mansabdar died, all his property was confiscated by the Emperor.

Jahangir (1605-1627)

- Jahangir was the son of Akbar. He welcomed Sir Thomas Roe and Captain Hawkins to his court.
- He executed Guru Arjun Dev and established Zanjir-i-Adal at Agra Fort for justice.

Shah Jahan (1627-1658)

- Shah Jahan, son of Jahangir, led the Mughal Empire's Golden Age and built iconic structures like the Taj Mahal, Red Fort, Jama Masjid, and Moti Mahal.
- Mughal architecture peaked under his rule. His court was visited by Manucci, Bernier, and Tavernier.

Aurangzeb (1658-1707)

- Aurangzeb ascended to the throne after a long and fierce struggle with his father and three brothers.
- He ruled for almost 50 years and was called Zinda Pir and Alamgir.

- His empire stretched from Kashmir in the North to Jinji in the South and from the Hindu Kush in the West to Chittagong in the East.
- In the first ten years of his rule, Aurangzeb led many military campaigns.
- The Jats and Satnamis along with Sikhs revolted during his reign. These revolts were a result of his harsh religious policy.
- Many oppressive land revenues and taxes were abolished by him.
- He also abolished Octroi tax and Inland transit duty taxes.
- He stopped the rituals like Jharokha darshan and weighing the emperor on his birthday were stopped.
- He re-introduced Jazya and Pilgrim tax. His deccan policy ruined the treasury of the Mughal Empire.
- He died in 1707 and after his death, the Mughal Empire was on the verge of collapse.

Later Mughal Emperors

- The later Mughal emperors were weak and controlled by nobles and warlords. The empire declined, ending with British rule in the 19th century.
- Weak rulers included Jahandar Shah (1712-1713), Furrukhsiyar (1713-1719), Muhammad Shah (1719-1748), and Shah Alam II (1760-1806).
- The last Mughal emperor was Bahadur Shah II (1837-1857). He was exiled to Burma after the Revolt of 1857.

Administrative System of the Mughals

1. Central Administration

- The head of the Mughal administration was the Emperor. He appointed a number of officers in different departments of the government. These were
  - (i) The office of Wazir or Wakil was responsible for civil and military affairs.
  - (ii) The Diwan or Diwan-i-ala was the head of revenue department and the sole incharge of income and expenditure.
  - (iii) Mir Bakhshi was the officer responsible for military pay and accounts. He was also responsible for recruiting the soldiers of the army and for maintaining a list of Mansabdars and other high officials.
  - (iv) Khan-i-Saman was the officer of the imperial household department.
  - (v) The Judicial department was headed by the Chief Qazi. Sometimes this post was combined with that of the Chief Sadar who was the head of religious endowments and charity, and also the minister of education and royal alms (Charity).

2. Provincial Administration

- For the purpose of smooth administration and revenue collection, the Mughal Empire was divided into several provinces known as Subas.
- Akbar divided his empire into 12 Subas (Provinces) which gradually rose to 21 during the reign of Aurangzeb.
- There were following officers in the provincial administration
  - (i) **Subahdar** was head of the Subah, appointed directly by the Emperor. He was the head of the civil as well as military administration.
  - (ii) **Diwan** was the head of the revenue department of the province.
  - (iii) **Bakhshi** looked after the military establishment. He kept an account of the salaries and emoluments of all mansabdars.
  - (iv) **Daroga-i-Dak Chowki** conducted an intelligence and postal system.
  - (v) **Waqai Navis** and Waqai Nigars delivered reports directly to the king.

3. Local Administration

- The Subahs were divided into Sarkars and the Sarkars were sub-divided into Parganas or mahals at the village level.
- The officers in local administration include
  - (i) **Faujdar** was the chief executive head of a Sarkar, to maintain law and order.
  - (ii) **Amalguzar** was the revenue collector.
  - (iii) **Shiqdar** was incharge of general administration, who had to maintain law and order of a Pargana. He was assisted by an Amil (revenue collector), an Amin (revenue assessor), a Potadar (treasurer), Qanungo (record keeper of land) and few Bitikchis (writers or clerks).
  - (iv) The village head was known as Muqaddam. He was assisted by the Patwari, who took care of village revenue records.

4. Judicial Administration

- The king was at the top of the judicial administration.
- The courts of Sadr-us-Sudur and Qazi-ul-Qzat were next to the king's court.
- Sadr-us-Sudur handled the religious cases and the Qazi-ul-Qzat handled all other cases.
- The cases of the Muslims were decided on the basis of Quranic injunctions, Hadis or sayings of the prophet, Fatwas or decrees of the eminent judges, etc.
- In the case of the Hindus, the cases were decided in accordance with their customary and traditional laws.

5. Military Administration

- Mir Bakhshi was incharge of the military department.
- He managed the recruitment of the soldiers, branding of the horses and the elephants, supplies to the army and training of the soldiers.
- Daroga-i-Dak Chauki was the head of the spy department of the state.

Land Revenue System

- A proper land revenue system was founded by Akbar.
- Todar Mal drew up schemes for effective tax collection.
- A uniform system of measurement was established for calculating the land tax.
- Akbar made the following corrections and precisions in the existing system of land revenue
  - (i) Standardisation of measurement of land.
  - (ii) Ascertaining the produce per Bigha (half acre) of land.
  - (iii) Fixing the share of produce.
  - (iv) Fixing rate of assessment or dahsala or zabti system.

EXAM ORIENTED QUESTIONS

TYPE - 1 1 Mark

Multiple Choice Questions

Q.1 The Ain-i-Akbari is primarily a description of
(a) Akbar's relations with Rajputs.
(b) The administration, economy and culture of Akbar's Empire.
(c) The architectural achievements of the Mughal Empire.
(d) The religious policies of Akbar.

Ans. (b) The administration, economy and culture of Akbar's Empire.

Q.2 Which of the following statements is most likely about the Taj Mahal?
(a) It was built by Shah Jahan as a memorial for his wife.
(b) The Taj Mahal was constructed using red sandstone.
(c) The Taj Mahal was completed in 1600 after 20 years of construction.
(d) Ustad Isha Khan was the master architect of the Taj Mahal.

Ans. (a) It was built by Shah Jahan as a memorial for his wife.

Exp. The Taj Mahal was constructed by Shah Jahan in memory of his wife Mumtaz Mahal, who passed away during childbirth. It is renowned for its stunning white marble architecture.

Q.3 Which of the following ruler is responsible for the construction of Red Fort?
(a) Iltutmish (b) Shah Jahan (c) Akbar (d) None of these

Ans. (b) Shah Jahan

Exp. Shah Jahan built the Red Fort in Delhi in 1648. It was his grand palace and a symbol of Mughal power. Made of red sandstone, it remains an important historical monument today.

Q.4 Which of the following statements about Babur is not true?
(a) Babur was the founder of the Mughal Empire in India.
(b) Babur succeeded his father Umar Shaikh Mirza at the age of 11.
(c) Babur defeated Ibrahim Lodhi in the Second Battle of Panipat.
(d) Babur was related to Timur and Genghis Khan.

Ans. (c) Babur defeated Ibrahim Lodhi in the Second Battle of Panipat.

Exp. Babur defeated Ibrahim Lodi in the First Battle of Panipat in 1526. The Second Battle of Panipat, fought in 1556, was between Akbar and Hemu.

Q.5 Which of the following is most likely to have been the reason for the success of Akbar's rule?
(a) His aggressive foreign policy
(b) His religious tolerance and administrative reforms
(c) His military conquests in Europe
(d) His economic policies favouring trade

Ans. (b) His religious tolerance and administrative reforms.

Q.6 Which of the following was not a feature of Akbar's Rajput policy?
(a) Religious freedom for Rajputs
(b) High-ranking appointments for Rajputs
(c) Complete annexation of Rajput territories
(d) Respect for Rajput traditions and autonomy

Ans. (c) Complete annexation of Rajput territories

Q.7 In 1575, Akbar built a hall called Ibadat Khan at which of the following place?
(a) Fatehpur Sikri (b) Delhi
(c) Shahjahanabad (d) Agra

Ans. (a) Fatehpur Sikri

Exp. Fatehpur Sikri was a place for religious discussions and debates among scholars of different religions, reflecting Akbar's interest in spiritual tolerance.

Q.8 Complete the given analogy.
Battle of Panipat : 1526 :: Battle of Haldighati : ?
(a) 1556 (b) 1576
(c) 1610 (d) 1680

Ans. (b) 1576

Q.9 Which of the following is not true about the Mansabdari System?
(a) The Mansabdari System was introduced by Akbar to organize the military and civil administration.
(b) A mansabdar's rank determined his responsibilities in both military and civil spheres.
(c) Mansabdars were paid in land grants, not in cash.
(d) The Mansabdari System was an integral part of Akbar's policy of centralization and military control.

Ans. (c) Mansabdars were paid in land grants, not in cash.

Q.10 Choose the correct answer to the question from the given options.

"This ruler's reign marked the zenith of Mughal architecture, especially through the construction of a grand tomb for his wife, the Taj Mahal. He also faced internal challenges, including conflicts with his sons, which ultimately led to the weakening of his rule."

Which ruler of the Mughal Empire is described above in the given description?

(a) Babur (b) Shah Jahan
(c) Humayun (d) Aurangzeb

Ans. (b) Shah Jahan

Q.11 Which of the following is not true about Aurangzeb's reign?

(a) Aurangzeb expanded the Mughal Empire to its greatest territorial extent.
(b) Aurangzeb's reign saw the introduction of policies of religious intolerance, leading to internal strife.
(c) Aurangzeb was known for his efforts to integrate Hindus into the Mughal administration.
(d) Aurangzeb's military campaigns drained the Empire's resources, leading to economic and political difficulties.

Ans. (c) Aurangzeb was known for his efforts to integrate Hindus into the Mughal administration.

Q.12 The Mughal Empire began to decline after the death of which emperor?

(a) Akbar (b) Jahangir
(c) Aurangzeb (d) Shah Jahan

Ans. (c) Aurangzeb

Q.13 Identify the odd one out regarding Mughal rulers

(a) Akbar (b) Aurangzeb
(c) Babur (d) Qutb-ud-din Aibak

Ans. (d) Qutb-ud-din Aibak

Q.14 Identify the following statements regarding the different rulers of the Mughal Empire and choose the correct option.

P : Babur founded the Mughal Empire after his victory at the Battle of Panipat in 1526.
Q : Akbar imposed harsh religious restrictions on non-Muslims and promoted Islam as the state religion.
R : Shah Jahan's reign is best known for its remarkable architectural achievements, including the construction of the Taj Mahal.
S : Aurangzeb was known for his tolerant policies towards non-Muslims, which helped maintain peace within the Empire.

Codes

(a) P and Q (b) P and R (c) Q and S (d) P and S

Ans. (b) P and R

Q.15 Who was responsible for military pay, accounts, recruiting soldiers, and maintaining a list of Mansabdars in the Mughal Empire?

(a) Dewan (b) Wazir
(c) Mir Bakhshi (d) Subedar

Ans. (c) Mir Bakhshi

TYPE - 2 1 Mark

Assertion-Reason Questions

Q.1 Read the two statements given below about the Taj Mahal and select the option that shows the correct relationship between (A) and (R).

Assertion (A) The Taj Mahal is built at Agra on the banks of river Yamuna.

Reason (R) The method of decoration used in Taj Mahal is called Pietra dura.

(a) R contradicts A
(b) R is the reason for A
(c) A is true but R is false
(d) A and R are independent of each other

Ans. (d) (A) and (R) are independent of each other

Q.2 Read the two statements given below about Babur and select the option that shows the correct relationship between (A) and (R).

Assertion (A) Babur defeated Ibrahim Lodhi at First Battle of Panipat in 1526 and occupied Delhi and Agra.

Reason (R) He wrote his memoirs in Tuzuk-i-Baburi in Turkish language, describing the flora and fauna of India and detailed record of his entire career.

(a) R contradicts A
(b) R is the reason for A
(c) A is true but R is false
(d) A and R are independent of each other

Ans. (d) A and R are independent of each other

Q.3 Read the two statements given below about the Jama Masjid and select the option that shows the correct relationship between (A) and (R).

Assertion (A) The Jama Masjid in Delhi is the largest mosque in India.

Reason (R) It was built by Emperor Aurangzeb using red sandstone and white marble.

(a) R contradicts A
(b) R is the reason for A
(c) A is true but R is false
(d) A and R are independent of each other

Ans. (c) A is true but R is false

Q.4 Read the two statements given below about the administration of the Mughals and select the option that shows the correct relationship between (A) and (R).

Assertion (A) The Mughal Emperor established a centralised state based on military power.

Reason (R) The centre appointed the officials of the provinces, sarkars and parganas.

(a) R contradicts A (b) R is the reason for A
(c) A is true but R is false
(d) A and R are independent of each other

Ans. (b) R is the reason for A

Q.5. Read the two statements given below about the Mughal Empire and select the option that shows the correct relationship between (A) and (R).

Assertion (A) There was no Mughal land revenue system before Akbar.

Reason (R) Akbar's predecessors continued with the existing land revenue system.

(a) R contradicts A (b) R is the reason for A
(c) A is true but R is false
(d) A and R are independent of each other

Ans. (a) R contradicts A

TYPE - 3 2 Marks

Very Short Answer Type Questions

Q.1 Who wrote Ain-i-Akbari? and How many books are there in the Ain-i-Akbari?

Ans. The Ain-i-Akbari was written by Abul Fazl, who was one of the nine jewels of Akbar's court.
There are five books in the Ain-i-Akbari.

Q.2 Give two reasons for the establishment of the Mughal Empire in India.

Ans. The two reasons of the establishment of the Mughal Empire in India include

(i) Babur's victory at the Battle of Panipat (1526) laid the foundation of Mughal rule in India.

(ii) The Mughal Emperors, especially Akbar, were skilled in political alliances and military strategies, which helped consolidate their power across India.

Q.3 Name two important sources that provide information about Mughals.

Ans. The two important sources that provide information about Mughals include

(i) Ain-i-Akbari

(ii) The Taj Mahal, Agra

Q.4 Mention the two taxes which were abolished by Akbar.

Ans. The two taxes which were abolished by Akbar include

(i) Jazya tax (ii) Pilgrim tax

Q.5 Mention any two features of educational reforms of Akbar.

Ans. The two features of educational reforms of Akbar include

(i) Akbar emphasised the study of secular subjects such as mathematics, history and astronomy apart from the study of religious scriptures.

(ii) During the Mughal period, female education also existed.

Q.6 Mention two important campaigns led by Akbar.

Ans. Two important campaigns led by Akbar were

(i) **The Conquest of Gujarat** (1572-1573) Akbar defeated the Gujarat rulers, expanding his empire's territory.

(ii) **The Battle of Haldighati** (1576) Akbar fought against Maharana Pratap of Mewar, although it was inconclusive, it marked a significant attempt to control the region.

Q.7 Imagine you were a Mansabdar during Akbar's reign. Give details of your powers and the salary received by you.

Ans. As a Mansabdar during Akbar's reign, I held a rank in the imperial administration. My duty was to maintain a specified number of cavalrymen and horses, ensuring they were properly registered.

I received my salary through Jagirs, which were revenue assignments. Additionally, I had the right to collect the revenue from these Jagirs, which was managed by my servants.

Q.8 Name any two architectural achievements of Shah Jahan.

Ans. The two architectural achievements of Shah Jahan include

(i) Taj Mahal, Agra (ii) Red Fort, Delhi

Q.9 Read the extract given below and answer the question which follows.

Aurangzeb Alamgir was a complex and polarising figure who left an indelible mark on Indian history. As the longest-reigning Mughal Emperor, Aurangzeb's rule was marked by a series of military conquests, political maneuverings, and religious policies that have ignited debates and controversies among historians and scholars for centuries. *The Economic Times*

(i) What were the geographical boundaries of Aurangzeb's Empire?

(ii) How did Aurangzeb's policies contribute to the weakening of the Mughal Empire?

Ans. (i) His Empire stretched from Kashmir in the North to Jinji in the South and from the Hindu Kush in the West to Chittagong in the East.

(ii) His policies, such as the re-imposition of the Jazya tax and strict religious policies, caused unrest and dissatisfaction among the people, leading to the weakening of the Empire.

Q.10 How did Aurangzeb's reign differ from that of his predecessors?

Ans. Aurangzeb's reign differed from his predecessors as he focused more on expanding the empire through military conquests, especially in the South. Unlike his predecessors, who promoted religious tolerance, Aurangzeb enforced strict Islamic laws and reimposed taxes on non-muslims, which led to growing resistance and internal conflicts.

TYPE - 4 — 3 Marks

Short Answer Type Questions

Q.1 Explain briefly about the political history of Babur.

Ans. Babur was the founder of the Mughal Empire in India. His original name was Zahir-ud-din Muhammad. Babur defeated Ibrahim Lodhi in the First Battle of Panipat in 1526 and established Mughal rule in India.

In 1527, Babur defeated Rana Sanga of Mewar in the Battle of Khanwa near Agra. In 1529, he defeated the Afghans in the Battle of Ghaghra in Bihar. Babur was succeeded by his son Humayun who was further succeeded by his son Akbar.

Q.2 "Akbar is known for his policy of religious tolerance and his efforts to foster good relations between Hindus and Muslims". Justify this statement by mentioning any four points.

Ans. The given statement can be justified with the following three points

(i) Akbar abolished the Jazya tax, which was previously imposed on non-Muslims, easing their financial burden.

(ii) Akbar also formed marriage alliances with Rajputs, like marrying Harkha Bai, which strengthened relations between Hindus and Muslims.

(iii) Akbar also promoted religious debate by setting up the Ibadat Khana, where scholars from different religions, including Hinduism, Islam, Christianity, and Jainism, could discuss ideas.

(iv) Akbar even attempted to create a new faith, Din-i-Ilahi, to foster harmony among various communities in his empire.

Q.3 Mention the three features of social reforms of Akbar.

Ans. The three features of social reforms of Akbar include

(i) He prohibited the practice of 'sati' though he allowed it is done voluntarily and he also legalised the remarriage of widows.

(ii) He did not encourage child marriages. The minimum age for the marriage of girls was raised to 14 years, while the age of the marriage of boys was raised to 16 years.

(iii) He abolished all inland customs and taxes on trades and professions.

Q.4 Mention any three reasons why Akbar built Ibadat Khana.

Ans The three reasons why Akbar built Ibadat Khana include

(i) To hold religious discussions between scholars and religious leaders of different faiths.

(ii) To promote religious tolerance and foster understanding among various communities.

(iii) To establish a platform for interfaith dialogue and to explore ideas for governance based on religious principles.

Q.5 Analyse how Aurangzeb's administrative, religious, and military policies contributed to both the expansion and eventual decline of the Mughal Empire.

Ans. Aurangzeb expanded the Mughal Empire to its largest size, stretching from Kashmir to Chittagong. He abolished some oppressive taxes and rituals, improving governance in parts of the empire. However, his harsh religious policies, like reintroducing Jazya tax, angered non-muslims and caused widespread revolts by Sikhs, Jats and Marathas.

His costly Deccan campaigns drained the treasury, creating financial problems. These policies weakened the empire's unity and administration. By the end of his 50-year reign, frequent rebellions and economic strain left the Mughal Empire unstable. After his death in 1707, the Empire began to decline rapidly, leading to its eventual collapse.

Q.6 Mention three key features of the judicial administration under the Mughal rule.

Ans. The three key features of the judicial administration under the Mughal rule include

(i) The king was at the top of the judicial administration. The courts of Sadr-us-Sudur and Qazi-ul-Qzat were next to the king's court. Sadr-us-Sudur decided the religious cases and the Qazi-ul-Qzat decided all other cases.

(ii) No codified laws existed in the Mughal judicial system.

(iii) The cases of the Muslims were decided on the basis of Quranic injunctions, Hadis or sayings of the prophet, Fatwas or decrees of the eminent judges, etc. In the case of the Hindus, the cases were decided in accordance with their customary and traditional laws.

TYPE - 5 4 Marks

Long Answer Type Questions

Q.1 Mention any four architectural features of Jama Masjid.

Ans. The four architectural features of Jama Masjid include

(i) It is the largest Mosque in India.

(ii) There are three gateways to the Jama Masjid mosque i.e. on the South, East and North sides. On the North and South sides, there are two elegant tapering minaret.

(iii) The central dome is the largest and highest, made of white marble, decorated with stripes of black colour.

(iv) The face of its large prayer hall has eleven arches, with the middle one rising higher than the roof level.

Q.2 Explain the following terms.

(i) Akbar's Rajput Policy (ii) Mansabdari System

Ans. (i) **Akbar's Rajput Policy** According to this policy, Akbar married Harkha Bai, the daughter of Raja Bharmal, thus maintaining friendly relations with Rajputs. He followed the policy of religious tolerance and gave the Rajputs noble positions in the Mughal government and thus ended the centuries old hatred between Muslim rulers and the Rajputs.

(ii) **Mansabdari System** It was a military and administrative system introduced by Akbar, where officers (Mansabdars) were assigned ranks based on the number of soldiers they were required to maintain. These officials were responsible for both military duties and collecting revenue, and their salary was paid through land assignments called Jagirs.

Q.3 Describe the steps taken by Akbar towards the integration of people.

Ans. The steps taken by Akbar towards the integration include

- **Religious Tolerance** Akbar followed a policy of religious tolerance, abolishing the Jazya tax on non-Muslims and engaging in discussions with scholars of different faiths, such as Hindus, Muslims, Christians, and Zoroastrians, to foster mutual understanding.
- **Marriage Alliances** Akbar formed matrimonial alliances with Rajput rulers and other local leaders, integrating them into the Mughal administrative system and ensuring their loyalty to the Empire.
- **Sulh-i-Kul (Universal Peace)** He introduced the policy of 'Sulh-i-Kul', which emphasised peace, tolerance, and the fair treatment of all people, regardless of their religion or ethnicity, ensuring social harmony across the Empire.
- **Inclusion of Hindus in Administration** Akbar appointed Hindus to high-ranking positions in his administration, including the powerful position of Prime Minister (Dewan-i-Ala) and military positions, thereby giving them a stake in the governance of the Empire.

Q.4 What were the key reforms introduced by Akbar in the land revenue system, and how did they improve tax collection and land measurement?

Ans. Akbar introduced important reforms in the land revenue system that helped improve tax collection and land measurement. These include

- He standardised the measurement of land, ensuring that all lands were measured in the same way.
- The produce of land per Bigha (half-acre) was determined, so the government could calculate taxes based on the crop yield.
- Akbar also fixed a share of the produce for the state, which made the tax system more predictable.
- He introduced the Dahsala or Zabti system, a method for assessing land tax based on average produce over ten years.

These reforms made the tax system fairer, easier to manage, and helped increase revenue for the Mughal Empire.

Q.5 Explain the significance of the Second Battle of Panipat in 1556, highlighting Akbar's conflict with Hemu, the role of Bairam Khan, and the outcome of the battle.

Ans. The Second Battle of Panipat, fought in 1556, was a crucial moment in Akbar's rise to power. Hemu, a general of Adil Shah, captured Delhi and Agra, threatening the Mughal Empire. Akbar's regent, Bairam Khan, led the Mughal army to confront Hemu.

Despite Hemu's bravery, he was defeated, and in the battle, he was injured by an arrow, which led to his capture. This victory allowed Akbar to regain control of Delhi and Agra, securing his rule over Northern India.

The battle also marked the beginning of Akbar's strong leadership and the consolidation of the Mughal Empire, setting the stage for his future conquests.

Q.6 **Explain the central and provincial administrative systems of the Mughal Empire. How did it ensure the efficient functioning of the empire?**

Ans. The Mughal Empire had a well-organised central and provincial administrative system to ensure smooth governance with officers such as

- **Wazir** At the central level, the Wazir was the chief minister who helped the emperor manage the empire.
- **Bakhshi** The Bakhshi was responsible for military matters and overseeing the army's welfare.
- **Subahdar** At the provincial level, the empire was divided into regions called Subahs, each governed by a Subahdar. The Subahdar acted as the governor and oversaw law, order, and revenue collection.

These officers played key role in maintaining stability. The Wazir made decisions on national issues, the Bakshi kept the army strong, and the Subahdar governed the provinces, ensuring that the empire's rules were followed locally. This division of responsibilities helped the Mughal Empire function smoothly and maintain control over vast territories.

Q.7 **Mention the four important officers who took charge in local administration during Mughal rule.**

Ans. The four officers in local administration included

(i) **Faujdar** He was the chief executive head of a Sarkar, to maintain law and order.

(ii) **Amalguzar** He was the revenue collector.

(iii) **Shiqdar** He was incharge of general administration, who had to maintain law and order of a Pargana. He was assisted by an Amil (revenue collector), an Amin (revenue assessor), a Potadar (treasurer), Qanungo (record keeper of land) and few Bitikchis (writers or clerks).

(Iv) **Muqaddam** He was the village head. He was assisted by the Patwari, who took care of village revenue records.

Q.8 **In the Mughal administration, revenue played a key role in maintaining the Empire. Explain the functions of the Diwan and how the revenue system was structured to ensure the smooth functioning of the Empire.**

Ans. The Diwan was an important official in the Mughal administration, responsible for managing the empire's finances and revenue. The Diwan supervised the collection of taxes, which were the main source of income for the empire. This income was used to fund the emperor's army, public works and other essential services.

The revenue system was well-organised, with land revenue being the largest source. Taxes were collected based on the land's fertility and produce. Officers like Amils and Qanungos helped in collecting these taxes. The system was carefully structured to ensure fair distribution and prevent corruption. This steady flow of revenue helped the Mughal Empire to maintain control over its vast territory and fund its administration efficiently.

TYPE - 6 — 10 Marks

Structured Questions

Q.1 Look at the picture given below and answer the following questions.

(i) How long did it take to complete this monument, and what was the main purpose of its construction? **(3)**

(ii) Mention the person who designed this monument. What is the method of decoration of this monument called? **(3)**

(iii) Describe the architectural features of this monument and explain how they contribute to its beauty. **(4)**

Ans. (i) It took about 22 years to complete the Taj Mahal, from 1632 to 1653.

The main purpose of building the Taj Mahal was to honour Mumtaz Mahal, the wife of Emperor Shah Jahan, who passed away. It was built as a symbol of his love and as a tomb for her in Agra, India.

(ii) The Taj Mahal was designed by Ustad Ahmad Lahori, the chief architect of the Mughal Emperor Shah Jahan.

The Taj Mahal is decorated using a technique called 'Pietra dura,' where semi-precious stones are inlaid into marble to create intricate patterns and designs. This decoration adds to its elegance and makes the monument a masterpiece of Mughal architecture.

(iii) The Taj Mahal is known for its stunning Mughal architecture, which blends Persian, Ottoman, and Indian styles.

- The main structure is made of white marble, giving it a beautiful shiny appearance. It has a large dome at the top, surrounded by four tall minarets, and is set in a beautiful garden.

- The entrance is marked by an impressive gateway with detailed carvings and floral designs. It is also famous for its intricate inlay work, with colourful stones decorating the walls.
- The symmetry of the design, where everything is perfectly balanced, adds to its elegance.

These features, along with the peaceful surroundings and the reflection of the Taj in the water, make it one of the most beautiful monuments in the world.

Q.2 Look at the picture given below and answer the following questions.

(i) Identify where this fort is located? Mention its ceremonial importance in the present. **(3)**

(ii) Describe the architectural style of the Red Fort and mention any three structures found within it. **(3)**

(iii) Describe any four architectural features of the fort. **(4)**

Ans. (i) The fort in the given picture is the Red Fort.

It is located in Delhi. This fort was built by Shah Jahan. Its ceremonial importance in the present lies in the fact that the Prime Minister of India every year unfurls the national flag from its ramparts on Independence day (15th August).

(ii) The Red Fort is an excellent example of Mughal architecture, blending Persian, Timurid, and Indian styles. It is known for its large, imposing walls made of red sandstone and beautiful decorative elements.

The important structures inside the fort are

- **Diwan-i-Aam** (Hall of Public Audience), where the emperor addressed the public.
- **Diwan-i-Khas** (Hall of Private Audience), where important meetings took place.
- **Moti Masjid** (Pearl Mosque) beautiful mosque made of white marble.

(iii) Four architectural features of the fort include

(a) The fort has massive walls and two gateways. The Western gateway is known as the Lahori Gate.

(b) It is surrounded by a strongly fortified wall.

(c) Red sandstone and marble were used in its construction.

(d) These buildings are decorated with pure white marble and inlaid with precious stones.

Q.3 With reference to the administrative system in the Mughal period, answer the following questions.

(i) Describe the role of the monarch in Mughal period. (3)

(ii) In the Mughal Empire, the ministers played crucial roles in the governance of the vast Empire. Who were the three important ministers? Also mention their roles in administration. (3)

(iii) Describe how the provincial government was set up. (4)

Ans. (i) The monarch or Emperor was the head of the Executive, Legislature, Judiciary and the Army. He was the supreme commander of armed forces and all other commanders were appointed and removed by him. He made laws and issued administrative ordinances.

(ii) The three ministers in Mughal Empire include

(a) **Wakil or Prime Minister** He was entrusted with great powers in civil and military affairs.

(b) **Diwan or Diwan-i-ala** He was the head of the revenue department. He was responsible for all income and expenditure.

(c) **Mir Bakhshi** He was the head of the military department and intelligence and information agencies of the Empire.

(iii) The Mughal Empire was organised into twelve large provinces known as subahs, which were further divided into sarkars, and each sarkar was split into parganas or mahal. Each subah was governed by a high-ranking official called the subahdar, who was usually a mansabdar of high rank.

The subahdar's responsibilities included maintaining law and order, implementing imperial orders, overseeing criminal justice, and ensuring the efficient collection of revenue. The Diwan of the province was responsible for managing the revenue administration of the province.

Other important officials at the provincial level included the faujdar (military officer), kotwal (chief of police), bakhshi (military paymaster), sadr qazi (religious judge), and muhtasib (market inspector). The officials at the provincial, sarkar, and pargana levels were all appointed by the central government, making them directly accountable to the emperor.

10

COMPOSITE CULTURE

- Composite culture is a diverse mixture of multiple cultures meeting and co-existing in one single religion.
- The composite culture was neither purely Indian nor entirely Persian, but a fusion of the best elements of the two religions.
- The interaction of the Turks with the Indians resulted in the development of a new composite culture, called the Indo-Islamic culture.

Sources of Composite Culture

Bijak

- Bijak (the seed book) is one of the earliest and most significant texts of the Bhakti movement. It is a compilation of the verses of Kabir, a 15th century Indian mystic poet and saint.
- The Bijak is divided into three main sections
  (i) **Ramaini** written in the chaupai form and is based upon a musical raga.
  (ii) **Shabda** is a flowing form of poetry.
  (iii) **Sakhi** composed in the doha or couplet form.
  Additionally, there is a fourth section containing miscellaneous folk-song forms.
- Kabir's teachings in Bijak focus on the idea that all religions are the same and that everyone is equal in the eyes of God.
- He rejected idolatry, meaningless rituals, and the caste distinctions that sustain social inequality. Instead, Kabir promoted devotion to a singular God, who may be worshipped under many names.
- In Bijak, Kabir highlighted that to find salvation, we must have a pure heart and avoid being cruel, dishonest, hypocritical or insincere.
- He imagined a society where true spirituality was measured by devotion and inner purity, not by rituals or the control of priests.

Guru Granth Sahib

- Guru Granth Sahib (Adi Granth) is the holy book of the Sikh religion.
- The fifth Sikh Guru, Guru Arjan Dev compiled Guru Nanak Dev's hymns in Guru Granth Sahib, along with those of his four successors and other religious preachers like Ravidas, Kabir and Baba Farid.
- The text has 1430 pages and 6000 verses, which are sung in a poetic style.
- Guru Granth Sahib contains the teaching of Guru Nanak Dev. He laid emphasis on the oneness or unity of God. His concept of God was Nirguna (attribute less) and Nirankara (formless).
- He emphasised the importance of devotion to God and the repetition of Satnam (god's name) which should be combined with meditation.
- He criticised the caste system of the Hindus as it was against the will of God.
- He believed in the doctrine of Karma and the theory of the reincarnation of the soul.

Ajmer Sharif

- Ajmer Sharif or Ajmer Dargah is the holy shrine built over the grave of the Sufi saint Hazrat Khawaja Moinuddin Chishti which is located in Ajmer, Rajasthan.
- Khawaja Moinuddin was a religious Persian Sufi saint who came to India and made Ajmer as his base until his death in AD 1236.
- He was well-known for his secular preachings which were accepted by all sections of the society.
- The construction of the shrine was started by Iltutmish and completed by the Mughal emperor Humayun.

Ajmer Sharif Dargah

- Nizam gate is the main gate to the dargah followed by Shahjahani gate (built by Shah Jahan) and Buland Darwaza that leads to the dargah courtyard.
- There are two huge degs (type of big pot) in the courtyard fixed into solid masonry, one of the degs was presented by Akbar and the other by Jahangir.
- The tomb of Khwaja Moinuddin is made of white marble inlaid with pieces of precious stones and is daily covered with sandalwood-paste and perfume.
- Urs, a yearly carnival is held in Ajmer for six days in the honour of Khawaja Moinuddin Chishti.

St. Francis Assisi Church

- St. Francis Assisi (1181-1226) was an Italian Roman Catholic priest and preacher.
- The Church of St. Francis in Fort, Kochi was originally built in 1503.
- It is one of the oldest European Churches in India and serves as the monument to the composite culture of India.

St. Francis Assisi Church

Factors Responsible for Composite Culture

Political Factors

- The Delhi Sultanate (1206–1526) and Mughal Empire (1526–1857) introduced Persian, Turkish, and Central Asian influences.
- Rulers like Akbar promoted Sulh-i-kul (universal peace) and patronised scholars from different faiths.
- Regional kingdoms like the Bahmani and Vijayanagara empires fostered cultural fusion.

Religious and Social Factors

- Sufi and Bhakti movements emphasised love, devotion and unity, bridging Hindu-Muslim traditions.
- Saints like Kabir, Guru Nanak, and Mirabai rejected religious orthodoxy and promoted spiritual equality.

Economic and Trade Factors

- India's role as a major trade hub facilitated cultural exchanges between Arabs, Persians, Turks and indigenous merchants.
- Cities like Delhi, Agra, Lahore, and Ahmedabad became centers of diverse cultural interactions.

Art, Architecture and Music

- Indo-Islamic architecture blended Persian, Turkish and Indian elements (e.g., Qutub Minar, Taj Mahal, Gol Gumbaz).
- Hindustani classical music developed through Persian and Indian influences, with contributions from Amir Khusrau.

Bhakti Movement

- Bhakti means devotion to God. It has its roots in the revival of the Indian philosophy.
- The Bhakti movement was founded in South India which later began to spread to the North during the late medieval period.
- It was led by devotional mystics (later revered as Hindu saints) who praised devotion and love to God as the chief means of spiritual perfection.
- It originated as a reaction against caste division and ritualism in India.

Principles of the Bhakti Movement

- Bhakti movement saints believed that intense love and devotion is the only way to salvation which can be attained through the repetition of the true name of the God only.
- They were against religious rites, rituals, ceremonies and blind faith.
- They didn't believe in distinction between different castes, higher or lower.
- They emphasised the need of a guru for guidance and realisation of God.
- They preached in local and regional languages. They travelled from place-to-place for spreading the religious message.

Sant Jnaneshwar or Dnyaneshwar (1275-1296 AD)

- Jnaneshwar was a 13th century Marathi saint poet, philosopher and yogi of the Nath tradition.
- His works of Jnaneshwari or Bhavartha Dipika (a commentary on Bhagwad Gita) and Amrutanubhav are considered to be most important achievements of Marathi literature.
- He emerged as a first original philosopher who wrote in Marathi language.
- He popularised yoga and believed in Vithala or Lord Vishnu.
- He criticised religious degeneration, sectarianism, superstition and ritualism, etc.
- He regarded bhakti as the means to liberation.
- In his famous work Abhangas, Namdev has given a graphic description of Jnaneshwar's visit to the holy places.
- Under the influence of Namdev, he joined the Varkari movement which combined jnana (knowledge) and bhakti (devotion) with teaching from the Vedas.
- Dnyaneshwar attained sanjerwan (alive) samadhi in 1296 AD at Alandi, Pune.

Mira Bai (1498-1546 AD)

- Mira Bai was a great woman saint of the Bhakti movement.
- She was born at the village of Kudki in the Merta district of Rajasthan in a royal rajput family.
- She was married to Raja Bhojraj in 1516.
- She was highly religious from her childhood and a follower of the Krishna culture of Vaishnavism.
- After the death of her husband, she devoted herself completely to religious pursuits. Her brilliant poetry is known as Padavali.
- Her songs were full of devotion and love, written in Rajasthani and Braj Bhasha.

Sufism

- Sufism is a mystic movement in Islam. Sufism began in Persia and Arabia to act as a bridge between Shia and Sunni Muslims.
- Sufis promoted an egalitarian society based on universal love, tolerance and divine unity. They believed all religions lead to the same God.
- Sufis lived in Khanqah (monastic communities) led by a Pir, with his successor called Wali and their followers known as Murids.

- By the 12th century, Sufis were divided into 12 orders or Silsilas. In India, Sufis belonged to the Chishti and Suhrawardi orders.

Principles of Sufism

- It emphasised love for God (Ishq-e-Haqiqi) and compassion for all human beings, regardless of religion or social status.
- It stressed upon monotheism and the idea that God is present in all beings.
- It rejected formal religious rituals, emphasising internal devotion, self-discipline, and sincerity in worship.
- It advocated helping the poor, orphans, and needy as a form of worship, encouraging selfless acts of kindness.
- It encouraged simple living and renunciation of worldly desires to focus on spiritual growth.

Hazrat Nizamuddin Auliya (1238-1325 AD)

- Hazrat Nizamuddin Auliya also known as Garib Nawaz was a Sufi saint of the Chishti order. He was born in Budaun, Uttar Pradesh.
- He followed the footsteps of Baba Farid, Bakhtiyar Kaki and Khwaja Moinuddin Chishti and succeeded Baba Farid after his death.
- He built a Khanqah in Delhi, a place where people from all backgrounds were provided food and taught spiritual lessons.
- His open-minded and tolerant beliefs were not liked by the religious leaders who followed strict traditions. However, this helped to spread his message across the country, and he earned the popular title Mehboob-e-Ilahi, (beloved of God).

Hazrat Nizamuddin's Teachings

- He believed in social work, helping the needy, feeding the hungry and being sympathetic to oppressed.
- He believed in renunciation and complete trust in God.
- He strongly disapproved integration with the service of the state.
- He believed in the unity of mankind and avoiding distinctions based on social, economic and religious status.

Impact of Composite Culture

Religious Harmony and Social Integration

- Bhakti and Sufi movements promoted religious tolerance and unity.
- Saints like Kabir and Guru Nanak rejected religious barriers and emphasised devotion over rituals.
- Intermarriages and social interactions led to cultural assimilation.

Development of Language and Literature

- Urdu evolved as a blend of Persian, Arabic, and Hindi.
- Regional languages like Bengali, Marathi, and Punjabi incorporated Persian and Arabic elements.
- Poets like Amir Khusrau merged Persian and Indian traditions in literature.

Evolution of Music and Dance

- Hindustani classical music emerged from Indian and Persian traditions.
- New instruments like the sitar and tabla were developed. Qawwali, a devotional Sufi music form, gained popularity.
- Kathak evolved as a fusion of Hindu storytelling and Persian court traditions.

Impact of Bhakti and Sufi Movements

Religious Tolerance and Harmony

- Bhakti and Sufi movements bridged Hinduism and Islam, fostering unity.

- Saints like Kabir and Guru Nanak preached oneness of God, beyond religious differences.
- Sufi saints like Khwaja Moinuddin Chishti and Nizamuddin Auliya emphasised universal brotherhood.

Social Reforms and Caste Equality

- Bhakti saints opposed caste divisions and promoted equality.
- Women saints like Mirabai and Akkamahadevi challenged gender discrimination.
- Sufis advocated for social justice and welfare of the poor.

Growth of Vernacular Literature

- Bhakti and Sufi saints popularised regional languages (e.g., Hindi, Marathi, Bengali, Punjabi, Tamil).
- Works like Guru Nanak's Gurbani, Kabir's Doha, and Tulsidas's Ramcharitmanas made teachings accessible.
- Urdu developed as a fusion of Persian, Arabic and local languages.

Reform in Religious Practices

- Both movements rejected rituals, idol worship, and priestly dominance.
- Bhakti emphasised personal devotion, while Sufism promoted Ishq-e-Haqiqi (divine love).

Influence on Indian Society and Politics

- Akbar's Sulh-i-Kul policy was inspired by Sufi ideals.
- The Bhakti movement influenced Sikhism, founded by Guru Nanak.
- Hindu-Muslim communities coexisted peacefully, shaping India's composite culture.

Influence of Christianity in India

- The arrival of Vasco da Gama in Calicut in 1498 AD is an important event in the history of Christianity.
- The visits of Roman Catholic Missions to India became more organised with the arrival of Portuguese to India.
- St. Francis Xavier was the first Jesuit Missionary to arrive in India.
- These missions were mainly established in coastal areas like Goa, Cochin, Tuticorin, and other regions along the coast.
- The Portuguese were motivated by the Pope's command to spread Christianity and baptise people across the world.
- They fought wars against the local Indian rulers and also tried to enforced their Roman Catholic prayers on Syrian Christians which paved way to the Christian missionaries.
- The Portuguese colonial government in Goa supported the mission in India by giving rewards to people who converted to Christianity, donating rice to the poor, and offering good jobs in the Portuguese colonies to the middle class.
- They also helped local rulers by providing military support.

St. Francis Xavier

- Francis Xavier was born on 7th April, 1506 in the Castle of Xavier, in the Kingdom of Navarre, Spain.
- He arrived in Goa, the then capital of Portuguese in India on 6th May, 1542.
- The primary mission of Francis, as ordered by King John III, was to bring Christianity back to the Portuguese settlers.
- Xavier spent the first five months preaching and helping the sick in hospitals.
- He was invited to head Saint Paul's College, a seminary for the education of secular priests. It became the first Jesuit headquarters in Asia.
- Francis was the first Jesuit to come to India, but he faced many challenges in his missionary work and did not achieve much success. He died on 2nd December, 1552, when he was on a sea voyage to China.
- The body of St. Francis Xavier is still enshrined in the Basilica of Bom Jesus in Goa.

EXAM ORIENTED QUESTIONS

TYPE - 1 1 Mark

Multiple Choice Questions

Q.1 Which of the following statements is correct about Bijak?
(a) Bijak is a collection of hymns written by Guru Nanak Dev.
(b) Bijak emphasise devotion to a personal god and rejection of ritualistic practices.
(c) The Bijak contains teachings focused solely on the caste system.
(d) Kabir's teachings in Bijak mainly promote the importance of idol worship.

Ans. (b) Bijak emphasise devotion to a personal god and rejection of ritualistic practices.

Q.2 Identify the correct statement about teachings of Kabir.
(a) Kabir was a follower of the Hindu beliefs and idol worship.
(b) Kabir's teachings emphasised the unity of God, rejecting religious divisions.
(c) Kabir was known for his support of the caste system and social hierarchy.
(d) Kabir's writings are mainly focused on the practices of Jainism.

Ans. (b) Kabir's teachings emphasised the unity of God, rejecting religious divisions.

Exp. Kabir believed in one God, rejecting idol worship and religious differences. He opposed caste discrimination and rituals, teaching that true devotion comes from a pure heart and love for God.

Q.3 His name means 'Great' in Arabic, a Quranic name - was a part of the Julaha caste, a weaver's son who started on his journey to become a poet, a philosopher, a guru, and a saint. He personified inclusivity through his Doha (Couplets). *The Indian Express, 14th June, 2022*
Which of the following saints is being discussed in the News above?
(a) Guru Nanak (b) Sant Tukaram
(c) Kabir (d) Sant Eknath

Ans. (c) Kabir

Q.4 Which of the following best reflects the teachings found in the Bijak?
(a) "The path of devotion is the only way to salvation".
(b) "God resides in all hearts, not in temples or idols".
(c) "Knowledge is power".
(d) "Love for all, hatred for none".

Ans. (b) "God resides in all hearts, not in temples or idols".

Q.5 Identify the odd one out statement about the Guru Granth Sahib.
(a) The Guru Granth Sahib is considered the eternal Guru by Sikhs.
(b) It contains hymns from Sikh Gurus and saints from various religions.
(c) The Guru Granth Sahib was compiled by Guru Nanak Dev alone.
(d) The Guru Granth Sahib is written in Gurmukhi script.

Ans. (c) The Guru Granth Sahib was compiled by Guru Nanak Dev alone.

Q.6 Read the description and identify the text.
It has 1430 pages and 6000 verses.
(a) Bijak
(b) Guru Granth Sahib
(c) Quran
(d) Abhangas

Ans. (b) Guru Granth Sahib

Exp. Guru Granth Sahib is the holy book of Sikhism. It includes hymns by Guru Nanak and other saints, promoting devotion to one God.

Q.7 Which of the following best describes the central philosophy of Guru Nanak Dev's teachings?
(a) The importance of rituals and ceremonies to achieve salvation.
(b) The belief in a formless, Nirguna God and the unity of all people.
(c) The idea of divine incarnation and idol worship.
(d) The superiority of the Hindu caste system over other social structures.

Ans. (b) The belief in a formless, Nirguna God and the unity of all people.

Q.8 Based on the image given below answer the following question.

Who among the following started the construction of this monument?

(a) Akbar (b) Humayun
(c) Iltutmish (d) Kabir

Ans. (c) Iltutmish

Q.9 Identify which of the following pairs are correct.

P : God is formless and resides in every being is conveyed in Saint Kabir's teaching.

Q : Equality, humility and love for all is conveyed by the Guru Nanak Dev ji.

R : Promotion of rituals and idol worship is advocated in Guru Granth Sahib.

S : The goal is spiritual liberation through practicing rituals.

Options

(a) P and Q (b) R and S (c) P and S (d) Q and R

Ans. (a) P and Q

Q.10 Which regional kingdoms played a significant role in fostering cultural fusion in medieval India?

(a) Chola and Rashtrakuta
(b) Bahmani and Vijayanagara
(c) Gupta and Maurya
(d) Maratha and Rajput

Ans. (b) Bahmani and Vijayanagara

Q.11 Which of the following is associated with the teachings of Sant Jnaneshwar?

(a) Worship of idols
(b) Belief in caste hierarchy
(c) Bhakti and Jnana
(d) Rejection of all scriptures

Ans. (c) Bhakti and Jnana

Exp. Sant Jnaneshwar taught that a person can achieve liberation through devotion (Bhakti) and knowledge (Jnana), rejecting idol worship, caste divisions, and focusing on the love for God and self-realisation.

Q.12 Which of the following is not the significance of Sufism?

(a) Their goal is union with god.
(b) Many sufis were strict vegetarian.
(c) The sufi was derived from the word 'Safa'.
(d) They focused on spiritual practices rather than worldly pleasures.

Ans. (d) They focused on spiritual practices rather than worldly pleasures

Q.13 What was a significant contribution of the Bhakti and Sufi saints to literature?

(a) Promotion of Sanskrit as the only language of religious texts
(b) Popularisation of regional languages through poetry and teachings
(c) Restriction of literary expression to elite classes
(d) Introduction of Latin in Indian literature

Ans. (b) Popularization of regional languages through poetry and teachings

Q.14 Who is recognised as the first Jesuit missionary to arrive in India?

(a) St. Francis Xavier (b) Vasco da Gama
(c) King John III (d) St. Thomas

Ans. (a) St. Francis Xavier

Exp. St. Francis Xavier was the first Jesuit missionary to come to India in 1542. He worked to spread Christianity and helped the sick, establishing the first Jesuit mission in Goa.

Q.15 Complete the given analogy.

Ajmer Sharif: Rajasthan:: St. Francis Church : ?

(a) Kochi (b) Delhi (c) Kolkata (d) Goa

Ans. (a) Kochi

TYPE - 2 — 1 Mark

Assertion-Reason Questions

Q.1 Read the two statements given below about the Bhakti movement and select the option that shows the correct relationship between (A) and (R).

Assertion (A) The Bhakti Movement promoted the worship of a formless God.

Reason (R) Saints like Kabir and Nanak rejected idol worship and emphasised devotion to a single, formless deity.

(a) R contradicts A (b) R is the reason for A
(c) A is true but R is false
(d) A and R are independent of each other

Ans. (b) R is the reason for A

Q.2 Read the two statements given below about the role of Sufism in India and select the option that shows the correct relationship between (A) and (R).

Assertion (A) Sufism played an important role in promoting religious tolerance in India.

Reason (R) Sufi saints were largely focused on spreading the teachings of the Quran without incorporating local traditions.

(a) R contradicts A
(b) R is the reason for A
(c) A is true but R is false
(d) A and R are independent of each other

Ans. (c) A is true but R is false

Q.3 Read the two statements given below about the impact of the Bhakti movement and select the option that shows the correct relationship between (A) and (R).

Assertion (A) The Bhakti movement led to the weakening of the caste system in India.

Reason (R) Bhakti saints like saint Jnaneshwar encouraged the idea of devotion to a personal god but did not openly challenge the caste system.

(a) R contradicts A
(b) R is the reason for A
(c) A is true but R is false
(d) A and R are independent of each other

Ans. (c) A is true but R is false

Q.4 Read the two statements given below about the composite culture in India and select the option that shows the correct relationship between (A) and (R).

Assertion (A) India's composite culture is a blend of various regional and religious traditions.

Reason (R) The interaction of different religious communities and their cultural practices, especially during the Mughal period, led to the development of a shared cultural identity.

(a) R contradicts A (b) R is the reason for A
(c) A is true but R is false
(d) A and R are independent of each other

Ans. (b) R is the reason for A

Q.5 Read the two statements given below about saints role in the Bhakti movement and select the option that shows the correct relationship between (A) and (R).

Assertion (A) The Bhakti movement emphasised personal devotion over ritualistic practices.

Reason (R) Saints like Ramanuja, Guru Nanak, and Sant Tukaram only promoted external rituals and did not advocate for personal devotion.

(a) R contradicts A
(b) R is the reason for A
(c) A is true but R is false
(d) A and R are independent of each other

Ans. (c) A is true but R is false

TYPE - 3 2 Marks

Very Short Answer Type Questions

Q.1 Name any two sections of the Bijak and explain them briefly.

Ans. The two sections of the Bijak are

(i) **Ramaini** It is written in a fixed poetic form (chaupai).

(ii) **Sakhi** It is written in couplets (doha). It contains teachings emphasising devotion to one God and rejection of rituals.

Q.2 Imagine you are a follower of Kabir and reading the Bijak. You come across verses that reject idolatry, rituals and caste distinctions, promoting devotion to a singular God.
How would you explain the message of equality and devotion in the Bijak to someone unfamiliar with Kabir's teachings?

Ans. In the Bijak, Kabir teaches that all people are equal, regardless of caste or rituals. He believes true devotion is about love for one God, not worshipping idols or following meaningless practices. It's about inner purity and sincerity.

Q.3 Mention two teachings of Guru Nanak Dev in the Guru Granth Sahib.

Ans. The two teachings of Guru Nanak Dev in the Guru Granth Sahib are

(i) **Oneness of God** He believed in one God who is formless and beyond human understanding.

(ii) **Equality of all people** He rejected the caste system and emphasised treating everyone equally.

Q.4 How did trade and economic interactions help in the development of composite culture?

Ans. Trade and economic interactions help in the development of composite culture in the following ways

- India's strategic location made it a key hub for trade, attracting merchants from Arab, Persian and Turkish regions.
- Exposure to foreign markets introduced new textile patterns, jewellery designs and handicraft techniques, enriching Indian art forms.

Q.5 **State any two important literary works of Jnaneshwar.**

Ans. The two important literary works of Jnaneshwar are Janeshwari (a commentary on Bhagwad Gita) and Amrutanubhav, which are considered to be milestones in Marathi literature.

Q.6 **Name the languages Mira Bai used for her poetry and mention the reason for her devotion to Krishna.**

Ans. Mira Bai wrote her poetry in Rajasthani and Braj Bhasha.

The reason for her devotion to Krishna is that she believed in his divine love and grace.

Q.7 **Name any two famous Sufi saints in India and the impact of Sufism in India.**

Ans. Hazrat Nizamuddin Auliya and Khawaja Moinuddin Chishti were two famous Sufi saints in India.

The two major contributions of Sufism are as follows

(i) Sufism neutralised the Hindu-Muslim tension in society. The belief of Sufi saints in equality led people to protest against caste domination, consumption of alcohol, gambling and slavery.

(ii) The Sufi saints made Islam a part of Indian culture by living and teaching in India, mixing with local traditions and practices.

Q.8 **Discuss the social reforms brought about by the Bhakti and Sufi movements.**

Ans. The social reforms brought about by the Bhakti and Sufi movements are as follows

- Female saints like Mirabai and Akkamahadevi defied societal norms and promoted gender equality in spiritual practices.
- Sufis emphasized helping the needy, orphans, and oppressed, promoting the idea of service to humanity as worship.

Q.9 **How did the Bhakti and Sufi movements influence Indian society and politics?**

Ans. The Bhakti and Sufi movements influence Indian society and politics in the following ways

- The Mughal emperor Akbar adopted the Sulh-i-Kul (universal peace) policy, influenced by Sufi ideals of religious harmony.
- The Bhakti movement played a role in the emergence of Sikhism, founded by Guru Nanak, which combined elements of both Hinduism and Islam.

Q.10 **Name the two places where Christian missions were established in India and why?**

Ans. Two places where Christian missions were established in India were Cochin and Tuticorn.

These coastal areas were key locations for Portuguese missionaries like St. Francis Xavier to spread Christianity, build churches, and educate people about the Christian faith.

TYPE - 4 — 3 Marks

Short Answer Type Questions

Q.1 **Explain the significance of Ajmer Sharif as a symbol of composite culture in India. How did Khwaja Moinuddin Chishti's teachings promote harmony among different communities?**

Ans. Ajmer Sharif, the shrine of Hazrat Khawaja Moinuddin Chishti, represents India's composite culture by embracing people from all communities, irrespective of their religious backgrounds. Khawaja Moinuddin Chishti's teachings focused on love, equality and service to humanity, emphasising that all religions lead to the same God.

His message promoted unity, tolerance and respect for diversity. The annual Urs festival at Ajmer Sharif symbolises this inclusivity, where people from different faiths come together to honor the saint's legacy, reflecting the harmony and shared values among different religious communities in India.

Q.2 **Mention any three teachings of Hazrat Nizamuddin Auliya.**

Ans. The three important teachings of Hazrat Nizamuddin Auliya are as follows

(i) Auliya believed in social work, helping the needy, feeding the hungry and being sympathetic to the oppressed.

(ii) Auliya believed in renunciation and complete trust in God.

(iii) Auliya strongly opposed mixing with sultans, princes, and nobles to avoid any kind of influence or dependence.

Q.3 **What is the importance of Sufism in creating a composite culture? Mention two key beliefs of Sufi saints.**

Ans. Sufism played an important role in creating a composite culture by promoting love, tolerance, and unity across different religions. Sufi saints believed that all religions lead to the same God and emphasised the importance of inner spirituality over rituals. They encouraged a peaceful society, focusing on love and devotion to God rather than religious divisions.

Two key beliefs of Sufi saints were

(i) They believe in God's love, mercy, and light as the ultimate quality.

(ii) They believe in the practice of devotion through chanting and music to strengthen the connection with God.

Q.4 The saints of Bhakti and Sufi movement promoted Hindu-Muslim unity in India. Justify the statement with suitable examples.

Ans. The saints of Bhakti and Sufi movement promoted Hindu-Muslim unity in India by emphasising devotion to God, love, and equality in the following ways

- **Guru Nanak** He promoted unity between Hindus and Muslims by advocating for the oneness of God, religious tolerance and rejected caste barriers.
- **Sant Kabir** He criticised both Hindu and Muslim rituals, and taught about direct devotion to God and emphasised on fostering unity through shared spiritual values.
- **Hazrat Nizamuddin Auliya** (Sufi) Auliya emphasised love, tolerance and equality by getting followers from both Hindu and Muslim communities.
- **Khwajah Moinuddin Chishti** (Sufi) Chisti's teaching of love, peace, and charity united people from diverse backgrounds by fostering interfaith harmony.

Q.5 Mention any four contributions of St. Francis Xavier in the growth of Christianity.

Ans. Saint Francis Xavier made significant contributions to the growth of Christianity in India in the following ways

(i) He played a key role in spreading Christianity by converting many people, especially along the coastal regions like Goa.

(ii) He established the first Jesuit mission in India, where he focused on education and community service.

(iii) He worked to restore and strengthen the Christian faith among the Portuguese settlers.

(iv) He introduced Christian teachings to the local people in their own languages, making the faith more accessible. His missionary work laid the foundation for the expansion of Christianity in India.

TYPE - 5   4 Marks

Long Answer Type Questions

Q.1 With reference to the influence of Christianity in India, explain about the following.

(i) Background of Christianity in India

(ii) Life of St. Francis Xavier

Ans. (i) The background of Christianity in India is associated with the arrival of Vasco da Gama in Calicut in 1498 AD. It is a landmark in the history of Christianity in India. With the arrival of Portuguese to India, the visits of Roman Catholic Missions to India became more organised and were initially concentrated to Goa, Cochin, Tuticorin and other coastal areas.

The Portuguese Colonial government in Goa supported Christian missions in India by giving rewards to people who were converts. They offered rich donations for the poor, good positions in the Portuguese colonies for the middle class and military support for local rulers.

(ii) Francis Xavier was born on 7th April, 1506, in the Castle of Xavier, Kingdom of Navarre, Spain. He played an important role in spreading Christianity, especially in India. He arrived in Goa, the capital of Portuguese on 6th May, 1542. Francis' primary mission, as ordered by King John III, was to restore Christianity among the Portuguese settlers.

Q.2 The arrival of Portuguese missionaries, particularly St. Francis Xavier, marked an important chapter in the history of Christianity in India. How did their efforts to spread Christianity shape the religious landscape of coastal India during the colonial period?

Ans. The arrival of Portuguese missionaries, especially St. Francis Xavier, in the 16th century significantly impacted the religious landscape of coastal India during the colonial period.

- St. Xavier arrived in Goa in 1542 and began spreading Christianity, particularly among the local population and Portuguese settlers.
- The Portuguese used their colonial power to support these efforts, offering rewards for conversions and promoting Christianity through schools and hospitals.
- Xavier's mission helped establish Christianity in regions like Goa, Cochin, and Tuticorin.
- These efforts led to the growth of Christian communities along the coastal areas, influencing local cultures.
- However, the missionaries also faced resistance from local rulers and traditional beliefs, creating both opportunities for new religious practices and tensions between different communities.

Q.3 Analyse the significance of the Bhakti movement in reformation of the contemporary society.

Ans. The significance of the Bhakti movement in reformation of the contemporary society were as follows

- **Rejection of the Caste System** Bhakti saints rejected the rigid caste system, promoting the idea that devotion to God was open to all, regardless of social status, fostering social equality.
- **Promotion of Religious Tolerance** The Bhakti movement emphasised the unity of all religions, as many saints, like Kabir, preached that God is one, fostering religious harmony and reducing communal divisions.
- **Simplification of Worship** Bhakti saints emphasised personal devotion over complex rituals, making spirituality accessible to everyone, regardless of their education or social standing.
- **Social Reform and Equality** Bhakti saints advocated for the rights of marginalised groups and fought against social injustice like untouchability, promoting a just society.

Q.4 Explain the significance of the Bhakti movement in promoting social equality. Mention any two saints associated with it and their contributions.

Ans. The Bhakti movement played a crucial role in promoting social equality by rejecting caste distinctions and rituals, emphasising love and devotion to God. It encouraged people from all social backgrounds to participate in spiritual practices, making religion accessible to everyone.

Two important saints of the Bhakti movement were Sant Jnaneshwar and Mirabai. Jnaneshwar criticised religious rituals and promoted devotion in Marathi.

Mira Bai expressed her deep love for Lord Krishna through devotional songs, inspiring many with her message of equality and devotion.

TYPE - 6 — 10 Marks

Structured Questions

Q.1 Look at the picture given below and answer the following questions.

(i) Identify the saint in the given image. Give some details of his early life. **(3)**

(ii) Highlight the relevance of his teachings in the contemporary socio-political conditions in India? **(4)**

(iii) Analyse the importance of Bijak in understanding the meaning of his philosophical ideas about God. **(3)**

Ans. (i) The given image is of Saint Kabir. He was a disciple of the Bhakti saint Ramananda.

Kabir was born in the 15th century, around 1398, in Varanasi, India. Some sources suggest that he was born to a Brahmin widow, while others claim he was found as an infant by a Muslim weaver couple, Niru and Nima.

(ii) Saint Kabir's teachings played a significant role in spreading the idea of Nirguna Bhakti (devotion to a formless God) in India. His relevance in this context is as follows

- **Rejection of Idol Worship** Kabir rejected the worship of idols and rituals, advocating for devotion to a formless God, emphasising that God transcends physical representations.
- **Universal God** He believed in a single, formless, omnipresent God that could not be confined to any religious structure or rituals. This idea resonated with the concept of Nirguna Bhakti, which focuses on a God beyond attributes.
- **Equality and Inclusivity** Kabir's focus on a formless God who does not differentiate between castes, religions, or social status spread the message of universal love and equality. Nirguna Bhakti reflects this by stressing that all can reach God through true devotion, irrespective of their background.
- **Simplicity in Devotion** Kabir's teachings emphasised simplicity in spirituality, encouraging individuals to connect with God through love, sincerity, and inner devotion, rather than through complex rituals.
- Kabir's spread of Nirguna Bhakti shaped spiritual practices in India, particularly in the Bhakti movement, by focusing on a personal and direct connection with the divine.

(iii) The Bijak is crucial for understanding Kabir's philosophy of God. It highlights his belief in a formless God (Nirguna) and rejection of idol worship and rituals. Kabir emphasises inner devotion over external practices, advocating for a personal connection with the divine. The Bijak promotes the idea of religious unity showing that God transcends all boundaries of caste, religion, and rituals.

Kabir's simple and direct spirituality is reflected in the text, urging followers to seek truth and devotion through sincerity rather than formal worship. It remains key to understanding the core of Kabir's philosophical ideas.

Q.2 With reference to the composite culture, explain the following.

(i) Explain the contribution of Sant Jnaneshwar to Marathi literature and philosophy. Highlight his major works and their significance in the Bhakti movement. (3)

(ii) Mirabai's devotion to Lord Krishna and her rejection of social norms are central to her poetry. How did Mirabai's songs contribute to the Bhakti movement, and what role did they play in promoting social change? (3)

(iii) How did the arrival of Vasco da Gama and the Portuguese paved the way for the spread of Missionaries in India? Highlight the role of the Portuguese colonial government in supporting missionary activities. (4)

Ans. (i) Sant Jnaneshwar was a 13th century Marathi saint, poet, and philosopher who made a lasting impact on Marathi literature and the Bhakti movement. His main work, Jnaneshwari (a commentary on the Bhagavad Gita), simplified complex spiritual ideas into the Marathi language, making them accessible to common people. Another key work, Amrutanubhav, discussed the union of devotion and knowledge.

He emphasised equality, devotion to God, and the rejection of rituals and caste discrimination. Jnaneshwar's teachings spread the message of love and unity, inspiring people to focus on personal spirituality. He also played a key role in popularising the Varkari tradition in Maharashtra.

(ii) Mirabai's songs played a crucial role in the Bhakti movement by emphasising devotion to Lord Krishna and rejecting traditional social norms, particularly the rigid caste system and gender roles. Her poetry expressed deep love and surrender to Krishna, encouraging people to focus on inner devotion rather than external rituals.

Mirabai's songs were a form of protest against societal constraints, especially the suppression of women. By singing in Rajasthani and Braj Bhasha, she made her messages accessible to the common people. Her poetry inspired many to challenge social injustice, promoting equality and devotion over caste or gender, and helped in the spread of the Bhakti movement across India.

(iii) The arrival of Vasco da Gama in 1498 marked the beginning of Portuguese influence in India. With the Portuguese colonisation, they established control over key coastal areas like Goa and Cochin.

The Portuguese colonial government supported missionary work by providing military aid, encouraging conversions, and offering rewards like jobs and donations to those who accepted Christianity. They sent missionaries, including St. Francis Xavier, to spread Christianity. The government helped the missionaries by offering resources, such as schools, churches, and protection, which allowed Christianity to grow in India during this time.

Q.3. With reference to the composite culture in India, answer the following questions.

(i) Discuss the role of Ajmer Sharif Dargah in promoting religious harmony and social unity. Explain how Khawaja Moinuddin Chishti's teachings influenced people of various communities and helped bridge the gap between Hindus and Muslims. (3)

(ii) Describe the influence of St. Francis Xavier in spreading Christianity in India during the Portuguese period. How did his missionary work contribute to the development of Indo-European relations? (3)

(iii) The concept of composite culture in India reflects the blending of diverse cultural elements from various communities. How did the Bhakti and Sufi movements contribute to the development of this culture, and what were two key elements that shaped it? (4)

Ans. (i) For answer, refer to Q.1 of Short Answer Type Questions.

(ii) For answer, refer to Q.2 of Long Answer Type Questions.

(iii) The Bhakti and Sufi movements played a crucial role in the development of India's composite culture by promoting unity, equality, and devotion over rituals and caste divisions. The Bhakti movement, led by saints like Kabir and Mirabai, emphasised love and devotion to God, transcending religious boundaries. Similarly, Sufi saints like Khawaja Moinuddin Chishti focused on universal love and tolerance, accepting people from all religions.

Two key elements that shaped this composite culture were the rejection of social inequalities (like the caste system) and the emphasis on spiritual devotion, which brought together different religious communities under shared values.

THE MODERN AGE IN EUROPE : RENAISSANCE

- The term Renaissance is derived from the French word meaning rebirth or revival.
- Renaissance was the revival of European art and literature under the influence of classical models.
- The Renaissance period dated from 14th century in Italy and lasted till 17th century. It spread across Europe from Italy.

Causes of Renaissance

1. Capture of Constantinople

- Constantinople (present day Istanbul) was the capital of the Eastern Roman Empire (Byzantine Empire) and centre of learning for Greek and Roman culture.
- On 29th May, 1453, the Ottoman Empire captured Constantinople, ending the Byzantine Empire. As a result, the Greek intellectuals left Constantinople and entered into cities of Italy like Venetia, Naples, Milan, Sicily, Rome, etc.
- They became famous by teaching Greek language and literature to the people.
- They taught mathematics, history, geography, philosophy, astronomy, medicine to the people of Italy.
- They spread their ideas and revived the interest of the people in the study of Greek philosophy, science, art and literature. This led to the foundation of the Renaissance.

2. Decline of Feudalism

- Feudalism was a way of structuring European society on the basis of land tenure which meant the holding of land in exchange for service and labour.
- In feudalism, Kings were at the highest level of feudal lords, subordinated by Dukes and Earls and they were subordinated by Barons. The knights were at the lower level.
- The rise of the middle class of traders and businessmen played a dominant role in the decline of feudalism.
- The decline of feudalism led to freedom and peace which further led to growth of new learning and development in the field of art, literature, philosophy and science.

3. New Trade Routes

- Due to the capture of Constantinople by the Turks in 1453, the trade routes between the West and East were closed. So, the European traders and navigators felt the need to discover new sea-routes.
- This led to the various sea expeditions or voyages, such as
  (i) Prince Henry, the navigator of Portugal was the first to discover a sea route to Africa.
  (ii) In 1488, Bartholomew Dias reached the Cape of Good Hope at the Southernmost point of Africa and proved that access to the Indian ocean was possible.
  (iii) In 1492, Christopher Columbus found the mainland of Central and South America on three later voyages.

(iv) In 1498, Vasco da Gama reached Calicut in India.

(v) In 1519, Ferdinand Magellan sailed from Spain to Brazil.

These voyages helped to create new trade routes that bring wealth to Europe. This led to the Renaissance in art, science and education.

4. Spirit of Enquiry

In the Medieval age, scholars developed a spirit of enquiry and a sense of curiosity among the people. They also questioned the authority of Church. These thoughts made the way for Renaissance.

- The factors responsible for the development of the spirit of enquiry were

(i) **Role of Crusades** The Crusades were religious expeditionary wars where people fought to gain control of holy places in and around Jerusalem, Israel. The Crusades brought ideas to Western Europe from the East. It helped them see life in a broader way. People began to rely on reason rather than on blind faith.

(ii) **Role of Original Thinkers** During the medieval Age, the Church discouraged original thinking and called upon scholars to put faith in the Church dogmas (principles).

Independent thinkers were called forerunners of Renaissance, as they criticised the Church and asked the people to develop their own thinking. The thought process was revolutionised by thinkers like Abelard, Roger Bacon and Thomas Aquinas and they laid stress on reasoning.

(iii) **Development of Science** Roger Bacon contemplated the use of horseless carriages and flying machines. Copernicus proved that the Earth moves around the Sun. Galileo invented the telescope.

5. Invention of the Printing Press

- In 1456, Johannes Gutenberg of Germany invented the printing press and set up the first printing press in Germany.
- In the middle of the 15th century, William Caxton brought this machine to England in 1476.
- With the passage of time, printing press was established in Italy, France, Belgium and other European countries.
- Printing and distribution of books influenced the attitude of people towards life and brought about a new awakening in Europe.

Impact of Renaissance

The Renaissance had a great impact on the various fields of art, architecture, painting, sculpture, literature and science. Its spirit led to significant developments in art, thought and literature.

Art and Architecture

- Artists started to focus more on people and their lives, paying more attention to nature, humanity, and similar topics.
- Artists started using new techniques like frescoes (wall paintings), oil paints, and woodcuts.
- The architects rejected the old Gothic style and accepted the Greeco-classical architecture.

Paintings

- The painters of Italy during Renaissance brought excellence and became world famous.
- They had a humanistic secular approach and produced life-like paintings.
- One of the most famous painter of Renaissance period was Leonardo da Vinci.

Leonardo da Vinci

The Last Supper by Leonardo da Vinci

- He was a great painter, sculptor, musician and a scientist.
- He had become immortal for his famous painting of the Mona Lisa.
- 'The Last Supper', 'The Virgin of the Rocks' and 'The Virgin and Child with Saint Anne' are his other famous paintings which are appreciated all over the world.

Sculpture

- Sculpture also underwent a significant change during the Renaissance period. Some artists copied the works of Greek and Romans, while others produced the works that could not match Greek works.
- The first famous sculptor of the Renaissance was Donatello, who created the bronze statue of David standing victorious over the body of the defeated Goliath.
- Lorenzo Ghiberti, a famous Italian sculptor during the Renaissance, carved the beautiful bronze doors for the Church in Florence, known for their stunning artistry.
- **Michelangelo's** huge marble statue of 'David' at Florence, give an idea about his greatness as a sculptor.

Literature

- The Renaissance literature originated in Italy.
- The first notable creation was Dante's 'Divine Comedy'. In the book, Dante describes about the heaven, hell and the other world.
- The famous philosopher of Italy was Machiavelli who described the principle of 'the lion and the fox' in his famous book The Prince.
- Ariosto's 'Orlando Furioso' and Tasso's 'Jerusalem Delivered' were two other great works of the Italian literature.
- By this time, Martin Luther of Germany translated the 'Bible' into German language.

William Shakespeare

William Shakespeare

- He was born in England, and was an English poet, playwright and actor. He is widely regarded as the greatest writer in the English language and world's pre-eminent dramatist.
- He is often called England National Poet and the Bard of Avon.
- His works include 38 plays, 154 sonnets, two long narrative poems and few other verses.
- His early plays were primarily comedies and histories but later, he wrote mainly tragedies including Hamlet, Othello, Macbeth, King Lear, Julius Caesar which are considered the finest works in English language.

Science

- The development in astrology, medicine and other branches of science made Renaissance distinct.
- Francis Bacon was a great scientist who advised to explore nature. He advised that truth was to be noticed by experiment.
- Another famous scientist of Renaissance period was Nicolaus Copernicus.

Nicolaus Copernicus

Nicolaus Copernicus

- He was born in Poland. He was a mathematician and astronomer of Renaissance and reformation-era.
- He formulated a model of the universe that placed the Sun instead of the Earth at the centre of the universe. This is called the heliocentric theory of universe.
- He was a polyglot (knowing or using several languages) and polymath (a person with wide-ranging knowledge) and obtained a degree in Canon Law.

Consequences of Renaissance

Changes in Government

- Kings and queens became more powerful, while feudalism (where lords controlled land) weakened.
- Some thinkers, like Machiavelli, introduced new ideas about leadership and politics in his book *The Prince*.
- Many European nations began forming strong centralised governments.

Religious Changes

- People started questioning the Church, leading to the Protestant Reformation with the spread of Martin Luther's ideas.
- The Catholic Church responded with the Counter-Reformation to regain followers.
- Religious conflicts, like wars between Catholics and Protestants, spread across Europe.

Growth in Trade and Money

- Cities like Florence and Venice became rich from trade.
- Banking became important, with rich families like the Medici supporting artists and scientists.
- More people like Columbus, Vasco da Gama started exploring new lands, leading to the Age of Discovery.

Social Changes

- More people learned to read and write because books became cheaper.
- The middle class (merchants, traders) grew stronger, while nobles lost some power.
- People started valuing individual talents and achievements more than before.

EXAM ORIENTED QUESTIONS

TYPE - 1

1 Mark

Multiple Choice Questions

Q.1 Which of the following was not a result of the fall of Constantinople?

(a) Discovery of new trade routes (b) Crusades
(c) Decline of feudalism (d) Revival of learning

Ans. (b) Crusades

Q.2 Which event led to the capture of Greek manuscripts and the spread of Greek philosophy during the Renaissance?

(a) Fall of Rome (b) Capture of Constantinople
(c) Rise of Feudalism (d) Invention of the Printing Press

Ans. (b) Capture of Constantinople

Exp. When the Turks captured Constantinople in 1453, Greek scholars fled with valuable manuscripts, spreading Greek philosophy and knowledge to Italy.

Q.3 Which invention led to the exploration of new trade routes during the Renaissance?

(a) Telescope (b) Mariner's Compass
(c) Printing Press (d) Telescope

Ans. (b) Mariner's Compass

Exp. The Mariner's compass enabled sailors to determine direction accurately, facilitating exploration of new trade routes during the Renaissance.

Q.4 Identify the odd one out of the following sea expeditions during the Renaissance:

(a) Christopher Columbus discovered America
(b) Vasco da Gama reached Calicut
(c) Ferdinand Magellan's voyage to Brazil
(d) Marco Polo's journey to China

Ans. (d) Marco Polo's journey to China

Exp. Marco Polo's journey to China occurred between 1271 and 1295, which predates the Renaissance period (14th to 17th centuries).

Q.5 Which of the following was not an impact of the Renaissance on art?

(a) A focus on the human form
(b) A shift away from religious themes
(c) The development of perspective in paintings
(d) Rejection of classical artistic methods

Ans. (d) Rejection of classical artistic methods

Exp. The Renaissance was actually marked by a revival of classical artistic methods from ancient Greece and Rome, rather than a rejection of them. Artists like Leonardo da Vinci and Michelangelo blended classical techniques with new innovations such as perspective and realism.

Q.6 Which of the following is the most likely reason for the spread of Renaissance ideas across Europe?

(a) Invention of the printing press
(b) The exploration of the New World
(c) The rise of Protestantism
(d) The creation of the Roman Empire

Ans. (a) Invention of the printing press

Q.7 Identify the following statements regarding the Renaissance and choose the correct pairs.

P : The Renaissance began in Italy and spread throughout Europe.

Q : The Renaissance rejected classical Greek and Roman ideas.

R : Humanism, which emphasised human potential and achievements, was a key idea during the Renaissance.

S : Artists during the Renaissance focused on abstract art and rejected realism.

(a) P and Q (b) P and R (c) Q and S (d) P and S

Ans. (b) P and R

Q.8 Which of the following was not likely a medium used by Renaissance artists?

(a) Oil paints (b) Frescoes
(c) Digital technology (d) Marble sculptures

Ans. (c) Digital technology

Q.9 The religious expeditionary wars with the goal of restoring the Church's access to holy places in and near Jerusalem was referred to

(a) Brisades (b) Black wars
(c) Agnar (d) Crusades

Ans. (d) Crusades

Q.10 Read the description and identify the person

'The last super' and the 'Virgins of the Rocks' are his famous paintings.

(a) Michelangelo (b) Raphael
(c) Leonardo da Vinci (d) Donatello

Ans. (c) Leonardo da Vinci

Q.11 Which of the following is the artist of this art work?

(a) Michelangelo (b) Raphael
(c) Leonardo da Vinci (d) Donatello

Ans. (c) Leonardo da Vinci

Q.12 Complete the given analogy.

Dante : Divine comedy : : Torquato Tasso : ?

(a) The Prince (b) Utopia
(c) King Lear (d) Jerusalem Delivered

Ans. (d) Jerusalem Delivered

Q.13 Complete the given analogy.

William Shakespeare : England : : Nicolaus Copernicus : ?

(a) Poland (b) Russia
(c) Denmark (d) Hungary

Ans. (a) Poland

Q.14 The book 'The Prince', written by Niccolò Machiavelli, is considered a key work of political theory. Which of the following ideas does it endorse?

(a) The ideal ruler should be guided by moral virtues.
(b) The ruler should be pragmatic and sometimes use deception to maintain power.
(c) The ruler should be a philosopher-king.
(d) The ruler should always act in the best interest of the people.

Ans. (b) The ruler should be pragmatic and sometimes use deception to maintain power.

Q.15 Look at the image below and choose the correct answer of the following question.

Which of the following theories in Science, was formulated by the person in the above image?

(a) Multiverse theory of universe
(b) Heliocentric theory of universe
(c) Steady state theory of universe
(d) None of the above

Ans. (b) Heliocentric theory of universe

Q.16 How did the Catholic Church respond to the Protestant Reformation?

(a) It ignored the changes
(b) It started the Counter-Reformation
(c) It encouraged more religious questioning
(d) It stopped all religious wars

Ans. (b) It started the Counter-Reformation

TYPE - 2 1 Mark

Assertion-Reason Questions

Q.1 Read the two statements given below about the Feudalism and select the option that shows the correct relationship between (A) and (R).

Assertion (A) The decline of feudalism contributed to the growth of Renaissance ideas.

Reason (R) The middle class gained power and provided funding for artistic and intellectual pursuits.

(a) (R) contradicts (A)
(b) (R) is the reason for (A)
(c) (A) is true but (R) is false
(d) (A) and (R) are independent of each other

Ans. (b) (R) is the reason for (A)

Q.2 Read the two statements given below about the Renaissance and select the option that shows the correct relationship between (A) and (R).

Assertion (A) Renaissance, which means rebirth or revival, was a complex transitional movement that began in Europe in the 14th century in Italy and lasted till 17th century.

Reason (R) Many Greek and Roman scholars shifted to Rome and revived the learning of Greek classics and paved the way for Renaissance.

(a) R contradicts A
(b) R is the reason for A
(c) A is true but R is false
(d) A and R are independent of each other

Ans. (b) R is the reason for A

Q.3 Read the two statements given below about the Renaissance and select the option that shows the correct relationship between (A) and (R).

Assertion (A) The wealthy merchants of Italy patronised the artists and literary figures for the revival of classical culture and literature.

Reason (R) The opening of new trade routes between the East and the West led to the revival of feudalism in Europe.

(a) R contradicts A
(b) R is the reason for A
(c) A is true but R is false
(d) A and R are independent of each other

Ans. (c) A is true but R is false

Q.4 Read the two statements given below about the Renaissance and select the option that shows the correct relationship between (A) and (R).

Assertion (A) Renaissance led to the use of local languages instead of Latin.

Reason (R) During Renaissance, the authors dwelt on spiritual themes.

(a) R contradicts A
(b) R is the reason for A
(c) A is true but R is false
(d) A and R are independent of each other

Ans. (c) A is true but R is false

Q.5 Read the two statements given below about the Renaissance and select the option that shows the correct relationship between (A) and (R).

Assertion (A) Renaissance led to the Reformation Movement in England and in Europe.

Reason (R) During the Renaissance period, there occurred a division of the Church into two sects - Catholics and the Protestants.

(a) R contradicts A
(b) R is the reason for A
(c) A is true but R is false
(d) A and R are independent of each other.

Ans. (b) R is the reason for A

Q.6 Read the two statements given below and select the option that shows the correct relationship between (A) and (R).

Assertion (A) Many European nations formed strong centralised governments.

Reason (R) The weakening of feudalism and the rise of powerful monarchs led to political unification.

(a) R contradicts A
(b) R is the reason for A
(c) A is true but R is false
(d) A and R are independent of each other

Ans. (b) R is the reason for A

TYPE - 3 — 2 Marks

Very Short Answer Type Questions

Q.1 Give two reasons why Renaissance began in Italy.

Ans. The two reasons why Renaissance began in Italy include

(i) Italy was the seat of the glorious Roman Empire and all the historical remains and relics of the Romans were found there.

(ii) As a result of fall of Constantinople, a large number of Greek scholars and thinkers migrated to Italy along with their original manuscripts and art treasures.

Q.2 Explain the role of Greek scholars in the Renaissance period.

Ans. Greek scholars played a key role in the Renaissance by bringing ancient Greek and Roman knowledge to Italy. They shared their writings on subjects like philosophy, science, and art, which sparked renewed interest and helped shape the Renaissance period.

Q.3 Who was Christopher Columbus? What did he discover during his voyages?

Ans. Christopher Columbus was an Italian explorer. In 1492, he sailed westward to find a new route to Asia but instead discovered America, landing in the Caribbean. His voyages helped connect Europe to the New World.

Q.4 Mention any two factors that led to the growth of the spirit of enquiry among the people of Europe.

Ans. Two factors that led to the growth of the spirit of enquiry in Europe were

(i) **Role of Original Thinkers** Thinkers like Roger Bacon, Abelard, and Thomas Aquinas encouraged people to think independently and question the Church's teachings. They promoted reasoning and critical thinking, which sparked intellectual growth.

(ii) **Development of Science** Scholars in the medieval period started adopting a scientific approach by observing nature. This led to new inventions and discoveries, fostering a spirit of enquiry and scientific temper.

Q.5 **Mention two scientific developments that contributed to the spirit of enquiry during the Renaissance.**

Ans. Two scientific developments that contributed to the spirit of enquiry during the Renaissance are:

(i) The invention of the telescope by Galileo, which allowed for improved observation of the heavens and contributed to a new understanding of the cosmos.

(ii) The heliocentric theory proposed by Copernicus, which challenged the traditional geocentric model and placed the Sun at the center of the universe, prompting further scientific investigation.

Q.6 **Imagine that you went to Rome during the period when the Renaissance movement was at its peak. Describe the spirit of Renaissance among the artists, scientists, authors and the masses.**

Ans. When I went to Rome during Renaissance, I saw that there was a vibrant energy of discovery and creativity. Artists, scientists, and authors were inspired by a renewed interest in classical knowledge, leading to groundbreaking work in art, science, and philosophy.

The masses welcomed the new ideas, human potential and the pursuit of knowledge. The city was alive with innovation, as people sought to explore and understand the world in deeper, and in more meaningful ways.

Q.7 **Mention any two voyages that took place during the era of exploration.**

Ans. Two of the voyages that took place during the era of exploration were

(i) In 1488, Bartholomew Dias rounded the Cape of Good Hope and proved that access to the Indian ocean was possible.

(ii) In 1498, Vasco da Gama reached Calicut in India.

Q. 8 **Name the inventor of the printing press and mention one impact of its invention.**

Ans. The inventor of the printing press was Johannes Gutenberg.

One impact of its invention was that it made books cheaper and faster to produce, allowing more people to access information and leading to the spread of knowledge in Europe.

Q.9 **Name two important artists of the Renaissance and their contributions.**

Ans. Two important artists of the Renaissance were Leonardo da Vinci and Michelangelo. Leonardo painted the famous Mona Lisa and The Last Supper, which are known for their lifelike details. Michelangelo created the David statue and painted the Sistine Chapel's ceiling, showing mastery in both sculpture and painting.

TYPE - 4 — 3 Marks

Short Answer Type Questions

Q.1 **"The decline of feudalism led to the rise of Renaissance". Justify this statement by mentioning any three points.**

Ans. The given statement can be justified by the following three points

(i) The decline of feudalism created a wealthy middle class, including merchants and bankers, who supported art, learning, and culture, which contributed to the Renaissance.

(ii) The decline of feudalism provided an impetus to free thinking.

(iii) The peace and freedom that prevailed after the decline of feudalism favoured the growth of new learning.

Q.2 **Name three explorers who contributed to the discovery of sea routes that expanded European trade during the Renaissance.**

Ans. Three explorers who contributed to the discovery of sea routes during the Renaissance were

(i) **Bartholomew Dias** He reached the Cape of Good Hope in 1488, opening the sea route to India.

(ii) **Vasco da Gama** He reached India in 1498, further expanding trade routes.

(iii) **Christopher Columbus** He discovered America in 1492, connecting new trading territories.

Q.3 **How did the discovery of new trade routes contribute to the expansion of the Renaissance period?**

Ans. The discovery of new trade routes during the Renaissance helped Europe connect with new regions, bringing in wealth, goods, and ideas. Explorers like Vasco da Gama and Christopher Columbus found new routes to Asia, America and trade grew. This increased wealth in countries like Italy, which funded art, literature, and learning.

The exchange of ideas and cultures boosted the Renaissance, making it a time of new discoveries in science, art, and philosophy.

Q.4 The Renaissance, which means 'rebirth' in French, typically refers to a period in European history from AD 1400 to AD 1600. Many historians, however, assert that it started earlier or ended later, depending on the country. *Live Science*

(i) How did the Crusades influence the Renaissance?

(ii) What invention helped sailors discover new trade routes during the Renaissance?

Ans. (i) The Crusades helped the Renaissance by bringing new ideas from the East to Europe. Europeans learned about new science, philosophy, and art from the Muslims and Byzantine Empire, which sparked a desire for knowledge and a cultural revival.

(ii) The mariner's compass, invented during the Renaissance, enabled sailors to determine direction accurately, facilitating long voyages and new trade routes.

Q.5 State any three impacts of the Renaissance brought in the field of sculpture.

Ans. The three impact of the Renaissance brought in the field of sculpture include

(i) The first great sculptor of Renaissance was Donatello, who made the bronze statue of David, triumphant over the body of the defeated Goliath.

(ii) The famous sculptor of Italy during Renaissance period was Lorenzo Ghiberti, who carved the bronze doors of the Church at Florence which was famous for its exquisite beauty.

(iii) Michelangelo's huge marble statue of 'David' at Florence, give an idea about his greatness as a sculptor. He had also made the grand statue of 'Moses' and completed the construction of 'Basilica of St. Peter' in Rome.

Q.6 Mention any three famous writers of Renaissance with their works.

Ans. The three famous writers of Renaissance with their works were

(i) The Italian philosopher, Machiavelli described the principle of 'the Lion and the Fox' in his famous book 'The Prince'.

(ii) Ariosto's 'Orlando Furioso' and Tasso's 'Jerusalem Delivered' were two other great works for the Italian literature.

(iii) Rabelais' 'Gargantua' and the writings of Racine, Sevigne and La Fontaine created golden age in the French literature.

TYPE - 5

4 Marks

Long Answer Type Questions

Q.1 Explain any four causes that led to the emergence of the Renaissance in Europe.

Ans. Four key causes that led to the emergence of the Renaissance in Europe are

(i) **Capture of Constantinople** Greek scholars moved to Italy, bringing ancient knowledge and ideas that sparked interest in Greek and Roman culture.

(ii) **Decline of Feudalism** As feudalism declined, the rise of middle class allowed the growth of trade, wealth, and new learning.

(iii) **New Trade Routes** The search for new sea routes to the East led to more exploration, bringing new knowledge and wealth to Europe.

(iv) **Spirit of Enquiry** The Crusades and the work of independent thinkers encouraged people to question old beliefs and explore new ideas in science, art, and philosophy.

Q.2 Explain the following terms.

(i) Fresco

(ii) Spirit of Enquiry

Ans. (i) **Fresco** It is a painting technique in which pigments are applied onto a wet plaster surface. The paint becomes an integral part of the wall as the plaster dries, creating durable and vibrant wall art. This technique was commonly used during the Renaissance to decorate large walls and ceilings of Churches and palaces.

(ii) **Spirit of Enquiry** It refers to the curiosity and desire to question, explore, and understand the world. During the Renaissance, it encouraged people to seek knowledge in science, philosophy, and art.

Q.3 "Renaissance artists tried to depict life on canvas and stone". With reference to this statement, describe the progress in the art of painting.

Ans. The painters during Renaissance established very high standards and showcased some of the greatest paintings of the time. The artists of the Renaissance period refused to abide by general rules, tradition and adopted new artistic methods such as frescoes for wall pictures, oil colors and woodcuts.

They studied optics and geometry and used their knowledge to develop perspective in their paintings. They also studied human anatomy to find the mechanism underlying gestures and expressions. They had a humanistic secular approach and produced highly artistic and life like paintings.

Q.4 Describe the life and contribution of William Shakespeare in the context of the Renaissance period.

Ans. William Shakespeare, born in England during the Renaissance, was a poet, playwright, and actor, widely regarded as the greatest writer in English. He is known as the 'Bard of Avon'.

William Shakespeare's contribution in the Renaissance period were

- His works include 38 plays, 154 sonnets, and two long narrative poems.
- His early works focused on comedies and histories, while later he wrote famous tragedies like Hamlet, Macbeth, and Julius Caesar.
- In his final phase, he wrote tragicomedies and collaborated with others, embodying the Renaissance ideals of creativity, humanism, and artistic excellence.

Q.5 Explain the importance of the spirit of enquiry during the Renaissance. How did developments in science, such as those by Galileo and Copernicus, challenge old beliefs and contribute to a new way of thinking about the world?

Ans. The spirit of enquiry during the Renaissance encouraged people to question old beliefs and seek new knowledge. Scientists like Galileo and Copernicus challenged the long-held idea that the Earth was the center of the universe. Copernicus proposed that the Sun was at the center, and Galileo supported this with observations through a telescope.

These discoveries led to a shift in how people viewed the world, moving away from religious explanations and focusing more on scientific evidence and reasoning. This new way of thinking helped lay the foundation for modern science and changed the course of history.

Q.6 "Renaissance or rebirth brought about drastic changes in art, literature and science". In this context, describe the contribution of Copernicus.

Ans. The Renaissance, known as the rebirth of art, literature, and science, sparked changes.

The contributions of Nicolaus Copernicus in this context were

- As a Renaissance-era mathematician and astronomer, Copernicus revolutionised science by introducing the heliocentric theory, which placed the Sun, not the Earth, at the center of the universe.
- This idea challenged old beliefs and inspired further discoveries by scientists like Kepler, Galileo, and Newton.
- A true Renaissance polymath, Copernicus also excelled as a physician, scholar, diplomat, and economist, embodying the spirit of inquiry and knowledge of the era.

TYPE - 6 — 10 Marks

Structured Questions

Q.1 Many factors contributed to usher in the spirit of Renaissance, which had far-reaching consequences for the entire world. In this context, answer the following questions.

(i) "The printing press, a spark that ignited the flames of knowledge and revolutionised the Renaissance." Justify the statement. (3)

(ii) How did the fall of Constantinople in 1453 contribute to the spread of Greek culture and the Renaissance? (3)

(iii) What was the reason behind the decline of feudalism? Mention any four. (4)

Ans. (i) The given statement can be justified, by highlighting the following three points regarding the invention of the printing press

- The invention of printing press in the middle of the 15th century in Europe made it possible to produce books in large numbers. The Bible and many other religious and classical books were printed and made available all over Europe.
- The printing press spread knowledge far and wide. Scholars found it easier to read printed books than hand-written manuscripts.
- The printing press enabled Europe to multiply books and put them within the reach of people. Printing and distribution of books influenced people's attitude to life and brought about a new awakening in Europe.

(ii) Constantinople was the capital of the Eastern Roman Empire and was a centre of Greek and Roman culture. It had valuable manuscripts of Greek and Roman writers. But Constantinople fell into the hands of Turks in 1453.

Many Greek and Roman scholars were forced to shift to Rome and other parts of Europe with their manuscripts. Rome then became the centre of Greek culture. These scholars were genius, men of liberal outlook, humanism and logical thinker. Wherever they went, they spread their new spirit and ideas.

They revived the interest of people in the study of Greek philosophy, science, art and literature. The revival of the learning of Greek classics paved the way for the Renaissance.

(iii) The reasons behind the decline of feudalism were

(a) **Rise of the Middle Class** The growth of a middle class of traders and businessmen provided the necessary funds to the king, reducing the power of feudal lords.

(b) **Growth of Towns and Cities** Increased trade and the rise of towns diminished the role of feudal estates as the main centers of economic activity.

(c) **The Black Death** The plague reduced the population, creating a labour shortage and leading to greater demands for workers, which weakened the feudal system's rigid structure.

(d) **Military Changes** The development of new military technology, like the longbow, made knights less important, reducing the reliance on the feudal military system.

Q.2 Look at the picture given below and answer the following questions.

(i) Identify the painting. Name the artist who made it. Name other famous painting by the same artist. (3)

(ii) "Paintings are the reflection of the personal experiences and imaginations". Explain the life and contributions of the artist who made this painting. (3)

(iii) Describe the changes occurred in the style of painting as a result of the Renaissance spirit in Europe. (4)

Ans. (i) The given painting is 'The Last Supper'.

Leonardo da Vinci was the artist who made it.

'Mona Lisa' is another famous painting by him.

(ii) Leonardo da Vinci was a talented painter, sculptor, musician, and scientist. He was interested in many things beyond art, including nature, mechanics, anatomy, physics, architecture, and weapons. He trained in painting and sculpture with Andrea del Verrocchio and learned about mechanical arts.

Da Vinci believed that art and science were connected, and ideas from one could help the other. He spent a lot of time studying nature, testing scientific laws, dissecting animals and humans, and writing about his findings.

In the 1490s, he started to focus on four main areas – painting, architecture, mechanics, and human anatomy and created thousands of detailed drawings. Some of his famous paintings include 'Virgin of the Rocks', 'The Last Supper', and the 'Mona Lisa'.

(iii) For answer, refer to Q.3 of Long Answer Type Questions.

Q.3 With reference to the rise of the Renaissance, answer the following questions.

(i) The Renaissance saw a flourishing of literature, with major literary figures shaping the cultural and intellectual development of the period.

Explain the role of major literary figures during the Renaissance. How did writers like Dante, Petrarch, and Boccaccio help shape the cultural and intellectual landscape of the time? (3)

(ii) In what ways did the Crusades contribute to the spread of Renaissance ideas? (3)

(iii) Why did cities like Florence and Venice become wealthy during the Renaissance period? (4)

Ans. (i) During the Renaissance, writers like Dante, Petrarch, and Boccaccio played a key role in shaping literature and culture in the following ways

- Dante's Divine Comedy explored themes of the afterlife, introducing new ideas about life and the world.
- Petrarch promoted humanism with his poetry, focusing on individual emotions and human experiences, which encouraged people to think beyond religious beliefs.

- Boccaccio's Decameron questioned traditional views on religion and society, promoting a more secular outlook.

These writers helped bring about a shift in thinking, encouraging people to focus on human experiences, reason, and the beauty of the world, marking the start of the Renaissance.

(ii) The Crusades helped spread Renaissance ideas by bringing Western Europeans into contact with the cultures of the East. During their journeys to the Holy Land, Crusaders encountered advanced knowledge in science, philosophy, and art from the Arab world, including Greek and Roman texts. Many of these ideas were brought back to Europe, where they influenced scholars and artists.

The Crusades also opened up new trade routes, allowing goods and ideas to flow more freely between East and West. This exchange of knowledge and culture helped lay the foundation for the intellectual awakening that became the Renaissance.

(iii) Florence and Venice became wealthy due to the following reasons

- Florence and Venice thrived due to their strategic locations. Venice, a key Mediterranean port, traded silk, spices, and metals from the East, while Florence, positioned along major trade routes, prospered through its profitable wool and silk industries.
- Banking boosted the wealth of Florence and Venice. Florence, led by the Medici, financed trade and introduced financial innovations, while Venice used its wealth to support maritime trade and a strong navy.
- The economic success of Florence and Venice allowed their wealthy elites, including the Medici family in Florence and the Doges in Venice, to sponsor artists, architects, and scholars.
- Both cities had stable political structures that promoted economic growth. Venice was ruled by an oligarchy of wealthy merchant families, while Florence was controlled by powerful banking dynasties like the Medici.

12

THE MODERN AGE IN EUROPE : REFORMATION

Meaning of Reformation

- The Reformation was a group of religious movement launched by the Christians that opposed the authority and practices of the Church and the objectionable practices of the clergyman.
- It was a protest against corruption and wrong practices in the Church, monasticism, such as its rituals, sacraments (holy ceremonies), and the Pope's involvement in non-religious matters.
- The people who opposed the Pope were called Protestants, while those who supported him were known as Roman Catholics.
- The Reformation began in countries like England, France, Germany, Switzerland, Scotland and Czechoslovakia. It played an important role in ending blind faith and outdated beliefs of that time.

Causes of the Reformation

The immediate cause of the reformation was Martin Luther, a German priest, who challenged the Pope's authority and protested against Church abuses. Apart from this, the two most prominent causes behind reformation were

(i) Dissatisfaction with the practices of the Catholic Church

During the early medieval period, the Church had become a hierarchical organisation headed by the Pope as its head in Rome. However, during the 14th century, many people were dissatisfied with certain practices of the Church. This growing dissatisfaction led to the Reformation. These church practices were the following

- Church priests and high-ranking officers gained positions through corrupt practices. They led lives of luxury and immorality.
- Priests and Church officers issued indulgences (a way to reduce the amount of punishment), or pardon certificates, in exchange for payment. This practice was described as the 'sale of licenses to commit sin'.
- The Church imposed taxes such as Peter's Pence and the tithe which was one-tenth of a person's income.
- The Popes interfered in political matters, which was opposed by kings. European kings, like French King Philip IV and King Henry VIII of England, disagreed with the Pope over the royal right to tax Church property.

(ii) New Learning

- The spread of learning and spirit of enquiry developed by the Renaissance scholars, greatly contributed to the Reformation.
- The invention of the printing press and the translation of the Bible into local languages encouraged people to question blind faith and unnecessary religious rituals.
- People began to believe they could connect with God without a priest's mediation.

- Nobles and merchants envied the wealth of the Church, while ordinary people in Europe were upset about paying Church taxes.
- The changing attitude of people towards the Church contributed to the growth of secular ideas.

Contribution of Martin Luther in Reformation

Martin Luther

- Martin Luther (1483-1546) started the Reformation in Germany. He was the first reformer to lead a large movement against the Church.
- In 1512, after visiting Rome, he was shocked by the luxurious lives of Church officials. This made him a strong critic of the Church.
- In 1517, he publicly challenged the sale of indulgences by agents of Pope Leo X, who were raising money to finish building St. Peter's Church in Rome.
- In 1517, he wrote Ninety-five Theses in Latin on the Wittenburg Church door. His theses challenged the Church practices.
- Luther's movement spread to other parts of Europe, including Sweden, Norway, and Denmark. This movement came to be known as German Protestant Movement.
- To face the Emperor, Luther and his followers formed the Schmalkaldic League, which led to a religious civil war (1546-1553).
- Nine years after Luther's death in 1555, the Peace of Augsburg treaty was signed.
- Lutherism was accepted as another legal form of Christianity.

Counter Reformation

- In response to the Protestant Reformation in Germany, Switzerland and Scandinavia, some devoted Christians, including some Popes, tried to make changes in the Catholic Church in Italy, Austria, France and Spain.
- The Counter Reformation aimed to defend Catholic practices and reorganise the Church, involving five major elements
  (i) Reactionary defence of Catholic sacraments
  (ii) Structural reconfiguration of the Church
  (iii) Formation of religious orders
  (iv) Spiritual movements
  (v) Political actions

  The Counter Reformation included the following reforms

The Council of Trent (1545-1563)

- The council summoned by Pope Paul III in 1545, aimed to explain Catholic beliefs and make changes in areas like finance and education.
- The Church updated its service books and released a new version of the Vulgate and the Latin Bible.
- Catholics were prohibited from reading certain heretical books (religious opinion). These books were listed in a list called the Index.
- The Council of Trent set up seminaries to train priests. It also stopped the sale of indulgences, fees that was charged for religious services, and encouraged the use of local languages for preaching in the Church.

The Society of Jesus

- It was founded by Ignatius Loyola, a Spanish noble, in 1534. Its members were called the Jesuits. Jesuits worked to spread reformed Catholic teachings across Europe, as well as in China, India, Africa and America.
- The hard work and dedication of Jesuits like Loyola and St. Xavier had a big impact on the Counter Reformation. This helped to restore the reputation of the Roman Catholic Church.

EXAM ORIENTED QUESTIONS

TYPE - 1 — 1 Mark

Multiple Choice Questions

Q.1 Which of the country was not the part of this image?

Protestant Reformation

(a) China (b) France
(c) Germany (d) Scotland

Ans. (a) China

Q.2 Identify the reason behind the reformation movement.
(a) Caste system (b) Colonial rule
(c) Social inequality (d) Corruption

Ans. (d) Corruption

Exp. The reformation movement protested against corruption in the Catholic Church, such as the sale of indulgences, luxurious lives of Church officials, and political interference by the Pope. It aimed to reform these practices.

Q.3 Read the following and identify the person.
He issued pardon certificates called indulgences.
(a) Martin Luther
(b) Pope Leo X
(c) Philip IV
(d) King Henry VIII

Ans. (b) Pope Leo X

Exp. Pope Leo X issued indulgences, which were certificates sold to people, promising forgiveness for sins. Martin Luther criticised this practice, sparking the reformation movement.

Q.4 Identify the causes of the Reformation.
P : Dissatisfaction with the practices of the Catholic Church
Q : Corruption and immoral practices within the Church
R : Purchasing of indulgences by the Church
S : Murder of the priests of the Church.

Codes
(a) P and Q (b) R and S (c) P and R (d) Q and S

Ans. (a) P and Q

Q.5 Which of the following was not part of the corruption criticised by reformers during the reformation?
(a) Selling indulgences to forgive sins
(b) Priests charging fees for religious services
(c) Pope's involvement in political matters.
(d) Establishing monasteries to accumulate wealth

Ans. (d) Establishing monasteries to accumulate wealth

Q.6 Identify the odd one out from the following factors that led to criticism of the Church during the Reformation.
(a) The sale of indulgences
(b) The Church's wealth
(c) Church taxes on common people
(d) The secular perspective of the Renaissance

Ans. (d) The secular perspective of the Renaissance

Q.7 Luther was a professor of theology at the University of Wittenburg in Germany and a Catholic monk. He authored ninety-five Theses, or doctrines

Norwegian SciTech News

In which year did Martin Luther write the Ninety-five Theses?
(a) 1520 (b) 1517 (c) 1512 (d) 1521

Ans. (b) 1517

Q.8 What was Martin Luther's primary objection to the Catholic Church that led to the Reformation?
(a) The Church's rejection of feudalism
(b) The authority of kings over the clergy
(c) The belief that salvation could be bought through indulgences
(d) The Church's refusal to translate the Bible into Latin

Ans. (c) The belief that salvation could be bought through indulgences

Q.9 Which of the following best describe the role of the Jesuits in the Counter-Reformation?

(a) They led violent uprisings against Protestant rulers.

(b) They spread Catholic teachings and established educational institutions.

(c) They promoted secularism and scientific discoveries over faith.

(d) They attempted to merge Catholic and Protestant beliefs.

Ans. (b) They spread Catholic teachings and established educational institutions.

TYPE - 2 1 Mark

Assertion-Reason Questions

Q.1 Read the two statements given below about the Catholic Church and select the option that shows the correct relationship between (A) and (R).

Assertion (A) The dissatisfaction with the practices of the Catholic Church was one of the main causes of the Reformation.

Reason (R) Church practices like selling indulgences and corruption led to a loss of faith among the people.

(a) R contradicts A

(b) R is the reason for A

(c) A is true but R is false

(d) A and R are independent of each other

Ans. (b) R is the reason for A

Q.2 Read the two statements given below about the printing press and select the option that shows the correct relationship between (A) and (R).

Assertion (A) The invention of the printing press contributed significantly to the Reformation.

Reason (R) It helped spread ideas against the Church and made it easier for people to access the Bible in local languages.

(a) R contradicts A

(b) R is the reason for A

(c) A is true but R is false

(d) A and R are independent of each other

Ans. (b) R is the reason for A

Q.3 Read the two statements given below about Martin Luther and select the option that shows the correct relationship between (A) and (R).

Assertion (A) Martin Luther was sheltered by Duke Frederick of Saxony after his trial at the Diet of Worms.

Reason (R) Martin Luther's translation of the Bible into German helped people understand Christian teachings without relying on the clergy.

(a) R contradicts A

(b) R is the reason for A

(c) A is true but R is false

(d) A and R are independent of each other

Ans. (d) A and R are independent of each other

Q.4 Read the two statements given below about King Henry VIII and select the option that shows the correct relationship between (A) and (R).

Assertion (A) King Henry VIII broke away from the Catholic Church and established the Church of England.

Reason (R) He opposed the teachings of Martin Luther and wanted to preserve Catholic traditions.

(a) R contradicts A

(b) R is the reason for A

(c) A is true but R is false

(d) A and R are independent of each other

Ans. (c) A is true but R is false

Q.5 Read the two statements given below about the Council of Trent and select the option that shows the correct relationship between (A) and (R).

Assertion (A) The Council of Trent was convened to address the issues raised by the Protestant Reformation.

Reason (R) The Council of Trent rejected Catholic doctrines and adopted Protestant beliefs.

(a) R contradicts A (b) R is the reason for A

(c) A is true but R is false

(d) A and R are independent of each other

Ans. (c) A is true but R is false

TYPE - 3 2 Marks

Very Short Answer Type Questions

Q.1 Mention any two corrupt practices of the Catholic Church during the Reformation period.

Ans. Two corrupt practices of the Catholic Church during the Reformation period were

(i) **Simony** Church offices were sold to the highest bidder and unsuitable men were often appointed as priests.

(ii) **Selling Indulgences** The Church sold certificates to buy forgiveness for sins, which many viewed as a way to exploit people's faith for financial gain.

Q.2 **Imagine you were a peasant in the year 1517. Mention any two ways in which the policies of the Catholic Church during the Reformation would have impacted your life.**

Ans. If I were a peasant in the year 1517, the Catholic Church's policies would have greatly affected my life. First, the Church's heavy taxation, including the tithe, would have financially burdened me, as I would have to give a portion of my income.

Second, the sale of indulgences would have left me feeling helpless, as I would have to rely on the clergy for spiritual salvation, which limits my direct connection with God.

Q.3 **Mention any two economic factors that led to the Reformation.**

Ans. Two economic factors that led to the Reformation were

(i) **Corruption in the Church** Church officials lived luxurious lives, and positions were bought and sold.

(ii) **Sale of Indulgences** The Church sold pardons certificates and issued indulgences, which upset many people. These practices led to growing dissatisfaction and the call for change.

Q.4 **Give two reasons for Martin Luther's opposition to the sale of indulgences.**

Ans. The two reasons for Martin Luther's opposition to the sale of indulgences were

(i) He believed that selling indulgences, which promised forgiveness of sins, went against the real Christian idea of sorrow and faith.

(ii) He saw the practice indulgences as a form of corruption, as a way for the Church to take advantage of people's fear of going to hell for money.

Q.5 **How did the spirit of new learning from the Renaissance contribute to the Reformation?**

Ans. The spirit of new learning from the Renaissance contributed to the Reformation by making people question old religious practices.

The printing press and translation of the Bible allowed people to connect with God on their own. It weakened the Church's power.

Q.6 **List two outcome of the Peace of Augsburg treaty.**

Ans. The two outcome of 'The Peace of Augsburg' treaty were

(i) It allowed rulers to choose either Catholicism or Lutheranism as the official religion of their territories.

(ii) It officially recognised Lutheranism as a legal form of Christianity, ending religious conflicts in Germany.

Q.7 **Describe two key changes introduced by the Council of Trent.**

Ans. Two key changes introduced by the Council of Trent were

(i) **Training of Priests** The Council established seminaries to train priests more effectively, to make them knowledgeable and morally upright.

(ii) **Reformation of Church Practices** The sale of indulgences was stopped, and the Church prohibited charging fees for religious services.

TYPE - 4 — 3 Marks

Short Answer Type Questions

Q.1 **What were the causes of the Reformation? Briefly explain each one.**

Ans. The causes of the Reformation were

- **Dissatisfaction with the Church** People were unhappy with the Church's corrupt practices, like selling indulgences and the luxury of priests.
- **New Learning** The Renaissance encouraged people to think critically, and the printing press helped spread ideas that questioned the Church's authority.

These factors led to a movement for change, challenging the power and practices of the Catholic Church.

Q.2. **What was the Great Western Schism and how did it affect the Catholic Church?**

Ans. The Great Western Schism (1378-1417) was a split within the Catholic Church when two Popes were elected-one by French cardinals in Avignon and the other by Italian cardinals in Rome. This division caused confusion and weakened the Church's authority.

The Schism led to a loss of faith in the papacy, as people struggled to accept which Pope was the legitimate one. This weakened the Church's unity and influence across Europe.

Q.3 **European kings opposed the Pope's political interference. Justify this by mentioning any three points.**

Ans. European kings opposed the Pope's political interference for several reasons

- The Pope's control over church lands and wealth limited the power of monarchs.
- The Church's influence over taxation, such as Peter's Pence, burdened common people and weakened royal authority.

- Conflicts like King Philip IV forcing Pope Clement V to move to Avignon showed the growing tension between the Church and Kings, as Kings wanted more independence and control over their own affairs.

Q.4. **Mention the major establishments born out of the Council of Trent?**

Ans. The Council of Trent was responsible for many major establishments such as

- Appointed seminaries to educate and train priests.
- Catholics were prohibited from reading certain heretical books.
- No fees were to be charged for religious services.
- Started preaching in the local language in the Church.

TYPE - 5 4 Marks

Long Answer Type Questions

Q.1 **Discuss the role of political interference in the Church's decline during the Reformation. How did the action of European Kings, such as King Philip IV and King Henry VIII, contribute to the spread of the Reformation?**

Ans. Political interference played a significant role in the Church's decline during the Reformation as follows

- Kings like King Philip IV of France and King Henry VIII of England disagreed with the Pope's control over their countries in political and financial matters.
- King Philip IV had conflicts with the Pope over taxes, and King Henry VIII wanted to control the Church in England.
- These actions weakened the Pope's authority and helped spread Reformation ideas. European rulers saw the Reformation as a way to gain more power and reduce the Church influence over their kingdoms, which turned out to be a great support for the movement.

Q.2 **Examine how internal divisions within the Catholic Church and new learning contributed to the reformation.**

Ans. Internal divisions within the Catholic Church, like the election of multiple Popes, caused confusion and weakened people's faith. This made many people to question the Church authority.

At the same time, the Renaissance sparked a new spirit of learning and questioning. The invention of the printing press allowed ideas to spread quickly, and people began to challenge the Church's teachings and rituals. These factors together led the Reformation, as people sought religious change and reform.

Q.3 **Mention any four contributions of Martin Luther in the reformation movement.**

Ans. The four contributions of Martin Luther were

(i) Publishing of the the Ninety-five Theses in 1517, challenging the sale of indulgences.

(ii) In 1520, he ignored Pope Leo X's order and publicly burned the Papal Bull.

(iii) Translating the Bible into German, which makes it comprehensible to the common people.

(iv) His actions inspired many German princes to leave the Catholic Church, leading to the creation of Lutheran Churches across Europe.

Q.4 **Read the extract given below and answer the questions which follows.**

The Counter Reformation was a response to the Protestant Reformation, where devoted Christians, including some Popes, initiated reforms in Italy, Austria, France and Spain to restore the Catholic Church's reputation.

(i) What were the main goals of the Counter Reformation?

(ii) What role did the Society of Jesus play in the Counter Reformation?

Ans. (i) The main goal of the Counter Reformation were to defend Catholic doctrines and practices against Protestant criticism to restore the authority of the Catholic Church, and address internal corruption. It sought to reform Church structures, promote education, and strengthen spiritual movements.

(ii) The Society of Jesus, founded by Ignatius Loyola in 1534, played a pivotal role in the Counter Reformation. Jesuits helped spread Catholic teachings in Europe and other parts of the world.

They focused on education, missionary work, and encouraged people to stay loyal to the Church. They established schools and seminaries, helped restore the Catholic faith, and strengthened the Church's influence in regions like China, India, and America.

TYPE - 6 10 Marks

Structured Questions

Q.1 With reference to the Reformation answer the following questions.

(i) Who were called protestants during the Reformation and what were their main beliefs and actions? **(3)**

(ii) What role did the printing press play in the Reformation? **(3)**

(iii) How did the Reformation challenge the Pope's authority? **(4)**

Ans. (i) During the Reformation, people who opposed the authority and practices of the Catholic Church were called protestants. They criticised issues like the sale of indulgences, the Pope's power, and corrupt practices within the Church. The movement began with figures like Martin Luther, who challenged Church practices and sought reforms.

Protestants believed in direct communication with God and rejected the idea that only the Church could provide salvation. They formed new Christian groups, such as Lutheranism and Calvinism, that spread across Europe and led to the division of Christianity.

(ii) The printing press played an important role in spreading the ideas of the Reformation.

- It allowed books like Martin Luther's Ninety five Theses and other religious writings to be printed and shared with many people rapidly.
- Printing allowed books to be printed in languages that people spoke. This helped them to understand religious ideas on their own instead of depending on the Church to explain everything.
- People could read the Bible in their own language, which helped them understand it differently. This led to more people questioning the Church and its corrupt practices, like selling indulgences.

(iii) The Reformation challenged the Pope's power by questioning both his spiritual and political authority. Martin Luther, for example, disagreed with the Pope's right to sell indulgences and his role as the only one who could interpret the Bible.

The Reformation taught that faith alone could bring salvation and that the Bible was the highest authority, not the Pope. This caused a split from the Catholic Church, as many European kings supported the Reformation to reduce the Pope's control over their countries.

Q.2 With reference to the given picture, answer the following questions.

(i) Explain about the personality shown in the above picture. **(3)**

(ii) What were the political and religious consequences of Martin Luther's actions in Germany and Europe during the Reformation? **(4)**

(iii) Lutheranism was recognised as a legal form of Christianity. How Lutheranism was accepted as legal form? **(3)**

Ans. (i) Martin Luther is shown in the given picture. He was the first reformer who led a large number of people to openly break ties with the Church. He was a native of German and became monk at the age of 22. In 1517, he wrote 'Ninety-five Theses' on the Wittenburg Church door, which challenged the Church practices.

(ii) Martin Luther's actions had significant political and religious consequences in Germany and Europe. Religiously, his challenge to the Catholic Church led to the spread of Protestantism, with many German princes supporting Lutheranism and establishing Lutheran Churches. This divided Europe into Catholic and Protestant regions.

Politically, it weakened the power of the Pope and the Catholic Church, as monarchs like King Henry VIII of England used the Reformation to assert more control over religious matters in their kingdoms. Luther's actions also sparked religious conflicts, such as the Thirty Years' War, and eventually led to the Peace of Augsburg, allowing religious freedom in the Holy Roman Empire.

(iii) Luther and some German princes formed the Schmalkaldic League to face the challenge of Emperor Charles V. This led to a religious Civil War during 1546-1553 AD. Finally, nine years after the death of Luther, a treaty known as 'The Peace of Ausburg' was signed by which Lutheranism was accepted as another legal form of Christianity. The Northern states of Germany accepted Lutheranism while the Southern states remain loyal to the Catholic Church.

Q.3. The Reformation was a religious movement sparked by internal divisions within the Catholic Church, political interference, and corruption, with figures like Martin Luther challenging Church practices. With reference to this, answer the following questions.

(i) Describe the major reforms introduced during the Counter Reformation, focusing on the role of the Council of Trent and the Society of Jesus in defending Catholic practices. **(3)**

(ii) Explain the significance of the Great Western Schism in weakening the authority of the Catholic Church. **(3)**

(iii) Martin Luther's challenges to Church practices, especially the sale of indulgences, sparked widespread religious reform across Europe. **(4)**

What were Martin Luther's key contributions to the reformation movement?

Ans. (i) The Counter Reformation brought key reforms to the Catholic Church such as

- **The Council of Trent** (1545-1563) It aimed to clarify Catholic beliefs and improve the Church's practices. It stopped the sale of indulgences, trained priests, and encouraged the use of local languages in sermons.
- **The Society of Jesus** It was founded by Ignatius Loyola. It played a major role in spreading Catholic teachings. Its members were called 'Jesuits' Their work was to restore the reputation of the Church and spread Catholic teachings across Europe.

(ii) For answer, refer to Q.2 of Short Answer Type Questions.

(iii) For answer, refer to Q.3 of Long Answer Type Questions.

13

INDUSTRIAL REVOLUTION

Definition and Meaning of Industrial Revolution

- The Industrial Revolution can be described as the period of rapid industrialisation characterised by the transition from hand made production to machine made production. The term Industrial Revolution was first used by a British historian, Arnold Toynbee.
- The **first stage of revolution**, from 1750 to 1870 in England, saw a move from slow expensive hand production to faster and cheaper machine production.
- The **second stage of revolution**, started after 1870, mainly involved the application of science to industry and mass production techniques. It spread in countries like France, Belgium, North America, Germany and Russia to meet growing demands for goods.

Causes of Industrial Revolution

The Industrial Revolution was driven by the following key factors

1. **Agricultural Growth** Improved agriculture resulted in population growth which lead to surplus workforce.
2. **Development of Transportation** New and improved roads, canals and railways facilitated the movement of raw materials and goods.
3. **Expansion of Trade and Capital** Colonial trade, banking and investment provided funding for factories.
4. **Discovery of Natural Resources** Discovery of natural resources like iron, coal and other resources fueled machinery and infrastructure.
5. **Spread of Education and Awareness** Beginning of the Renaissance and the Reformation made people aware and educated which helped in the growth of industries.

Capitalism

- Capitalism is an economic system where businesses and industries are owned and run by private individuals with an aim to make profit and gain wealth.
- In common language, the wealth used for making more wealth is known as capital and the owner of this capital is known as Capitalist.
- Capitalism increases productivity through the division of labour. It breaks tasks into smaller parts.

Causes for the Rise of Capitalism

1. **Population Growth** Improved wealth, healthcare and purchasing power during the Industrial Revolution led to a population increase. People moved from rural to urban areas for jobs and better opportunities.
2. **Growth of Towns** New towns and cities developed near coalfields and supplied fuel to the factories. It led to the rapid growth of new towns and cities.
3. **Mass Production** Machines helped produce goods on a large scale. Mass production allowed capitalists to gather huge wealth, leading to the rise of capitalism.

4. **Decline of Small Farmers** Many small farmers moved to new industrial towns for work after industrialists bought their land. Reformers began to speak of the mills and factories as dark, evil places.

Socialism

- Socialism emerged as a response to the negative effects of capitalism and aimed to improve workers' conditions.
- It is an economic system where the means of production are owned by the community to ensure fair wealth distribution.
- Socialism is based upon three principles as follows
  - (i) It is opposed to private capitalism.
  - (ii) It is the voice of all workers and the working class.
  - (iii) It demands a fair distribution of wealth.
- The key socialists were
  - (i) **Early Socialists** Babeuf, Saint-Simon, Charles Fourier, Robert Owen (father of British socialism), and Louis Blanc.
  - (ii) **Scientific Socialists** Karl Marx and Friedrich Engels.
  - (iii) **Democratic Socialists** Bernstein, Jean Jaurès, Bernard Shaw, and Sidney Webb, supported socialism by promoting peaceful and democratic methods.

Causes for the Rise of Socialism

- **Reaction to the Evils of Capitalism** The Industrial Revolution created two classes: Capitalists and Socialists. Capitalists became rich by exploiting workers and lived luxurious lives. On the other hand, socialists fought for workers' rights, aiming to protect them from capitalist exploitation.
- **Trade Union Movement** A strong trade union movement developed in India which forced the British Government to acknowledge the rights of the workers. It highlighted the growing division between the rich and poor. This led to the shift in perspective among many workers.
- **Chartist Movement** This movement took place from 1836 to 1848, led by workers who presented their demands to Parliament in the form of a charter. The movement aimed to secure voting rights for workers but this resulted in riots and strikes. It declined in the mid-19th century.

This created clear divisions between the rich capitalists and the poor workers, leading to the idea of socialism.

Comparative Study Between Socialism and Capitalism

Capitalism	Socialism
Its economic model allows free market conditions to drive innovation and wealth creation.	It incorporates elements of centralised economic planning, utilised to ensure conformity and to encourage equality of opportunity and economic outcome.
The means of production such as labour, raw-materials, tools and machines are owned by the private individuals or capitalists.	The state owns and controls the major means of production.
Wealth is distributed unequally.	Focuses on equal distribution of wealth.
State does not employ the workforce directly.	State is the primary employer.
The motto of capitalism is profit maximisation and accumulation of wealth.	The motto of socialism is to bring changes through revolution and abolition of social classes.
It led to the unfair treatment of the poor and divided the society into two classes- the rich and the poor	It seeks to end all forms of exploitation and give equal opportunities to all classes of people.

EXAM ORIENTED QUESTIONS

TYPE - 1 — 1 Mark

Multiple Choice Questions

Q.1 Read the following and identify the person.
He was the first person to use the term 'Industrial Revolution'.
(a) James Watt (b) Abraham Darby
(c) Karl Marx (d) Arnold Toynbee

Ans. (d) Arnold Toynbee

Exp. Arnold Toynbee was the first person to use the term 'Industrial Revolution' to describe the shift from hand-made to machine-made production during the 18th century.

Q.2 Undergirding the development of modern Europe between the 1780s and 1849 was an unprecedented economic transformation that embraced the first stages of the great Industrial Revolution and still more general expansion of commercial activity. *Britannica*

Why Industrial Revolution was different from other revolutions?
(a) It was quick and violent
(b) It was gradual and peaceful
(c) It was driven by wars
(d) It was limited to rural areas

Ans. (b) It was gradual and peaceful

Q.3 Identify the country where the first stage of the Industrial Revolution occurred between 1750 and 1870.
(a) Germany (b) England
(c) France (d) Russia

Ans. (b) England

Exp. During this stage, England shifted from hand-made to machine-made production, making goods faster and cheaper.

Q.4 Identify the key factors that led to the rise of capitalism during the Industrial Revolution.
P : Population growth and urban migration
Q : Development of mass production techniques
R : Equal distribution of wealth
S : Decline of small farmers and traditional jobs
(a) P and Q (b) R and S (c) P and R (d) P and S

Ans. (a) P and Q

Q.5 In a capitalist economic model, who owns the means of production?
(a) The state
(b) The government
(c) Private individuals or capitalists
(d) The working class

Ans. (c) Private individuals or capitalists

Exp. In capitalism, businesses and industries are owned by private people who aim to make a profit.

Q.6 Which of the following was not a reason for the spread of capitalism during the Industrial Revolution?
(a) Mass production of goods
(b) Population migration to urban areas
(c) Equal wealth distribution
(d) Growth of towns near industrial centers

Ans. (c) Equal wealth distribution

Q.7 Which of the following best describes the primary goal of Socialism?
(a) Maximisation of profits for capitalists
(b) Revolution and abolition of social classes
(c) Free markets and private business ownership
(d) Increase in imperialism and colonialism

Ans. (b) Revolution and abolition of social classes

Q.8 Identify the odd one out from the following key socialist leaders.
(a) Karl Marx
(b) Friedrich Engels
(c) Robert Owen
(d) Adam Smith

Ans. (d) Adam Smith

Exp. Adam Smith is known for his capitalist ideas, while Karl Marx, Friedrich Engels, and Robert Owen were socialists who advocated for workers' rights and equal wealth distribution.

Q.9 Read the description and identify the person.
He was known as the father of British socialism.
(a) Charles Fourier
(b) Robert Owen
(c) Louis Blanc
(d) Karl Marx

Ans. (b) Robert Owen

Q.10 Complete the given analogy.

Capitalism : Wealth accumulation : : Socialism :?

(a) Class division (b) Social equality

(c) Profit maximisation (d) Market competition

Ans. (b) Social equality

Exp. In capitalism, wealth accumulation is a key goal, while in socialism, the focus is on creating social equality by ensuring fair distribution of resources and opportunities for everyone.

Q.11 Socialism, which is opposite to capitalism, is most likely emphasised which of the following principles?

(a) Centralised control of the means of production

(b) Promotion of private property rights above all else

(c) Focus on individual wealth accumulation

(d) Promotion of competition in the marketplace

Ans. (a) Centralised control of the means of production

Q.12 What was the main impact of the Trade Union Movement in India?

(a) It promoted the interest of the British Government.

(b) It forced the British Government to acknowledge the rights of the workers.

(c) It led to the establishment of new industries.

(d) It increased the division between rich and poor.

Ans. (b) It forced the British Government to acknowledge the rights of the workers.

TYPE - 2 — 1 Mark

Assertion-Reason Questions

Q.1 Read the two statements given below about the rise of capitalism and select the option that shows the correct relationship between (A) and (R).

Assertion (A) The rise of capitalism was fueled by the population growth during the Industrial Revolution.

Reason (R) Population growth led to a higher demand for goods, which increased the need for mass production and factory labour.

(a) R contradicts A

(b) R is the reason for A

(c) A is true but R is false

(d) A and R are independent of each other

Ans. (b) R is the reason for A

Q.2 Read the two statements given below about the growth of capitalism and select the option that shows the correct relationship between (A) and (R).

Assertion (A) The growth of capitalism during the Industrial Revolution contributed to imperialism and colonial expansion.

Reason (R) Capitalists sought new colonies for raw materials and new markets to sell their goods, leading to competitive imperialism.

(a) R contradicts A

(b) R is the reason for A

(c) A is true but R is false

(d) A and R are independent of each other

Ans. (b) R is the reason for A

Q.3 Read the two statements given below about the socialism and select the option that shows the correct relationship between (A) and (R).

Assertion (A) Socialism emerged as a response to the negative impacts of capitalism.

Reason (R) Socialists aimed to improve workers' condition and reduce the wealth disparity caused by capitalism.

(a) R contradicts A

(b) R is the reason for A

(c) A is true but R is false

(d) A and R are independent of each other

Ans. (b) R is the reason for A

TYPE - 3 — 2 Marks

Very Short Answer Type Questions

Q.1 Mention any two factors that led to the rise of capitalism.

Ans. Two factors that led to the rise of capitalism are

(i) **Population Growth** Improved wealth, healthcare, and purchasing power during the Industrial Revolution led to a population increase. As a result, people moved from rural areas to urban centers in search of jobs and better opportunities.

(ii) **Mass Production** The development of machines for large-scale production allowed capitalists to produce goods at a lower cost, leading to increased wealth accumulation and the rise of capitalism.

Q.2 Capitalism has fuelled the industrial, technological and green revolutions, reshaped the natural world and transformed the role of the state in relation to society. *Greenly Earth*

What was the main goal of capitalism? How did capitalism impact workers during the Industrial Revolution?

Ans. The main goal of capitalism is to make as much profit as possible. Capitalists aim to increase wealth by owning businesses, controlling production, and using workers to earn more money.

Capitalism during the Industrial Revolution led to workers earning low wages, working long hours in poor conditions. Many faced exploitation, overcrowded living spaces, and the loss of traditional jobs to machines.

Q.3 **Imagine you are a worker in an English factory during the early stages of the Industrial Revolution. How would the working conditions, such as long hours and low wages, affect your daily life and overall well-being?**

Ans. As a factory worker during the Industrial Revolution, long working hours and low wages would make my daily life very difficult. I would be tired, stressed, and have little time for rest. Poor pay would make it hard to meet basic needs, affecting my health and happiness.

Q.4 **Give two reasons for the rise of socialism during the Industrial Revolution.**

Ans. Two reasons for the rise of socialism during the Industrial Revolution were

(i) **Exploitation of workers** Workers faced low wages and poor working conditions, that gave rise to the movement for workers' rights.

(ii) **Wealth gap** The rich capitalists became wealthier, while the poor suffered. This led to the demand for fair wealth distribution.

Q.5 **Mention any two key socialist leaders who advocated for the welfare of workers.**

Ans. Two key socialist leaders who advocated for the welfare of workers were

(i) **Karl Marx** A German philosopher who co-authored 'The Communist Manifesto' and called for a society where workers would control the means of production.

(ii) **Robert Owen** A British social reformer who worked to improve workers' conditions and promoted the idea of cooperative communities.

Q.6 **What was the purpose of the Chartist Movement?**

Ans. The Chartist Movement aimed to secure better rights for workers, particularly the right to vote. It started in the 1830s and pushed for political reforms, including universal male suffrage, equal electoral division, and annual parliaments. Workers wanted a fairer and more democratic society.

Q.7 **What is the difference between capitalism and socialism regarding wealth distribution?**

Ans. In capitalism, wealth is distributed unevenly, with the rich owning most resources.

In socialism, wealth is shared more equally, the aim is to reduce the gap between the rich and poor by controlling production and ensuring fair distribution for everyone.

TYPE - 4 — 3 Marks

Short Answer Type Questions

Q.1 **Describe briefly about first and second stages of the Industrial Revolution. How did the second stage, started after 1870, build upon the earlier changes?**

Ans. The first stage of the Industrial Revolution (1750-1870) focused on shifting from hand-made to machine-made production, mainly in England. It involved inventions like the steam engine and machines for spinning and weaving.

The second stage, starting after 1870, saw the application of science and mass production techniques in industries. It introduced improvements in steel production and new technologies, like electricity.

The second stage built upon earlier changes by enhancing production efficiency, expanded industries, and spread to countries like France, Germany, and the US. This increased global trade and production.

Q.2 **Explain how the rise of capitalism during the Industrial Revolution led to the growth of new towns and cities. What role did mass production and the decline of small farms play in this transformation?**

Ans The rise of capitalism during the Industrial Revolution led to the growth of new towns and cities because factories needed workers, and people moved from rural areas to urban areas for jobs.

Mass production made goods cheaper and increased the need for more factories, which attracted workers. The decline of small farms also contributed, as many farmers sold their land to industrialists and moved to cities in search of work. This shift created overcrowded cities with rapidly growing populations and changed landscape and economy.

Q.3 **"Capitalism led to significant social and economic changes during the Industrial Revolution". Justify this by mentioning any three points.**

Ans. Capitalism led to significant social and economic changes during the Industrial Revolution such as

- **Growth of Industries** Factories were built, leading to mass production and an increase in the availability of goods, which boosted the economy.
- **Urbanisation** People moved from rural areas to cities for work, leading to the rapid growth of towns and cities near factories.
- **Exploitation of Workers** Capitalists profited from cheap labour, with workers, including women and children, being paid low wages and working long hours in poor conditions.

These changes helped shape modern economies but also led to social inequalities.

Q.4 **Explain the relationship between the rise of capitalism and imperialism.**

Ans. The rise of capitalism and imperialism are closely connected because as factories in capitalist countries needed more raw materials, they began to look for new colonies. These colonies provided resources like rubber, coal, and cotton, which were essential for production.

Capitalist countries also sought new markets in these colonies to sell their goods. This competition for resources and markets led to imperialism, where powerful countries controlled weaker ones to benefit economically.

Q.5 **How did socialism emerge as a response to the negative effects of capitalism, and how did early socialists like Karl Marx and Robert Owen contribute to the spread of socialist ideas?**

Ans Socialism emerged as a response to the harsh conditions created by capitalism, where workers were exploited and lived in poor conditions.

Karl Marx and Robert Owen contributed to the spread of socialist ideas in the following ways

- Karl Marx believed that workers should control production, aiming for a society where the working class holds power.
- Robert Owen worked to improve the lives of workers by creating better working conditions and developing cooperative communities.
- Both Marx and Owen believed in the idea of wealth being shared equally among all people, striving for a fair society without exploitation or class differences, where everyone had equal opportunities and resources.

TYPE - 5 — 4 Marks

Long Answer Type Questions

Q.1 **Discuss the rise of imperialism in capitalist countries during the Industrial Revolution. How did the need for raw materials and new markets for mass-produced goods contribute to the search for colonies and the spread of competitive imperialism?**

Ans During the Industrial Revolution, capitalist countries needed more raw materials like coal, cotton, and rubber to keep their factories running. At the same time, they produced goods on a large scale and needed new markets to sell these products. To meet these needs, they began to explore and take control of foreign lands, especially in Africa and Asia, creating colonies.

The search for resources and markets led to the spread of imperialism, where powerful nations took control of weaker countries. This competition between nations to gain colonies was known as competitive imperialism. Countries like Britain, France, and Germany competed to expand their empires, aiming to secure resources and profits from the colonies.

Q.2 **Compare capitalism and socialism in any four points.**

Ans. The comparison between capitalism and socialism are

Capitalism	Socialism
In capitalism, the businesses are owned by private individual.	In socialism, the businesses are owned by the government or are cooperatively managed.
The means of production such as labour, raw-materials, tools and machines are owned by the private individuals or capitalists.	The state owns and controls the major means of production.
Capitalism encourages innovation and competition for profit.	Lack of innovation and competition due to social welfare schemes.
The motto of capitalism is profit maximisation and accumulation of wealth.	The motto of socialism is to bring changes through revolution and abolition of social classes.

TYPE - 6   10 Marks

Structured Questions

Q.1 With reference to the Industrial Revolution, answer the following questions.

(i) Define the term Industrial Revolution. **(3)**

(ii) "Socialism emerged as a response to the exploitation and inequality caused by capitalism during the Industrial Revolution". Analyse this statement by discussing the key principles of socialism. **(3)**

(iii) In what ways did the capitalist system create a division between the wealthy and the working class during the Industrial Revolution? Describe the conditions faced by workers under capitalism. **(4)**

Ans. (i) The Industrial Revolution was a period of major changes in industries, where hand-made products were replaced by machine-made ones. It began in England in the 18th century and led to new inventions, faster production which led to a massive change in society and economy.

These factors created the perfect environment for industrial growth, making England the starting point of the revolution.

(ii) The statement highlights that socialism was created to address the unfairness caused by capitalism.

The three key principles of socialism are

(a) **Opposition to Capitalism** Socialism believes that industries should not be owned by private individuals, as it leads to exploitation of workers

(b) **Voice of the Workers** Socialism supports the working class and aims to protect workers' rights from capitalist exploitation.

(c) **Wealth Distribution** Socialism calls for fair distribution of wealth, ensuring everyone has equal access to resources, rather than a few capitalists owning everything.

These principles aimed to create a fair and just society, where wealth and power were shared more equally.

(iii) During the Industrial Revolution, capitalism created a clear division between the wealthy capitalists and the working class. The capitalists, who owned factories and businesses, became very rich by exploiting workers. The working class, on the other hand, had to work long hours for low wages in poor conditions.

Under capitalism, workers faced poor conditions. They worked long hours, sometimes 12-14 hours a day and got low wages. Many worked in dangerous factories with no safety measures. Women and children were often employed because they could be paid even less.

Workers lived in overcrowded and unhealthy conditions, which led to the spread of diseases. There was no job security, and workers had little control over their work, which makes it difficult for them to improve their living conditions.

Q.2 With reference to socialism and capitalism, answer the following questions.

(i) How did the Industrial Revolution contribute to the rise of capitalism, and what were its major impacts on society? **(3)**

(ii) How did socialists aim to improve workers' conditions? **(3)**

(iii) Explain the key features of capitalism. **(4)**

Ans. (i) The Industrial Revolution led to the rise of capitalism by fostering mass production, increasing productivity, and creating new industries. With the increased use of machinery, factory owners sought profit maximisation, leading to wealth concentration in private hands.

It resulted in the growth of urban centers, exploitation of workers, and a growing division between the rich and poor. The working class faced poor conditions, low wages, and overcrowded living spaces, while capitalists accumulated wealth, further emphasising social and economic inequalities.

(ii) Socialists believed that the state or the government should control the means of production, such as factories and land, to ensure fair wealth distribution. They aimed to improve workers' condition by advocating for better wages, justified working hours, and safer working environments.

Socialists also pushed for workers' rights, including the right to vote and form trade unions. They sought to create a fairer society where wealth and resources were shared equally, reducing the gap between the rich capitalists and poor workers.

(iii) The key features of capitalism are

- Businesses and industries are owned by private individuals.
- The main goal is to make profits by selling goods and services.

- Encourages competition between businesses to improve products and services.
- Wealth is distributed unevenly.
- Workers are paid wages for their labour.
- Prices are determined by supply and demand in free markets.

Q.3. The Industrial Revolution was a period of profound social, economic, and technological change, marked by the shift from hand-made to machine-made production, transforming industries, cities, and society. With reference to this, answer the following questions.

(i) What was the impact of socialism on the condition of workers during the Industrial Revolution? (3)

(ii) 'How did capitalism bring about significant social and economic changes during the Industrial Revolution? Justify your answer with three points.' (3)

(iii) Capitalism and socialism are two contrasting economic systems with different approaches. Mention any four differences between socialism and capitalism. (4)

Ans. (i) Socialism had a positive impact on workers' conditions during the Industrial Revolution by advocating for better wages, shorter working hours, and safer working environment.

Socialists pushed for laws to protect workers from exploitation, ensuring they were treated fairly. They also promoted the idea of wealth redistribution to reduce income inequality.

As a result, workers gained more rights, including the right to vote and form unions, leading to improved living and working conditions. These changes helped create a more balanced society, reducing the gap between the rich and the poor.

(ii) For answer, refer to Q.3 of Short Answer Type Questions.

(iii) For answer, refer to Q.2 of Long Answer Type Questions.

ICSE SAMPLE QUESTION PAPER
(FULLY SOLVED)
HISTORY & CIVICS

General Instructions

Maximum Marks : 80

Time allowed : Two hours

Attempt all questions from **Part I** (Compulsory).

A total of 5 questions are to be attempted from **Part II**, 2 out of 3 questions from **Section A** and 3 out of 5 questions from **Section B**.

The intended marks for questions or parts of questions

Part - I (30 Marks)

Attempt all questions from this section.

Question 1

Select the correct answers to the questions from the given options

(i) The Fundamental Rights in the Indian Constitution are enforceable by the .... **(1)**

(a) President
(b) Supreme Court and High Court
(c) Prime Minister
(d) Speaker of Lok Sabha

(ii) Given below are details of a few individuals. **(1)**

Person	**Age** (in years)	**Description**
W	21	Is a professor in government college
X	36	Is a doctor
Y	19	Has declared insolvency
Z	24	Has taken citizenship of Nepal

Who among them is eligible to become a member of the State Legislative Council?

(a) W
(b) X
(c) Y
(d) Z

(iii) With reference to the Directive principles, complete the following. **(1)**

Directive Principles : Not justiciable :: Fundamental Rights : ....

(a) Enforceable by courts
(b) Justiciable
(c) Obligatory
(d) Mandatory

(iv) Who do you think supervises and resolves disputes regarding the information you obtained in the cartoon below? **(1)**

(a) The President
(b) The Prime Minister
(c) The Election Commission of India
(d) None of these

(v) Which one of the following options given below is not a part of the State Legislature? **(1)**

(a) The Governor
(b) The Legislative Assembly
(c) The Legislative Council (in some states)
(d) Gram Panchayat

(vi) Who is known as the 'First Citizen'; and represents the city at various ceremonies? **(1)**

(a) The Alderman
(b) The Mayor
(c) The President
(d) The Commissioner

(vii) Read the two statements given below and select the option that shows the correct relationship between (A) and (R).

Assertion (A) The Harappan Civilisation is considered as the first civilisation that arose in the North-Western regions of the Indian subcontinent.

Reason (R) The Harappan Civilisation is also known as the Indus Valley Civilisation. **(1)**

(a) (A) is true and (R) is false
(b) (R) is true but (A) is false
(c) Both (A) and (R) are independent of each other
(d) (A) is the reason for (R)

(viii) Identify the odd one out of the following aspects of the Rig Veda. **(1)**

(a) First Testament of Mankind
(b) Collection of 1028 hymns
(c) Deals with spells and charms
(d) Divided into 10 Mandalas

(ix) Which of the following statements is most associated with the edict shown in the picture? **(1)**

(a) It promotes military conquest as a way to expand the empire.
(b) It emphasises Ashoka's policy of Dhamma, including non-violence and religious tolerance.
(c) It announces the creation of new tax laws for the subjects.
(d) It marks the location of Ashoka's palace in Pataliputra

(x) Identify the correct statements from the following options. (1)

P : The Sangam Age is known for the creation of Tamil literature, which includes works composed by Tamil poets.

Q : The Chola dynasty was the only dynasty that ruled during the Sangam Age.

R : The Sangam Age saw the establishment of trade relations between Tamil kingdoms and the Roman Empire.

S : The Sangam literature does not include Akam and Puram.

(a) P and Q
(b) P and R
(c) R and S
(d) Q and S

(xi) Read the description and choose the correct answer. (1)

This ruler's reign marked the peak of the Gupta Empire's cultural achievements. He is known for his patronage of the arts and he promoted Sanskrit literature. He was also a lover of poetry and drama, and Kalidasa's works flourished during his rule.

Who is being described in the above description?

(a) Chandragupta I
(b) Samudragupta
(c) Chandragupta II
(d) Harsha

(xii) Which of the following is not associated with the reign of Chandragupta II (Vikramaditya)? (1)

(a) Expansion of the Gupta Empire to its greatest territorial extent.
(b) Patronage of arts, literature, and science.
(c) The support for Buddhism as the state religion.
(d) Military victories over the Shakas.

(xiii) Which person is associated with this picture (1)

(a) Balban
(b) Qutub-ud-din Aibak
(c) Iltutmish
(d) Ala-ud-din Khilji

(xiv) Which dynasty was the last ruling family of the Delhi Sultanate before its fall? (1)

(a) Khilji Dynasty
(b) Tughlaq Dynasty
(c) Lodi Dynasty
(d) Sayyid Dynasty

(xv) What does this structure tell us about the Harappan Civilisation? (1)

(a) The Harappans were skilled in building large-scale irrigation canals.
(b) It was a ceremonial structure used for religious or social gatherings.
(c) The Great Bath was used primarily for grain storage.
(d) The Harappans lacked advanced construction techniques.

(xvi) Read the description and identify the artist. (1)

"A famous artist of the Renaissance who painted the Mona Lisa and The Last Supper. He was not just a painter but also an inventor, scientist and architect and is often referred to as the Renaissance man for his wide range of interests and talents".

(a) Michelangelo (b) Raphael (c) Leonardo da Vinci (d) Donatello

Question 2

(i) Mention any two sources of information about the Sangam Age. (2)

(ii) Imagine you were to bring certain reforms in the system of elections to Lok Sabha and Vidhan Sabha in States, which ones would you like to introduce and why? (2)

(iii) Mention two religious beliefs of the Harappan people. (2)

(iv) Mention any two main causes for the spread of Jainism. (2)

(v) Mention any two sources of information about the Mauryan Empire. (2)

(vi) What are Constituencies? How many types of constituencies exist? (2)

(vii) "Delimitation is the process of redrawing the boundaries of constituencies to ensure that each constituency has an equal representation based on population. This process is carried out by the Delimitation Commission, which is appointed by the President of Indi(a)" *The Hindu (Editorial), February 6, 2024*

From the above passage, define the purpose of delimitation. Also mention who carries out the delimitation process in India? (2)

Part - II

Section - A

(20 Marks)

Attempt any two questions from this section.

Question 3

(i) Fundamental Rights are provided to all citizens irrespective of their caste, creed, color, sex, faith, religion, property, qualifications, place of residence or education. With reference to the Fundamental Rights, answer the following questions.

Mention any three circumstances under which the Fundamental Rights of citizens can be restricted by the government. (3)

(ii) Explain the following terms related to Fundamental Rights (3)

(a) Right to Freedom of Religion (b) Cultural and Educational Rights

(c) Right to Constitutional Remedies

(iii) When can the Fundamental Rights of citizens be suspended? Mention any three ways in which the Right to Constitutional Remedies empowers citizens to protect their rights. (4)

Question 4

The Directive Principles are the guidelines to be followed by the Government in the governance of the country. With reference to the Directive Principles, answer the following questions

(i) Explain briefly any two Articles that are enlisted in the Directive Principles of the Indian Constitution. (3)

(ii) Mention any three important roles of the Directive Principles of State Policy. (3)

(iii) With reference to the DPSPs, explain the concept of a Welfare State. (4)

Question 5

In India, constituencies are the basic units of elections and they ensure the representation of people in both the Parliament and State legislatures. There are different types of constituencies based on the electorate and specific needs. With reference to the constituencies, answer the following questions

(i) Explain the different types of constituencies in India and the role they play in the electoral process. **(3)**

(ii) Discuss how these constituencies ensure representation of all sections of society in the Parliament and State Legislatures. **(3)**

(iii) 'Reserved constituencies play a crucial role in ensuring political representation and social justice for historically marginalised communities, fostering inclusivity and empowering underrepresented sections of society in India's democratic framework'. What is the significance of Reserved Constituencies in India? Discuss their purpose and importance in promoting social justice. **(4)**

Section - B

(30 Marks)

Attempt any three questions from this section.

Question 6

"Renaissance was not a sudden or spontaneous development". With reference to this statement, answer the following questions.

(i) Describe the life and contributions of William Shakespeare in the context of the Renaissance period. **(3)**

(ii) Renaissance was not a sudden or spontaneous development. Mention the three principles which caused the Renaissance. **(3)**

(iii) Explain any four causes that led to the emergence of the Renaissance in Europe. **(4)**

Question 7

"The Chola dynasty was known for its remarkable contributions to art, architecture and administration". With reference to the Cholas, answer the following questions.

(i) The temple in the Chola Kingdom was the center of social activity, besides being a place of worship. How did the temples gain this position of eminence? **(3)**

(ii) Mention any three significant features of inscriptions for providing information about the Cholas. **(3)**

(iii) Give any three reasons why Rajaraja I undertook a naval expedition against Ceylon and Maldives? **(4)**

Question 8

Look at the picture given below and answer the following questions.

(i) Identify the name of this fort. Where is it located? Mention its ceremonial importance in the present. **(3)**

(ii) Mention three important buildings within the fort. **(3)**

(iii) Describe any four architectural features of the fort. **(4)**

Question 9

Read the passage given and answer the following questions.

"The period between 1206 AD and 1526 AD in the Indian history is known as the period of Delhi Sultanate. During this period, rulers belonging to five different dynasties, the Slaves, the Khiljis, the Tughlaqs, the Sayyids and the Lodhi's, ruled over India".

(i) Mention three key features of the judicial administration under the Mughal rule. **(3)**

(ii) Mention the three features of social reforms of Akbar. **(3)**

(iii) Mention any four architectural features of Jama Masjid. **(4)**

Question 10

The Gupta Empire, which flourished in India from around 320 to 550 CE, is often referred to as the "Golden Age" of ancient Indian civilisation. With reference to this, answer the following questions.

(i) How did the Guptas contribute to the field of medicine? **(3)**

(ii) Mention any two titles adopted by the Gupta rulers. **(3)**

(iii) What role did the Gupta Kings play in promoting religion? Do you think that the religion followed by the rulers gained prominence? Give reasons to support your answer. **(4)**

Answers

1. 1. (b) Supreme Court and High Court

2. (b) X

3. (b) Justiciable

4. (c) The Election Commission of India

5. (d) Gram Panchayat

6. (b) The Mayor

7. (c) Both (a) and (a) are independent of each other

8. (c) Deals with spells and charms

9. (b) It emphasises Ashoka's policy of Dhamma, including non-violence and religious tolerance.

10. (b) P and R.

11. (c) Chandragupta II

12. (c) The support for Buddhism as the state religion.

13. (b) Qutub-ud-din Aibak

14. (c) Lodi Dynasty

15. (b) It was a ceremonial structure used for religious or social gatherings.

16. (c) Leonardo da Vinci

2. (i) Two sources of information about the Sangam Age are

- **Sangam Literature** Ancient Tamil texts like Tolkappiyam and Ettuthokai provide detailed insights into the social, cultural, and political life of the Sangam period.
- **Archaeological Evidence** Excavations at sites like Arikamedu and Keeladi reveal information about trade, urban settlements, and daily life during the Sangam Age.

(ii) If I were to bring reforms in elections to the Lok Sabha and Vidhan Sabha, I would introduce state funding of elections to reduce the influence of black money and ensure fair competition, and implement Right to Recall Representatives to hold leaders accountable for non-performance or corruption. These reforms would promote transparency, equality and accountability in the electoral process.

(iii) Two religious beliefs of Harappan people were

- They worshipped trees like Pipal. They worshipped animals like - Bull, Buffalo and Tiger.
- They believed in magic and charms.

(iv) The two main causes for the spread of Jainism are

- **Local Dialect** Mahavira adopted the language of common people, i.e, Prakrit instead of Sanskrit to preach his doctrines.
- **Royal Patronage** Jainism received royal patronage of Chalukyas and Rashtrakutas. Chandragupta Maurya is also said to have converted to Jainism. Kharvela helped in the spread of Jainism in Eastern India.

(v) Two key sources of information about the Mauryan Empire are

- **Arthashastra** Written by Kautilya (also known as Chanakya), the Prime Minister of Chandragupta Maurya, this text serves as an extensive guide on political theory, diplomacy, administration and governance.

- **Indica** Composed by Megasthenes, a Greek ambassador at Chandragupta Maurya's court, the work offers a detailed account of the culture, society and politics of the Mauryan Empire. It also provides a unique foreign perspective on the Indian subcontinent during that era.

(vi) For ease in elections, the entire area of a country is divided into fixed electoral areas with specific bodies of registered voters. These areas are called Constituencies. There are mainly three types of constituencies exist - Single member constituency, multi-member constituency and reserved constituency.

(vii) The purpose of delimitation is to redraw the boundaries of constituencies to ensure equal representation based on the population of the country. This process is carried out by the Delimitation Commission, which is appointed by the President of India.

3. (i) Three circumstances under which the fundamental rights of citizens can be restricted by the government are as follows

- **National Emergency (Article 352)** Fundamental rights can be suspended when a national emergency is declared due to war or external aggression.
- **Automatic Suspension (Article 358)** Article 19 (Right to Freedom) is automatically suspended during such emergencies.
- **Presidential Power (Article 359)** The President can suspend the enforcement of other fundamental rights during the emergency through an official order.

(ii) (a) **Right to Freedom of Religion**

The Right to Freedom of Religion, enshrined in Articles 25 to 28 of the Indian Constitution, ensures that all individuals have the freedom to practice, profess and propagate any religion of their choice. It guarantees religious freedom while maintaining the secular nature of the state. It also prohibits forced religious conversion and ensures that the government does not favour or discriminate against any religion.

(b) **Cultural and Educational Rights**

Cultural and Educational Rights, mentioned in Articles 29 and 30, aim to protect the interests of minority communities by ensuring their right to preserve their language, culture and traditions. These rights allow minorities to establish and administer their own educational institutions to promote and protect their cultural identity.

(c) **Right to Constitutional Remedies**

The Right to Constitutional Remedies, provided under Article 32, empowers citizens to directly approach the Supreme Court or High Court if their fundamental rights are violated This right is considered as the "Heart and Soul" of the Constitution. The courts can issue writs such as Habeas Corpus, Mandamus, Prohibition, Certiorari and Quo Warranto to enforce fundamental rights and provide justice.

(iii) Fundamental Rights can be suspended during a national emergency declared under Article 352 of the Indian Constitution. Ways in which the Right to Constitutional Remedies empowers citizens are

- **Writs** Citizens can approach courts for writs like Habeas Corpus and Mandamus.
- **Judicial Review** The judiciary can strike down unconstitutional laws.
- **Enforceability** Courts ensure rights are upheld against state violations.

4. (i) Two Articles that are enlisted in the Directive Principles of the Indian Constitution are as follows

- **Article 49** This aims to protect the country's cultural heritage by ensuring the preservation of monuments, places and objects of national importance. They enable people to study and understand various aspects of history, architecture, art and culture.
- **Article 51** This is based on Liberal-Intellectual principles. It states that the State should advance global harmony and security. It has significant implications for India's foreign policy.

(ii) The three important roles of the DPSPs are

- **Shaping laws and policies** The DPSPs help the government create laws and policies that promote social and economic democracy, environmental protection and fair wages.
- **Establishing a welfare state** The DPSPs aim to create a welfare state by promoting social and economic justice and ensuring social equality for all citizens.
- **Serving as a moral compass** The DPSPs are not legally enforceable, but they serve as a moral compass for the government. They are intended to be a guide for the ruling party in legislative and executive acts.

(iii) A Welfare State is a state which seeks to ensure the maximum happiness of the maximum number of people living within its territory.

- It is a political system where the government is responsible for the economic and social well - being of its citizens. The Constitution of India seeks to establish India as a Welfare State.
- The words 'Welfare State' are not specifically mentioned in the Constitution, however the aims and objectives of a Welfare State are clearly pointed out in the Directive Principles of State Policy.

5. (i) In India, there are different types of constituencies, each serving a distinct purpose to ensure fair and diverse representation. These are as follows

- **General Constituencies** These constituencies are open to all citizens, where any eligible voters can elect a representative regardless of their social or economic background General constituencies form the majority of the electoral divisions in India and ensure representation from all sections of the population.
- **Reserved Constituencies** Reserved constituencies are specifically set aside for candidates from the Scheduled Castes (SCs) and Scheduled Tribes (STs). This system is aimed at ensuring political empowerment for historically marginalized communities, promoting social justice and giving them a platform for active participation in governance.
- **Nominated Constituencies** Though this provision has been discontinued after the 104th Constitutional Amendment, nominated constituencies were once created to give representation to the Anglo-Indian community in the Lok Sabha and state assemblies. These seats were filled by appointments made by the President, ensuring that the community had a voice in the legislature.

(ii) The different types of constituencies in India ensure representation of all sections of society in the Parliament and state legislatures by creating a more inclusive and equitable electoral system.

- General constituencies are open to all voters and elect representatives from the general population. These constituencies ensure that the diverse voices of the Indian electorate, regardless of caste, creed, or social background, are heard.
- Reserved constituencies guarantee that members from Scheduled Castes (SCs) and Scheduled Tribes (STs) are given the opportunity to participate in governance and have their voices heard in the Parliament and state assemblies.
- Nominated Constituencies originally allowed for the representation of the Anglo-Indian community in the Lok Sabha and state assemblies. This ensured that a minority community, whose interests might otherwise be overlooked, had a direct voice in shaping national and state policies.

(iii) Reserved constituencies are significant in India because they give members of weaker sections of society a chance to participate in politics and address historical Marginalisation. Reserved constituencies are important because of the following purposes

- **Promote political inclusivity** They ensure that underrepresented groups have a voice in legislative processes.
- **Address historical inequalities** They help to address the historical marginalization of communities like Scheduled Castes (SC), Scheduled Tribes (ST) and Other Backward Classes (OBC).
- **Provide opportunities to influence policy** They give these communities the opportunity to influence policy and decision-making.

6. (i) William Shakespeare was born in England He was an English poet, playwright and actor, widely regarded as the greatest writer in the English language. He is often called England National Poet and the Bard of Avon. His works include 39 plays, 154 sonnets, two long narrative poems and a few other verses. He wrote Hamlet, Othello, Macbeth, King Lear, Julius Caesar which are considered the finest works in the English language.

(ii) The three principles which caused the Renaissance include

- **Humanism** The word humanism was derived from the Latin words 'Studia humanitatis' or 'the studies of mankind'. It is an idea of rationality or reason. It disagrees with the ideas of faith or believing something because you have faith in it. The humanists looked deep into the ancient classics for ideas on humanism like those of Plato, Virgil, Aristotle, Cicero and Quintilianus.

- **Glorification of human form** The Renaissance scholars and artists glorified the human body. The Renaissance artists took their subjects from the Bible but portrayed the human form in all its earthly beauty and vigor.
- **Spirit of Enquiry** The Spirit of Enquiry extended from scientific enquiry into nature, explorations and expeditions to probe into every realm of knowledge. It was the principal cause of the Renaissance.

(iii) Four key causes that led to the emergence of the Renaissance in Europe are

- **Capture of Constantinople** Greek scholars moved to Italy, bringing ancient knowledge and ideas that sparked interest in Greek and Roman culture.
- **Decline of Feudalism** As feudalism declined, the rise of middle class allowed the growth of trade, wealth, and new learning.
- **New Trade Routes** The search for new sea routes to the East led to more exploration, bringing new knowledge and wealth to Europe.
- **Spirit of Enquiry** The Crusades and the work of independent thinkers encouraged people to question old beliefs and explore new ideas in science, art, and philosophy.

7. (i) The temples in the Chola Kingdom gained their position of eminence as centers of social activity for several reasons

- **Religious and Cultural Hub** Temples were not only places of worship but also centers for cultural activities
- like music, dance and literature, promoting artistic expression and community participation.
- **Economic and Administrative Importance** Temples were major landholders and received donations and land grants. They became centers for economic activity, including the management of revenue, distribution of resources and conducting local governance.
- **Social Welfare** Temples provided food, shelter, and education to the poor and needy, becoming key institutions for social welfare and charity.
- **Educational Centers** Temples were centers of learning where scholars, poets and artists gathered, fostering the growth of knowledge, including Tamil literature and philosophy.

(ii) Three significant features of inscriptions for providing information about the Cholas include

- These inscriptions tell us about the Chola administration. For example, the Uttaramerur inscription gives information on the village administration, taxation and land revenue.
- Some inscriptions have royal orders on taxation and land revenue, resolutions of village assemblies, judgements delivered against persons guilty of theft, murder and other crimes.
- The inscriptions of contemporary rulers like Cheras, Pandyas, Rashtrakutas and Gangas give information about the Cholas' records of land grants villages, plots of farmland or other privileges given by the kings to private individuals or institutions.

(iii) The three reasons why Rajaraja I undertook a naval expedition against Ceylon and Maldives include

- Rajaraja aimed to extend the Chola Empire's power and influence over neighbouring regions, especially Sri Lanka and the Maldives, which were strategically important for controlling maritime trade routes in the Indian Ocean.
- He sought to control the lucrative trade routes in the Indian Ocean, and by conquering these areas, he ensured dominance over maritime trade, which boosted the empire's wealth and prosperity.
- He wanted to defeat the local rulers of Ceylon and the Maldives who were resisting the Chola authority, asserting the Cholas' supremacy in the region.

8. (i) The fort in the given picture is the Red Fort. It is located in Delhi. This fort was built by Shah Jahan. Its ceremonial importance in the present lies in the fact that the Prime Minister of India every year unfurls the national flag from its ramparts on Independence day (August 15).

(ii) Three important buildings within the fort include

- Diwan-i-Aam (Hall of Public Audience)
- Diwan-i-Khas (Hall of Private Audience)
- Moti Masjid (Pearl Mosque)

(iii) Four architectural features of the fort include

- The fort has massive walls and two gateways. The Western Gateway is known as the Lahori Gate.
- It is surrounded by a strongly fortified wall.

- *Red sandstone and marble were used in its construction.*
- *These buildings are decorated with pure white marble and inlaid with precious stones.*

9. *(i) The three key features of the judicial administration under the Mughal rule include*

- *The king was at the apex of the judicial administration. The courts of Sadr-us-Sadur and Qazi-ul-Qzat were next to the king's court. Sadr-us-Sadur decided the religious cases and the Qazi-ul-Qzat decided all other cases.*
- *No codified laws existed in the Mughal judicial system.*
- *The cases of the Muslims were decided on the basis of Quranic injunctions, Hadis or sayings of the prophet, Fatwas or decrees of the eminent judges, etc. In the case of the Hindus, the cases were decided in accordance with their customary and traditional laws.*

(ii) The three features of social reforms of Akbar include

- *He prohibited the practice of 'sati' and legalised the remarriages of widows.*
- *He did not encourage child marriages. The minimum age for the marriage of girls was raised to 14 years, while the age of the marriage of boys was raised to 16 years.*
- *He abolished all inland customs and taxes on trades and professions.*

(iii) The four architectural features of Jama Masjid include It is the largest Mosque in India.

- *There are three gateways to the Jama Masjid mosque i.e. on the South, East and North sides. On the North and South sides, there are two elegant tapering minaret.*
- *The central dome is the largest and highest, made of white marble, decorated with stripes of black colour.*
- *The face of its spacious prayer hall consists of eleven arches of which the central arch rises till above the roof level.*

10. *(i) The Guptas made significant contributions to the field of medicine, particularly in surgery, anatomy, and the treatment of diseases. Sushruta, known as the 'Father of Surgery' wrote the 'Sushruta Samhita', which is one of the earliest texts on surgery and medical procedures. He described surgical techniques for various procedures, including plastic surgery and discussed the importance of hygiene and sterilization in medical practice.*

(ii) Two titles adopted by the Gupta rulers were

- ***Parameshvara*** *This title means 'Supreme Lord' and was used by Gupta rulers to emphasize their status as the highest authority, symbolizing their divine right to rule.*
- ***Maharajadhiraja*** *This title translates to 'King of Kings' and was used by the Gupta emperors to indicate their supremacy over other regional kings and rulers in the empire.*

(iii) The Gupta kings played a key role in promoting Hinduism. They were devoted followers of Lord Vishnu and constructed several complicatedly designed temples, such as the Dashavatara temple. They also practiced Vedic rituals like the Ashwamedha Yajna. While they were tolerant of other religions, their primary focus was on the welfare and growth of their people, rather than on promoting a specific religion.

Yes, Hinduism gained prominence during the Gupta period. The belief in the divine nature of kings became widespread, with Gupta rulers being compared to gods like Vishnu, Indra, and Varuna. The construction of elaborate temples further promoted Hinduism, and the decline in royal patronage contributed to the weakening of Buddhism and Jainism during this period.